Structured Products and Related Credit Derivatives

The Frank J. Fabozzi Series

Structured Products and Related Credit Derivatives

A Comprehensive Guide
for Investors

BRIAN P. LANCASTER
GLENN M. SCHULTZ
FRANK J. FABOZZI

WILEY

John Wiley & Sons, Inc.

ISBN: 978-0-470-12985-2

Printed in the United States of America.

10 9 8 7 6 5 4 3 2 1

Contents

  Credit Derivatives and Synthetic CDOs   **231**
  Brian McManus, Steven Todd, Dave Preston, and Anik Ray

    Single-Name Credit Default Swaps   232
    CDS Indexes   240
    Index Tranches, Swaps, Synthetic Equity, and CDOs   248
    Synthetic CDOs   252
    Correlation   255
    Summary   259
    Appendix A: Index Eligibility Rules   259
    Appendix B: The Mechanics of Cash Settlement   262

CHAPTER 12
  CDO Performance   **267**
  Steven Todd, Brian McManus, Anik Ray, and Dave Preston

    Upgrade/Downgrade Statistics Suffer from a Vintage Bias   268
    Return Performance Data May Not Be Informative   269
    What Does the Market Tell Us about Managers?   269
    Some Case Studies   271
    What Do the Rating Agencies Have to Say about Managers?   274
    Should Equity Investors Look for Managers with Equity Stakes?   275
    Is Good Performance the Result of Luck or Skill?   277
    Market Efficiency and Manager Performance   277
    No CDO Benchmarks   278
    CDO Ratings Transitions   278
    Liquidity Considerations   280
    So What Should Investors Do?   280
    Conclusion   282
    Appendix: Rating Agency Reports   282

CHAPTER 13
  CDO Equity   **289**
  Brian McManus, Steven Todd, Anik Ray, and Dave Preston

    What Is CDO Equity?   290
    What Are the Advantages of CDO Equity?   291
    What Are the Risks of CDO Equity?   292
    How Can Investors Gain Exposure to CDO Equity?   292
    What Are the Sources of Equity Cash Flows?   292
    What Is the Best Time to Invest in CDO Equity?   295
    What Is the Typical Life Cycle for Equity?   297

SECTION FOUR
Commercial Real Estate   311

CHAPTER 14
Commercial Mortgage-Backed Securities   313
Brian P. Lancaster, Anthony G. Butler, and Greg Laughton

CHAPTER 15
Understanding Managed CRE CDOs   333
Brian P. Lancaster, Anthony G. Butler, and Greg Laughton

Foreword

Innovation has been the hallmark of the structured products market since its inception in the mid-1980s. Frank Fabozzi is an acknowledged expert in this space, having witnessed the growth, development, and reach of this market. Along the way, he has assembled some of the most talented analysts in the structured products market to contribute their insight and experience. His efforts over the years have produced the most prolific fixed income reference library in existence today.

Now, in cooperation with Frank Fabozzi, Brian Lancaster and Glenn Schultz and other members of the Structured Products Research team at Wachovia Capital Markets, LLC have produced *Structured Products and Related Credit Derivatives*. This book presents a comprehensive overview of both the assets and the structures used to finance these assets in the capital markets.

At Wachovia, our overall goal in research is to give investors the full 360 and a balanced perspective on the opportunities and risks embedded in each of our investment recommendations. To that end, we strongly encourage our analysts across the capital structure to collaborate with one another and to share information.

This book was written over a time frame that spans the pinnacle of the structured products market through to its most challenging period. Such roller coaster volatility has crystallized the interdependence of the markets and the benefits of Wachovia's holistic approach.

The use of structured products by consumer finance, banking, insurance, and manufacturing companies, as a part of their overall corporate financing strategies, makes this book an invaluable reference not only for fixed income analysts and portfolio managers, but also for their equity counterparts seeking to understand how this market can influence the revenue, capital structure, and financing costs of the companies within their coverage universe.

As the technology for securitizing and financing assets is exported across the globe, it is important to understand the state of the art as it exists today as well as the challenges that this unique market faces going forward. These instruments are highly complex, both from a financial and a legal perspective. Issues such as bankruptcy remoteness and perfection of interest become even more intricate when one considers the different cultures and legal frameworks under which securitization will evolve in the future.

Diane Schumaker–Krieg
Managing Director
Global Head of Research
Wachovia Capital Markets, LLC

Acknowledgments

The editors thank each contributing Wachovia analyst, including Tony Butler, Brian McManus, Steven Todd, and Chris VanHeerden. This book reflects the enthusiasm and dedication of the authors and of Wachovia's structured products research team. We are equally indebted to Steve Cummings, Head of Wachovia's Corporate and Investment Bank, and Ben Williams, Head of Global Markets and Investment Banking, for fostering an environment within Wachovia that strongly supports independent published research.

About the Editors

Brian P. Lancaster is a Managing Director at Wachovia Securities where he heads a 19-member Structured Products Research team. Before joining Wachovia Securities, Mr. Lancaster was a Managing Director (Principal) in Structured Products at Bear, Stearns & Co. Inc., Vice-President in New Financial Products and Engineering at Chemical Securities Inc., and Senior Capital Markets Economist at both the Federal Reserve Bank of New York and the Bank of England in London. From 1996 to 1999, he served as an Adjunct Professor of Finance in Columbia University's MBA program and periodically lectures at Harvard, Wharton, and New York University business schools. Mr. Lancaster was voted to Institutional Investor's All-America Fixed Income Research Team in 2001, 2000, and 1999, and was voted best CMBS Analyst of the Year in 2003 by *Real Estate Finance & Investment*, an Institutional Investor publication. In 2006, *National Real Estate Investor* magazine named him a "CMBS Pioneer" and one of "Ten to Watch" in real estate. Mr. Lancaster is on the Commercial Real Estate/Multifamily Finance Board of Governors of the Mortgage Bankers Association where he consults periodically with senior government policy makers. He has been a contributing author to numerous books and reports. He holds an MBA from New York University, a Masters in International Affairs from Columbia University (where he was selected as an International Fellow), and a BS from MIT.

Glenn M. Schultz is a Managing Director and the Head of ABS and Non-Agency Mortgage Research a Wachovia Capital Markets, LLC. Mr. Schultz has over 18 years of Capital Markets experience focused on structured finance and fixed income analytics, particularly focused in the ABS and MBS markets. Prior to joining Wachovia, he held positions at the Royal Bank of Canada Financial Group and JPMorgan/Banc One. He and his group have received several professionally recognized awards: including individually ranked in the top 10 Home Equity Loan Analysts 2003 Institutional All-Star Analyst Survey, ASR/IDD 2003 deal of the year for the Bullet Line of Credit structure created for the securitization of Home Equity Line of Creditloans, and Senior Home Equity Loan Analyst on JPMorgan's top ranked II All-Star team 2004, and 2005. Glenn completed his undergraduate degree in Business Administration and his MBA from the University of Louisville and has earned the designation of Chartered Financial Analyst.

Frank J. Fabozzi is Professor in the Practice of Finance and Becton Fellow in the School of Management at Yale University. Prior to joining the Yale faculty, he was a Visiting Professor of Finance in the Sloan School at MIT. Professor Fabozzi is a Fellow of the International Center for Finance at Yale University and on the Advisory Council for the Department of Operations Research and Financial Engineering at Princeton University. He is the editor of the *Journal of Portfolio Management* and an associate editor of the *Journal of Fixed Income*. He earned a doctorate in economics from the City University of New York in 1972. In 2002, Professor Fabozzi was inducted into the Fixed Income Analysts Society's Hall of Fame and is the 2007 recipient of the C. Stewart Sheppard Award given by the CFA Institute. He earned the designation of Chartered Financial Analyst and Certified Public Accountant. He has authored and edited numerous books about finance.

Contributing Authors

Anthony G. Butler	Senior CMBS Analyst	Wachovia Capital Markets, LLC
Frank J. Fabozzi	Professor in the Practice of Finance	Yale School of Management
Landon C. Frerich	CMBS Analyst	Wachovia Capital Markets, LLC
Brian P. Lancaster	Senior CMBS Analyst	Wachovia Capital Markets, LLC
Greg Laughton	Analyst	Wachovia Capital Markets, LLC
Stephen P. Mayeux	CMBS Analyst	Wachovia Capital Markets, LLC
John N. McElravey	Senior Analyst	Wachovia Capital Markets, LLC
Brian McManus	Senior CDO Analyst	Wachovia Capital Markets, LLC
Dave Preston	Associate CDO Analyst	Wachovia Capital Markets, LLC
Anik Ray	Associate CDO Analyst	Wachovia Capital Markets, LLC
Glenn M. Schultz	Senior Analyst	Wachovia Capital Markets, LLC
Garret Sloan	Short-Term Debt Analyst	Wachovia Capital Markets, LLC
Steven Todd	CDO Analyst	Wachovia Capital Markets, LLC
Chris van Heerden	Vice President	Wachovia Capital Markets, LLC
Erin K. Walsh	Associate Analyst	Wachovia Capital Markets, LLC
Shane Whitworth	Associate Analyst	Wachovia Capital Markets, LLC
Chris van Heerden	Analyst	Wachovia Capital Markets, LLC

Background

CHAPTER 1

Introduction

Brian P. Lancaster
Senior Analyst
Wachovia Capital Markets, LLC

Glenn M. Schultz, CFA
Senior Analyst
Wachovia Capital Markets, LLC

Frank J. Fabozzi, Ph.D., CFA
Professor in the Practice of Finance
Yale School of Management

Since the summer of 2007 and as this book goes to press in late 2007, it has been difficult to ignore the news on television, in the print media, and online without one or more of the following financial instruments mentioned: "subprime ABS CDOs," "structured finance products," and "credit derivatives." Even the popular web site YouTube.com has seen the posting of numerous comedy skit videos and music videos about these financial instruments.

This greater awareness of the new media, comedians, and would-be musicians was obviously due to the 2007 subprime residential mortgage-backed security crisis. These terms have been referred to in some media reports as financial "toxic waste." While real credit issues have surfaced in subprime ABS and some CDOs, it is important to keep the current turmoil roiling the structured product markets in perspective. Securitized subprime mortgage backed securities represent 6% of the approximately $10 trillion structured products markets which consists of a wide variety of assets ranging from commercial real estate loans, to credit card debt to equipment leases, most of which have performed as well as if not better than equivalent rated corporate bonds. Put another way 94% or about $9.4 trillion of structured products have generally been money good, stable credit quality securities with upgrade downgrade ratios equal to or better than the corporate bond market.

Beyond the generally high quality of the investments, structured finance has played a critical role in improving the efficiency, liquidity, and availability of capital in the United States and abroad. At the simplest level through the transformative powers of statistical analysis and credit tranching, structured products efficiently connect pools of capital around the world to various financial markets and assets that heretofore only had access to localized specialty lenders. Borrowers are provided with the best possible borrowing rates and investors are provided with greater and more diverse investment opportunities to maximize their investment performance. Moreover, structured products allow for the distribution of risk to a wider variety of financial institutions both domestically and internationally than could otherwise be achieved through traditional balance sheet lending, a feature not lost on regulatory authorities.

The four obvious risks in the structured product endeavor are that (1) the rating agencies, the main arbiter of asset and bond credit quality get it wrong; (2) the originators of the original assets turn into "toll takers" not caring about credit quality but only fees; (3) the investors don't understand the risks and opportunities embedded in the securities they are acquiring; and (4) risk transfer and dispersion is not actually as clear cut as originally expected.

This book, written over a period spanning the greatest bull market in structured products history to arguably its most challenged period by some of Wall Street's top ranked and most seasoned analysts, offers the reader the unique insights that can only come from such a phenomenal roller coaster ride. With many structured finance spreads at or well beyond their historically widest spreads and defaults falling in some sectors and rising in others, there is more investment risk and opportunity in these markets than ever before. This comprehensive book is designed to help the reader identify the opportunities and mitigate the risks in what is perhaps the most fascinating and complex financial market in the world.

Section One of this book includes the forward, this introduction (Chapter 1) and Chapter 2 which provides an analysis of what is arguably one of the most critical and controversial topics in the entire structured products market: *structured finance operating companies* (SFOCs), which includes *structured investment vehicles* (SIVs) and *structured lending vehicles* (SLVs). SFOCs started in the late 1980s and have grown exponentially since 2002.

This chapter also analyzes vehicles of consumer asset backed securities (ABS), their role in the structured products markets as well as their trademark feature, *dynamic leverage*, which allows them to reduce or increase leverage in response to, or in anticipation of, market movements or collateral quality. SFOCs have purchased significant amounts of floating rate bonds across the structured products markets. In 2007, difficulties with these vehicles stemming from sector-level illiquidity and market value declines led to the effective closure of a range of structured products markets. To remain viable, SFOCs will need to learn from the events of 2007 and address both the liquidity and market value risks inherent in the structures.

Section Two (Chapters 3 through 8) starts off with analysis of *residential asset-backed securities* (RABS), the market at the center of the 2007 subprime mortgage crisis (Chapter 3). The market is covered from its inception in the 1990s through the creation of *credit default swaps* (CDSs) referencing RABS transactions. It includes a discussion of the loan level drivers of both voluntary repayment and default, providing an excellent starting point for anyone interested in modeling home equity loan cash flows. Combined with a detailed examination of the structures employed in a RABS securitization and a discussion of the mechanics of pay as you go CDSs, the chapter provides the investor with a solid understanding and methodology for valuing single-name CDS referencing RABS transactions.

Chapters 4 and 5 examine two of the largest and oldest nonresidential consumer ABS markets—credit-card-backed securities and auto-loan-backed securities. Each chapter serves as a guide to understanding the characteristics and credit quality of the respective underlying collateral as well as the structures that were adapted to suit the unique cash flow characteristics of the collateral. An investor approach to evaluating these securities as well as the delinquency and loss performance of credit cards, prime, near-prime, and subprime auto deals are also discussed.

The student-loan-backed securities sector, generally acknowledged as one of the most stable sectors of the ABS market, has grown at a steady pace as the cost of college education continues to rise and demand for loans has increased. In Chapter 6 securitization of both government-guaranteed student loans and private student loans are discussed. Generic structures and underlying collateral characteristics including prepayments and risk associated with this asset class are provided.

Small businesses are often viewed as one of the fundamental contributors to the growth and success of economies and consequently financing is one of the keys to their success. In the United States, the U.S. Small Business Administration (SBA) provides assistance to entrepreneurs by guaranteeing portions of loans to borrowers that may not have otherwise qualify for financing. Chapter 7 provides a guide to understanding the securitization of the unguaranteed portions of SBA loans as well as conventional small business loans, techniques which could have applications in a variety of countries wishing to accelerate their own small business development.

The correct valuation of subprime ABS credit default swaps is one of the hottest topics in the structured product markets and was the driver behind many of the large write-offs being taken by major financial institutions in 2007. Chapter 8 focuses on the techniques required for investors that are looking to consider whether going long or short subprime ABS CDS. The chapter argues that Subprime ABS CDS can be valued in a risk neutral framework using scenario analysis. Multiple scenarios are useful for valuation of ABS CDS and bonds because of the complex nature of the ABS deal structure. Investors cannot derive the price of the CDS by looking simply at the expected mortgage performance of a deal. Rather, the full distribution of mortgage performance probabilities are needed in order to generate the fundamental price of an ABS CDS.

Section Three (Chapters 9 through 13) are devoted to perhaps one of the most misunderstood structured products, *collateralized debt obligations* (CDOs) and their many forms. Chapter 9 serves as an introduction for the novice, describing the different CDO structures (managed versus static, synthetic versus cash flow) and the purposes for which they are created (arbitrage verus balance sheet). The chapter also gives a step-by-step guide to the CDO life cycle. Included in the life cycle description is an explanation of the major phases of a cash flow CDO: ramp-up, reinvestment, and amortization. The cash flow waterfalls, various features that impact the waterfall (such as overcollateralization and interest coverage tests, interest diversion tests, and turbo and pay-in-kind tranches), various covenants and tests, and controlling class rights are explained in this chapter. Chapter 9 should help investors distinguish among truths, half-truths, and myths that have appeared in the popular press as well as commentators in professional investment publications who have attacked CDOs.

Chapter 10 builds on the introduction given in Chapter 9, describing and analyzing the various types of CDOs and the underlying assets that make up the collateral. The chapter highlights the special risks and considerations for various collateral classes. The focus is on the most prominent CDO sectors found in the primary market in the summer of 2007. The new issue mix that will be used as CDO collateral, however, can change significantly over time. As an example, high-yield corporate bonds were the most prevalent assets of new issue CDOs in the 1990s, while by 2006 ABS was the most prominent collateral. Investors must strike a balance between the higher yield they will be offered for an emerging asset class or innovative structure with the risk that the product will remain illiquid and possibly obsolete.

The sometimes complex and counterintuitive terminology and mechanics of credit default swaps on corporate entities, ABS, and CDOs, one of the most ubiquitous structured product types, are examined in Chapter 11. The chapter explores actively traded CDS indices, tranche trading strategies, and the dynamics of synthetic CDOs concluding with a discussion of correlation.

Chapter 12 takes on the controversial topic of how CDO managers can be evaluated. Along the way, investors are provided with a toolkit to appraise CDOs as potential or current investments. Some of the challenges in comparing managers, including timing biases and the lack of benchmarks, are discussed. Investors should also be aware of the conflicting interests of note and equity holders, as well as how a manager's interest can be aligned with a particular investor class. By using historical rating transition data and equity cash flow studies, a more complete picture of investor concerns when examining CDOs is provided. Finally, the rating agencies' various reports and research are described. Details about that material is described in the chapter along with an explanation of how they can aid portfolio managers in assessing their CDO investments.

CDO equity—one of the most opaque and potentially profitable corners of the structured products markets—is explored in Chapter 13. After first discussing the advantages and risks of CDO equity investments, an analysis of the drivers of CDO equity cash flows and investment timing issues is provided. The chapter concludes with an analysis of equity return performance.

Commercial mortgage-backed securities (CMBS)—born out of the troubled Resolution Trust Corporation era of the early 1990s when commercial banks and insurance companies shut down commercial real estate lending—have grown to become a significant part of many fixed income indexes and provided 40% of U.S. commercial real estate finance in 2007. Section Four (Chapters 14 through 18) is devoted to this market sector. Chapter 14 discusses in detail what a CMBS is and how investors should appropriately analyze and value the product. In addition, the chapter takes a look at how CMBS has performed with respect to defaults and losses historically and discusses who should and does invest in CMBS.

Like CMBS, *commercial real estate CDOs* (CRE CDOs) were born at a time of crisis—the Russian default induced liquidity crunch of 1998. Evolving from simple static structures which provided nonmark to market, match funded financing for lower-rated CMBS, managed CRE CDOs allowed for the inclusion of a broad array of commercial real estate debt assets including short-term whole loans, bridge loans, B-notes, mezzanine debt, and preferred equity. Chapter 15 analyzes managed CRE CDO structures and examines in detail the legal and credit issues of the primary collateral types such as B-notes, rake bonds, mezzanine loans, and preferred equity.

While synthetic CDOs were first used by European banks in the early 1990s as a means of transferring on balance sheet corporate risk while maintaining client relationships, their application to commercial real estate finance only began in 2005. Chapter 16 explores the growth and development of synthetic CRE CDOs including such topics as what constitutes an event of default, the negative basis trade, monoline insurer involvement, as well as how they may be used by financial institutions to reduce commercial real estate capital requirements and transfer risk. Synthetic CRE CDOs had been growing in popularity prior to the dislocation in the structured products markets in 2007 and could show much promise in helping diversify and transfer commercial real estate risk from the balance sheet of financial institutions.

In Chapter 17, we extend our tour of commercial real estate securitization techniques with a trip abroad—the European commercial real estate CDO market. An American import, CDO technology was first applied to European commercial property finance in 2006. The active management framework of the CDO structure has increased the accessibility of European *commercial real estate* (CRE) investments by addressing (1) the high prepayment velocity synonymous with European CRE; (2) the lack of transparency in investments; and (3) the regulatory morass and country-specific investment nuances. Although the number of transactions to market has been limited, the variation in managers, collateral, and structures make these deals useful benchmarks for developing an understanding of the market. This chapter reviews European CRE CDO collateral types and structures, and outlines an investor approach to uncovering the opportunities and risks in the sector.

Chapter 18, the last chapter in Section Four, is designed to educate the newcomer about the Government National Mortgage Association (GNMA) multifamily securities market and provide the seasoned investor with an updated view of the sector. After a brief history, the chapter first takes a look at how the securities are created. It then looks at the underlying collateral, how the securities are valued, and the inherent risks. The chapter concludes with an analysis of both historical prepayments and defaults for GNMA deals.

Commercial ABS are covered in the three chapters that comprise Section Five (Chapters 19 through 21) which include aircraft securitization, intermodal equipment, and life insurance reserve securitization.

Pooled lease-aircraft-backed securitizations have been used since the early 1990s to finance the aircraft portfolios of leasing companies. Chapter 19 reviews the development of the aircraft ABS market and its overall place in aircraft financing. This is followed by an overview of deal modeling.

The use of intermodal shipping containers has grown rapidly based on the gains to efficiency in cargo transportation. Chapter 20 explains how one of the smaller asset securitization markets provide container lessors with match-term funding against assets while allowing for growth, as additional assets can be funded via the master indenture structure. Generally taking the form of wrapped bonds with significant overcollateralization, bonds in this sector have performed consistently to their structuring assumptions.

Securitization has been used by life insurers and reinsurers to meet statutory reserve requirements in a match-term funded form. Chapter 21 shows how life insurance reserve securitizations provide investors with a diversification opportunity where the primary drivers of performance, lapsation and mortality, perform independently of business cycles.

CHAPTER 2

Structured Finance Operating Companies: SIVs, SLVs, and Other Structured Vehicles

Garret Sloan, CFA
Short-Term Debt Analyst
Wachovia Capital Markets, LLC

The growth of structured finance operating companies, including structured investment vehicles, structured lending vehicles, credit derivative product companies, and other forms of structured vehicles continues to increase with new programs, technologies, and asset classes being introduced. The trademark feature of structured finance operating companies is dynamic leverage, which allows structured vehicles to reduce or increase leverage in response to, or in anticipation of, market movements, collateral quality, and liquidity. Structured assets have grown as a proportion of most structured finance operating companies due to their historically low relative volatility, credit quality, and return profile. Within structured assets, residential mortgage-backed securities are the most prevalent asset type.

The purpose of this chapter is to explain the technology of the different types of structured finance operating companies. Our primary focus will be on one type of structured finance company: a structured investment vehicle.

STRUCTURED FINANCE OPERATING COMPANY DEFINED

The term *structured finance operating company* (SFOC) began at Moody's when, in reviewing the number of structured companies entering the market and the breadth of product types seeking ratings, the agency decided to consolidate its ratings approach when dealing with these structures. The name of the category represents a blanket functional title for a number of different types of structured companies attempting to earn returns through the structuring of cash flows and risk. The vehicles give investors, who may not otherwise be able to gain exposure to certain product markets, the opportunity to allocate capital without exceeding their risk parameters. The following is Moody's definition of the category:

> Structured Financial Operating Companies (SFOCs) are companies that depend upon detailed, pre-determined parameters to define and restrict their business activities and operations. Moody's ratings issued on SFOCs rely heavily upon these parameters and generally apply to the issuer's debt programs rather than to specific debt issues.[1]

In short, SFOCs come up with a set of operating guidelines that are reviewed by the rating agencies and are then given an issuer or counterparty rating based on the operating principles that the SFOC submits. The guidelines are conservative enough that the rating agencies provide these companies with relatively high ratings. If SFOCs were not able to improve their credit ratings through structure, their value would be eliminated because the primary reason for a SFOC is to earn a return between the spread on its asset portfolio and its funding cost, and the company's funding costs are largely determined by strong credit ratings. As long as the company's investment guidelines are adhered to, the SFOC should be able to maintain its rating indefinitely. However, in the event that an SFOC begins to deviate from its guidelines, or extreme market conditions persist, remedial action must be taken to bring the company back into alignment with the model, or wind down of the structure commences.

Many investors worry that rating agencies lag the market in their responses to credit and/or liquidity events, and they may have cause for that belief. However, one of the main stipulations for the SFOC is to perform a set of recurring tests that are frequently reported to the rating agencies to ensure that there is as small a lag as possible between what is happening within the company and what is communicated to the agencies. Each SFOC will approach a test failure differently, and although the rating agencies approve the corporate structure in general, the way in which each SFOC addresses a shortfall in capital adequacy (collateral), liquidity (cash flow) or interest rate neutrality can differ dramatically, exposing investors to potentially different risks.

---

[1] *Moody's Ratings Methodology: A Framework For Understanding Structured Finance Operating Companies.* (April 2005), p. 1.

TYPES OF STUCTURED FINANCE OPERATING COMPANIES

The blanket term SFOC encompasses a number of different structures, the details for many of which are beyond the scope of this chapter, but it is important to mention a few of the different structures in the market for comparison purposes.

Structured Investment Vehicle

The vast majority of SFOCs are *structured investment vehicles* (SIV). An SIV purchases securities, holds them within the operating structure and generally issues two classes of securities: senior notes and capital notes to fund its asset purchases. Its primary purpose is the creation of leveraged returns for the capital note (subordinated) investors by way of spread arbitrage between the return on assets and the cost of funding. Securities are selected by the SIV manager.

Structured Lending Vehicle

A *structured lending vehicle* (SLV) purchases securities and then enters into a repurchase agreement or repo (as the asset buyer), *total return swaps* (TRS) or funding agreements. The primary purpose of these vehicles is again to provide leveraged returns for clients. The senior-subordinated structure is similar to the SIV except that the subordinated investor (similar to the SIV capital note holder) is the counterparty to the repurchase agreement/total return return swap. Returns from the SLV assets are passed to the subordinated investor and the investor, in turn, pays the SLV a predetermined interest rate. The commitment of the counterparty to the SLV is similar to that of the capital note holder in an SIV program described later in this chapter. Securities are selected by the various counterparties and then approved by the SLV manager.

Credit Derivative Product Companies

A *credit deriviative product company* (CDPC) sells synthetic credit protection on single company names or a portfolio of companies as well as structured assets. It issues equity and debt classes and then takes synthetic credit exposure. The few CDPCs in the market average around 40 to 45 credit default swap counterparties and are leveraged at approximately two to four times the typical SIV. The efficiency and flexibility with which these vehicles operate is making them one of the fastest-growing SFOC technologies in the market.

Collateralized Swap Programs

At the outset, a *collateralized swap program* (CSP) is not an operating company; it is a sponsor program. A CSP obtains favorable counterparty ratings by entering into collateral posting arrangements rather than segregating a pool of capital, collateral and/or swap receivables. So, the CSP, in an effort to improve the exposure it poses to its counterparties, will post collateral with that counterparty, thereby reducing the exposure and improving the counterparty rating. The rating a CSP would receive only pertains to the swap transactions that are eligible under the rating. A CSP only issues equity, there are no classes of debt in these programs.

Interest Rate Arbitrage Vehicles

Data on interest rate arbitrage vehicle structures is so scarce and the programs so few that it is not practical to discuss in detail the nuances of this structure. In its initial SFOC ratings methodology article, Moody's listed two programs, and as of October 2007 the rating on one of them has been withdrawn.

Guaranteed Investment Contracts

A *guaranteed investment contract* (GIC) in the context of structured finance is a contract through which an issuer helps municipalities invest the proceeds of bonds issues until the funds are required for a civil project. The size and maturities are generally predetermined at the time of the municipal bond issuance. The insurance company issuing the GIC takes the proceeds of the issuance from the municipality, purchases assets, and enters into a contract with the municipality to repay the funds at maturity plus a set return. The insurance company issuing the GIC assumes all credit and interest rate risk on the assets it purchases to fund the GIC. The purchaser can exit the GIC at any time at book value.

Synthetic GICs provide the same basic function, except that the GIC enters into an insurance agreement with a bond insurer that guarantees the book value of the asset before maturity.

Why Asset-Backed Conduits Are Not SFOCs

One of the interesting classes missing from the list above is the traditional asset-backed conduit (multiseller, securities arbitrage, or hybrid). After all, conduits are special purpose vehicles that finance third-party borrowers, they are bankruptcy remote and conduits, like SFOCs, are managed as operating entities. However, Exhibit 2.1 may help illustrate why conduits are not typically included in SFOC nomenclature, and explains some of the differences.

EXHIBIT 2.1 Differences Between SFOCs and Asset-Backed Conduits

SFOCs	Asset-Backed Conduits
Investors can purchase different parts of the risk pool (senior/substructure)	Investors purchase a share of the full-risk pool (all note holders pari passu)
Initial rating based on a formulaic capital model (asset haircuts)	Rating relies primarily on credit and liquidity structure and support provider(s)
Investors look for adherence to capital model to gain comfort	Investors look through vehicle to credit and liquidity structure and provider(s)
Collateral Marked to Market Daily, value is published monthly to investors	Collateral value reviewed monthly through servicer reports, but not required to be marked to market
Daily liquidity, capital adequacy, and Interest rate sensitivity tests ensure viability (F/X tests are also possible)	Strength of Credit support provider, and periodic collateral review ensure viability
Collateral is highly rated and priced securities	Collateral is pools of cash flows or securities, or both
Can issue MTNs for liquidity relief	Generally issues Commercial Paper
Monthly *pricing*, liquidity, and test result reports	Monthly *pool* or *default* reports, pricing does not affect conduit performance
Monitor asset, geographic, and industry concentrations	Monitor concentrations (per credit provider limits)
Portfolio haircut models created by SFOC manager to obtain rating	Portfolio haircut models created by sponsor and provided by loan servicers
0%–15% third-party liquidity support (daily liquidity tests allow this)	Up to 100% third-party liquidity support

As Exhibit 2.1 shows, there are many differences that make the SFOC technology unique from traditional asset-backed conduit. Some market participants believe that these differences make SFOCs too similar to market value *collateralized debt obligations* (CDOs) with commercial paper tranches for their liking.

The reality is that the technologies of asset-backed conduits, SFOCs, and market value CDOs overlap in some respects, but their differences make each product unique enough not to lump any one product into the risk bucket of any other. Asset-backed conduits generally escape this comparison, but SFOCs do not. Many investors look at SFOCs as market value CDOs with a new name. However, Exhibit 2.2 outlines some of the differences between SFOCs and CDOs.

EXHIBIT 2.2   Differences between SFOCs and CDOs

SFOCs	CDOs with CP Tranches
Dynamic capital/Funding management	Static capital/Asset management
No legal final maturity	Specific legal final maturity; collateral is sold and investors are paid out
Issuer/Counterparty ratings and instrument rating	Transaction rating
Continuous monitoring relationship with agencies	Transaction relationship with agencies
Monitor liquidity, interest rate sensitivity, and asset/geography/industry concentrations	Strength of credit support provider and periodic collateral review ensure viability
Limited liquidity facilities	Full liquidity facilities
Daily or weekly reporting to ratings agencies	Flexible reporting and risk management
Majority of underlying collateral rated AA or higher, ranging from A to AAA	Majority of underlying collateral highly rated but can range from B to AAA
No specific ramp-up period; program limit is approved and assets/liabilities ramp up in tandem	Typically one-year ramp-up to reach desired collateral level
Collateral and capital are both managed	Collateral can be managed or static, but capital is static
Subordination levels can be maintained by raising additional capital or adjusting collateral	Subordination levels must be maintained by adjusting collateral

In general, the SFOC structure must respond to market movements quickly because its ability to fund depends on its rating, which in turn is based on its capital adequacy (which is market value dependent), liquidity, and interest rate neutrality. This differs from a market value CDO that ramps-up one time, has full liquidity for the CP tranche, and in the event of a market value drop takes interest from lower tranches to amortize senior tranches.

STRUCTURED INVESTMENT VEHICLES

The *structured investment vehicle* (SIV) has been around in the market since the late-1980s when banks and asset managers began using the structure to generate leveraged returns, exploiting the difference in short-term liabilities and long-term investments in capital markets. Exhibit 2.3 identifies the SIV landscape as of July 2007.

Growth in the SIV Market

The SIV market has grown slowly over time, given that the first SIV was underwritten in 1989. However, recent growth has been substantial. Since 2002, the number of programs and the authorization limits have grown exponentially (see Exhibit 2.4). Since 2002, the market has almost tripled by number of programs and more than doubled by authorized assets, showing that there are many smaller players coming into the market with numerous smaller programs. Between 2002 and 2006, the average program size has declined to $25.1 billion from $29.5 billion (see program sizes in Exhibit 2.3).

Not only has the size of the market grown, but the types of assets have moved as well. Exhibit 2.5 shows that SIVs have always been partial to structured assets, but the proportion of structured assets in newer programs is now almost 3:1 compared to all other asset classes. The growth of structured assets as the predominant class was largely a function of managers seeking sectors with low volatility, high credit quality and good relative returns in markets where credit spreads were systematically compressing over a number of years. Market familiarity with structured assets had grown significantly at the institutional level, and it was reasonable to conclude that SFOCs would continue to buy many different types of structured assets.

Exhibit 2.6 makes it clear that residential mortgages make up the majority of underlying collateral within the structured asset sector, although the exposure is not evenly distributed among SFOCs. As Exhibit 2.5 shows, newer SIVs are more exposed to structured assets, especially mortgage assets, than their more seasoned counterparts.

Even though most SIVs purchased structured assets at the AAA level, prices even at those credit ratings fell precipitously in mid-2007, forcing many SIVs to sell assets and create headline risk in a market that was believed to have no headline risk. As a result, the market for SIV-issued *commercial paper* (CP) and *medium-term notes* (MTNs) fell almost to zero by the end of August 2007. Even though Exhibit 2.7 shows that ratings on underlying assets in most SIVs remain quite high.

The SIV Structure

Exhibit 2.8 shows the general structure of an SIV's operating process. First, the SIV purchases assets with funds it is able to obtain from MTN and CP

EXHIBIT 2.3 SIV Programs

SIV	Sponsor	Authorized ($ millions)	Balance (July 2007)	Inception
Abacas Investments	III Offshore Advisors	5,000	1,008	12/1/1999
Axon Financial Funding	Axon Asset Management	3,540	11,194	11/1/2005
Beta Finance	Citibank International PLC	15,000	20,176	9/1/1989
Rhinebridge	IKB Credit A.M. GmbH	1,638	2,199	1/1/2005
Carrera Capital	HSH Nordbank/JPM Chase	20,000	4,283	6/1/2006
CC USA / Centauri Corp.	Citibank International PLC	25,000	21,839	9/1/1996
Cheyne Finance	Cheyne Capital	20,000	9,726	8/1/2005
Cortland Capital	Ontario Teachers/QSR Mgt.	20,000	1,344	11/1/2006
Cullinan Finance	HSBC	50,000	35,142	7/1/2005
Dorada Finance	Citibank International PLC	25,000	12,484	9/1/1998
Eaton Vance VLF	Deutsche Bank	4,000	546	11/1/2005
Five Finance	Citibank International PLC	20,000	12,843	11/1/1999
Nightingale Finance	Banque AIG	1,500	2,330	11/1/2005
Harrier Finance	WestLB	20,000	12,343	1/1/2002
K2 Corp.	Dresdner Kleinwort Wasserstein	54,000	29,056	2/1/1999

EXHIBIT 2.3 (Continued)

SIV	Sponsor	Authorized ($ millions)	Balance (July 2007)	Inception
Kestrel Funding	WestLB	20,000	3,316	8/1/2006
Links Finance	BMO Bank of Montreal	40,000	22,301	6/1/1999
Asscher Finance	HSBC Bank	4,000	7,330	6/1/2006
Orion Finance (formerly ABC)	Eiger Capital	40,000	2,298	5/1/1996
Parkland Finance	BMO Bank of Montreal	13,080	3,414	9/1/2001
P.A.C.E.	Société Générale	20,000	4,313	7/1/2002
Sedna Finance	Citibank International PLC	15,000	14,415	6/1/2004
Sigma Finance	Gordian Knot	65,947	52,642	2/1/1995
Stanfield Victoria Finance	Stanfield Global Strategies	40,000	13,243	7/1/2002
Tango Finance	Rabbobank	40,000	14,039	9/1/2002
Whistlejacket Capital	Standard Chartered Bank	30,000	8,845	7/1/2002
White Pine Corp	Standard Chartered Bank	20,000	7,854	2/1/2002
Vetra Finance	Citibank International PLC	40,000	2,617	11/1/2006
Zela Finance	Citibank International PLC	40,000	4,189	9/1/2006
Hudson-Thames Capital	MBIA	40,000	1,767	12/1/2006

Source: Pool reports, Moody's Investors Service, and Standard & Poor's.

EXHIBIT 2.4   Growth in the SIV Market

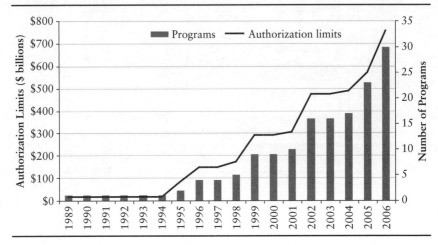

Source: Exhibit constructed by author from data obtained from Moody's Investors
Service and Standard & Poor's.

EXHIBIT 2.5   SIVs and Structured Assets

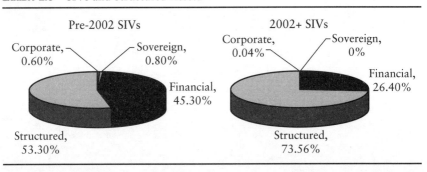

Source: Exhibit constructed by author from data obtained from Moody's Investors
Service and Standard & Poor's.

investors. The ratings are given to the SIV as an issuer and to each program
it issues (CP or MTN). In addition to MTN and CP funding, the SIV issues
capital notes, which are a subordinated class to the senior MTNs and CP.
The SIV attempts to maximize the returns to the capital note investors by
earning a spread between the return on assets and the senior funding costs.
The credit, liquidity and interest rate risk tolerances of the structure are
clearly defined at the outset by the capital model and tested daily, giving the
SIV limited ability to chase yield outside of its investment parameters.

EXHIBIT 2.6   Structured Asset Breakdown

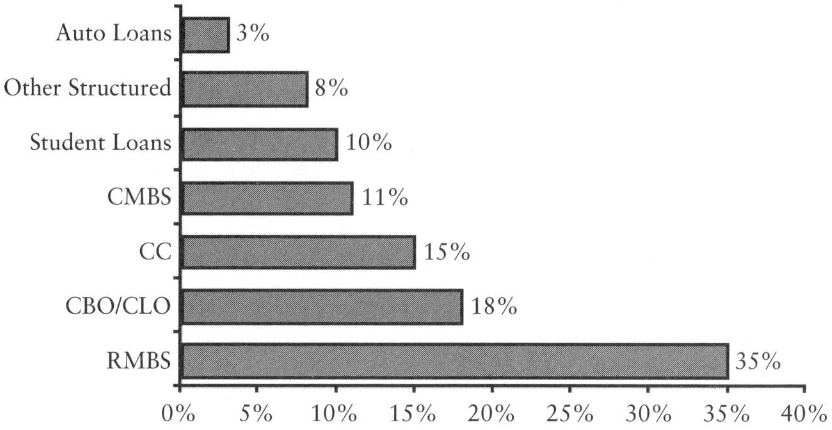

Auto Loans 3%
Other Structured 8%
Student Loans 10%
CMBS 11%
CC 15%
CBO/CLO 18%
RMBS 35%

0%   5%   10%   15%   20%   25%   30%   35%   40%

Source: Exhibit constructed by author from data obtained from Moody's Investors Service.

EXHIBIT 2.7   Average Underlying Rating of SIV Collateral

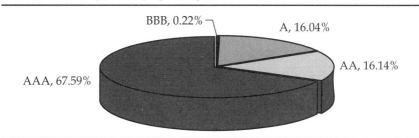

BBB, 0.22%
A, 16.04%
AA, 16.14%
AAA, 67.59%

Source: Exhibit constructed by author from data obtained from Standard & Poor's.

The SIV is also able control the leverage within the vehicle through the purchase of asset classes that require more or less capital cushion or through the issuance of capital notes. At times when the market is unfavorable, the SIV can reduce leverage and increase program flexibility to respond to market movements. Exhibit 2.9 shows the average leverage in SIVs from December 2003 to February 2007. The upward trend is not necessarily the result of new SIVs adding leverage to the system, as would be the case with CDOs that have static capital structures. An SIV's dynamic capital structure allows any single program to leverage up or down based on the assets in the underlying portfolio.

Capital note holders are generally paid a coupon out of the residual spread that is left after all MTN and CP investors are paid and costs are

EXHIBIT 2.8 General Structure of an SIV

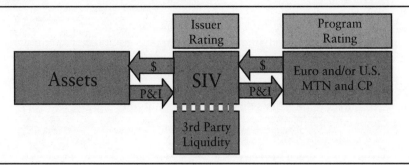

Source: Wachovia Capital Markets, LLC.

EXHIBIT 2.9 Average SIV Leverage

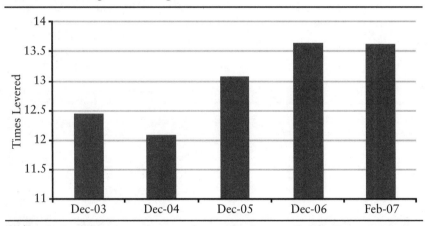

Source: Exhibit constructed by author from data obtained from Standard & Poor's.

recovered.[2] After the capital note holders are paid their fixed residual spread, the remaining residual spread is split between sponsors and the capital note holders at a predetermined level.

An SIV attempts to eliminate any interest rate risk, currency risk and other external risk beyond basic credit risk through active hedging programs. Interest rate and F/X risk in most SIVs are tested daily and must remain within the operating limits to comply with the SIV's operating guide-

---

[2] Recent SIVs have begun "short portfolio" programs that take the residual spread payable to capital note holders and purchase synthetic "protection" during tight spread environments. The belief is that spreads will widen and returns to capital note holders will be augmented. However, if spreads remain tight the cost of carry can become a drag on subordinated capital note holders' returns.

lines. Exhibit 2.10 shows a complete SIV schematic, which shows an SIV with both U.S. and non-U.S. funding vehicles. The diagram also outlines the various operating relationships that the SIV maintains.

SIVs, while mainly relying upon the inherent liquidity of the underlying collateral, also maintain third-party liquidity support sized from 10% to 15% of the outstanding senior debt to ensure that there are no shortfalls during extreme portfolio fluctuations. But unlike *asset-backed commercial paper* (ABCP) conduits, SIVs do not have full liquidity support or program-wide credit enhancement.

The example in Exhibit 2.11 shows how SIVs generally deal with collateral shortfalls and surpluses to maximize capital efficiency within the structure.

SIVs have endured multiple market disruptions without incident because the asset makeup of most SIVs has generally been considered quite liquid due to their relatively stable prices and credit ratings. Each SIV discloses the types of assets it may purchase in its offering memorandum. This list is often quite broad, and an SIV does not always hold every approved asset class. However, the capital model adjusts the amount of leverage the SIV can maintain based on asset-specific considerations.

In the situations above, the capital model assigns a specific "lending value" to each asset based on the asset's risk profile, assuming that the SIV could hold up to 100% in a single asset class. Although the operating models of each SIV are different, they are created to standards that allow ratings

EXHIBIT 2.10 SIV Schematic

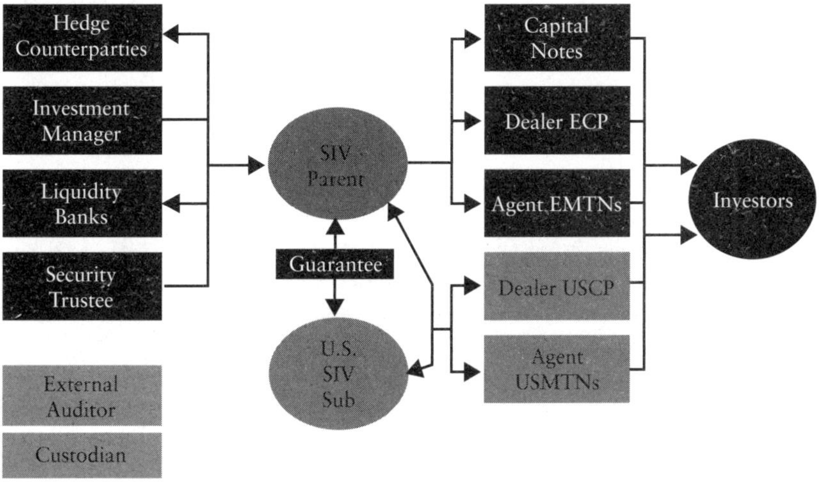

Source: Wachovia Capital Markets, LLC.

EXHIBIT 2.11   Dynamics of an SIV

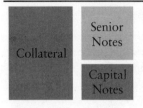 **Situation 1:** SIV is adequately funded with senior and junior pieces. The ratio of capital notes to senior notes (leverage) is set according to the "advanced rate" capital model.

Situation 2: Collateral shortfall. The issuer must add collateral or retire senior/capital notes. This can be done by adding collateral that fits the current leverage ratio in the SIV or by adding other collateral and adjusting the leverage ratio to match the new collateral composition.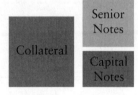

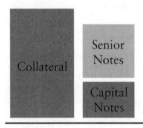 **Situation 3:** Excess collateral. The SIV should issue senior/capital notes to optimize the leverage for the collateral held by the SIV. The ratio of senior/capital notes issued is determined by the collateral being held and the capital model.

agencies to rate the vehicles ex ante as long as they adhere to their respective capital (operating) models. Ratings are based on the historical volatility profile of the assets and then the assets are stressed beyond the observed volatility levels to provide a cushion against even more extreme market scenarios.

SLVs AND HYBRID SLVs

A variation on the original SIV structure is the SLV, which is a much less developed market. The list of SLVs and hybrid SLVs in Exhibit 2.12 and 2.13 is much shorter than the list of SIV vehicles in Exhibit 2.13, but the similarities between SIV and SLV programs will become apparent.

Exhibit 2.14 shows the structure of a standard SLV and illustrates the structural differences between SIVs and SLVs, including:

1. The absence of the capital note class of investor (may have a very small capital note holder that provides initial operating capital).
2. The addition of a counterparty to the SLV (replacing the capital note holder as the subordinated investor).

3. The addition of a TRS/repo transaction between a counterparty and the SLV.
4. The rating on the SFOC is a "counterparty" rating, not an "issuer" rating.

One of the primary ways in which an SIV maintains its rating is through its adjustments of leverage and liquidity. An SLV also adjusts its leverage and liquidity to remain flexible in unstable market environments. The difference is not in the use of leverage but in the identity of the subordinated investor who becomes more or less exposed to fluctuations in the market value of

EXHIBIT 2.12 SLV Programs

SLV	Sponsor	Authorized ($ million)	Balance	Inception
Atlas Capital Funding	Wachovia	$10,000	$6,800	Nov 25, 2005
Liquid Funding	Bear Stearns	$10,000		Nov 1, 2004
William Street Funding	Goldman Sachs	$20,000		Apr 1, 2003
Grand Central Funding	HypoVereinsbank	$5,000		Dec 22, 2000

Source: Pool reports, Moody's Investors Service and Standard & Poor's.

EXHIBIT 2.13 Hybrid SLV Programs

Hybrid SLV	Sponsor	Authorized ($ million)	Balance	Inception
Chesham Finance	BSN Holdings	$25,000	$21,333	Aug 19, 2004
Halkin Finance	BSN Holdings	$20,000	$6,733	Feb 28, 2006
Ebury Finance	BSN Holdings	$30,000	$21,756	Feb 23, 2005

Source: Pool reports, Moody's Investors Service and Standard & Poor's.

EXHIBIT 2.14 Structure of a Standard SLV

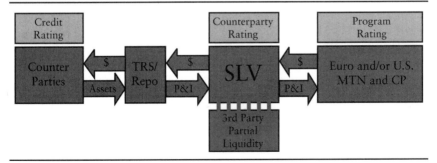

Source: Wachovia Capital Markets, LLC.

assets. The comfort that senior SIV investors receive from their subordinated note holders is altered somewhat in the SLV structure, but the result is a similar layer of subordination. However, in SLVs the subordination is created through a TRS/repo arrangement with a swap or repo counterparty, which gives the counterparty exposure to changes in asset values.

In a traditional SIV, the company acquires assets and finances the purchases through a combination of senior CP/MTNs and subordinated Capital Notes. In an SLV, the vehicle acquires assets and finances its purchases through a combination of senior CP/MTNs and an injection of capital through repo and/or TRS margin.

How does this work? When an SLV purchases assets, it simultaneously enters into a repo or TRS with a third party who then (as a result of the TRS/repo) is exposed to the market risk of the assets held by the SLV. The SLV assigns a specific lending value to the assets it purchases, just as an SIV does, meaning that if collateral is valued at $100 the SLV will only issue CP for $95 and the remaining $5 must be supplied by the TRS/repo counterparty. In an SIV, the difference between the lending value and the asset value is made up through capital notes. In an SLV, the difference between the asset value and the lending value is paid to the SLV in the form of equity by the counterparty. The margin that must be posted is similar in value to the capital note from an SIV and is dynamic based on the asset type, the composition of the SLV portfolio, and the asset seller's counterparty rating. This means that if a counterparty is rated A1+/P1/F1 by the rating agencies, it allows higher leverage in the structure.

Exhibit 2.14 showed that the SLV is given a counterparty rating, similar to an SIV's issuer rating. The entity with whom the SLV enters the TRS or repo may also be rated,[3] and the lending value that an asset is given is not only based on the strength of the collateral and the portfolio, but, because the assets are swapped to an external counterparty, the rating of that counterparty factors into the leverage that the SLV can maintain.

A structured vehicle that intends to enter derivative transactions will generally receive a counterparty rating as opposed to an issuer rating, whereas "SFOCs issuing senior liabilities would typically request an issuer rating."[4] The *counterparty* rating expresses the rating agencies' "opinions of the financial capacity of an obligor to honor its senior obligations under financial contracts, given appropriate documentation and authorizations."[5]

---

[3] In hybrid SLVs, the asset seller's counterparty rating is the primary source of comfort for investors.

[4] Moody's *Ratings Methodology: A Framework for Understanding Structured Finance Operating Companies*, April 2005.

[5] Moody's *Ratings Methodology: A Framework for Understanding Structured Finance Operating Companies*.

EXHIBIT 2.15   Dynamics of an SLV

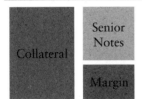

Situation 1: SLV adequately funded with senior notes and margin. Margin amount set according to "advance rate" capital models.

Situation 2: SLV collateral shortfall. Counterparties must post extra collateral or reduce senior notes/margin to maintain adequate capital haircuts (leverage). Margin level set according to "advance rate" capital models.

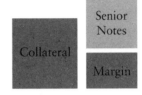

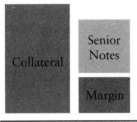

Situation 3: SLV has excess collateral. SLV can issue new senior notes or return margin cash and collateral to the counterparty to leverage the SIV back to rating agency "advance rate" levels. If additional securities are issued, the ratings agencies must affirm the current rating on the program. Margin level is set according to "advance rate" capital models.

Source: Wachovia Capital Markets, LLC.

An *issuer* rating is an "opinion of the ability of entities to honor senior unsecured financial obligations and contracts."[6] The caveat with the counterparty rating is the assumption that all documents are in order. Because the TRS/repo documentation is an integral part of the subordination present in SLVs, they have a unique risk that is not present in SIVs. The risk in SIVs is more focused on balancing the interests of senior and subordinated investors.

Exhibit 2.15 summarily explains the dynamics of an SLV and how it maintains capital efficiency using dynamic leverage.

From the SIV and SLV examples the main change in funding dynamics is, again, the identification of the subordinated investor. In an SIV capital notes can be sold into the market to adjust leverage, while reducing leverage in the SLV results in contacting the swap/repo counterparty to post extra collateral, which is why counterparty credit ratings figure into the assessment of lending values in SLV capital models. Senior investors that purchase notes from SLVs with highly rated counterparties get comfort first from the

---

[6] See http://www.moodysasia.com/mdcsPage.aspx?section=ir&template=ratingdefi nitions&mdcsId=10.

counterparty and subsequently from the collateral, whereas investors purchasing notes from SLVs with lower-rated or unrated counterparties primarily rely on the integrity of the collateral and then the counterparty.

Variations of the SLV

Some issuers have built SLVs and issued GICs instead of CP as a funding source (Grand Central Funding Corp.), others have set up funding note companies to fund the existence of committed lines of credit to investment-grade companies (William Street Commitment Corporation/William Street Funding Corporation). Each of these variations are built on a similar capital model, but funding and asset sources are chosen differently.

A third variation takes it a step further, and we call these hybrid SLVs (Ebury Finance, Chesham Finance, and Halkin Finance), which does not employ any kind of liquidity backstop to ensure the timely payment of investors. Instead, it operates by balancing the funding and repo maturities through extendible notes and through call/put provisions on the notes. Exhibit 2.16 shows the general structure of the hybrid SLV and the source of liquidity that it uses to ensure timely payment of its maturing and periodic obligations. In performance reviews of these structures, the agencies consider these hybrid SLVs fully supported programs.

THE RISK HISTORY OF SFOCs TO 2006

During the 19-plus-year history of SFOCs, the market has suffered severe macroeconomic shocks and sector-specific shocks in SFOC-invested areas. The results for the structures overall have been very favorable. In fact, un-

EXHIBIT 2.16   Hybrid SLVs

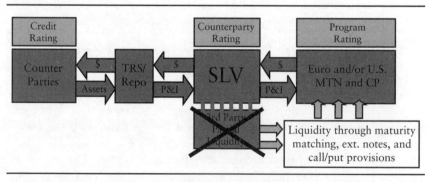

Source: Wachovia Capital Markets, LLC.

til 2007 there had been no *senior* debt downgrades on any publicly rated classes of debt issued by SFOCs or on any public issuer ratings such as counterparty ratings, despite collateral downgrades.[7]

The main reason these structures are so strong in the face of economic downturn is their ability to dynamically leverage the structure. The capital models by which these structured companies operate test collateral daily. If collateral is downgraded, management must adjust the company's leverage to stay within the operating guidelines. If the company fails one of the daily tests required by the capital model, it has a brief window to correct it and take curative action.

Looking back on the history of SFOCs, there have been several severe downgrades in underlying collateral. Exhibit 2.17 shows some of the major events and the outcomes of each of these events.

THE 2007 LIQUIDITY CRISIS

The history of SFOCs up until 2007 was characterized by low volatility, strong asset growth, and little to no headline risk. That all changed in 2007 and SFOCs have become one of the most widely discussed sectors in the financial world.

The general decline of the ABCP market as shown in Exhibit 2.18 dramatically impaired the SIV market's ability to issue ABCP and MTNs. In the 18+ year history of the SIV market, there has never been a time when investors were generally unwilling to lend to SFOCs. The primary factor underlying the liquidity crisis has been the uncertainty surrounding U.S. subprime mortgage-backed securities.

Typically, if an SIV is unable to roll commercial paper or issue MTNs within five days[8] it calls on committed liquidity facilities and then, if liquidity and cash on hand are insufficient to repay liabilities the SIV must begin selling assets to repay liabilities. If asset prices are severely depressed at the time of sale, the vehicle realizes losses that are directed first to capital note holders, and if asset values continue to fall, to senior note and CP investors.

As shown in Exhibit 2.17, sector or company specific price declines can be cured quickly with limited impact on the SIV itself. However, in an environment characterized by restrictive secondary markets and secular

---

[7] *Moody's Ratings Methodology: A Framework for Understanding Structured Financial Operating Companies.*

[8] Liquidity or *net cumulative outflow* tests require an SIV to maintain sufficient cash and liquidity facilities to repay the maximum amount of maturing liabilities over a given five-day period. A similar test is calculated for any given 15-day period but includes securities that are considered liquid for testing purposes.

EXHIBIT 2.17   Major SFOC Events and Outcomes

SFOC	Event	Outcome
Asset-Backed Capital (Orion Finance)	Invested in Hollywood Funding, which was initially rated AAA. Wrap provider refused to honor agreement, notes downgraded to "D" then to "unrated" by S&P.	ABC maintained its AAA/A-1+/P-1 counterparty credit rating on ABC and any related senior-secured, subordinated, and CP ratings.
Asset-Backed Capital (Orion Finance)	Invested in Korean debt which was rated A1/A by Moody's/S&P and subsequently downgraded to noninvestment grade status in 1997.	ABC maintained its AAA/A-1 Aaa/P-1 counterparty credit rating on ABC and any related senior-secured, subordinated and CP ratings.
Dorada Corporation	Issued credit-linked notes tied to Mirant Corp. BBB senior notes. Mirant subsequently filed for Ch. 11 bankruptcy protection, and the CLNs were downgraded.	Dorada maintained its AAA/A-1+ Aaa/P-1 counterparty credit rating on Dorada and any related senior-secured and CP ratings.

Source: This exhibit was created by the author based on a presentation in which Dr. Douglas Long of Principal Partners discussed multiple events in the SIV market ("Converging Developments in ABCP Conduits and SIV Markets").

EXHIBIT 2.18   Asset-Backed Commercial Paper Assets

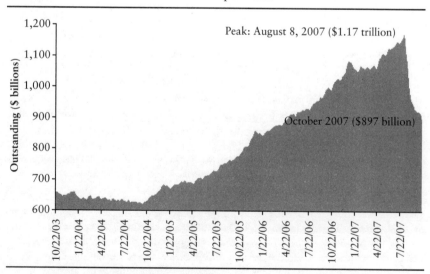

Source: Federal Reserve.

credit spread widening, liquidity and capital adequacy[9] may be so impaired as to accelerate asset sales and realized losses. These losses can cause SIVs to breech operating tests and enter restricted and even forced-wind-down operating states.

Those SIVs that have been most affected by the market turmoil of 2007 are also those that are most heavily exposed to structured products, which also happens to be the newest SIVs in the market (see Exhibit 2.5).

Other nonsector specific risks include:

1. Counterparty risk in SLVs that rely on third parties to post collateral/ margin.
2. Documentation risk for repo and TRS contracts on which collateral enters and exits certain types of vehicles.
3. Timing risk in SIVs in the event that subordinated investors wish to liquidate their holdings and new capital note investors must be found.
4. Liquidity matching risk for those structures that do not carry any type of external liquidity support.
5. Prepayment risk and extension risks for senior notes and CP with call and extension features.
6. Model risk (reliance on a capital model to identify asset volatility, concentration risk and lending values, which has turned out to be one of the biggest risks to which the SFOC market has shown vulnerability).
7. Management risk (although the events in Exhibit 2.17 did not result in downgrades, the inability of a structured vehicle to respond to collateral rating downgrades, and make portfolio funding and collateral adjustments in response to reasonable forecasts is critical).
8. Concentration risk (investors should be aware that investing in multiple SIVs may expose them to correlated underlying assets, especially considering the high concentration of MBS in the current SIV market).

CONCLUSION

In *static* leverage structures, the depletion or downgrade of underlying collateral can represent a significant risk to investors if there are not specific supports in place. In such structures, capital losses that have been realized cannot be replenished by issuing more capital.

---

[9] Capital adequacy or net asset value is tested daily to ensure that it complies with operating guidelines. It is calculated by subtracting the value of the senior debt from the asset value of the portfolio, divided by capital. Moody's states that the average NAV was 102% at the beginning of June 2007, 101% at the beginning of July, 94% at the beginning of August, 85% at the beginning of September, with an NAV range amongst SIVs from close to par down below 50%.

In contrast, the dynamic leverage in SFOCs allows senior note holders to enjoy a more consistent risk profile as the underlying leverage acts as a stabilizer to movements in credit quality and market conditions. However, the inability to attract investors in certain market conditions may preclude vehicles from adjusting leverage even though they have the structural ability to do so. When market deterioration becomes protracted and systemic, SFOCs may be unable to withstand market inertia and triggers will eventually be breeched. The events of 2007 illustrate such a scenario.

However, even given the experiences of 2007, SFOC technology may evolve into new collateral types and structures, providing highly conservative investors access to credit exposure in sectors that may be too volatile without the innovative structural enhancements that SFOCs provide.

SECTION Two

Consumer ABS

CHAPTER 3

Residential Asset-Backed Securities

Glenn M. Schultz, CFA
Senior Analyst
Wachovia Capital Markets, LLC

This chapter provides a guide to the *residential asset-backed securities* (RABS) sector, including collateral performance and modeling; the evaluation of alternative structures; and an introduction to the related credit derivative markets.

From its inception in the early 1990s, the *home equity loan* (HEL) market has experienced a dramatic evolution from a market representing predominantly second lien loans to prime borrowers to first lien loans to credit impaired borrowers, including a wide variety of loan types, for example, fixed rate, hybrid adjustable rate and interest-only loans. As lending practices evolved and investor acceptance of the product grew, the structures used to securitize loans in this sector also evolved. The earliest securitizations employed financial guarantees from third-party wrap providers. By the mid-1990s, the structures evolved to employ senior/subordinate tranching of credit risk, seller-paid mortgage insurance or deep *mortgage insurance* (MI) and *net interest margin* (NIM) transactions to monetize the front-end residual.

Recently, the advent of both single-name *credit default swaps* (CDS) and the ABX.HE credit index have increased notional trading volume and allowed investors to express directional opinions (long or short) regarding issuer origination and servicing practices, relative vintage performance and capital structure arbitrage.

OVERVIEW OF THE MARKET

The consumer ABS market consists of securities backed by pools of assets such as credit card receivables, auto loans and leases, student loans and

HELs. The HEL market has evolved from securitizations of traditional second lien mortgages to prime borrowers in the early 1990s to include several different types of mortgage products to credit impaired borrowers.

The HEL sector has experienced outstanding growth, especially over the past few years (Exhibit 3.1). Growth in the sector was driven by the following:

- The historically low mortgage rates that prevailed over the period.
- Unprecedented home price appreciation.
- Increased consumer leverage.
- Greater investor acceptance of nontraditional mortgage products.
- Demand for mortgage credit exposure in the form of deeper subordination.

The origins of the residential ABS market lie in the development of the nonagency mortgage market in the mid- to late-1980s. Many of the mortgage loans made by lenders exceeded the underwriting guidelines established by Fannie Mae (FNMA) and Freddie Mac (FHLMC), typically by either original loan balance or underwriting criteria. The nonconforming product encompassed Jumbo-A and Alternative-A (Alt-A loans to prime borrowers). The nonconforming market developed as a means to securitize these loans and generally made use of internal credit enhancement via the senior/subordinated structures used in the residential ABS market today.

EXHIBIT 3.1   Home Equity Issuance, 1996 through September 2006

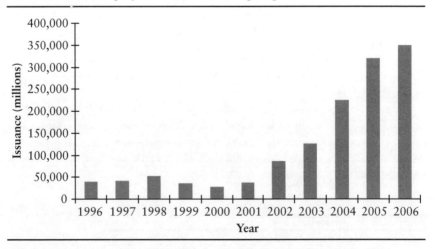

Source: Created from data obtained from Asset Backed Alert and Wachovia Capital Markets, LLC.

Because the earliest residential ABS securitizations were collateralized by second lien loans to prime borrowers, the sector earned the name "home equity loan." During the early to mid-1990s, monoline lenders extended the second lien lending practice to subprime and nonprime borrowers, assuming a first lien position when financing a subprime borrower to his or her limit.

Today, cash-out refinance loans still dominate the collateral backing most residential ABS transactions (Exhibit 3.2). These loans allow borrowers to access the equity in their homes to consolidate debt, lower their monthly payments, finance home improvements, pay for education or purchase consumer durables. The loans may be fixed, adjustable rate (2/28, 3/27 or 5/25 hybrid ARMS) or interest-only loan structures.

EXHIBIT 3.2   Loan Purpose and Product Type
Panel A. Loan Purpose

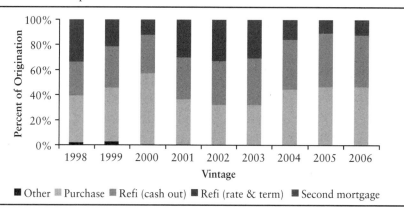

Panel B. Product Type

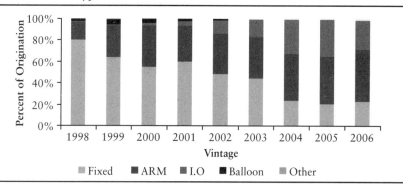

Source: Created from data obtain from Loan Performance and Wachovia Capital Markets, LLC.

EXHIBIT 3.3 Standard & Poor's Subprime Underwriting Guidelines

| Characteristic | Standard & Poor's Rules Based Credit Classification | | | | |
	A	A–	B	C	D
Mortgage credit	0×30	2×30	3×30	4×30 1×60	5×30 2×60 1×60
Consumer credit		2×30 1×60	3×30 2×60	4×30 3×60	4×30 3×60
Revolving	2×30				
Installment	1×30				
Debt/Income ratio	36%	45%	50%	55%	60%
Notice of default/ Bankruptcy	None in past 7 yrs.	None in past 5 yrs.	None in past 3 yrs.	None in past 2 yrs.	None in past year

Note: Each cell indicates × times the borrower was days delinquent.
Source: U.S. Residential Subprime Mortgage Criteria, 1999, Issuer Reviews for Subprime Mortgage Transactions, Table 1- Standard & Poor's Rules Based Credit Classifications, Standard& Poor's Ratings Services, a division of The McGraw-Hill Companies, Inc. This material is reproduced with permission of Standard & Poor's, a division of the McGraw-Hill Companies, Inc.

Defining the Subprime Borrower

Standard & Poor's rules based on credit classifications (Exhibit 3.3) provide guidance when discussing the qualities of a subprime borrower. The rules established by Standard & Poor's reflect a generalized view of the under-writing criteria used by many subprime originatiors.

Borrowers below A quality in the matrix are considered subprime. As a general rule, subprime borrowers have had some mortgage delinquencies and seriously delinquent consumer debt. Debt service ratios as measured by debt to income are higher than for prime borrowers.

Many subprime lenders also make use of Fair Isaac & Co. (FICO) credit scores. These scores may be used to numerically quantify a borrower's credit-worthiness. A lower credit score is associated with a higher frequency of default (Exhibit 3.4). The frequency of default by credit score decreases exponentially as the borrower's credit score increases. While the Office of the Comptroller of the Currency suggests that subprime borrowers are defined at 660 FICO or lower,[1] in practice, borrowers are generally classified by credit score as follows:

[1] Office of the Comptroller of the Currency, *Expanded Guidelines for Subprime Lending Programs*, January 31, 2001.

EXHIBIT 3.4 FICO Score and Default Frequency

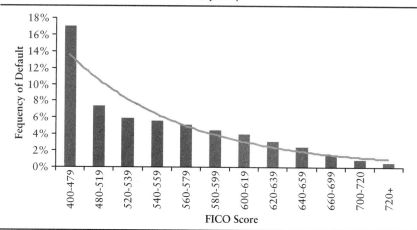

Source: Created from data obtained from Loan Performance and Wachovia Capital Markets, LLC.

- Subprime: 620 FICO and below
- Near prime: 621–679 FICO
- Prime: 680 or greater FICO

COLLATERAL PERFORMANCE

In this section, we provide an overview of subprime collateral performance. We evaluate the voluntary repayment rates (referred to as *conditional repayment rates*, CRR) and involuntary repayment rates (defaults; referred to as *conditional default rates*, CDR). Our discussion addresses both the borrower's sensitivity to refinancing incentives and the influence of prepayment penalties on the baseline repayment assumptions. In addition, we examine the variables that influence repayment rates, including loan purpose, property type, documentation program, risk grade, and lien status.

Next, we discuss roll rates, default frequencies and default timing curves. Throughout the discussion, we examine the influence of borrower characteristics and underwriting practices on the baseline assumptions presented.

VOLUNTARY REPAYMENT

Subprime borrowers exhibit a greater propensity to both voluntarily prepay or involuntarily prepay their mortgages. Both the CRR and CDR rates are influenced by a number of borrower and econometric variables, including the rate of home price appreciation. From the first quarter of 2000 through the first quarter of 2005, the U.S. housing market has experienced a dramatic rate of home price appreciation (Exhibit 3.5).

As mentioned earlier, homeowners often access the equity in their homes for a number of reasons including debt consolidation, durable goods or education spending. Borrowers who have taken cash-out refinance loans have demonstrated a propensity to access the equity in their homes and, given the opportunity, these borrowers will most likely do so again.

The loan-to-value (LTV) repayment risk multipliers presented in Exhibit 3.6 are based on the borrower's original loan-to-value ratio and provide an indication of a borrower's propensity to voluntarily repay at various LTV thresholds. The multipliers exhibit an inverse relationship to the LTV ratio. This indicates that rising home prices and the subsequent increase in homeowner's equity result in a greater propensity to voluntarily repay.

The analysis presented in Exhibit 3.7 suggests that a strong and persistent upward trend in home prices, like that experienced between 2000 and 2005, combined with scheduled principal paydown, can quickly alter a borrower's propensity to voluntarily repay.

For example, the risk repayment multiplier for a 2/28 hybrid ARM loan originated with the characteristics presented in Exhibit 3.7 increased over the three years of 2004, 2005, and 2006 from 1.00 to 1.26, assuming the home's value increased in step with the national home price index reported by OFHEO.

EXHIBIT 3.5   OFHEO Home Price Appreciation

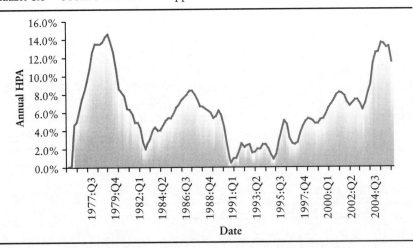

Source: Created from data obtained from the Office of Federal Housing Enterprise and Oversight (OFHEO) and Wachovia Capital Markets, LLC.

EXHIBIT 3.6 Loan-to-Value Repayment Risk Multipliers

Loan-to-Value Ratio	Risk Multiplier	95% Confidence	
		Lower	Upper
Less than 25%	2.10	1.78	2.49
25.01% to 55%	1.43	1.37	1.49
55.01% to 65%	1.26	1.22	1.30
65.01% to 75%	1.16	1.13	1.18
75.01% to 85%	1.00	1.00	1.00
85.01% to 95%	0.89	0.87	0.91
Greater than 95%	0.94	0.80	1.10

Source: Wachovia Capital Markets, LLC.

EXHIBIT 3.7 Updated LTV Risk Multipliers

Rate:	8.00%	Orig. Date:	2003:Q1
Term:	360.0	Orig. LTV:	80%
Orig. Balance:	$200,000	Appraisal Value:	250,000
Starting HPI:	285.96	Loan Type:	2/28 hybrid ARM

Loan Age	HPI	Home Price	Curr. Balance	Updated LTV Risk	Multiplier
3	289.55	$253,139	$199,595	79%	1.000
6	294.49	$257,457	$199,045	77%	1.000
12	309.52	$270,597	$198,055	73%	1.160
18	332.17	$290,399	$197,024	68%	1.160
24	349.73	$305,751	$195,951	64%	1.260
36	394.84	$345,188	$193,835	56%	1.260

Source: Wachovia Capital Markets, LLC, and OFHEO.

ADJUSTABLE RATE REPAYMENT ANALYSIS

Interest Rate Sensitivity

The borrower's sensitivity to refinancing incentives (see Exhibit 3.8) is measured by the loan rate less the Fannie Mae conforming rate adjusted for credit grade. The minimum and maximum refinancing CRRs *before the first rate reset* exhibit the following behavior:

EXHIBIT 3.8   Hybrid ARM Refinancing Sensitivity

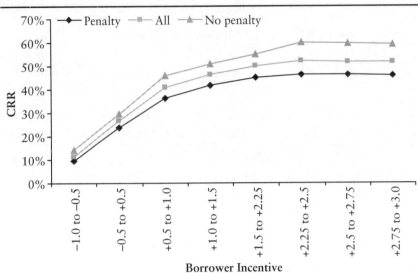

Source: Wachovia Capital Markets, LLC.

- For all hybrid ARMs, the minimum and maximum refinancing CRRs are 11.3% and 46.7%, respectively.
- The prepayment penalty cohort's minimum and maximum CRRs are 9.5% and 40.9%, respectively.
- The absence of a prepayment penalty raises both the minimum and maximum refinancing CRRs to 14.2% and 59.6%, respectively.

Generally speaking, the presence of a prepayment penalty reduces the CRR rate by 4.7% at the minimum and 18.7% at the maximum relative to no-penalty loans. Of particular note is the convergence/divergence of CRR as the borrower's incentive declines/increases. This is due to the following: once the borrower's incentive is "out-of-the-money," the prepayment penalty is a secondary consideration. Conversely, due to the presence of a prepayment penalty, the "incentive hurdle" is greater and the penalty cohort's refinancing response lags that of the no-penalty cohort.

Baseline Repayment Functions

The baseline loan cohort is defined by the following loan characteristics (this applies to all cohorts and loan types discussed): single family, owner occupied, full documentation, refinance (cash-out), AA risk grade, 575–625

FICO score, 75% to 85% LTV, 40% to 45% *debt-to-income ratio* (DTI) and original balance $100,000 to $150,000. The baseline no-penalty hybrid ARM cohorts exhibit the following CRR curves (Exhibit 3.9):

- The 2/28 hybrid ARM cohort's CRR curve begins at 3.5% in the first month and increases to a peak of 56.8% in month 12. The CRR exhibits a modest downward bias leading to the first rate reset (month 24) before peaking again at 71.0%. Thereafter, the CRR declines to around 50.0%.
- The 3/27 hybrid ARM cohort's CRR curve begins at 1.1% in the first month and increases to a peak of 56.2% in month 12. The CRR gradually declines to around 40.0% CRR before peaking coincident with the first rate reset at 57.3%.

Influence of Prepayment Penalties

Loans to subprime borrowers are predominantly originated with a prepayment penalty tenor matching the time to the first rate reset (Exhibit 3.10). An analysis of the prepayment penalty loans originated between 1998 and September 2006 shows that most prepayment penalty expirations were structured to coincide with the loan's first rate reset.

The presence of a prepayment penalty significantly alters the shape of the hybrid ARM seasoning ramp. The peak in the seasoning ramp (around 13 months) is lower than the no-penalty cohort, and the CRR tends to decline

EXHIBIT 3.9 Baseline Hybrid ARM No-Penalty CRR

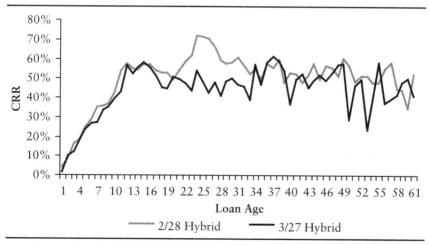

Source: Wachovia Capital Markets, LLC.

EXHIBIT 3.10 Prepayment Penalty Tenor and Loan Type

	Penalty Tenor			
	1-year	**2-year**	**3-year**	**5-year**
6-month ARM	22.1%	29.0%	32.1%	16.8%
1-year ARM	54.5%	5.6%	25.3%	14.6%
2-year hybrid	6.6%	79.8%	12.0%	1.6%
3-year hybrid	5.1%	6.0%	84.1%	4.8%
5-year hybrid	10.5%	9.9%	55.8%	23.8%
7-year hybrid	25.6%	2.7%	40.3%	31.4%
10-year hybrid	45.1%	0.4%	31.6%	22.9%

Source: Created from data obtained from Loan Performance and Wachovia Capital Markets, LLC.

EXHIBIT 3.11 Hybrid ARM Penalty Loan Baseline

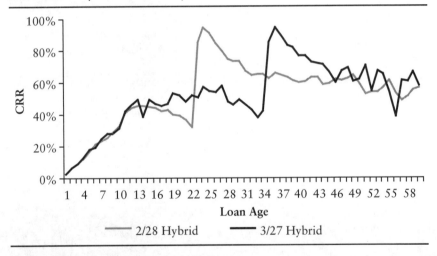

Source: Wachovia Capital Markets, LLC.

before penalty expiry. In addition, a prepayment penalty tenor matching the time to the first rate reset results in a greater prepayment peak coincident with the first rate reset owing to pent-up refinancing demand (Exhibit 3.11).

- The 2/28 hybrid ARM cohort seasoning ramp begins at 2.1% CRR in the first month and increases to a peak of 44.6% in month 13. The CRR exhibits a downward bias until month 24, when the CRR peaks again at 94.0%, coincident with the first rate reset and two-year prepayment-penalty expiration. Thereafter, prepayments decline to around 50% CRR.

- The 3/27 penalty hybrid ARM cohort seasoning ramp begins at 1.7% CRR in the first month and increases to a peak of 48.6% CRR in month 13. The CRR remains somewhat stable through month 30 before exhibiting a downward bias before the first rate reset and penalty expiration. Commensurate with both the first rate reset and penalty expiration, the CRR peaks at 94.2%. Thereafter, the CRR declines to around 50%.

INTEREST-ONLY REPAYMENT ANALYSIS

In response to the dramatic home price appreciation rates experienced between 2000 and 2005 and the commensurate decline in affordability, subprime lenders introduced *interest-only* (IO) loans as part of a strategy to support their origination volume. These loans delay scheduled amortization for a predetermined amount of time, lowering the borrower's initial payment. Most (86.4%) are adjustable rate and structured with a prepayment penalty (Exhibit 3.12). Of the adjustable rate loans, 55.1% are structured with a prepayment penalty. Typically, both the prepayment penalty and the amortization period are structured to expire and begin coincident with the first rate reset.

Baseline Repayment Functions

The IO baseline is very similar to that of the hybrid ARM loan with a prepayment penalty, suggesting similar borrower motivation for taking the loan.

- The interest-only cohort's seasoning ramp begins at 3.5% in the first month and ramps to a peak of 47.9% in month 11. The CRR exhibits a modest downward bias leading to the first rate reset, amortization and penalty expiration. Coincident with these, the CRR peaks at 97.5%.

EXHIBIT 3.12   Interest-Only Rate Type and Penalty Tenor

	Penalty	No Penalty	Row Total
Adjustable	47.71%	38.78%	86.48%
Fixed rate	3.90%	9.62%	13.52%
Column total	51.60%	48.40%	100.00%

Source: Created from data obtained from Loan Performance and Wachovia Capital Markets, LLC.

EXHIBIT 3.13 Interest-Only Baseline

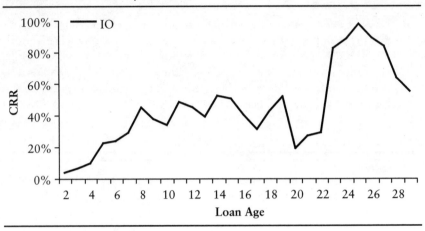

Source: Wachovia Capital Markets, LLC.

Both the adjustable rate and interest-only loans introduce borrower "payment shock." Payment shock occurs when the borrower's payment adjusts upward due to rate reset and/or the beginning of amortization. The implications of payment shock are discussed in greater detail later in this section.

FIXED RATE REPAYMENT ANALYSIS

Interest Sensitivity Analysis

The borrower's sensitivity to refinancing incentives is measured by the loan rate less the FNMA conforming rate, adjusted for credit grade. The minimum and maximum refinancing CRRs exhibit the following:

- For all fixed rate loans, the minimum and maximum refinancing CRRs are 9.5% and 45.3%, respectively.
- The prepayment penalty cohort's minimum and maximum refinancing CRRs are 8.2% and 40.7%, respectively.
- The no-penalty cohort's minimum and maximum refinancing CRRs are 14.2% and 59.2%, respectively.

The presence of a prepayment penalty reduces the CRR rate by 4.7% CRR at the minimum and 13.9% CRR at the maximum. Again, the minimum and maximum CRRs exhibit a convergence when "out-of-the-money"

EXHIBIT 3.14 Fixed-Rate Refinancing Sensitivity

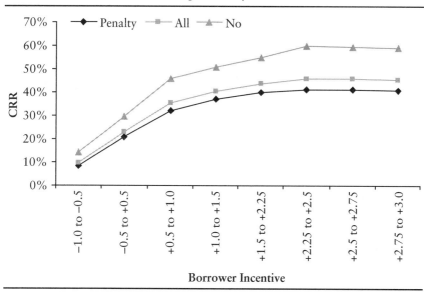

Source: Wachovia Capital Markets, LLC.

and a divergence when "in-the-money," attributable to the decreasing and increasing value of the prepayment penalty.

Baseline Repayment Functions

The baseline fixed rate cohorts (Exhibit 3.15) exhibit the following voluntary repayment rates (CRRs):

- The penalty fixed rate cohort begins at 0.84% CRR in the first month and increases to a peak of 41.7% CRR in month 12. Thereafter, the repayment rate exhibits spikes around months 36, 48 and 60, commensurate with the expiration of prepayment penalties.
- The no-penalty cohort begins at 3.5% CRR in the first month and increases to a peak of 38.7% CRR in month 12. Thereafter, the repayment rate steadily declines to around 30% CRR.

OTHER FACTORS INFLUENCING VOLUNTARY REPAYMENT

Additional factors influencing CRRs are property type, occupancy type, documentation program, loan purpose, risk grade, lien status, debt-to-in-

EXHIBIT 3.15   Fixed-Rate Baselines

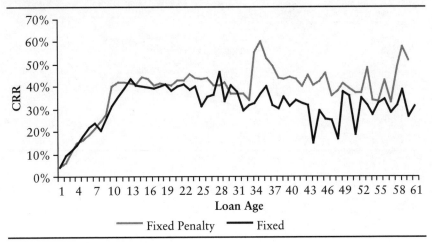

Source: Wachovia Capital Markets, LLC.

come ratio, loan-to-value ratio and original balance. Each of these variables either increases or decreases the CRR (Exhibit 3.17).

Original Loan Amount

The original loan amount influences the borrower's propensity to voluntarily repay (Exhibit 3.16). Specifically, loans with a higher original balance up to about $600,000 exhibit greater risk multipliers relative to the baseline cohort original loan amount ($150,000). The borrower's propensity to repay (risk repayment multiplier) initially increases with the loan amount, but then declines beyond $225,000. Similarly, as the original loan amount declines, the repayment risk multiplier declines.

- Borrowers with original loan amounts lower than the baseline tend to be payment sensitive rather than rate sensitive. As a result, these borrowers are less likely to turn over.
- Borrowers with original loan amounts higher than the baseline amount tend to be less payment sensitive and are more responsive to external incentives and, as a result, exhibit higher turnover rates.

Of particular note is the behavior of the repayment risk multipliers at the super-jumbo balance threshold (greater than $600,000). At first blush, this may seem counterintuitive to the discussion above and the conventional

EXHIBIT 3.16   Original Loan Amount Risk Multipliers

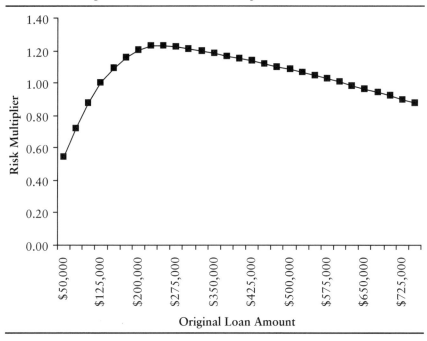

Source: Wachovia Capital Markets, LLC.

wisdom that states that a borrower's propensity to repay increases with the original loan amount. The intuition behind this result is as follows:

- First, the origination liquidity for jumbo subprime loans is lower than that of conforming balance subprime loans.
- Second, the credit curing effect, the tendency of a borrower's credit profile to improve over time, is extended because the greatest source of origination liquidity for jumbo loans is found in the prime and Alt-A sectors, which are often underwritten to more stringent criteria.

Property Type

Property type influences the propensity to voluntarily repay as follows:

- The *planned unit development* loan purpose exhibits a repayment rate roughly equivalent to the single-family cohort. The adjustable and fixed rate multipliers are 1.03 and 0.99, respectively. However, both confidence intervals include 1.0, indicating that voluntary repayments are not significantly different from the single-family cohort.

EXHIBIT 3.17   Repayment Risk Multipliers

Risk Set	Hybrid ARM			Fixed Rate		
	Risk Multiplier	95% Confidence		Risk Multiplier	95% Confidence	
		Lower	Upper		Lower	Upper
Property Type						
PUD	1.03	1.00	1.06	0.99	0.93	1.06
2–4 Units	1.19	1.15	1.24	1.11	1.05	1.17
Condo	1.46	1.42	1.51	1.50	1.40	1.61
Single family	1.00	1.00	1.00	1.00	1.00	1.00
Manufactured housing	0.58	0.54	0.62	0.55	0.49	0.63
Occupancy Type						
Owner occupied	1.00	1.00	1.00	1.00	1.00	1.00
Nonowner (investor)	0.96	0.92	1.01	0.75	0.70	0.80
Second home	0.87	0.81	0.93	0.81	0.71	0.92
Documentation Program						
Full doc	1.00	1.00	1.00	1.00	1.00	1.00
Low doc	1.09	1.07	1.11	0.93	0.90	0.97
Loan Purpose						
Purchase	1.06	1.04	1.08	0.97	0.93	1.01
Refi (cash out)	1.00	1.00	1.00	1.00	1.00	1.00
Refi (no cash out)	0.89	0.86	0.91	0.83	0.79	0.87
Risk Grade						
AA+	0.75	0.72	0.78	1.18	1.13	1.24
AA	1.00	1.00	1.00	1.00	1.00	1.00
A	1.08	1.05	1.10	0.98	0.94	1.02
B	1.18	1.15	1.21	0.95	0.90	1.00
C	1.45	1.39	1.51	0.93	0.83	1.03
CC	1.89	1.79	2.00	1.08	0.93	1.24
Lien Status						
First lien	1.00	1.00	1.00	1.00	1.00	1.00
Second lien	1.40	0.35	5.61	2.50	2.35	2.66

Source: Wachovia Capital Markets, LLC.

- The 2–4 unit (multifamily) and *condominium property* types exhibit repayment risk multipliers greater than 1.0, indicating faster voluntary repayments relative to the baseline cohort (single family).
- The *manufactured housing property* type's risk multiplier (0.58 and 0.55) indicates slower voluntary repayments relative to the single-family cohort.

Occupancy Type

The baseline repayment rate is set by owner-occupied status. Both investor and second home occupancy status voluntarily repay at a rate slower than the baseline.

- With respect to the investor occupancy loan type, hybrid ARMs exhibit a higher multiplier relative to fixed rate loans (0.96 versus 0.75). This indicates that the fixed rate borrower exhibits a slower turnover rate relative to hybrid ARM borrowers. We believe this is due to the speculation versus rental decision. Speculative investors most likely choose financing that closely matches their holding period (hybrid ARM), while investors seeking to rent choose fixed rate funding, reflecting their longer holding period. To the extent that the hybrid ARM cohort contains a greater proportion of speculators relative to renters, the risk multiplier should be higher than that of the fixed rate cohort.

Documentation Program

Full documentation programs require verification of income, assets and employment. Asset verification is required for purchase transactions and corroborates both the seasoning and the source of funds. With respect to income, full documentation generally requires applicants to submit a written form of verification from the employer for stable income for a period up to 12 months. A wage earner may document income by a current pay stub reflecting year-to-date income and the applicant's most recent W-2 or IRS Form 1040. Self-employed applicants may document income with either their most recent federal tax returns or personal bank statements.

Limited or stated documentation is for borrowers who are otherwise unable to meet the full documentation standards. Limited documentation requires applicants to submit at least three months of bank statements, and no documentation is generally available only to the highest credit grade borrowers.

- The low documentation (limited or stated) risk multiplier for hybrid ARMs and fixed rate loans are 1.09 and 0.93, respectively.

Loan Purpose

As shown in Exhibit 3.2, the majority of subprime loans are refinanced (cash out), meaning that borrowers are extracting equity from their homes.

- The purchase cohorts differ according to loan type. Specifically, the purchase ARM repayment risk multiplier is 1.06; conversely, the fixed multiplier is 0.97. This suggests that the hybrid ARM purchase borrower demonstrates faster turnover than the cash-out borrower, whereas the fixed rate purchase borrower exhibits a slower turnover.
- Rate and term (no cash out) hybrid ARM and fixed rate borrowers exhibit lower voluntary repayment multipliers of 0.89, and 0.83, respectively. This suggests that rate and term borrowers refinance based on an expectation of living in their homes for a longer period than either refinance cash out or purchase cohort.

Borrower Risk Grade

Lower credit grade borrowers exhibit higher risk multipliers relative to the baseline (risk grade AA). This is due to the "credit curing effect."

- Credit curing refers to the improvement in a borrower's credit score or profile as the borrower makes and maintains a schedule of timely payments. As the borrower's credit improves, he or she could become eligible for a prime or near-prime loan with a favorable rate relative to a subprime loan. As a result, the borrower is "in-the-money" and faces a positive economic incentive to refinance.
- The credit curing effect increases as the borrower's risk grade declines. This is because the lowest risk grade borrowers (C, CC) are paying the highest rates and, as a result, realize the greatest economic benefit from credit curing.

Lien Status

Second lien loans may represent either financing of the down payment, referred to as a silent second, or equity extraction. The trend from 2004 to 2006 has been toward the use of silent seconds as a means of down payment financing.

- Adjustable and fixed rate second lien loans risk multipliers are 1.40 and 2.50, respectively. Irrespective of the purpose of a second lien (silent for down payment or equity extraction), a borrower realizes a significant economic incentive to pay down the loan, either directly or through subsequent refinancing due to the second lien's higher rate.

COLLATERAL CREDIT PERFORMANCE

In this section, we examine the delinquency and roll rates, and the default and loss severity of subprime loans. The delinquency status of a loan indicates the number of days the borrower is contractually past due (i.e., days past due or dpd). The loan delinquency statistics may be calculated using either the Mortgage Bankers Association (MBA) method or the Office of Thrift Supervision (OTS) method.

- Using the MBA method, a loan is considered contractually delinquent if the payment is not received by the end of the day immediately preceding the loan's next due date (generally the end of the month). For example, a loan due on November 1, 2006 with no payment received on November 30, 2006 *would be* reported delinquent on the November statement to bondholders.
- Using the OTS method, a loan is considered contractually delinquent if the payment is not received by the close of business on the loan's due date in the following month. For example, a loan due on November 1, 2006 with no payment received on November 31, 2006 would not be reported delinquent on the November statement to the bondholders.

The OTS method delays the reporting of delinquent loans by one month relative to the MBA method. It is important to know which reporting method is used by each originator or servicer when comparing delinquency statistics.

Roll Rate Analysis

A roll rate matrix (Exhibit 3.18) is read by rows (from state) across columns (to state) and provides transition probabilities. The roll rate matrix presented in Exhibit 3.18 includes both fixed- and adjustable rate subprime loans originated between the first quarter of 2000 and second quarter of 2006. A roll rate matrix may be stratified by product type (ARM, fixed and IO) as well as seasoning intervals. Exponentiation of the matrix (Exhibit 3.19) provides estimates of delinquency, foreclosure, and *real estate owned* (REO) stated as a percentage of the original balance. Because transition probabilities are not constant across time, a roll rate matrix model tends to overstate delinquencies. Nonetheless, it can be instructive for investors to examine roll rate matrixes by issuer or product type.

- The first row of the matrix describes the roll rate of loans that are current. Of the current loans, 95.1% remain current in the next period. The balance of the loans roll to the next delinquent state.
- The second row provides the transition probabilities for loans that are 30 days delinquent. Of the 30-days delinquent loans, 41.0% remain delinquent (rolling delinquency), 36.3% cure, returning to the current state, and the balance roll to the next delinquency state.
- The matrix shows that loans are remitted to foreclose beginning at 60 (9.0%) and 90 days delinquent (20.8%).

EXHIBIT 3.18 Roll Rate Analysis

From/To	Current	30-dpd	60-dpd	90-dpd	Foreclosure	REO
Current	95.1%	4.7%	0.2%	0.0%	0.0%	0.0%
30-dpd	36.3%	41.0%	21.6%	0.6%	0.5%	0.0%
60-dpd	16.2%	19.3%	26.4%	29.1%	9.0%	0.0%
90-dpd	4.7%	2.4%	4.6%	67.0%	20.8%	0.5%
Foreclosure	4.7%	1.1%	0.8%	7.2%	81.1%	5.2%
REO	0.1%	0.0%	0.0%	1.5%	0.6%	97.7%

Source: Created from data obtained from Loan Performance and Wachovia Capital Markets, LLC.

EXHIBIT 3.19 Roll Rate Model of Delinquency

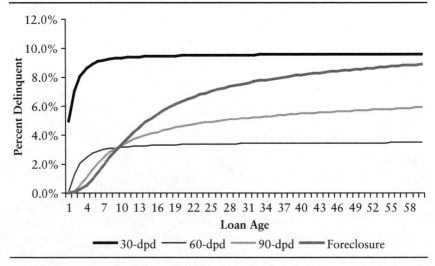

Source: Wachovia Capital Markets, LLC.

INVOLUNTARY REPAYMENT (DEFAULT)

The baseline default rate, as measured by CDR, for both hybrid ARM and fixed rate loans (Exhibit 3.20) illustrate the difference between loans with prepayment penalties and those without by amortization type.

■ The penalty loan hybrid ARM default curve approaches its maximum (around 10.0%) in month 38. Defaults range between 10.0% and 11.0% through month 55 before beginning to decline. The penalty loan default curve reaches a plateau around 6.0% in month 72.
■ The no-penalty loan hybrid ARM default curve reaches its maximum at month 40 around 8.5%. Defaults range between 8.5% and 10.0% through month 52 before beginning to decline. The no-penalty loan default reaches a plateau around 5.0% in month 72.
■ The fixed rate default curve reaches its peak at month 38 around 5.0%. Defaults range between 5.0% and 6.0% through month 52 before beginning to decline. The fixed rate default curve reaches a plateau around 4.0% in month 72. Like its hybrid ARM counterpart, the absence of a prepayment penalty reduces the frequency of default.

The hybrid ARM default baselines presented in Exhibit 3.20 show that during the first rate reset window, months 24 through 36, the hybrid ARM default baseline increases relative to its fixed rate cohort.

EXHIBIT 3.20 Hybrid ARM Default Curve

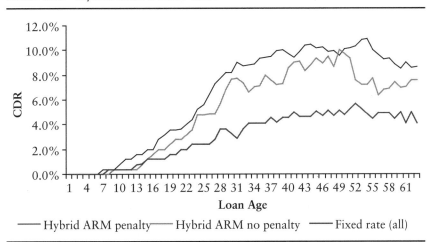

Source: Wachovia Capital Markets, LLC.

OTHER FACTORS INFLUENCING INVOLUNTARY REPAYMENT RATES

We examined the influence of the following variables on the default function: property type, occupancy type, documentation program, risk grade, debt-to-income ratio, loan-to-value, and FICO (Exhibit 3.21).

Property Type

The property-type risk multipliers indicate that, with the exception of manufactured housing (adjustable and fixed rate) and 2–4 units (fixed rate), all other property types default at a rate slower than the baseline (single family).

- The manufactured housing property type defaults at a rate 7.0% (hybrid ARM) and 34.0% (fixed rate) faster than the baseline.
- The 2–4 units property type defaults at a rate equal to (hybrid ARM) and 13.0% faster (fixed rate) than the baseline.

Occupancy

The investor and second home risk multipliers are directionally the same across product type. The investor risk multipliers of 1.48 (hybrid ARM) and 2.53 (fixed rate) indicate that investor occupancy types default at a rate 48.0% and 153.0% greater than the baseline (single family). The second home cohorts default at a rate 50.0% and 29.0% less than the baseline (single family). The intuition for the lower risk multiplier of the second home cohort is as follows:

- Borrowers who are unable to continue to make payments on a second home due to a financial disruption are easily able to dispose of the property without concern for their current living situation (owner occupied) or the presence of renters in the case of investor property. As a result, we believe that these homes are most often voluntarily liquidated (sold) before the event of default.

Documentation Program

Generally, lower levels of documentation tend to be associated with a higher incidence of default. The borrower's inability to fully document income suggests a potentially weaker borrower or overstatement of income.

- Low documentation adjustable and fixed rate loans default at rates 35.0% and 41.0% faster than the baseline (single family).

Loan Purpose

In the case of hybrid ARMs, both the purchase and rate and term refinance (no cash out) risk multipliers are greater than 1.0. At first blush, this seems counterintuitive, especially in the case of the purchase loan, which is generally perceived to be stronger. However, we believe the findings are due to the following:

- Purchase borrowers may be first-time borrowers or "stretching" to purchase their home. In addition, they may employ a second lien loan to finance their down payment. In either case, they may be overleveraged. In addition, purchase borrowers have, by definition, no time in property, and this may influence the propensity to default.
- Rate and term borrowers are not extracting equity but rather seeking to lower monthly payments. The reluctance to extract equity or the absence of equity available for extraction may signal a weaker borrower relative to a cash-out refinance.
- Fixed rate and term refinance default risk is less than refinance cash out or purchase. This borrower is most likely reducing rate and/or extending term. This, in turn, lowers the borrowers and reduces the probability of default.

Borrower Risk Grade

The risk grade multipliers exhibit an inverse relationship, mostly increasing as the borrowers risk grade declines. At risk grades B and lower, the confidence intervals do not overlap one another, an indication of effective credit scoring. Both the adjustable and fixed rate grade-A risk multipliers straddle 1.0, this suggests that the A risk grade does not default significantly different than the risk grade AA.

Debt-to-Income

The borrower's DTI ratio expresses the mortgage payment as a percentage of the borrower's income (front-end ratio). In addition, lenders consider mortgage payment and other obligations such as car payments, credit card payments, and the like, to determine the debt-to-income (back-end ratio). Generally speaking, the ideal DTI ratio (back end) is 36%. As borrower DTI passes 40%, he or she has little financial flexibility and is vulnerable to financial shocks (Exhibit 3.22).

- The borrower's risk of default increases 4.8% for every 5.0% increase in the borrower's DTI ratio.

EXHIBIT 3.21 Involuntary Repayment Risk Multipliers

	Hybrid ARM			Fixed Rate		
	Risk	95% Confidence		Risk	95% Confidence	
Risk Set	Multiplier	Lower	Upper	Multiplier	Lower	Upper
Property Type						
PUD	0.77	0.70	0.86	0.46	0.31	0.67
2–4 units	0.99	0.89	1.11	1.13	0.90	1.43
Condo	0.66	0.57	0.75	0.48	0.31	0.75
Single family	1.00	1.00	1.00	1.00	1.00	1.00
Manufactured housing	1.07	0.95	1.20	1.34	1.01	1.77
Occupancy Type						
Owner occupied	1.00	1.00	1.00	1.00	1.00	1.00
Nonowner (investor)	1.48	1.33	1.68	2.53	2.09	3.06
Second home	0.50	0.37	0.68	0.71	0.35	1.42
Documentation Program						
Full doc	1.00	1.00	1.00	1.00	1.00	1.00
Low doc	1.35	1.28	1.42	1.41	1.24	1.61
Loan Purpose						
Purchase	1.12	1.06	1.18	1.33	1.15	1.54
Refi (cash-out)	1.00	1.00	1.00	1.00	1.00	1.00
Refi (no cash-out)	1.05	0.98	1.13	0.84	0.69	1.01
Risk Grade						
AA+	0.75	0.61	0.94	0.67	0.51	0.88
AA	1.00	1.00	1.00	1.00	1.00	1.00
A	0.93	0.88	1.00	1.11	0.94	1.31
B	1.32	1.23	1.41	2.11	1.77	2.52
C	1.84	1.66	2.04	3.56	2.77	4.59
CC	3.12	2.72	3.57	6.64	4.42	9.98

Source: Wachovia Capital Markets, LLC.

EXHIBIT 3.22 Debt-to-Income Default Risk Multipliers

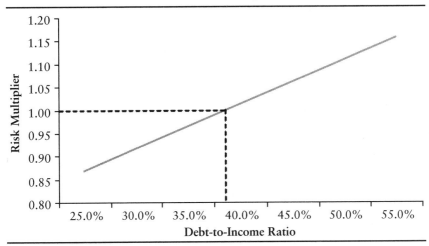

Source: Wachovia Capital Markets, LLC.

Loan-to-Value

LTV risk multipliers exhibit a positive relationship, increasing as the LTV increases and decreasing as the LTV decreases.

- The LTV default risk multiplier function indicates that borrowers with an LTV of 90.0% or higher default at a rate 80% greater than those with an 80% LTV.

FICO Score

The FICO risk multipliers exhibit an inverse relationship, decreasing as the FICO score increases.

- A borrower with an 800 FICO score is expected to default at 38%, the rate of the baseline (600 FICO score). Conversely, a borrower with a 450 FICO score is expected to default at a rate two times the baseline.

STRUCTURAL CONSIDERATIONS

The loans that collateralize residential ABS structures may be all adjustable, all fixed rate or separate collateral groups of adjustable and fixed rate loans. The loans may support adjustable, fixed rate or a combination of adjustable and fixed rate liabilities (bonds).

EXHIBIT 3.23   Loan-to-Value Default Risk Multipliers

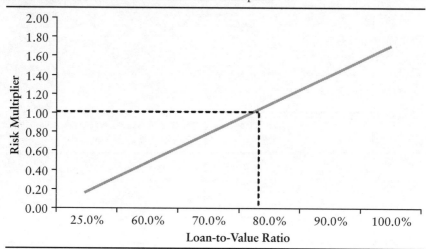

Source: Wachovia Capital Markets, LLC.

EXHIBIT 3.24   FICO Default Risk Multipliers

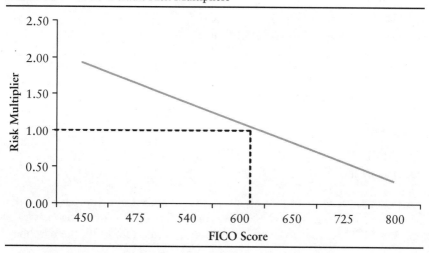

Source: Wachovia Capital Markets, LLC.

The early subprime securitizations mostly relied on monoline insurance providers for credit enhancement despite the fact that self-insuring structures were widely used in the prime nonagency market. This was largely due to limited investor experience in the sector, and a relative dearth of collateral performance statistics with respect to defaults, recoveries, and cumulative losses. In 1997, the first senior/subordinated structure was introduced in the residential ABS market.

Over time, issuers adopted the structure. As liquidity in the AAA sector continued to improve, a market for credit-sensitive bonds developed and more issuer-specific performance data with respect to repayment, default and recovery rates became available.

Senior-Subordinated Structures

Senior-subordinated structures are referred to as self-insuring structures because they rely on internally generated credit support to protect the investor from losses. Typically, senior-subordinated bonds employ a combination of excess spread, overcollateralization and subordination. Losses are absorbed in reverse priority through the capital structure (Exhibit 3.25), first by excess spread, then *overcollateralization* (OC) and finally via the principal writedown of the subordinated bonds.

As mentioned previously, collateral may be either all fixed or adjustable rate or consist of both fixed and adjustable rate. Credit enhancement structures may be designed to accommodate the different collateral groups. These structures are referred to as I-, H-, or Y-structures.

Type I credit enhancement structures (Exhibit 3.25) accommodate a single collateral group of either fixed rate, adjustable rate, or mixed loan types. Both the H (Exhibit 3.26) and Y (Exhibit 3.27) credit enhancement structures may be used with multiple collateral groups. The H-structure allows two collateral groups and two distinct subordinated bond groups.

The H-structure can be thought of as two distinct transactions, except that excess interest may be shared between collateral groups (Exhibit 3.26) to maintain target OC levels and cross coverage of subordinate bonds for triple-A support. Because excess interest is shared between groups, the H-structure is said to be cross collateralized.

For example, if Group 2's excess interest is insufficient to cover losses and maintain target OC levels and Group 1 has sufficient excess interest to cover its losses and maintain excess interest, then Group 1's excess interest may be used to bring Group 2's OC to the target level.

The Y-structure also allows two distinct collateral groups. However, unlike the H-structure, the Y-structure employs a single subordination group to support both the Group 1 and the Group 2 senior tranches.

Shifting Interest

Like other nonagency mortgage securitizations, subprime transactions employ a "shifting interest" mechanism that increases the credit enhancement avail-

EXHIBIT 3.25   Representative Credit Enhancement at Deal Inception

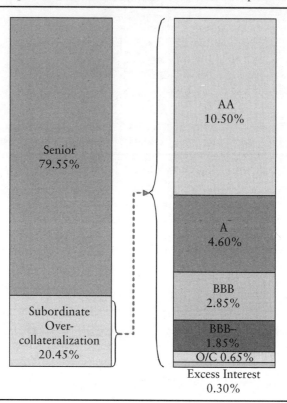

Source: Wachovia Capital Markets, LLC.

able to the senior bonds. Early in the transaction, principal collections and, in some cases, excess interest are paid to the senior bonds only, and the subordinated bonds are "locked out" from receiving principal during this time.

For example, consider the structure presented in Exhibit 3.25; the triple-A rated class, mezzanine, and subordinated classes, and OC and excess interest account for 79.55%, 19.50% and 0.95% of the capital structure, respectively. During the "lockout" period, the triple-A bonds amortize and their percentage interest in the underlying collateral pool decreases. Concurrently, the relative interest of the subordinated bonds in the collateral pool increases. For the most part, the subordinated bonds are "locked out" from receiving principal for the first 36 months or until the credit enhancement level for the senior bonds has doubled, whichever is later. This point is called the *step-down date*, referring to the reduction (step-down) of the dollar amount of subordination as credit enhancement. In the case of our

EXHIBIT 3.26   H-Structure Credit Enhancement

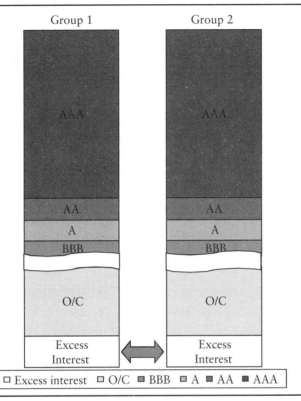

Source: Wachovia Capital Markets, LLC.

transaction, with multiple classes assigned different ratings, the mezzanine and subordinated classes would receive their pro rata share of principal collections and begin to amortize.

The 36-month lockout period is based on historic default experience. Typically, a pool of subprime loans will experience about 60% of its total expected cumulative defaults by month 36, with the majority of the defaults most likely occurring from months 24 to 48 (Exhibit 3.28). Given the timing of losses, the early lockout of the subordinate bonds increases the amount of credit enhancement available concurrent with the peak in default timing.

Deep Mortgage Insurance

Mortgage insurance (MI) purchased by the issuer at the time of securitization may be used as a form of credit enhancement. The presence of deep

EXHIBIT 3.27   Y-Structure Credit Enhancement

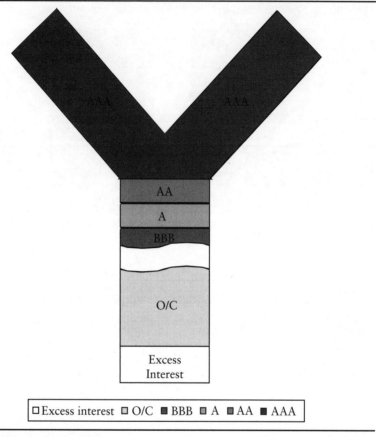

Excess interest   O/C   BBB   A   AA   AAA

Source: Wachovia Capital Markets, LLC.

MI has the effect of reducing realized losses. As a result, the rating agencies view deep MI as a significant source of credit enhancement that reduces the amount of upfront credit support needed to achieve the desired ratings on the bonds compared with a straight senior-subordinated bonds structure. In a transaction employing "deep MI," the issuer pays a premium, which may come out of the cash flow of the securitization, for a policy that covers losses on a portion of the mortgage pool.

It is important to note that loan level mortgage insurance differs from a monoline wrap. A wrap from one of the bond insurance companies is an unconditional guarantee of timely payment of interest and the ultimate repayment of principal. Thus, the investor's credit exposure is directly

EXHIBIT 3.28 Expected Default Timing of Residential ABS

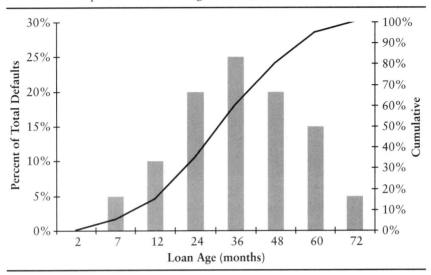

Source: Created from data obtained from Standard & Poor's Corp. and Wachovia Capital Markets, LLC.

linked to the monoline insurer. In a deep MI structure, the loans must meet the insurer's criteria. The insurer specifies the characteristics, such as minimum and maximum LTV, property type, minimum and maximum borrower credit, and so on. When an insured loan defaults, the issuer submits a claim to the insurer and the insurer reviews the claim. The insurer may cover all or a portion of the claim or may reject the claim if the insurer determines that its underwriting guidelines have been violated by the issuer.

Mortgage insurance covers a portion of the principal balance of the loan to a prespecified LTV ratio, typically 60% to 65%. In addition, a deep MI policy covers accrued interest and expenses incurred during the foreclosure and liquidation process. Consequently, deep MI makes a loan look like it has a lower LTV ratio because the insurance takes a second loss position behind the borrower's equity.

Exhibit 3.29 illustrates a loan at origination covered by deep MI. The original LTV ratio of the loan is 90%, and deep MI brings the effective LTV down to 65%. The mortgage insurance covers one-quarter of the outstanding loan balance and has a second loss position in the loan. Effectively, this loan now has a 65% LTV. In practice, loans with different LTV ratios and levels of coverage will have different mortgage insurance coverage ratios. Finally, over time this loan will amortize and the amount of borrower equity in the property will increase, assuming no change in the property market value. The mortgage insurance policy is designed to still cover one-quarter of the outstanding balance as the loan amortizes.

Excess Interest

Excess interest represents the difference between the collateral weighted average mortgage rates and the weighted average cost of the liabilities, net of fees and expenses. Generally, the mortgage loans are expected to generate more interest than required to pay the liabilities.

- To the extent that excess interest (net of fees, expenses or derivative payments) is positive, it is used to absorb losses on the mortgage loans.
- After the financial obligations of the trust are covered, excess interest is used to maintain overcollateralization at the target level.

EXHIBIT 3.29 Loan Covered by Deep Mortgage Insurance

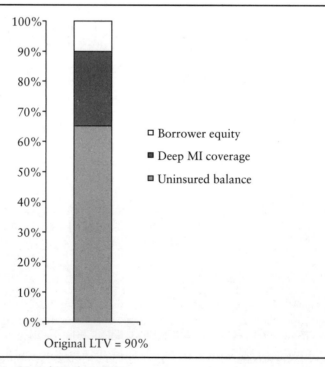

Original LTV = 90%

Source: Wachovia Capital Markets, LLC.

Several factors could affect the extent to which excess interest is available to maintain overcollateralization:

- Full or partial repayments and defaults may reduce the amount of excess interest. This is because borrowers with mortgage loans carrying higher WACs have a greater tendency to repay. This, in turn, reduces the weighted average rate of the underlying mortgage loan pool (this is commonly referred to as WAC drift).
- If the rates of delinquencies, defaults or losses turn out to be higher than expected, excess interest will be reduced by the amount necessary to compensate for any shortfalls in the cash available to make required distributions to the senior and mezzanine certificates.

Overcollateralization

Overcollateralization is the excess of the mortgage pool balance over the certificate balance and acts as internally generated credit support. Excess spread is used to accelerate the amortization of the outstanding certificate's principal balance to a level lower than the mortgage pool balance.

Overcollateralization can either be allowed to build over time or be fully funded at closing. If the OC is built over time, excess spread is used to accelerate the paydown of the AAA classes until the target OC amount is achieved. The target OC amount is usually achieved in the early months of the transaction's life. Conversely, if the OC is fully funded at closing, then excess spread is used to maintain the OC amount. The target OC amount is generally established as a percentage of the original principal balance. The required OC amount varies depending on the underlying collateral composition, structured used and the level of spreads on the liabilities (bonds) issued.

An overcollateralized transaction can sustain losses equal to the amount of current available excess spread and overcollateralization before incurring principal writedowns in the capital structure. For example, assume the transaction structure presented in Exhibit 3.25 and a target OC building to 1.3%. Once cumulative losses exceed the OC amount, and if excess spread is insufficient to cover losses in a given period, then subordinated bond investors will incur principal losses.

Structural Credit Protection and Trigger Events

Trigger events are generally based on both seriously delinquent loans and cumulative losses. Seriously delinquent loans includes loans that are 60+

days past due (dpd), in foreclosure or REO. Trigger events are considered in effect on or after the step-down date if the various criteria are not passed.

There are two types of delinquency triggers: soft delinquency triggers and hard delinquency triggers.

Soft Delinquency Triggers

Soft delinquency triggers dynamically link credit enhancement to deal performance. There are two types of soft delinquency triggers. The first is a soft trigger based on the credit enhancement of the senior certificates. This trigger specifies a target value for delinquencies as a percentage of the senior certificate's enhancement. This type of trigger mostly protects the senior bondholders. However, as the senior classes pay down, the credit enhancement to those classes increases and the trigger becomes mechanically weaker, to the point that it may no longer be effective. Exhibit 3.30 illustrates the point; under the higher prepayment scenarios, the delinquency threshold increases faster than under slower prepayment scenarios.

The second type of soft delinquency trigger is based on the credit enhancement of the most senior outstanding bond. This kind of delinquency trigger will not step down if serious delinquencies exceed a target level that is tied to the credit enhancement available for the most senior outstanding class. The structure of this trigger partly addresses the weakness of the delinquency trigger discussed previously.

Hard Delinquency Triggers

The second type of trigger is a hard delinquency trigger. Hard delinquency triggers are not tied to the senior enhancement percentage. Rather, the threshold is a fixed percentage of the current collateral balance. The hard delinquency trigger offers several advantages over a soft delinquency trigger. First, it mitigates the adverse selection risk due to rapid repayments. Second, a hard delinquency trigger's ability to prevent step-down does not diminish with the increase in subordination to the senior bonds like a soft delinquency trigger.

The hard delinquency trigger equivalent of a soft delinquency trigger can be estimated as follows: multiply the soft trigger by two times the initial senior enhancement and the soft delinquency trigger threshold. Using the 30% CPR example in Exhibit 3.30, the equivalent hard trigger at year three would be (0.20 times 2 times 0.233) = 9.3%

EXHIBIT 3.30 Soft Trigger CPR Sensitivity Comparison

CPR	30%				40%			
	Pool	Aaa	SEP	Delinquency Threshold	Pool	Aaa	SEP	Delinquency Threshold
Initiation	100.00	80.0	20%	8.00%	100.00	80.0	20%	8.00%
Year 1	70.00	50.0	29%	11.43%	60.00	40.0	33%	13.33%
Year 2	49.00	29.0	41%	16.33%	36.00	16.0	56%	22.22%
Year 3	34.30	14.0	58%	23.32%	21.60	2.0	93%	37.04%
Year 4	24.00	4.0	83%	33.32%	12.96	0.0	100%	40.00%
Soft delinquency trigger			40% of Senior Enhancement Percentage (SEP%)					
Baa3 enhancement			8%					

Source: Navneet Agarwal and Gregory Besserman, *Moody's Overview of Triggers in U.S. Home Equity Transactions*, August 11, 2007, p. 2, Figure 1. © Moody's Investors Service, Inc. and/or its affiliates. Reprinted with permission. All Rights Reserved.

EXHIBIT 3.31   Overcollateralization Trigger Amounts

Distribution Date Occurring	Percentage
July 2008–June 2009	1.55% for July 2008, plus 1/12 of 1.90% thereafter
July 2009–June 2010	3.45% for July 2009, plus 1/12 of 1.95% thereafter
July 2010–June 2011	5.40% for July 2010, plus 1/12 of 1.55% thereafter
July 2011–June 2012	6.95% for July 2011, plus 1/12 of 0.85% thereafter
July 2012 and thereafter	7.80%

Source: Option One Mortgage Loan Trust 2006-2 Prospectus, page S-88.

Overcollateralization Step-Up Trigger

The overcollateralization step-up trigger increases the deal's OC target (rather than stop the release of OC) to a higher level if cumulative losses exceed a specified amount. This trigger provides the advantage of increasing OC in the later stages of a deal's life. However, due to WAC drift, it is possible that when losses cross the specified level, excess spread may be insufficient to build the additional OC. Exhibit 3.31 illustrates a typical overcollateralization trigger schedule.

Available Funds Cap

The term *available funds cap* (AFC) refers to the truism that a bondholder may only be paid interest up to the amount of net interest that can be generated by the mortgage pool. The AFC is due to the fact that home equity ABS are often collateralized by hybrid adjustable rate loans that have a fixed period (most commonly, from one to three years) as well as periodic and life caps that limit the interest that may be available to pay investors after trustee fees and transaction expenses.

Furthermore, floating rate ABS are, for the most part, indexed to one-month LIBOR and reset monthly. The ARMs included in these transactions may be indexed to several interest rate indexes such as six-month LIBOR or the one-year *constant maturity Treasury* (CMT). The differing indexes and reset periods relative to the liabilities create *additional basis risk.*

To calculate the initial available funds cap, subtract expenses (e.g., servicing fees, trustee fees, IO strip and net swap payments) from the original weighted average coupon on the underlying mortgage loans. After the liabilities are accounted for, the available excess spread generated by the mortgage pool can be calculated (Exhibit 3.32). In addition, the LIBOR strike or maximum LIBOR rate can be calculated (Exhibit 3.32) using the weighted average spread of the liabilities.

EXHIBIT 3.32   Calculating Available Funds Cap

Initial Available Funds Cap	
Weighted average gross coupon	8.726%
Less servicing fee	–0.300%
Less trustee fee	–0.003%
Less IO strip (if any)	0.000%
Less mortgage insurance	–0.250%
Less net swap payments (basis points)[a]	0.000%
Net available funds cap	8.173%
Weighted average bond coupon	–5.570%
Initial excess spread	2.603%

Life Cap	
Weighted average life cap	15.00%
Less servicing fee	–0.300%
Less trustee fee	–0.003%
Less IO strip (if any)	0.000%
Less mortgage insurance	–0.250%
Less net swap payments (basis points)[a]	0.000%
Net available funds life cap	15.55%
Weighted average bond spread	0.25%
Current 1 month LIBOR	5.32%
Maximum LIBOR increase	9.98%

[a] No swap hedge is assumed in this example.
Source: Wachovia Capital Markets, LLC.

Exhibit 3.32 illustrates the relationship between the net available funds cap, LIBOR strike and excess spread. Specifically, in a rising interest rate environment, as the liabilities reset and increase, the excess spread declines. Furthermore, the introduction of credit risk further complicates the AFC calculation because losses reduce the excess spread in the period when they are realized, which, in turn, reduces the available funds cap.

The AFC is a more significant component of the analysis for subordinated bonds than for senior bonds. Subordinated bonds tend to have longer average lives and, as a result, this gives the cap a longer time horizon over which to become binding. In addition, the potential for failing the triggers means that the subordinated bonds could extend their average lives further, increasing the cost of the available funds cap to the investor. Finally, the wider spread margin on subordinate bonds makes them more sensitive to changes in interest rates and the available funds cap.

Use of Derivatives to Hedge Asset/Liability Mismatches

Hedging can be done using either interest rate caps, interest rate swaps, or combination of both. Generally speaking, hedging with an interest rate swap is considered riskier than hedging with an interest rate cap. Asset/liability hedges are required in a transaction because, as stated previously, the available funds cap, or margin, refers to the fact that the coupon on a floating rate bond (liability) is limited to the weighted average rate on the underlying loans (assets), less the expenses of the trust. Trust expenses include trustee fees, servicing fees, bond surety fees, IO strip, and mortgage insurance fees. In addition, the timing mismatch between the adjustments to the liability rate, (generally monthly) and the asset rate, (generally semiannual or annual) may create temporary interest shortfalls due to the presence of periodic caps that may limit the weighted average asset rate relative to the liability rate.

In addition to the above issues, most residential ABS securitizations include hybrid ARM loans with fixed rate periods of two, three, and five years, and fixed rate loans. This creates an asset/liability mismatch of floating rate liabilities (bonds) and fixed rate assets (loans). As a result, this mismatch must be hedged to preserve the excess spread in a rising interest rate environment.

Hedging with Interest Rate Caps

Hedging with caps requires the issuer to purchase a cap to hedge the asset/liability mismatch and incur an upfront cost. The cap contract is not considered an asset of any Real Estate Mortgage Investment Conduit (REMIC). The cap payments are made to the distribution account after fees.

At the closing of the transaction, the trust enters into a cap agreement with a cap provider. The agreement states the LIBOR strike and the notional balance on which the cap contract is based. The cap contract may specify a LIBOR rate maximum beyond which the contract will not pay (a cap corridor). For example, Option One 2003-5 Mortgage Loan Trust employed a cap contract to hedge the basis risk in the transaction.

The cap contract covered the first 43 distribution dates; under the agreement, the cap provider or counterparty agrees to pay the trust the excess of the LIBOR strike up to a maximum of 9.25%, multiplied by the notional

EXHIBIT 3.33   Hedging with Interest Rate Caps

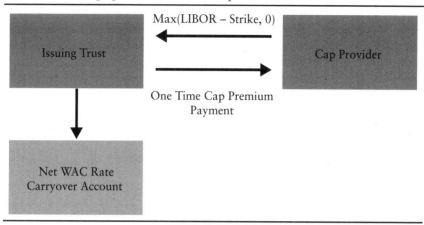

Source: Wachovia Capital Markets, LLC.

amount for the related distribution date on an actual/360 basis. The cap payment, if made by the cap counterparty, is deposited in a net WAC rate carryover account reserve account and made available for distribution to the certificates.

Hedging with Interest Rate Swaps

Swap payments become fees and expenses of the trust. The interest rate swap is held in a supplemental interest trust that is not considered an asset of any REMIC (see Exhibit 3.34). The net swap payments by the trust are withdrawn from amounts on deposit in the distribution account before distribution to certificate holders.

On the distribution date, the supplemental interest trust pays the swap provider a fixed rate and the swap provider pays the supplemental interest account a floating payment equal to one-month LIBOR. The swap amounts are calculated based on the amount of the senior class and mezzanine certificates.

A net payment, referred to as the *new swap payment*, will be made on the distribution date as follows:

- By the supplemental interest trust to the swap provider in the event that the fixed payment is greater than the floating payment.
- Or by the swap provider to the supplemental interest trust in the event that the fixed payment is less than the floating payment.

EXHIBIT 3.34 Hedging with Interest Rate Swaps

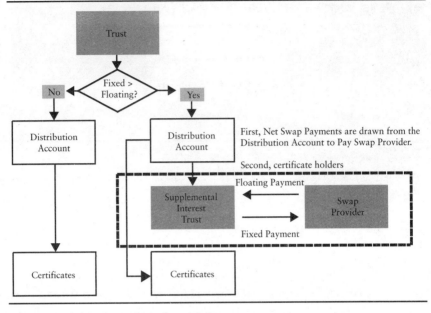

Source: Wachovia Capital Markets, LLC.

If the supplement interest trust is required to make a payment to the swap provider (the fixed payment is greater than the floating payment), the trust will be required to make a payment to the supplemental interest account from the distribution account before distributions to the certificate holders.

ASSET-BACKED CREDIT DEFAULT SWAPS

This section is not intended to be an exhaustive discussion of *asset-backed credit default swaps* (ABCDS) but rather provide a basic understanding of *credit default swaps* (CDS) and ABCDS with respect to home equity loan collateral. CDS are designed to isolate the risk of default and allow a party to either take or reduce default exposure on loans, bonds, sovereign, corporate and asset-backed securities.

Basics of CDS

Exhibit 3.35 illustrates a typical CDS structure.

EXHIBIT 3.35   CDS Mechanics

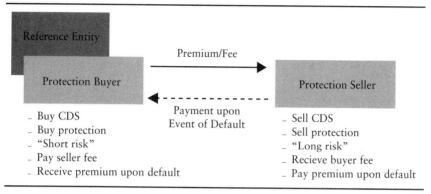

Source: Wachovia Capital Markets, LLC.

- The CDS buyer (protection buyer) pays a fee to the CDS seller (protection seller) on a reference security.
- Upon a credit event, the CDS seller (protection seller) pays the CDS buyer (protection buyer) a premium to cover any losses incurred by the protection buyer resulting from credit exposure to the reference entity.
- If there is no credit event, then there is no payment made to the protection buyer by the protection seller.

The payment received by the protection buyer from the protection seller arising from a credit event may take one of the following forms:

1. *Cash settlement.* The seller of protection pays the buyer of protection an amount based on the change in the price of the reference security. The change in price is the difference between the price of the reference security at the time the CDS contract was entered and the price of the asset immediately following the credit event.
2. *Physical settlement and delivery.* The buyer of protection delivers to the seller of the protection an agreed asset (usually the reference security) following a credit event. The seller of protection purchases the security from the protection buyer at the price agreed on at the time of entry into the CDS contract (this is the face value of the CDS).
3. *Fixed payment.* The seller of protection pays the buyer of protection a fixed payment (preagreed) upon an event of default, reflecting an estimate of loss between the protection buyer and protection seller. This arrangement is referred to as a digital or binary credit default swap.
4. *Actual workout recovery value.* The seller of protection pays the buyer of protection the full face value of the CDS. The buyer of protection is

required to collect and pay through to the seller of protection subsequent recoveries received from the reference entity during the workout following the credit event.

CDS Referencing ABS

ABCDS are reference-specific obligations. Credit events are specified with respect to a reference entity. Typically, the reference entity is an ABS issuer or a specific security issued by the reference entity. Most ABCDS transactions are settled either through physical settlement and delivery or cash settlement by reference to the payment performance or the market value of the specified security.

Typically, ABCDS for HELs are settled using pay-as-you-go cash settlement or physical settlement options (Exhibit 3.36). The pay-as-you-go promotes two-way settlement of credit events, reflecting the economics of home equity transactions. The PAUG structure differs from both the cash and physical settlement option in that a single payment may not take place. Rather, due to the recoverable nature of the losses in home equity transactions, the PAUG protection seller makes contingent cash payments to the protection buyer as writedowns on the reference bond occur. Conversely, the protection buyer makes contingent payments to the protection seller as losses are reversed (recoveries). As a result, the notional amount of the contract is adjusted throughout the life of the trade. Finally, the PAUG contract allows the protection buyer partial physical settlement in the event that full physical settlement cannot be executed.

EXHIBIT 3.36   Pay-As-You-Go CDS Settlement Mechanics

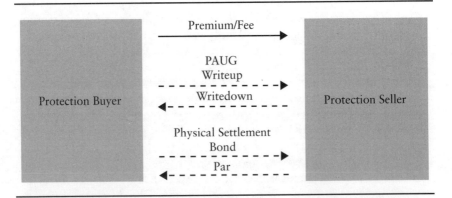

Source: Wachovia Capital Markets, LLC.

Available Funds Cap and CDS Contracts

The pay-as-you-go template allows parties to the transaction to elect either full or partial AFC risk transference. For full AFC risk transference, each party provides that the interest shortfall cap is not applicable. For partial transference, each party provides a fixed or variable cap.

Under the no-cap option, premium payments made by the protection buyer to the protection seller are netted against the floating payments. Under extreme interest rate scenarios, an unfunded protection seller may have to make out-of-pocket payments to the protection buyer when the floating (interest shortfall) payments are greater than the fixed premium paid by the protection buyer.

Under the fixed or variable rate option, the protection seller's liability is limited. In the case of a fixed cap, the protection seller's liability is limited to the premium paid by the protection buyer. In the case of a variable cap, the protection seller's liability is limited to the premium amount plus the base rate in the agreement, typically LIBOR.

ABX.HE INDEX

Credit indexes such as the ABX.HE are constituted from reference obligations on single-name CDS. The ABX.HE index is constituted from reference obligations on 20 transactions of residential mortgage-backed securities and led by 16 licensed market makers.

Differences between ABX.HE and Single-Name CDS

- The ABX.HE index does not allow for physical settlement or partial physical settlement because credit events, as they apply to the pay-as-you-go ISDA contract, do not form part of the index contract. As a result, all settlements occur through the floating payment mechanism covering interest shortfalls, principal shortfalls and writedowns.
- Also, unlike single name CDS, the ABX.HE does not allow for a coupon step-up at the call date if the transaction is not called.

To qualify for inclusion in the ABX.HE index, the reference obligation must meet the following criteria:

- The transaction must include tranches of securities rated by Moody's and S&P as follows: Aaa/AAA, Aa2/AA, A2/A, Baa2/BBB, Baa3/BBB-.

- Each tranche must be either a note or other security, pass-through certificate or similar security entitling the holder to receive payments that depend on the cash flow from a discrete pool of assets that substantially consists of loans (fixed or revolving) secured by a lien on one-to-four family residences or by security interests on proprietary leases on residential cooperative apartment units and the related stock of the cooperative apartment corporation.
- Each required tranche must have been issued within six months before the applicable roll date.
- The deal size of the RMBS transaction must be at least $500 million as of the issuance date.
- At least 90% of the residential mortgage loan assets collateralizing the RMBS transaction must have a priority first lien in favor of the holder. In the event that information necessary for the ABX.HE administrator to make such a determination is not readily available, then this criterion is satisfied if the prospectus states that the transaction is primarily backed by first liens.
- The weighted average FICO score of the obligors on the assets backing the securities issued in the transaction must not exceed 660 as of the issuance date.
- At least four of the required tranches must be registered pursuant to the U.S. Securities Act of 1933.
- The scheduled payment dates for the payment of interest under each required tranche must be the 25th calendar day of each month.
- The required tranche with an applicable rating of AAA must have an expected average life of greater than five years as of issuance and must have the longest average life of all tranches in the transaction with the same priority. Each other required tranche must have an expected average life greater than four years.
- Any required tranche with an applicable rating of AAA or its equivalent must have a principal amount at issuance of $15 million.
- Each required tranche must bear a floating rate indexed to one-month LIBOR.
- Each required tranche must bear publicly disclosed ratings from both Moody's and S&P.
- The identity and principal economic terms of each required tranche must be listed on Bloomberg.
- No tranche may be insured or guaranteed pursuant to a financial guarantee insurance policy, guarantee policy or similar instrument issued by a third party.
- The business day convention for each required tranche is based on New York business days only.

Originator and Servicer Exposure

Both originator and servicer exposure is limited by the ABX.HE administrator.

- The index may not contain more than four RMBS transactions with the same originator. The "originator" of the RMBS transaction is the entity that originated more than 60% of the aggregate principal balance of the RMBS transaction.
- Similarly, the index may not contain more than six RMBS transactions with the same servicer. The "servicer" of the RMBS transaction is the entity that is the master servicer of the mortgage loans collateralizing the transaction. If no master servicer is identified, then the servicer is defined as the servicer of more than 60% of the aggregate principal balance outstanding.

Rolling the Index

Index rolling occurs approximately every six months. Rolling into the most recent "on-the-run" ABX.HE index alters the investor's vintage exposure in six-month increments. Consequently, unlike the corporate indexes (CDX), rolling into the on-the-run index does not represent a means by which investors maintain a constant exposure to the sector. For example:

- The ABX.HE 06-1 represents vintage exposure to the second half of 2005 origination practices.
- The ABX.HE 06-2 represents vintage exposure to the first half of 2006 origination practices.
- The ABX.HE 07-1 represents vintage exposure to the second half of 2006 origination practices.

SUMMARY

The home equity loan sector has evolved from a market representing predominantly second lien loan prime borrowers to first lien purchase money market to credit-impaired borrowers including a wide variety of loan types such as fixed rate, hybrid adjustable rate, and interest-only loans. As the lending environment changed and the HEL sector gained greater investor acceptance, the structures also evolved.

The earliest HEL structures employed overcollateralization, excess spread and a financial guarantee from a third-party provider to achieve a triple-A rating. As the sector matured, the structures evolved to employ senior/subordinated tranching of credit risk. In addition, the issuers explored alternative means of enhancement to reduce their cost of funds by incorporating issuer-paid mortgage insurance (deep MI) and deeper tranching of credit risk—in some cases, down to Ba3/BB–.

The growth of the single-name CDS market changed pricing dynamics by allowing investors to express long or short opinions (before the advent of single-name CDS, the HEL market was predominantly long only). This allows investors in the HEL sector to express opinions regarding issuer origination and servicing practices, relative vintage performance and capital structure arbitrage.

We have no doubt that the market will continue to evolve and innovate on both the origination and servicing sides as well as with the securitization of the loans. As we complete this primer, there is a great deal of discussion surrounding the topics of affordable products, residual valuation and structuring, as well as refining the CDS market to better reflect the nuances of the reference obligations.

CHAPTER 4

Credit Card ABS

John N. McElravey, CFA
Senior Analyst
Wachovia Capital Markets, LLC

Credit cards have become ubiquitous in American society. Given their unique place in household transactions, it is not surprising that credit card asset-backed securities are generally acknowledged to be a benchmark *asset-backed securities* (ABS) sector. Credit card ABS made their first appearance in the public debt markets in 1987. The large dollar amount of new issue transactions introduced liquidity and drew many new investors to the ABS market. In addition, the strong credit ratings of the banks that make credit card loans and sponsor the securitizations eased the concerns of investors branching into a new asset class. Indeed, investors new to the ABS market will often begin by buying AAA rated credit cards.

As investors gain experience, they may move down in credit to subordinate credit card ABS or then branch out into other ABS sectors. For example, many Asian investors with dollars to invest started in the Treasury and agency markets, and then moved into credit cards to pick up additional yield without taking on undue credit risk. Pricing spreads of credit card ABS are often used as a point of comparison for other ABS sectors. In turbulent market conditions, the credit card sector will often recover first. Good liquidity in terms of overall investor demand and narrow bid-ask spreads from dealers make credit card ABS ideal as a source of liquidity in portfolios. This chapter summarizes the most important structural features of credit card ABS.

CREDIT CARD SECURITIZATION BACKGROUND

Credit card securitization began in the late 1980s as a way for commercial banks operating in this line of business to diversify their sources of funding. Banks also adopted ABS technology as a way to help meet the stricter risk-based capital standards being imposed by regulators during this period. Moving assets off the balance sheet freed capital for banks to improve their regulatory position and to grow other areas of their business. The overall credit card market has grown more rapidly as consumers started using credit cards to make payments for a growing list of products and services including groceries, doctor visits, and utility payments. These convenience users have changed the way credit card banks market their products to consumers.

Securitization also allowed specialty credit card banks to enter the market and fund themselves through the capital markets. This direct access to credit market investors helped to place these new competitors on an equal footing with the more established commercial bank players already dominant in the market. These specialty banks used the less expensive funding offered by the capital markets as a substitute for the retail deposits used by traditional commercial banks. MBNA, First USA, and Capital One were among the new entrants that became standalone credit card banking companies. In order to attract business away from larger commercial banks, these specialty banks used innovative products and services to compete aggressively for customers.

Teaser Rates and Balance Transfers

One of the most influential innovations of the 1990s was the one-two punch of low-price credit cards with no annual fee along with very low "teaser rates," and a balance transfer feature. Teaser rates are very low interest rates, as low as 0%, fixed for an initial period of 6 to 12 months. The interest rate on the account would then step up to the market rate for that borrower (the "go to" rate) at the end of the teaser period. These teaser rates are often combined with balance transfer options that allow the cardholder to move outstanding balances from other competing credit cards to take maximum advantage of the low initial rate. This strategy has been very effective at gathering assets and capturing market share.

However, consumers quickly became adept at arbitraging teaser rates and shifting balances promptly from one card to another as teaser periods would end. In addition, this marketing approach became expensive as lenders would spend money marketing and doing credit work on new borrowers, only to have them flee when the next teaser rate/balance transfer offer landed in their mailbox. Furthermore, cardholders with weaker credit are more likely to respond to an offer, but might not be able to move their balances at a later date. The potential for adverse selection and the credit problems that resulted in the past have influenced most lenders to be more targeted in their low-rate or balance transfer offers.

The competition that resulted from balance transfer offers and low teaser rates made customer retention key for credit card companies because of the costs associated with originating a new customer. Technological investments by credit card firms allowed them to tailor interest rates, credit limits, and other products and services to maximize their chances of keeping customers after the initial teaser period ended and to differentiate themselves from their competitors. Mass customization, as this process came to be called, was made possible by sophisticated systems that track the credit performance and spending habits of customers. Issuers can use this system to keep customers happy, and to maximize the profitability of their accounts.

Affinity and Cobranded Programs

Another way for credit card firms to compete is through "affinity" and "cobranded" programs. The specialty finance companies such as MBNA, Capital One, and First USA (later owned by Bank One and now Chase) were trailblazers in this regard. Affinity programs are credit cards issued by the bank in association with a group that has a common interest or tie. For example, sports teams, college alumni associations, or professional groups are popular affinity programs. The group receives a fee from the credit card issuer to allow that card company to market to the group's members. The credit card company can then target a specific demographic group to use their cards. Cobranded programs associate a bank's credit card with another commercial firm. Cardholders can earn rewards from the commercial firm for making purchases. Airlines are perhaps the most popular cobranding partners because cardholders can earn mileage points to be redeemed for free tickets or upgrades.

Over time, consolidation in the banking and finance sector reduced the number of competitors in the credit card business. Large commercial banks continue to dominate this arena. For example, Citibank, JPMorgan Chase, and BankAmerica have been on the acquiring end of significant credit card businesses. Many of the specialty consumer finance companies, such as MBNA, Household Finance, and Providian, have been acquired by large, diversified commercial banking firms. Capital One remains independent, though it has been an acquirer of full-service banking companies, and now more closely resembles its long-time, traditional competitors.

Credit Card Segments

The credit card market can be approximated by three broad segments: general purpose credit cards, independent networks, and private label credit cards. The first group, general purpose credit cards, is most often thought of as Visa and MasterCard. These cards are issued by the large banking companies and can be used in a wide variety of establishments and for almost any purpose. The independent networks are American Express and Discover. These two are widely accepted, but perhaps in a more limited way than Visa and MasterCard. They are generally not issued by the large commercial banks, but by their sponsoring companies. Finally, private label credit cards are a smaller segment of the market. They are cards sponsored by retailers for use in their own stores.

Private label cards were traditionally viewed by the retailer as a way to boost sales, and credit underwriting tended to be a secondary concern. As a result, credit charge-offs tend to be higher than they are on general purpose credit cards. The interest rates charged, however, are usually higher to help offset the credit risk. The largest private label issuer for many years was Sears, Roebuck & Co, accounting for about a third of the market. However, the Sears private label business was sold to Citibank in 2003. Indeed, Citibank and GE Capital have become significant issuers in the private label area. Economies of scale and the costs of underwriting have forced many stores to outsource their credit card marketing, underwriting, and servicing.

CREDIT CARD ABS STRUCTURES

The revolving nature of credit card loans presents a unique problem when it comes to their securitization. Until 1991, credit card ABS were structured as standalone trusts based on a pool of accounts and the receivables produced by those accounts. The advent of the master trust in 1991 solved the problem of creating new trusts each time an issuer wanted to securitize loans. Over time, clever investment bankers, lawyers, and accounts made improvements to the master trust structure to make it even more cost efficient and flexible.

The basics of credit card transactions are similar in many respects to other asset classes. A credit card issuer creates a master trust and pledges accounts to the trust. All receivables generated by those accounts become the property of the master trust. As the credit card bank opens new accounts, they, too, can be pledged to the master trust as long as they meet the eligibility requirements, and typically with the approval of the rating agencies. A master trust can issue numerous series of securities with a variety of ratings and maturities. The cash flows from all of the receivables (principal and interest) are used to support all of the securities issued by the master trust. Such a structure can be beneficial to both the issuer and the investor. The issuer gets lower costs and maximum flexibility to meet investor demands and market conditions. For the investor, the assessment of the underlying credit is facilitated by the fact that there is one pool of collateral to analyze. The characteristics of the pool change very gradually over time because of limitations on additions and the eligibility criteria. Furthermore, historical data on credit performance is readily available through a number of public sources.

Exhibit 4.1 summarizes a master trust structure as it has evolved over time into a master issuance trust structure that is used by most of the larger credit card ABS issuers. As noted earlier, the credit card lender pledges accounts, and their associated receivables, to the trust. The trust issues rated securities to investors. Under the classic master trust structure, the capital structure of each series of securities issued would include senior and subordinate classes, and perhaps a cash collateral account. The credit enhancement for each class was unique to that particular series. The master trust would then issue additional series over time as the receivables base would grow or to refund earlier series that matured.

EXHIBIT 4.1 Master Trust Structure

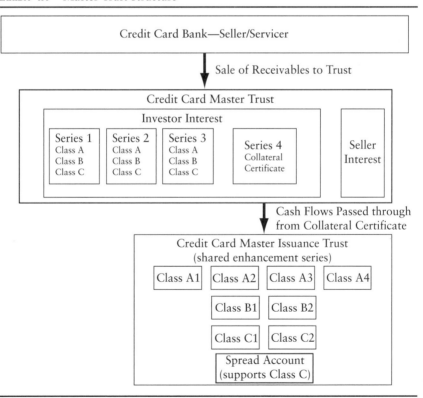

The cash flows from the receivables, principal and interest, are allocated on a pro rata basis to the outside bondholders (the investor interest) and to the originator of the receivables (the seller interest). The seller interest is the credit card bank's residual interest in the collateral pool. Finance charge collections are used to make interest payments to the bondholders, pay the ongoing expenses of the trust, and cover credit losses. Principal payments from the cardholders, if not used to redeem bonds at maturity, are used to purchase new receivables as they are generated by the credit card accounts. This process of using principal collections to purchase new receivables addresses the revolving nature of credit card loans.

Seller Interest

As noted above, the seller interest is the interest of the credit card bank in the receivables pool. One advantage of this structural feature is that it aligns the incentives of the credit card bank with those of the outside investors. All cash flows, as well as credit losses, are passed through on a pro rata basis. The rating agencies require a minimum amount of seller interest that tends to be in the 4% to 7% range. In practice, the proportion of the seller's interest is likely to be higher than the minimum depending on the bank's use of securitization for its funding of the credit card portfolio. In some cases, it may be cheaper to fund these assets on the bank's balance sheet, or through alternatives such as an asset-backed commercial paper conduit, rather than going directly to the capital markets.

From the ABS investor's point of view, the major benefit of the seller interest is to absorb the seasonal fluctuations in the amount of receivables outstanding, and to allocate dilutions from merchandise returns and ineligible receivables. Seller interest does not provide direct credit enhancement of credit losses for the ABS investors. Credit enhancement is provided by subordination, cash reserves, excess spread, or other measures as provided for in the master trust structure. The credit card bank would be obligated to add accounts and receivables if the seller interest falls below the minimum percentage. Large scale additions would require rating agency approval to make sure that the profile of the collateral pool does not change significantly. If the credit card bank cannot make an addition when required, then an early amortization event would be triggered and investors would receive principal repayments to wind down any outstanding securities. This risk of early amortization, and the loss of capital markets funding, means that the seller has an important incentive to make additions when needed, and to underwrite high quality loans for the master trust.

Master Issuance Trust

Credit card master trust structures have evolved over time so that issuers have a significant amount of flexibility when it comes to the issuance of new securities. Most issuers have moved to an issuance trust structure which incorporates existing master trusts along with the latest structured finance technology. In the second step depicted in Exhibit 4.1, an existing credit card master trust issues a collateral certificate to the issuance trust. The collateral certificate is treated like any other series issued out of the investor interest of the original master trust. It receives its proportional share of interest and principal cash flows, which are passed through the issuance trust.

The issuance trust structure has several important advantages for issuers. Different classes of notes can be issued in different sizes, with varying maturities, and at different times. This structure allows for the sort of flexibility found in corporate medium note programs. Issuers are able to bring to market bonds that best suit their needs at the time, as well as the needs of investors. For example, if an issuer finds that there is appetite in the market for 10-year single-A bonds, and the following week there is a need for five-year AAA bonds, then this structure can be flexible enough to meet those needs. As a result, an issuance trust is often referred to as a *delinked master trust* because the subordinate bonds offered need not be directly tied to any particular class of senior bonds. In the classic form of the master trust, the subordinate bonds would be offered at the same time as the senior bonds, and thus linked directly to them.

An issuance trust is designed so that all of the subordinate bonds (all the Class B's and Class C's) support all of the senior bonds issued by the trust. This is known as a *shared enhancement series*. The senior classes can only be issued to the extent that there is adequate subordination already in place. For example, a new issuer of a master issuance trust would need to place the Class C bonds and the Class B bonds in the required amounts before any Class A bonds could be issued. However, the Class B and Class C bonds may have different maturity dates than each other, and different from the Class A bonds that they support. In the classic master trust structure, each class in the series would have approximately the same average life and maturity. One important caveat is that the senior bonds will have the benefit of the required amount of the credit support available. If additional subordinate bonds have been issued in excess of what is required to support the senior bonds, the senior bonds would not have the benefit of the excess credit enhancement amount.

Credit Enhancement

Like any ABS transaction, credit card ABS achieve investment grade ratings through various forms of credit enhancement to cover credit losses and protect the more senior investors in the master trust. The amount of credit enhancement needed to earn a particular rating will depend upon the credit performance of an issuer's credit card program. The credit enhancement required for the major credit card companies to gain AAA rating ranges from about 12% to 17%. Single-A ratings require about 6% to 8%. Exhibit 4.2 shows a typical credit card ABS capital structure. Credit enhancement levels have declined somewhat over time as credit card usage by consumers has changed, card companies have become more sophisticated in their management of the business, and securitization structures have improved. Most master trusts utilize a senior-subordinate structure in which junior bonds provide credit support for the senior bondholders. Cash collateral accounts are also widely used, though mainly as enhancement for the Class C (BBB rated) securities. While these internal forms of credit enhancement are the normal practice, some issuers will use bond guarantees for achieve their desired ratings. The following sections describe different types of credit enhancement.

EXHIBIT 4.2   Credit Enhancement

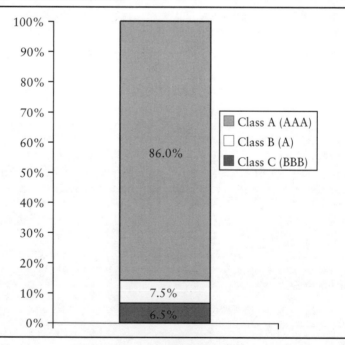

EXHIBIT 4.3 Excess Spread Calculation

Gross portfolio yield	18.0%
Less:	
Charge-offs	4.0%
Net portfolio yield	14.0%
Less:	
Investor coupon	5.5%
Servicing fee	2.0%
Excess spread	6.5%

Excess Spread

Excess spread is one of the most important gauges of the performance of any credit card master trust. It is the first line of defense against credit losses, and it is used as an early amortization trigger. Excess spread is calculated as the amount of interest collections less the ongoing costs and fees of the master trust, including the investor coupon, servicing fees, and any charge-offs allocated to the series. In some ways this measure can be thought of as the profitability of the trust. The data are usually presented as an annualized percentage as in Exhibit 4.3. The main early amortization trigger for a master trust is based on excess spread. Normally, the three-month moving average of excess spread must be greater than zero.

Spread Account/Cash Collateral Account

A cash reserve account may be in place to support the rated bonds. This may be in the form of cash funded upfront by the issuer, or it may be funded through the capture of excess spread generated by the receivables. The capture of excess spread is often triggered by the increase in delinquencies or losses. In most cases, the spread account only supports the triple-B rated class.

Subordination

As the market for ABS rated below AAA has broadened and deepened, subordination has displaced bond guarantees, letters of credit, or unrated classes as the credit enhancement of choice for most issuers. The development of the subordinate market allows issuers to receive a higher advance rate on the collateral being securitized. The typical structure of a credit card master trust includes AAA bonds supported by classes of single-A and triple-B bonds. On occasion an issuer will bring double-A bonds, as well.

Key Credit Data and Analysis

The amount of credit enhancement required will depend critically on the analysis of the historical credit performance of the issuer's credit card business. In addition, various structural provisions are required by the rating agencies in order to garner investment grade ratings. The agencies will determine the baseline credit performance of the credit card portfolio based on the key credit metrics, which include portfolio yield, charge-offs, monthly payment rate, monthly purchase rate, excess spread, and the investor coupon. Furthermore, the rating agencies will take into account the financial strength of the issuer, its ability to service the portfolio, and the potential for economic stress and changes in interest rates.

- *Portfolio yield* is the income generated by the portfolio of credit card receivables. It is primarily influenced by the weighted-average *annual percentage rate* (APR) charged to account holders, as well as any fees. The pattern of card usage will also have an important role in the level of portfolio yield. If more cardholders choose to carry a balance, that is a higher proportion of revolving accounts, then the portfolio yield will be higher that it would be for a portfolio that has a higher proportion of convenience users who pay off their entire balance on a monthly basis.
- *Charge-offs* are the defaults, net of any recoveries, experienced by the loan pool. Trends in credit card charge-offs are shown in Exhibit 4.4. Accounts tend to be charged off by most issuers at 180 days past due. Cardholders that have filed for bankruptcy are charged off within 60

EXHIBIT 4.4   Charge-Offs

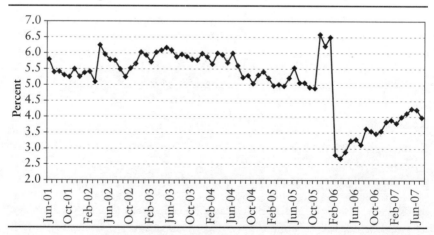

Source: Wachovia Capital Markets, LLC and Intex.

days. Because credit card loans are normally unsecured, recoveries do tend to be quite low. However, some issuers will offer secured credit cards to borrowers with weaker credit histories. The peak losses for static pools of credit card loans are usually seen between 18 and 24 months of seasoning.

- The *monthly payment rate* is one of the most important pieces of data to come out of the master trust, but it is often overlooked by many analysts. The payment rate is the proportion of outstanding loans that are repaid on a monthly basis, and Exhibit 4.5 illustrates its recent performance. A high monthly payment rate is a source of strength for the master trust and for investors in the pool. A higher payment rate means that investors would be repaid more quickly if the master trust hit an early amortization trigger. While convenience users may reduce the amount of portfolio yield generated by the loans, they offer an important source of internal credit enhancement. The monthly payment rate can also be used as an early warning indicator of trouble for the consumer. If it is getting harder to pay bills, or the household balance sheet is becoming more stressed, then payment rates are likely to slow.

- *Excess spread* is the amount of excess interest generated by the portfolio. As mentioned earlier, it is the first line of defense against losses. Excess spread is actually a calculated value. It is portfolio yield, less charge-offs, investor coupon, deal expenses, and servicing fees. Exhibit 4.6 indicates that excess spread for major credit card master trusts has been relatively stable. In the newer issuance trusts, the excess spread

EXHIBIT 4.5   Monthly Payment Rate

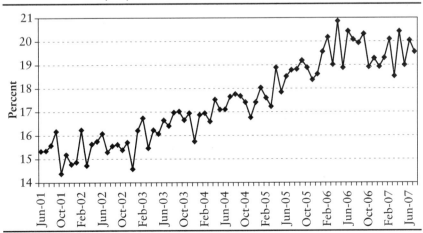

Source: Wachovia Capital Markets, LLC and Intex.

EXHIBIT 4.6   Excess Spread

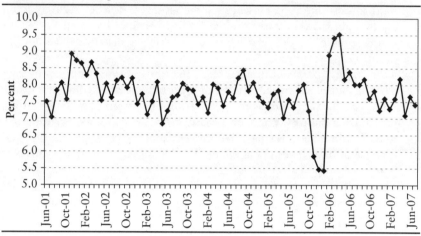

Source: Wachovia Capital Markets, LLC and Intex.

of all the series will be equal because the interest cash flows and trust expenses are applied at the top of the waterfall. All of the bond coupons, whether fixed or floating, are accounted for at this stage. A good way to track credit card performance is using a three-month average of excess spread and charge-offs.

- The *monthly purchase rate*, which is related to the monthly payment rate, is the amount of new receivables generated by the accounts pledged to the master trust. A higher purchase rate means that more new receivables are being generated faster to support the ABS issued by the master trust. Under a stressful scenario, the purchase rate may fall, leaving fewer receivables available and causing an early amortization of the ABS. The rating agencies will generally stress the purchase rate at the same time that the portfolio yield falls in order to test the resiliency of the trust structure. Purchase rate becomes a more critical element of private label credit card deals because those deals are more closely linked to the purchases at a retailer or group of retailers. If the retailer is having financial troubles, then cardholders may be less likely to shop there and outstanding receivables would decline. As a result, private label credit card ABS tend to have higher credit enhancement for the same credit rating than do deals from general purpose credit cards.
- *Credit limits, utilization rates,* and *the age of the accounts* (seasoning) are also useful information to be aware of when analyzing credit card transactions. Lenders will use credit limits as a way of adjusting the risk they take on any one borrower. Borrowers with better credit

histories may receive higher credit limits. New accounts may receive a lower credit limit initially, regardless of credit history, until they have proven themselves to the lender. Utilization rates are the proportion of the outstanding credit line that is currently being used. Lower utilization rates mean less current exposure to a borrower, but cardholders could borrower against their lines when times get tight and raise the risk of the lender. Card issuers that offer lower credit limits often have higher utilization rates, but lower overall risk exposure. The seasoning of accounts is also an important piece of information. More seasoning suggest cardholders with longevity, and less turnover suggests a more stable customer base and lower default rates.

■ *Economic stress* and *interest rates* will also play a role in the amount of credit enhancement required and the level of risk in a pool. Rapidly rising short-term interest rates would likely compress excess spread and reduce the amount of cushion available for charge-offs.

The rating agencies will apply their stress scenarios to varying degrees to these factors when analyzing a master trust. Geographic distribution, underwriting and servicing, marketing, and strategic objectives will all factor in to the rating agency analysis.

Cash Flow Allocations of Credit Card ABS

Credit card ABS transactions have two major components while they are outstanding: the *revolving period* and the *amortization period*. During the revolving period, investors only receive interest payments. All principal collections during this time are used by the master trust to purchase new receivables as they are generated by the accounts that have been pledged to the trust. The revolving period is a structural device that addresses the revolving nature of the collateral and allows them to be financed over a longer periods of time. The revolving period also helps maintain stable average lives for the ABS, and allows for the soft-bullet principal payment structure.

As the maturity of the ABS bonds approaches, the revolving period ends and the amortization period begins. During the amortization period, principal collections are no longer used to purchase new receivables, but instead are gathered by the master trust structure in an account used to repay the ABS investors. The length of the amortization period will depend on the monthly payment rate of the master trust. Slower monthly payment rates will require a longer amortization period, while faster monthly payment rates will require shorter periods. Given the payment rates of most credit card master trusts are in a range of 10% to 25%, the amortization period is most likely 4 to 10 months. For structural purposes, the amortization period is expected to be 12 months. For example, a credit card ABS bond with a five year expected maturity should revolve for 48 months and then amortize for 12 months. However, if the principal collections come in at a 20% rate on average, the length of the amortization period would be only 5 months. However, like most ABS deals, the legal final maturity of bonds will be about two years after expected maturity of the bonds to take into account any uncertainties as to the cash flows from the master trust.

Most credit card master trusts utilize a *controlled accumulation period* during which principal collections are deposited into a trust account each month until enough has been collected to fully repay the bonds. The cash is held until the maturity date and then repaid all at once, similar to the bullet payment of principal for a corporate bond. Taking our example above of a five year bond, suppose the revolving period lasts for 48 months and then the controlled accumulation period begins. Principal collections equal to 1/12 of the bond balance is deposited into an account for the remaining 12 months of the deal. Exhibit 4.7 depicts how a controlled accumulation would work. Excess principal collections would be used by the master trust to purchase new receivables. Interest payments continue to be made during the controlled accumulation period on the original principal balance of the bonds because they have not yet been retired.

A *controlled amortization period* may be used, but such a structure has become much less common. In this structure, principal is repaid to the ABS investors in equal installments (Exhibit 4.8). We revisit our ABS investor with a five-year expected maturity. The revolving period continues for 48

EXHIBIT 4.7   Controlled Accumulation (soft-bullet structure)

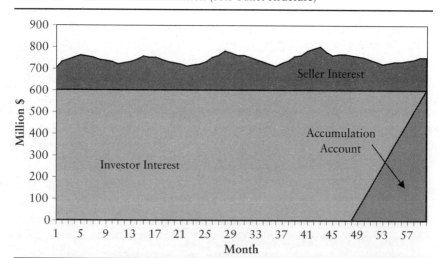

EXHIBIT 4.8 Controlled Amortization

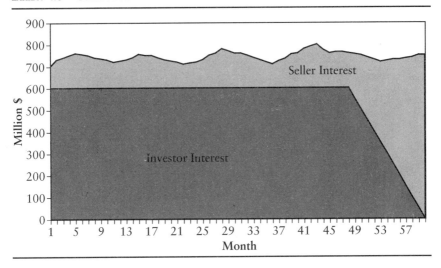

EXHIBIT 4.9 Common Early Amortization Triggers

Collateral Pool Credit

Three-month average excess spread less than zero.
Seller interest less than the minimum.
Collateral outstanding balance below the invested amount.

Seller/Servicer Events

Failure to make required deposits or payments.
Failure to transfer receivables to the trust when required.
Events of default, bankruptcy, or insolvency of the seller/servicer.
Breach of representations and warranties.

months where the investor receives only interest payments, and then the controlled amortization period begins at the beginning of year 5. The ABS investor receives principal payments in 12 equal installments. Principal collections not used to repay investors are used to purchase new receivables. Interest payments during amortization are based on the declining principal balance of the bonds.

In the event of certain credit or structural triggers being hit, an *early amortization event* may occur. These triggers are built into ABS transactions in order to reduce the amount of time that investors would be exposed to a weakened servicer or a troubled pool of credit card loans. Some common early amortization trigger events are listed in Exhibit 4.9. The most easily watched early amortization trigger is based on the level of three-month average excess spread. If the three-month average excess spread falls below zero, then an early amortization event occurs. Once the trigger is hit, then the revolving period ends immediately and all principal collections are passed through to pay off the ABS investors. An additional enhancement is for principal to be passed through on an uncontrolled, or rapid amortization, basis. This allows for principal due to the seller to be diverted to pay ABS investors and get them out of a troubled trust more quickly.

Cash Flow Groups

Master trusts employ a structural device called *grouping* to help allocate principal and interest cash flows. The ABS securities issued are assigned to a group, and one or more groups may be established. As noted earlier, the master trust allocates cash on a pro rata basis between the seller interest and the investor interest. The cash flows devoted to the investor interest are further allocated at the group level. While many credit card master trusts have only one group, some have two or more. For example, all of the fixed rate ABS could be in one group and all of the floating rate ABS could be in another. The sharing of excess interest or principal collections would be determined at the group level. This sharing of cash can be important if certain series are getting close to hitting early amortization triggers. Issuers utilizing the issuance trust structure, which is now the state of the art in the credit card ABS market, are likely to have only one group to allocate cash flows to, and largely avoiding some of the issues addressed in this section.

Principal collections are allocated to each series in the same group based on its relative size within the group. Series in their revolving period will get no principal allocated to them. Their principal collections can be reallocated and shared with other series that are in their accumulation periods. Sharing principal collections helps the master trust to make timely payment of principal to ABS investors. If no principal is needed to repay investors then it can be used to invest in new receivables.

Finance charge collections by credit card banks include the monthly interest on the account, any annual or late fees charged to the account, recoveries on charged-off receivables, interchange pledged to the trust, and discounted receivables. *Interchange* is a fee paid to the credit card bank that issues the card used in a transaction, and is often 1% to 2% of the value of a transaction. Interchange compensates the bank for taking credit risk and allowing for a grace period for the borrower. It is created when the receivables generated by a transaction are discounted before being paid out to the merchant. The interchange fee is shared by the bank issuing the credit card, the bank for the merchant, and Visa or MasterCard for clearing the transaction. Discounted receivables may also be put into a trust. The discount is typically between 1% and 5%, and can increase the portfolio yield of the portfolio when the face amount of the receivables is collected.

Historically, finance charge collections have been allocated most often by master trusts to each series based on its outstanding principal balance. The arrival of the issuance trust structure has shifted that process to a *socialized allocation method*. In a socialized trust, finance charges are allocated to each series based on their cost. The "socialized" nomenclature comes from the idea that each series gets finance charges based on its need. In this case, need is determined by the coupon, servicing fees, and charge-offs allocated to that series. Series with higher costs will get more of the finance charge collections. The advantage of such a socialized structure is that higher cost series are supported by the excess collections of other series, and thus they can avoid an early amortization that might have occurred under the historical method of allocating finance charge collections based on principal balance. However, all series in such a structure become linked and will remain outstanding or hit an early amortization trigger together.

Master trusts that allocate finance charges based on the size of the outstanding balance of the series are known as "nonsocialized" trusts. Prior to the advent of the issuance trust, most credit card ABS were issued by master trusts that operated in this manner. While much of the credit card ABS issued since 2002 is socialized, many outstanding ABS bonds issued before then are still affected by these cash flow rules. Like socialized deals, finance charges in nonsocialized trusts are used to pay the investor coupon, expenses, and cover its allocated credit losses. Moreover, excess finance charges may or may not be shared once the base expenses are covered. If they are shared, they are distributed based on need. The advantage of this type of structure is that the risk of an early amortization is more likely at the series level than it is at the group or trust level. The sharing of excess finance charges helps mitigate some of this risk, but it does not eliminate it. Over the years, several issuers have had to amend the documents to their master trusts so that the sharing of excess finance charges was easier to do. These measures were taken to avoid the early amortization of certain higher cost fixed rate series of bonds.

SUMMARY

Credit card ABS continues to act as one of the mainstays of the ABS market. Much relative value analysis is done using credit cards as the benchmark sector. For investors new to the securitization markets, credit cards are often the first sector where they put their money. Given its longevity, the credit card market has experienced periods of strong credit, as well as poor credit.

The structures have held up well, protecting investors in periods of rising credit losses. The credit card sector will remain one of the foundations of the ABS market.

CHAPTER 5

Auto Asset-Backed Securities

Glenn M. Schultz, CFA
Senior Analyst
Wachovia Capital Markets, LLC

John N. McElravey, CFA
Senior Analyst
Wachovia Capital Markets, LLC

Shane Whitworth, CFA
Associate Analyst
Wachovia Capital Markets, LLC

Erin K. Walsh
Associate Analyst
Wachovia Capital Markets, LLC

A uto loan *asset-backed securities* (ABS), which were introduced in 1985, have seen a steady growth in issuance over the years. This continual growth can be attributed to the evolution in the auto finance market as securitization has proven to be an attractive method of funding new loans for many auto lenders.

This chapter serves as a guide to understanding the characteristics of auto ABS and valuation. In addition, we provide subprime, near prime, and prime delinquency, and loss performance indexes. Because of the different legal nature of auto leases, we highlight the unique securitization challenges for these transactions.

ISSUANCE

Auto loans and leases are one of the mainstays of the ABS market. Americans love their cars. U.S. domestic auto sales have been running between 16 million and 17 million units annually since 1999, providing the ABS market with a steady stream of collateral to securitize. The auto ABS market began with securitizations of auto loans from prime quality borrowers, which were originated primarily by the captive finance arms of large automakers.

In the mid- to late 1990s, deals backed by loans from near prime and subprime borrowers, as well as auto leases, were introduced to the market. Moreover, investors showed a growing acceptance of the auto sector. This favorable reception brought more issuers to a market that included smaller, specialty finance companies. As a result, issuance jumped after 1998. This increase was driven by a number of factors, including the growing popularity of sport utility vehicles, deeper penetration by foreign automakers, and more financing options such as longer loan terms and a wider use of leases (see Exhibit 5.1).

The outstanding value of auto ABS was approximately $202 billion at the end of 2006. The amount of auto ABS outstanding debt declined after 2003 as existing deals paid down faster than new deals were created to replace them (see Exhibit 5.2). This trend resulted from a number of factors. First, low short-term interest rates created an environment where auto loans could be financed cheaper in asset-backed commercial paper conduits than they could in the term ABS market. Second, problems at the Big 3 U.S. automakers forced them to curtail issuance.

EXHIBIT 5.1   Yearly Auto ABS Issuance

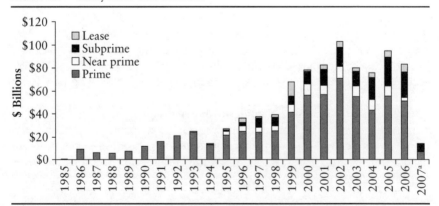

[a] As of 05/02/07.
Source: Asset Backed Alert, Intex Solutions, Inc.

EXHIBIT 5.2 Outstanding ABS by Sector

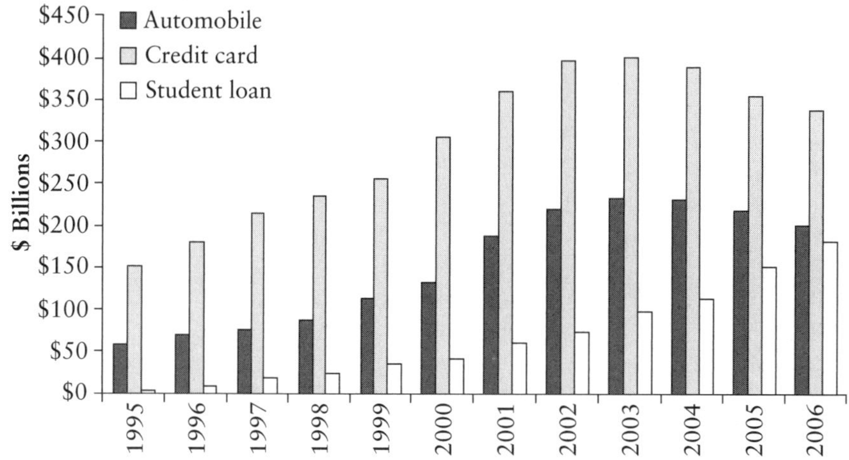

Source: Securities Industry and Financial Markets Association.

Finally, consumers substituted, to some extent, mortgage debt (which has tax deductible interest) for other types of borrowing during a period of record-low mortgage rates. This allowed some big-ticket purchases, like cars, to be financed on a tax-advantaged basis. Thus, excluding residential ABS, which overshadows the size of the other sectors, auto ABS rank second behind credit cards. However, because of their shorter loan terms, auto ABS pay down faster than other asset classes, such as student loans. Indeed, growth in the student loan sector has that asset class poised to surpass auto ABS outstanding.

Despite the various changes occurring in the auto finance market, the roster of issuers has not changed much over the past few years (see Exhibit 5.3). The largest issuers of prime auto ABS typically bring to market two to four deals per year. Ford Credit ranked as the largest issuer with three transactions in 2006 totaling $9.7 billion. DaimlerChrysler and GMAC (Capital Auto Receivables Asset Trust) followed as the next largest issuers with four and two transactions, respectively. The trend over the past several years has been for issuers to do fewer transactions, but at larger sizes.

Near prime issuance makes up only a small portion of the overall auto ABS market. Consolidation in the auto finance market has reduced the number of specialty lenders in this segment of the market. Prime lenders have the ability to go further down in credit, and have acquired near prime companies. For example, Wachovia Corporation purchased the former WFS, which was one of the largest and most active near prime auto lenders.

EXHIBIT 5.3   Top Prime Auto Issuers Ranked by 2006 Issuance ($ millions)

Prime Issuers	2005	2006	2007 YTD
Ford Credit Auto Owner Trust	$9,677	$9,003	
DaimlerChrysler Auto Trust	$4,002	$6,582	
Capital Auto Receivables Asset Trust	$3,070	$6,158	$1,882
USAA Auto Owner Trust	$4,535	$5,238	
Honda Auto Receivables Grantor Trust	$7,915	$4,123	$1,252
Nissan Auto Receivables Owner Trust	$5,642	$2,383	$1,071
Chase Auto Owner Trust	$3,622	$2,326	
Capital One Prime Auto Receivables Trust	$1,500	$2,250	
Hyundai Auto Receivables Trust	$774	$1,884	
CarMax Auto Owner Trust	$1,592	$1,875	
World Omni Auto Receivables Trust	$1,772	$1,872	$1,131
Banc of America Securities Auto Trust	$890	$1,616	
Wachovia Auto Owner Trust	$2,900	$1,300	
Pinnacle Capital Asset Trust	$0	$1,280	
BMW Vehicle Owner Trust	$1,439	$1,109	

Source: Intex Solutions, Inc.

EXHIBIT 5.4   Top Near Prime Auto Issuers in 2006 ($ millions)

Near Prime Issuers	2005	2006	2007 YTD
Wachovia Auto Loan Owner Trust (Inc. WFS)	$5,734	$2,700	
Franklin Auto Trust	$350	$355	$330
Credit Acceptance Auto Trust	$0	$100	

Source: Intex Solutions, Inc.

Wachovia was the largest issuer of near prime in 2006 with two transactions that totaled $2.7 billion (see Exhibit 5.4).

    The consolidation in the subprime auto sector is evident from some of the new names that are in the market. Larger, diversified banking firms are entering the market through the acquisition of specialty finance companies. For example, Capital One entered the market with its purchases of Summit Acceptance and Onyx Acceptance. With three transactions totaling $7 billion in issuance, Capital One ranked as the top issuer of subprime auto ABS in 2006 (see Exhibit 5.5). Household was acquired by HSBC, and Banco Santander acquired Drive Auto. Meanwhile, AmeriCredit purchased Long

EXHIBIT 5.5   Top Subprime Auto Issuers in 2006 ($ millions)

Subprime Issuers	2005	2006	2007 YTD
Capital One Auto Finance Trust	$5,600	$7,000	$1,500
AmeriCredit Auto Receivables (Inc. Long Beach)	$6,585	$5,949	$3,402
Household Automotive Trust	$2,848	$2,843	$859
Triad Auto	$2,832	$2,008	
Santander Drive Auto Receivables Trust	$1,600	$1,829	$1,200

Source: Intex Solutions, Inc.

EXHIBIT 5.6   Top Auto Lease Issuers in 2006 ($ millions)

Issuer	2005	2006	2007 YTD
Capital Auto Receivables Asset Trust	$1,970	$2,471	$0
Nissan Auto Lease Trust	$1,550	$1,719	$0
Volkswagen Auto Lease Trust	$1,685	$1,648	$0
Susquehanna Auto Lease Trust	$340	$590	$0

Source: Intex Solutions, Inc.

Beach Acceptance. AmeriCredit ranked second with six transactions and total issuance of approximately $6 billion.

Auto lease securitization volume is only a fraction of that seen from auto loans. The attractiveness of leasing to consumers seems to go through cycles and that affects the amount available for the ABS market. In general, auto lease deals enjoy somewhat less sponsorship among investors due to residual value risk and less liquidity. However, the most active issuers in the auto lease segment tend to be larger automakers (Exhibit 5.6).

STRUCTURE

Auto ABS are issued through one of two structures, either a grantor trust or an owner trust. In a *grantor trust*, certificates represent a proportionate beneficial interest in the trust, and principal and interest are passed through to the investors on a pro rata basis. Certificates issued by a grantor trust may be tranched into senior and subordinated classes, but no time tranching is allowed.

In contrast, *owner trusts* allow issuers to take advantage of differences in investor's maturity preferences by issuing multiple classes of senior bonds with different maturities. Owner trusts have a different legal form that allows for sequential bonds to be issued. For example, AAA bonds are

EXHIBIT 5.7   Grantor versus Owner Trust Issuance by Vintage

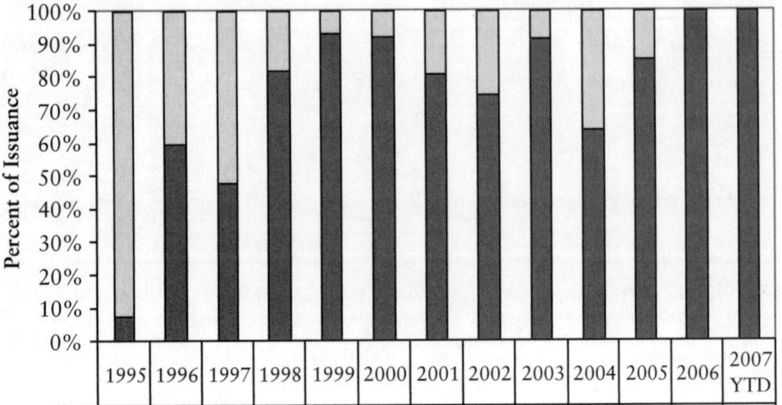

	1995	1996	1997	1998	1999	2000	2001	2002	2003	2004	2005	2006	2007 YTD
☐ Grantor Trust	92.6	40.3	52.0	18.3	6.9%	7.8%	19.4	25.5	8.7%	36.0	14.8	0.3%	0.0%
■ Owner Trust	7.4%	59.7	48.0	81.7	93.1	92.2	80.6	74.5	91.3	64.0	85.2	99.7	100.0

Vintage

Source: Intex Solutions, Inc., Wachovia Capital Markets, LLC.

offered with a money market tranche of less than a one-year maturity, and classes with average lives of one year, two years and three years. The Class A1 tranche is often structured so that it is Rule 2a-7 eligible, meaning that money market investors can buy them. The owner trust's ability to time the tranche has resulted in this type of trust being predominantly used over grantor trusts (Exhibit 5.7).

Cash Flows

The typical auto ABS deal is issued by an owner trust structure with senior and subordinate bonds offered to investors. Generally, four senior bonds with AAA ratings are offered, and tranched into classes with average lives from approximately 0.3 years to three to four years. The senior classes are structured to pay down sequentially, with all principal cash flow initially going to the money market tranche. This is necessary in order to pay it off within 13 months in accord with Rule 2a-7. The other senior tranches receive principal once the class before it is retired.

Exhibit 5.8 shows the principal cash flows for the senior classes from WFS 2004-2. Note that in month 4, the A1 tranche receives its final principal payment and the A2 bond receives its first. In month 18, the A2 bond is completely paid down and A3 begins receiving principal.

EXHIBIT 5.8 Principal Cash Flows for WFS 2004-2

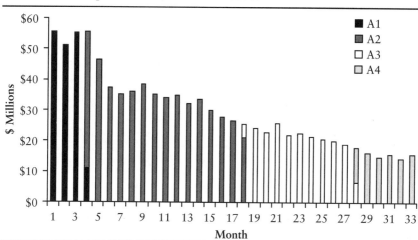

Source: Intex Solutions Inc., Wachovia Capital Markets, LLC.

Subordinate bonds are usually offered, and may be rated from AA down to BBB. In some cases, BB rated securities are issued to maximize the benefits from a higher advance rate that the issuer can garner. Subordinate bonds are often locked out from receiving principal until all of the senior bonds are paid off. When the subordinate bonds are locked out, the current amount of credit enhancement for each class grows as the deal amortizes. This type of structure is usually preferred by the AAA buyers because it creates the maximum credit protection for their classes. It can also make for more stable average lives among the subordinate bonds, which can be an attractive feature for those investors.

Alternatively, subordinate bonds might receive some principal payments at a point prior to the senior bonds being retired. However, for the subordinate bonds to receive principal, the deal will need to meet minimum credit enhancement requirements. This feature can be attractive for investors who prefer a shorter average life bond with an earlier return of capital. The market for subordinate bonds from auto ABS deals has become deep and liquid over time as more investors have taken the time to understand its credit and cash flow profile.

All tranches, both senior and subordinate, receive interest payments starting with the first payment date. Exhibit 5.9 shows a graph of the interest cash flows for WFS 2004-2. The last interest payment in month 4 for the A1 bond coincides with the last principal payment that retires the bond.

EXHIBIT 5.9 Interest Cash Flows for WFS 2004-2

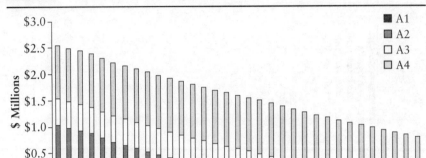

Source: Intex Solutions Inc., Wachovia Capital Markets, LLC.

Credit Enhancement

As with any ABS transaction, credit enhancement is required by the rating agencies to get to a desired credit rating, and is intended to reduce the risk of loss to the investor. For auto ABS, excess spread, *overcollateralization* (OC), reserve accounts, and subordination may be used separately or in some combination as forms of credit enhancement. Excess spread is the amount of interest collections exceeding the amount needed to pay interest on the bonds. This is the deal's first line of defense against credit losses.

Overcollateralization refers to the amount by which the aggregate principal balance of the collateral pool exceeds the aggregate principal amount of the bonds issued. This extra collateral can be a relatively cost effective way for an issuer to enhance a deal. It has the added benefit of increasing the amount of excess spread that flows through the deal.

Reserve funds provide liquidity to an ABS deal. They also offer limited protection against losses on the receivables. Amounts on deposit in a reserve fund are available to pay shortfalls in interest and certain principal collections. If the reserve fund needs to be tapped, then the deal will usually provide a mechanism for it to be replenished through excess interest collections in subsequent periods. These accounts are typically funded upfront with cash or securities in an amount equal to a given percentage of the aggregate principal balance of the initial receivables. The account will generally be required to maintain either a fixed dollar amount or an amount equal to a given percentage of the current pool balance down to a floor level.

As noted previously, subordination works by prioritizing the principal payments of the higher rated notes ahead of those of the lower-rated notes. The rating agencies require lower amounts of subordination for lower-rated bonds, and it is usually determined as a multiple of expected, baseline losses on the collateral pool. In the case of subordinate bonds that are locked out from receiving principal, the credit enhancement level of all the bonds increases as the collateral pool amortizes. Because of this increasing credit enhancement over the life of the transaction, it is common to see upgrades of subordinate bonds on auto ABS deals. According to data from Moody's Investor Service, the aggregate upgrade-to-downgrade ratio for auto ABS is 4.1:1 from 1986 to 2007. This trend toward upgrades is one of the most attractive features of subordinate auto ABS, and suggests a very good risk/reward trade-off compared to senior classes.

Cleanup Call Provisions

One of the most important features in an auto ABS deal is the *cleanup call*. Cleanup calls can have an important impact on the average lives of the bonds and their valuations. The cleanup call refers to the issuer's option (but not obligation) to repurchase the outstanding principal balance of the remaining collateral when the deal balance is paid down to a certain percentage of the original principal balance. This percentage is typically 10%, though it could vary from that level.

The issuer's call is on the *collateral*, and only indirectly on the bonds still outstanding when the threshold is met. The reason we emphasize this point is that market participants often focus on the bond's current price as a reason for or against exercise of the cleanup call.

There are several reasons why issuers would want to exercise cleanup calls despite movements in interest rates. A key reason is that there is value in the collateral pool, and the call is directly on the collateral. Reserve fund account balances can build up to a high percentage of the outstanding transaction balance as the bonds amortize. The same can be said for the extra loan collateral used as OC. This trapped capital could be used more efficiently by the issuer. An excellent example of this situation can be seen in GMAC's auto deals. Prior to GM's downgrade to below investment grade, GMAC was slow to exercise its cleanup call. It sometimes took several months for them to act. However, millions of dollars were locked up in the OC and reserve funds of its deals. Liquidity was a precious commodity for GMAC. After its downgrade to high-yield status, GMAC became very efficient in exercising its cleanup call at the soonest possible date to unlock that trapped capital.

In addition, the cost of servicing a deal becomes greater as the pool amount shrinks. It may be more cost efficient for the servicer to call the existing deal and reuse that collateral in a new deal. Reputation risk can be an important incentive for issuers to call deals as well. Market convention is to price auto ABS deals to the cleanup call. If an issuer does not exercise its call, then it risks having its new deals price cheaper. A few basis points on billions of dollars can add up to real money very quickly. Some transactions penalize the issuer for not calling the deal on time. Step-up coupons included in transactions add additional coupons if the transaction is not called as early as it could be.

Despite these reasons, and a substantial history of exercising calls, investors still question issuers' motivation for timely cleanup. As a result, bonds that would be affected by the cleanup call tend to trade at wider spreads, especially as the potential exercise date approaches. Investors can often find good value in auto ABS, where the issuer has a history of exercising calls and the credit performance of the collateral pool is good.

ISSUER COLLATERAL PROFILE

Auto ABS is usually divided into three subsectors by borrower type—prime, near prime and subprime. In general, transactions with a high *weighted average* (WAVG) FICO, usually 680 or higher, and low delinquency and loss rates would be considered prime. Near prime borrowers have characteristics close to prime borrowers (hence the name), and FICO scores between 620 and 680. Borrowers with a WAVG FICO below 620 and high delinquency and loss rates would be considered subprime (Exhibit 5.10).

The *weighted average coupon* (WAC) of a pool of loans tends to be a good indicator of the credit quality. In general, we would expect prime pools to have WACs in the 5% to 8% range, near prime to be in the 8% to 12% range, and subprime to be 12% to 20% or more.

EXHIBIT 5.10   Credit Quality

	Prime	Near Prime	Subprime
WAVG FICO	680+	620–680	<620
Typical WAC	5%–8%	8%–12%	12%–20%+
60+ Delinquencies at month 36[a]	0.36%	0.79%	3.15%
Cumulative Losses at month 48[a]	0.79%	4.75%	13.49%

[a] Wachovia Capital Markets Auto Index.
Source: Intex Solutions, Inc., Wachovia Capital Markets, LLC.

The rating agencies require greater credit enhancement for collateral pools composed of weaker borrowers than it does for pools of stronger borrowers. Expected losses would be lower for the prime pools, for example, and expected losses drive the level of credit enhancement.

As a general rule, prime borrowers populate auto receivable pools securitized by banks, and the finance companies owned or affiliated with automobile manufacturers. Near prime borrowers may be represented in bank and dealer receivable pools. However, most likely these borrowers populate receivable pools issued by specialty finance companies. Finally, subprime borrowers populate receivable pools that are issued primarily by specialty finance companies.

COLLATERAL PERFORMANCE

Auto loan ABS demonstrates relatively stable and well documented prepayment rates as measured by the ABS (absolute prepayment speed) scale. The ABS scale is used because auto loans tend to demonstrate rising prepayment speeds as measured on the CPR (constant payment rate) scale (Exhibit 5.11). As auto loans age, borrowers tend to accelerate their prepayments to eliminate a monthly bill or trade in their cars. ABS was developed to adjust for this upward trend.

EXHIBIT 5.11   Prime Auto Repayment Convention

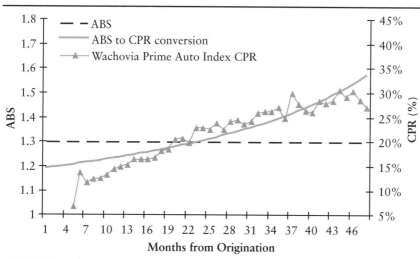

Source: Intex Solutions, Inc., Wachovia Capital Markets, LLC.

The ABS scale is calculated using the actual number (count) of loans in a pool. Next, a survivability factor is determined and expressed as the number of loans that have paid off as a percentage of the original number of loans in the pool. CPR, on the other hand, is calculated by comparing the current outstanding balance to actual monthly prepayments. For purposes of yield and average-life calculations, the original loan balance and loan rate are assumed to be equal to the average original balance and average loan rate of the pool. For example, a 1.5 ABS in any given period would indicate that 1.5% of the original balance paid off in that particular period.

Exhibit 5.11 suggests that, with respect to prime auto ABS, the ABS prepayment convention is representative of actual auto prepayment rates calculated on a CPR basis. However, this is not the case across all borrower credit grades.

Near prime borrowers exhibit a prepayment profile that is similar to that of the prime borrowers, although the upward drift in CPRs is not as pronounced. As a result, the ABS convention still works relatively well (Exhibit 5.12). In the case of near prime auto prepayment assumptions, a 1.5 ABS convention may be used. As a result the timing of short-dated cash flows may be modestly understated and the timing of the last cash flow may be modestly overstated.

EXHIBIT 5.12   Near Prime Auto Repayment

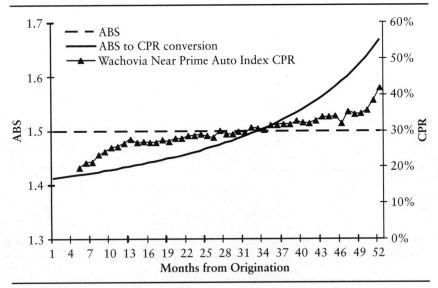

Source: Intex Solutions, Inc., Wachovia Capital Markets, LLC.

EXHIBIT 5.13 Subprime Auto Repayment

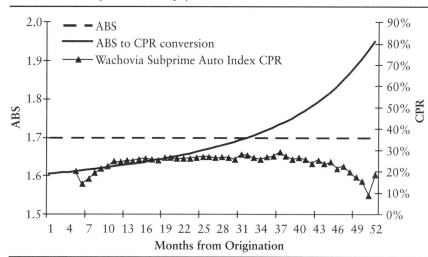

Source: Intex Solutions, Inc., Wachovia Capital Markets, LLC.

In the subprime sector, the ABS pricing convention diverges from pre-payment rates as measured by CPR (Exhibit 5.13). The divergence is particularly acute in the latter stages of the life of the deal. This situation has a larger impact on the last cash flow senior bonds and the subordinate bonds. This is due to the following:

- First, unlike both prime and near prime auto loans, subprime auto loans exhibit a relatively flat CPR curve as the loans age.
- Second, the relationship between the ABS assumption and the rate at which CPR rises in response to changes in the ABS assumption is not linear. Consequently, CPR increases at a faster rate as the ABS assumption is increased.

DELINQUENCY AND LOSS RATES

As expected, delinquency rates (60 days past due) increase as borrower credit risk increases (Exhibit 5.14). The prime auto delinquency rate seasons to around 36 basis points by month 36. The near prime sector exhibits a slightly higher delinquency rate seasoning to around 79 basis points at month 36. Finally, subprime auto delinquency rates season to about 315 basis points at month 36.

EXHIBIT 5.14   Wachovia Capital Markets Auto Index 60 Days Past Due

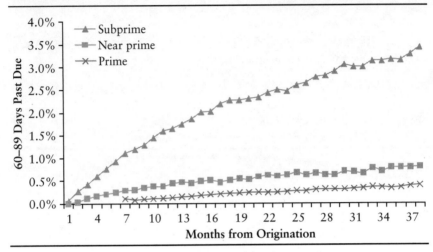

Source: Intex Solutions, Inc., Wachovia Capital Markets, LLC.

EXHIBIT 5.15   Wachovia Capital Markets Auto Indexes Cumulative Loss

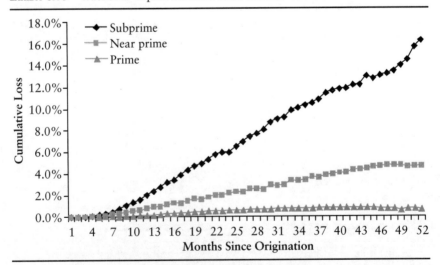

Source: Intex Solutions, Inc., Wachovia Capital Markets, LLC.

Naturally, cumulative losses exhibit a seasoning pattern similar to 60 days past due. Prime auto cumulative losses season to about 80 basis points around month 36. The near prime cumulative loss curve exhibits a more extended seasoning pattern reaching 475 basis points in month 48. The subprime cumulative loss curve exhibits a cumulative loss curve that maintains seasoning velocity through month 48. This seasoning pattern reflects the continuing evolution of the 60 days past due curve and suggests that subprime auto pools experience greater back-loaded losses relative to either near prime or prime auto pools.

VALUATION

Several factors affect auto ABS relative value analysis. The first of these factors is the quality of the originator/servicer. Over the life of an ABS transaction, an originator/servicer with a strong corporate credit profile is less likely than a weaker one to encounter financial problems that may interfere with its ability to effectively service the loans in the trust. Auto ABS supported by a financially strong originator/servicer should garner premium pricing because there is less risk of a servicing interruption.

Similarly, since timely collections from subprime obligors may be less certain than those from prime obligors, and because this uncertainty of collection translates into greater risk for the originator/servicer, auto ABS collateralized by subprime loans are priced to wider spreads vis-à-vis deals backed by prime loans. In addition, prime deals tend to have a broader investor base, which translates into tighter spreads.

The greater servicer risk posed by subprime loans or specialty finance companies is reflected in their respective ABS pricing (Exhibits 5.16 and 5.17). This is expressed as spread tiering, which is more pronounced in the three-year sector. Both banks and captive finance companies enjoy relative pricing spreads that are better than the benchmark average while independent finance companies price at wider spreads.

Another factor affecting relative value is the structure of the securitization and its effect on the cash flow profile of the bond. As discussed earlier, auto ABS may be structured as either a grantor trust or an owner trust, although the grantor trust structure is not as commonly used as in the past. Although there are significant legal and tax difference between the two trusts, these differences are largely irrelevant with respect to relative value analysis. However, the profile of expected cash flows implied by each trust significantly affects relative value.

Auto ABS issued through a grantor trust may be tranched into senior and subordinated bonds. However, no time tranching is allowed. As a

EXHIBIT 5.16   Historical Subprime Auto Loan ABS Spreads

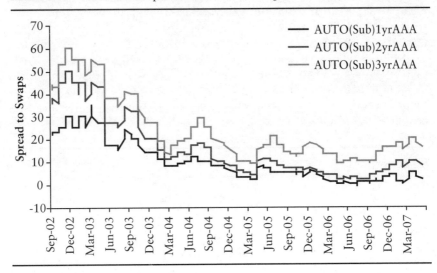

Source: Wachovia Capital Markets, LLC.

EXHIBIT 5.17   Historical Prime Auto Loan ABS Spreads

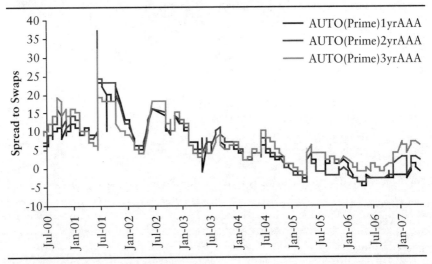

Source: Wachovia Capital Markets, LLC.

result, grantor trust bonds are paid over the life of the securitization and have "wide payment windows." In contrast to a grantor trust, the owner trust structure allows maturity tranching. The owner trust offers bonds with tighter principal payment windows.

When assessing relative value in auto ABS, investors need to be mindful of the relative merits of wide window (i.e., grantor trust) versus tighter window securities (i.e., owner trust). Wide window auto ABS will not "roll down" the curve as fast as tight window auto ABS.[1] Consequently, investors should require a higher spread for a wide window bond as compensation for the lesser price appreciation caused by the slower roll down the curve. The spread differential between wide window and tight window ABS increases as the yield curve steepens, and decreases as it flattens.

In addition to the preceding structural considerations, investors need to consider the effect of prepayments on the average life of the bond. Like other amortizing assets, the use of the appropriate prepayment assumption is critical when pricing auto ABS. Faster-than-expected prepayments result in a shorter average life, and conversely, slower-than-expected prepayments result in a longer average life. In addition, investors should consider the effect of the timing of the expected cash flows and the level and slope of the yield curve.

The most commonly used valuation framework to compare the equivalency of different amortizing structures is the *Z-spread*, or zero volatility *option-adjusted spread* (OAS) analysis. This analysis, also referred to as static spread, views the cash flows of an amortizing structure as a series of zero-coupon cash flows. It represents, using the basic bond pricing formula, the constant spread over the spot rate curve that equates the present value of the bond's cash flows to the current price of the bond plus accrued interest. The spot rate curve used for discounting may be derived from any term structure. Typically, either the U.S. Treasury or the U.S. Dollar Swap term structure is used for deriving the spot rate and discounting.

Exhibit 5.18 provides a graphic illustration of the Z-spread analysis. In the case of a normal, upwardly sloping yield curve, the cash flows occurring earlier than the pricing benchmark are undervalued when discounted at the benchmark yield plus the nominal spread. By extension, the cash flows occurring later than the pricing benchmark are overvalued under the same discounting scheme. The Z-spread analysis provides a framework under which cash flow valuations can be normalized and compared.

---

[1] *Roll down* refers to the rate at which a bond's average life shortens as the bond ages. Assuming a static, positively sloped yield curve, a fixed rate bond will appreciate in price as it ages because the benchmark used to price the bond will have a lower yield than its pricing benchmark. All else being equal, the greater a bond's rate of roll down the curve, the greater its period total return.

EXHIBIT 5.18   Z-Spread Analysis

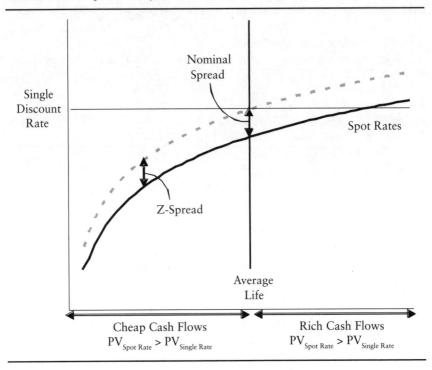

Source: Wachovia Capital Markets, LLC.

Using Z-spread analysis as part of a relative value framework is a straightforward exercise. If the Z-spread is less than the nominal spread, then a greater proportion of the cash flows are overvalued given the shape of the pricing curve and the timing of the cash flows. Conversely, if the static spread is greater than the pricing benchmark, then a greater proportion of the cash flows are undervalued given the shape of the pricing curve and the timing of the cash flows.

Changes in the shape of the curve can also affect the valuation of cash flows. For example, a flattening of the pricing curve led by the front-end of the curve (short-end twisting up) decreases the extent to which the earlier occurring cash flows are undervalued. Similarly, a steepening of the pricing curve led by the front-end (short-end twisting down) increases the extent to which the earlier occurring cash flows are undervalued. This in turn affects both spread differentials and the expected total return of tight widow (or principal locked-out) securities relative to wide window securities.

Total return analysis can further help quantify both relative value and the impact of changes in the shape of the pricing curve on investors expected holding period returns. The two major components of total return are price changes due to rolling down the curve and coupon income. For example, in the case of a positively sloped yield curve, the price appreciation associated with rolling down the curve contributes to an investor's expected horizon period return. Thus, total return analysis can be used to assess whether the higher yield typically associated with a wide window bond structure is sufficient to offset the superior roll down related to the price appreciation that may be experienced by a tighter window (or principal locked-out) structures.

AUTO LEASES

In a consumer auto lease transaction, the leasing company (lessor) purchases an automobile from the manufacturer or dealer and leases it to the consumer (lessee). The lessee pays the lessor for the right to use the automobile through the term of the lease. Lease terms are most often 24 to 48 months, though they can be longer. Auto lease-backed securities account for a relatively small percentage auto ABS securitizations making up 5.2%, 5.8%, and 7.7% of total auto ABS issuance in 2004, 2005, and 2006, respectively. Lease securitizations ebb and flow with the popularity of leasing among consumers.

The monthly lease payment reflects the following factors: net capitalized cost of the vehicle, residual value of the vehicle at lease termination, term of the lease, and the money factor (Exhibit 5.19). The monthly payment is calculated as the sum of the following:

The principal component(Net capitalized cost – Residual value)/Lease term

plus;

The interest component(Net capitalized cost + Residual value) × Money factor

The key risks in lease deals are somewhat different than loan deals. Credit losses, where the lessee defaults and stops making payments during the life of the lease, are a relatively small component of collateral losses. The major risk of loss is residual value risk, where the trust is subject to fair market prices in the used auto market at the disposition of the leased vehicle. In addition, the legal nature of auto leases represents unique structural challenges from vehicle titling requirements, perfection of security interests, and potential tort liability for the trust.

EXHIBIT 5.19   Typical Lease Calculation

Manufactured suggested retail price (MSRP)	$45,000
Negotiated price paid	$42,750
Taxes, title, delivery	$3,420
Down payment	$5,000
Net capitalized cost	$41,170
Residual value @ 65% MSRP	$29,250
Lease term (months)	48
Money factor	0.2719
Monthly payment	$439
Approximate APR	6.5%

Source: Fitch Rating, Moody's, Wachovia Capital Markets, LLC.

Residual Value Risk

Residual value risk arises when the actual market value of the leased vehicle is less than the assumed value at the termination of the lease. When used car prices are falling, the risk of a shortfall at disposition rises. In addition, higher-than-expected turn-in rates of leased vehicles results in greater residual value risk. The leasing company has an expectation of how many vehicles will be purchased by lessees at the point of lease expiration. If more consumers than expected turn their vehicles back to the lessor, then residual losses will be higher.

To put it in terms of an auto loan deal, turn-in rates are similar to defaults, and the actual residual value is similar to loss severity. For example, assume that the lease portfolio experiences a 55% turn-in rate and a loss per vehicle (loss severity) of $1,000. That is, the actual residual value at disposition is less than the expected residual value. In that case, a pool of 50,000 lease contracts would lose $27.5 million.

Vehicle Titling

A major hurdle in the securitization of auto leases is isolating both the leases and the automobiles from the assets of the lessor. Because the lessor is the owner of the automobile and titling laws vary from state to state, auto lease securitizations developed a titling trust structure illustrated in Exhibit 5.20.

EXHIBIT 5.20 Typical Auto Lease Securitization

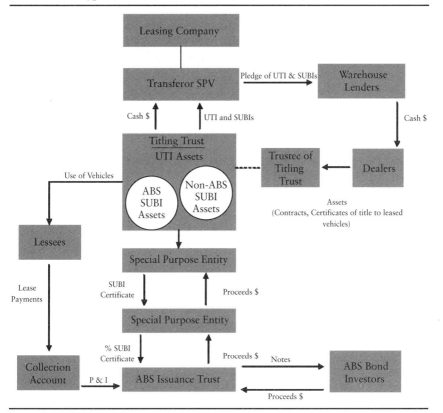

The titling trust is a bankruptcy remote special purpose entity that is formed to purchase both the lease contracts and automobiles from the manufacturer or dealer. The securitization sponsor/originator is engaged by the titling trust to act as the servicer on its behalf. The titling trust transfers to the sponsor/originator beneficial interest in its assets referred to as *undivided trust interest* (UTI assets). When the sponsor/originator securitizes the leases, the titling trust issues certificates representing a *special unit beneficial interest* (SUBI certificates). The automobile and lease assets remain in the titling trust and only the SUBI certificates and associated rights are transferred. Multiple SUBIs may be created from a single origination trust. However, the ABS issuance trust and bond investors only have rights in their SUBI designated portfolio.

A titling trust minimizes most of the hurdles associated with securitization of auto leases. However, the titling trust structure does give rise to other issues. Namely, priority of interest of the securitization trust against possible liens. In addition, the titling trust may be subject to liability for tort claims. This is because the titling trust is the owner of the automobile assets and anyone suffering an injury as a result of operating a leased vehicle could file a liability suit against the titling trust and owner of the vehicle.

SUMMARY

The auto ABS sector is one of the mainstays of the ABS market, with auto loans being one of the earliest asset classes tapped for securitization. Overall growth has coincided with increasing auto sales and the evolution of financing options. Furthermore, a wider array of asset classes, such as subprime loans or auto leases, gives investors a number of options. A deeper and more liquid subordinate bond market has developed as investors gained confidence in the sector. Indeed, the credit performance of most auto ABS has been very good, with upgrades outnumbering downgrades by a more than 4:1 ratio. One area for improvement seems to be in the realm of prepayments. The ABS prepayment curve was developed for the auto sector to compensate for a rising CPR profile. The current prepayment pricing convention works relatively well for prime and near-prime loan pools. However, the ABS curve fits less well for subprime loans.

CHAPTER 6

Student Loan ABS

Erin K. Walsh
Associate Analyst
Wachovia Capital Markets, LLC

T he increasing cost of education and rising college enrollments have pro-
pelled the rapid growth of student loan *asset-backed securities* (ABS).
The purpose of this chapter is to provide a guide to understanding the prepayments, risks and structural characteristics of student loans. In addition,
we discuss generic structures and provide statistics for the largest issuers.

BACKGROUND

Investing in a college education generally yields high returns for students.
The mean income is 74% higher for a bachelor's degree graduate versus a
high school graduate. The Higher Education Act (HEA) of 1965 opened
the gates for federal financing of post-secondary education. Under this act,
the Federal Family Education Loan Program (FFELP) was created. FFELP
is a public-private partnership that provides a federal guarantee for loans to
students and their parents.

As the cost of education has risen, limits on FFELP loans have remained
stagnant. This mismatch has increased the "funding gap," which is defined as
the cost of education minus the expected family contribution. Demand to fill
the funding gap has led to considerable growth in the private credit sector.

Prepayments for FFELP loans exhibit large, quarterly spikes due to
consolidations. Recent amendments to the HEA eliminate the number-one
reason to consolidate. In a rising interest rate environment, the opportunity
to consolidate floating rate loans into one fixed rate loan is very appealing;
however, this is no longer an option. FFELP student loans originated on or
after July 1, 2006, have a fixed interest rate. Prepayments will likely slow
due to the removal of this incentive.

Cost of Education

The cost of education has increased steadily over the past few decades. The growth in tuition, fees and room and board totals for four-year public and four-year private colleges indicates that (1) after adjusting for inflation, the *year-over-year* (YoY) increases for the total cost of private and public four-year colleges have averaged 2.4% and 3.5%, respectively, from academic years 1997–1998 to 2006–2007; and (2) even though the cost of attending a public college has increased faster than for a private college over the past decade, attending a private college is still more than double the cost of a public institution.

After adjusting for inflation, the tuition and fees in 2006 dollars contribute a higher proportion to the increasing cost of education. From academic years 1997–1998 through 2006–2007, tuition and fees for a private and public education have increased an average of 2.7% and 4.8%, respectively, YoY. Room and board costs for private colleges typically exceed public institutions by about 20%.

Growth in Financial Aid

Exhibit 6.1 shows aid from loans used to finance post-secondary education. The HEA amendment of 1992 included the addition of unsubsidized Staf-

EXHIBIT 6.1   Growth in Post-Secondary Aid

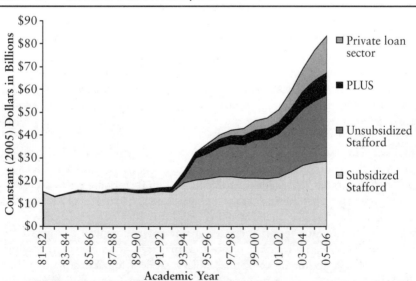

Source: Trends in Student Aid 2005, The College Board.

ford loans. We interpret the immediate rapid growth that followed as an indication of the strong demand to fill the funding gap. In addition, *parent loans for undergraduate students* (PLUS) limits were eliminated in the 1992 amendment and have seen steady growth.

The private loan sector has also seen increasing demand over the past decade. For the 2005–2006 academic year, private loans as a source of aid are estimated to be $16.3 billion.

Enrollment Projections

Fall enrollment is predicated to be almost 20 million by 2015. Undergraduate enrollment contributes approximately 16.8 million to this total with the remaining three million coming from graduate and first-professional.

Undergraduate enrollment spiked in 1991–1992, coinciding with the HEA addition of unsubsidized Stafford loans and the elimination of loan limits on PLUS loans. Enrollment for the following three years dropped 1.7%, 0.5% and 0.25% (1993, 1994, and 1995, respectively) before increasing again in 1996.

While enrollment growth averaged 2.1% per year for the decade prior to 2006, it is projected to slow for the upcoming decade (2006–2015) to an average of 1.17% per year.

TYPES OF LOANS

The U.S. Department of Education (DOE) makes financial aid available to all students and offers additional assistance to those students who demonstrate financial need. The DOE can act as the lender (Direct loans[1]) or as the guarantor for loans originated from private lenders (Federal Family Education Loan Program, FFELP). Below, we discuss loan types available and the FFEL program. Exhibit 6.2 provides a summary of these loans.

Perkins Loans

Federal Perkins loans are offered by participating schools to undergraduate or graduate students who demonstrate need. The school is the lender; therefore, borrowers repay the loan to the school or its agent. In contrast to other loan types, students are not required to be enrolled at least half time.

Graduate students can borrow up to $6,000 per year with a maximum of $40,000, including undergraduate loans. The interest is set at a fixed rate of 5% over the life of the loan, and the borrower has up to 10 years to repay, depending on the loan amount.

[1] William D. Ford Direct Student Loan Program.

EXHIBIT 6.2 Perkins, Stafford, PLUS, and Consolidation Loan Summary

	Perkins	Stafford — Subsidized	Stafford — Unsubsidized	PLUS	Consolidation
Loan Limits — Undergrad	$20,000 maximum total (up to $4,000 per year)	$3,500 freshman year; $4,500 sophomore year; $5,500 each remaining year; $23,000 maximum total		Up to the cost of attendance less other aid.	NA
Loan Limits — Graduate	$40,000 maximum inc. undergrad loans (up to $6,000 per year)	$8,500 per year; $65,500 maximum total including undergrad	$20,500 per year; $138,500 maximum total including undergrad	Up to the cost of attendance less other aid.	NA
Interest Rate	Fixed 5% for the life of the loan	See Exhibit 6.3		See Exhibit 6.3	Fixed rate equal to weighted average interest rate of loans consolidated rounded up to 1/8 of 1%
Maximum Interest Rate Caps	5%	8.25%	8.25%	9%	8.25%
In-School Payment	Interest paid by the government while in school and for a nine-month grace period.	Interest paid by the government while in school and for a six-month grace period.	Accrued interest paid by the student while in school or capitalized. Payments can be deferred for six months after graduation.	Repayment of principal and interest begins 60 days after final disbursement of loan.	NA
Repayment Period	Up to 10 years with possible extension for grace, deferment, and forbearance periods.	Up to 10 years with possible extension for grace, deferment, and forbearance periods.		Up to 10 years	Up to 30 years

Source: FinAid.org

Because the school is the lender, Perkins loans do not show up in student loan ABS transactions. It is somewhat undesirable to consolidate a Perkins loan, because forgiveness provisions[2] are lost. In addition, since the interest rate is already fixed, locking in a fixed rate via consolidation does not apply. However, students may consolidate their Perkins loans, and the consolidation loan could be included in a securitization.

Federal Family Education Loan Program

FFELPs include Parent Loan for Undergraduate Students Loans, Consolidation Loans, and Supplemental Loans to Students. We discuss each next. Historical interest rates for these loans are provided in Exhibit 6.3.

Stafford Loans

To qualify for a Stafford loan, students must be enrolled at least half time. Students borrow from either the DOE (Direct Stafford loans) or a bank or private lender where the funds are guaranteed by the federal government (FFELP Stafford loans).

EXHIBIT 6.3 Historical Interest Rates for Stafford and PLUS Loans

Period	Stafford–in School/ Grace/Deferment	Stafford Repayment	PLUS–in School/ Repayment
7/1/1995–6/30/1996	8.33%	8.93%	8.97%
7/1/1996–6/30/1997	7.66%	8.26%	8.72%
7/1/1997–6/30/1998	7.66%	8.26%	8.98%
7/1/1998–6/30/1999	6.86%	7.46%	8.26%
7/1/1999–6/30/2000	6.32%	6.92%	7.72%
7/1/2000–6/30/2001	7.59%	8.19%	8.99%
7/1/2001–6/30/2002	5.39%	5.99%	6.79%
7/1/2002–6/30/2003	3.46%	4.06%	4.86%
7/1/2003–6/30/2004	2.82%	3.42%	4.22%
7/1/2004–6/30/2005	2.77%	3.37%	4.17%
7/1/2005–6/30/2006	4.70%	5.30%	6.10%
7/1/2006–6/30/2012	6.80%	6.80%	8.50%

Source: FinAid.org, TreasuryDirect.gov, and Wachovia Capital Markets, LLC.

[2] Borrowers who teach or practice medicine in certain types of communities or perform volunteer work or military service can have all or part of a loan cancelled by the federal government.

Financial need is not a requirement for Stafford loans. However, for students who demonstrate need, the DOE will pay the interest that accrues while in school. These subsidized loans cannot exceed the amount of a student's financial need.

Unsubsidized Stafford loans can be used by students with or without financial need to cover the costs of education. Because the DOE does not pay the interest, students have the option to either pay the accrued interest while in school or have it added to the principal amount of the loan (capitalized).

The Stafford loan limits for undergraduate students increased July 1, 2007, allowing freshman to borrow up to $3,500 per year (previously $2,625) and sophomores up to $4,500 (previously $3,500). Loan limits for each remaining year are scheduled to stay at the current limit of $5,500, and the cumulative limit remains unchanged at $23,000 for undergraduate students.

For graduate students, the yearly limit increased to $20,500 per year from $18,500 with the amount that can be subsidized remaining at $8,500 per year. The maximum total for graduate students including undergraduate loans is $138,500 with a subsidized limit of $65,500.

Parent Loan for Undergraduate Students Loans

Parent Loan for Undergraduate Students (PLUS) loans are offered to parents with a dependent undergraduate student. It is important to note that these loans do not receive the benefit of a grace period[3] while the student is in school; therefore, repayment of these loans begins 60 days after the loan is fully disbursed. Typically, the cost of attendance exceeds the Perkins and Stafford loan caps. Fortunately, the loan amount for PLUS loans is not capped. Parents may borrow up to the amount of the student's cost of attendance, less any other financial aid received.

Consolidation Loans

One or more federal loans can be combined to create a single FFELP or Direct consolidation loan. This can benefit the borrower in several different ways including:

- Locking in a fixed rate for the life of the loan.
- Extending the loan term up to 30 years.
- Creating only one monthly loan payment.
- Possibly lowering the monthly payment.

---

[3] Under certain conditions, parents can receive a forbearance or deferral of the loan payment.

Supplemental Loans to Students

Supplemental loans to students (SLS) loans were created in 1986 for graduate, professional and independent students and have characteristics similar to the current PLUS loans. They are now virtually extinct in ABS transactions.

LOAN STATUS

Grace

Following graduation or withdrawal from school, Stafford, and Perkins borrowers are granted a period before the repayment of their loan begins. During the grace period, the government continues to pay the interest for subsidized and Perkins loans. For unsubsidized Stafford loans, the interest is still the responsibility of the student, who may request a shorter grace period to avoid additional accrual of interest. Grace periods for Stafford and Perkins loans are typically six and nine months, respectively.

Deferral

A deferral is a postponement of the loan repayment and acts similarly to the grace period. Interest accrues and the government pays it for subsidized and Perkins loans. However, for unsubsidized loans, the borrower is required to pay the interest or have it capitalized. Following are some circumstances in which students may receive deferment:

- Enrollment in postsecondary school at least half time.
- Economic hardship.
- Inability to find full-time employment.

Forbearance

A borrower, who cannot meet the repayment of his or her loan and does not qualify for a deferral, has the option of forbearance. During this period, payments are reduced or postponed; however, interest accrues and the borrower is responsible for paying it. To qualify, a borrower must provide documentation of why the borrower cannot meet the payments. Some of the conditions in which a borrower may be granted forbearance include the following:

- Payments on student loans are equal to or exceed 20% of monthly gross income.

- Inability to pay due to health problems.
- Residency in a medical or dental program.
- Service in a position under the National Community Service Trust Act of 1993.

INTEREST RATES

Prior to 1998, PLUS loans were indexed to the average one-year *constant maturity Treasury* (CMT). Since then, both PLUS and Stafford loan interest rates have been indexed to the 91-day Treasury bill. A margin plus the investment rate on the 91-day T-bill (from the last auction in May) equals the new interest rates, which reset on July 1 every year. Amendments to the HEA changed the floating rate to a fixed rate for loans originated on or after July 1, 2006. Exhibit 6.4 shows the formulas for calculating interest rates on FFELP loans.

The margin on PLUS loans does not depend on the loan status (i.e., school, repayment, grace and deferral). Conversely, the margin on Stafford loans adjusts depending on the period. The in-school, grace and deferral period margins are 60 basis points (bps) less than the repayment period for Stafford loans.

In 2001, interest rates on student loans dropped 220 bps and continued to drop through 2004. The July 1, 2005, interest rate reset increased rates a very significant 46% for FFELP loans. Exhibit 6.5 shows historical 91-day Treasury bill rates. Exhibit 6.6 shows the rate resets for student loans.

EXHIBIT 6.4   Historical Interest Rate Formulas for FFELP Loans

	Date Disbursed	In-School, Grace, Deferment Rate	Repayment Rate	Cap
Plus	10/1/1992–6/30/1994	CMT + 3.1%	CMT + 3.1%	10.00%
	7/1/1994–6/30/1995	CMT + 3.1%	CMT + 3.1%	9.00%
	7/1/1995–6/30/1998	CMT + 3.1%	CMT + 3.1%	9.00%
	7/1/1998–6/30/2006	91-day T-bill + 3.1%	91-day T-bill + 3.1%	9.00%
	7/1/2006–6/30/2012	Fixed rate of 8.5%	Fixed rate of 8.5%	NA
Stafford	10/1/1992–6/30/1994	91-day T-bill + 3.1%	91-day T-bill + 3.1%	9.00%
	7/1/1994–6/30/1995	91-day T-bill + 3.1%	91-day T-bill + 3.1%	8.25%
	7/1/1995–6/30/1998	91-day T-bill + 3.1%	91-day T-bill + 3.1%	8.25%
	7/1/1998–6/30/2006	91-day T-bill + 3.1%	91-day T-bill + 2.3%	8.25%
	7/1/2006–6/30/2012	Fixed rate of 6.8%	Fixed rate of 6.8%	NA

Source: FinAid.org.

EXHIBIT 6.5   91-Day Treasury Bill Rates

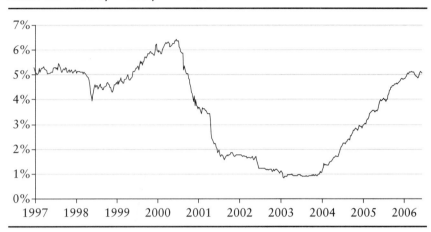

Source: TreasuryDirect.gov, Wachovia Capital Markets, LLC.

EXHIBIT 6.6   Historical Interest Rates for FFELP Loans

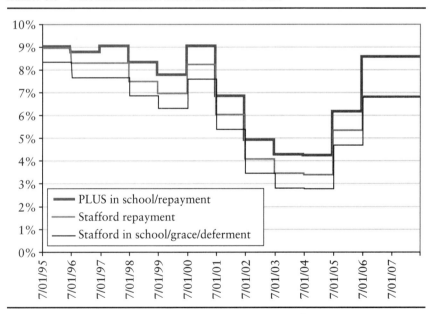

Source: FinAid.org, TreasuryDirect.gov, and Wachovia Capital Markets, LLC.

PREPAYMENTS

Prepayment analysis involves understanding the underlying components and the factors that affect them. Prepayments can be divided into the following four parts:

- Full repayment
- Curtailments
- Consolidations
- Default recoveries

Curtailment refers to principal paid by the borrower that exceeds the scheduled principal payment. It is important for borrowers to specify that extra payments made are to be applied to paying down the principal, and not treated as an advance for the next month's payment.

In *consolidation*, a new loan is created by combining and paying off one or more loans thus causing a prepayment of the loans consolidated. For FFELP loans, consolidations are the predominant factor contributing to prepayments.

Default recoveries are payments made by the insurer of student loans. The federal government is the guarantor for FFELP loans, whereas private insurers guarantee private credit loans.

Most issuers report prepayment speed on a quarterly frequency but as a cumulative measure. To determine quarterly prepayment speeds, we use the reported since-issued *constant prepayment rate* (CPR) from the current and previous quarter. The following calculation estimates quarterly prepayment speeds for student loan ABS where i represents the quarter.

$$\text{Quarterly CPR}_i = 1 - \left\{ \frac{[1 - \text{Since issued CPR}_i]^i}{[1 - \text{Since issued CPR}_{i-1}]^{i-1}} \right\}$$

Prepayments behave very differently depending on the collateral type. For comparison, in Exhibit 6.7, we show the estimated quarterly CPR for a private, consolidation and FFELP Sallie Mae transaction.

Estimated quarterly prepayments for private student loans are relatively low and do not exhibit any seasonality. Unlike FFELP, the option to lock in a fixed rate though consolidation does not exist for private credit. Typically indexed to either LIBOR or prime, private loans have a floating rate throughout the life of the loan.

Consolidation FFELP loans have slightly higher prepayments than private loans but are still low compared to nonconsolidation FFELP. A significant increase over the past year and a half can be attributed to unusual circumstances.

EXHIBIT 6.7 Estimated Quarterly CPR for Sallie Mae Transactions

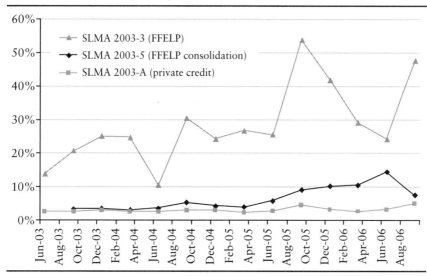

Source: Sallie Mae and Wachovia Capital Markets, LLC.

What caused the increase in consolidation loan prepayments? On May 16, 2005, the Department of Education published a "Dear Colleague" letter confirming a loophole that allowed for loans under the FFEL[4] program to enter into repayment status while in school, which made them eligible for consolidation. Previously, only loans in the Direct Loan[5] program allowed for in-school consolidation.

Once consolidated under the FFEL program, borrowers could reconsolidate under the Federal Direct Loan program and then reconsolidate again with a FFELP lender. This "super-two-step" consolidation option, coupled with historically low interest rates, caused an increase in prepayments on consolidation FFELP loans.

Exhibit 6.8 shows the estimated quarterly CPR for Sallie Mae consolidation transactions. These transactions display the same trends because the underlying collateral characteristics are parallel. The recent drop in prepayments is likely due to the repeal of "super-two-step" and the in-school consolidation option. Effective July 1, 2006, in-school consolidation for Direct Loans and FFELP loans is no longer an option.

The Dear Colleague letter and its repeal also had an effect on non-consolidation FFELP loans. During the allowance period for in-school consolidation, we see higher than normal prepayments. With historically low

---

[4] Bank or private lender backed by the federal government.

[5] U.S. Department of Education is the lender.

EXHIBIT 6.8   Estimated Quarterly CPR for SLMA Consolidation Transactions

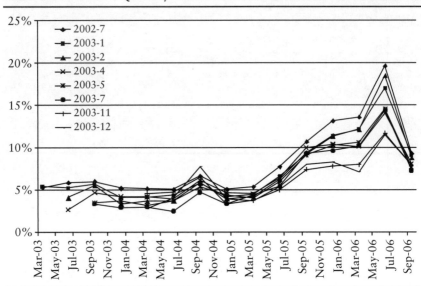

Source: Sallie Mae and Wachovia Capital Markets, LLC.

interest rates during this period, it is not surprising that students would take advantage of the last chance to consolidate while in school and lock in a lower rate.

Exhibit 6.9 shows estimated quarterly prepayments for FFELP transactions. We see seasonal prepayment spikes in these transactions due to consolidation action prior to interest rate resets (the largest proportion of FFELP prepayments comes from consolidations). In addition, borrowers who consolidate during the grace period benefit from a margin that is 60 bps lower.

We expect prepayments on new issue FFELP to be lower than current issues due to the interest rate change from floating to fixed for loans originated on or after July 1, 2006. There is no longer the motivation to consolidate for the purpose of locking in. However, students might still choose to consolidate to lower their monthly payment. Upon consolidating, the interest rate is set to a weighted average of all the loans, and the term of the loan is recast and extended thereby lowering the monthly payments. Also, the convenience of one monthly payment instead of several will likely continue to be an incentive to consolidate.

Prepayments for current vintages may also slow due to front-ended prepays for the in-school consolidation allowance. It would not be surprising to see the historically high prepayments of 2005 and 2006 slow to the levels seen prior to this period.

EXHIBIT 6.9   Estimated Quarterly CPR for SLMA FFELP Transactions

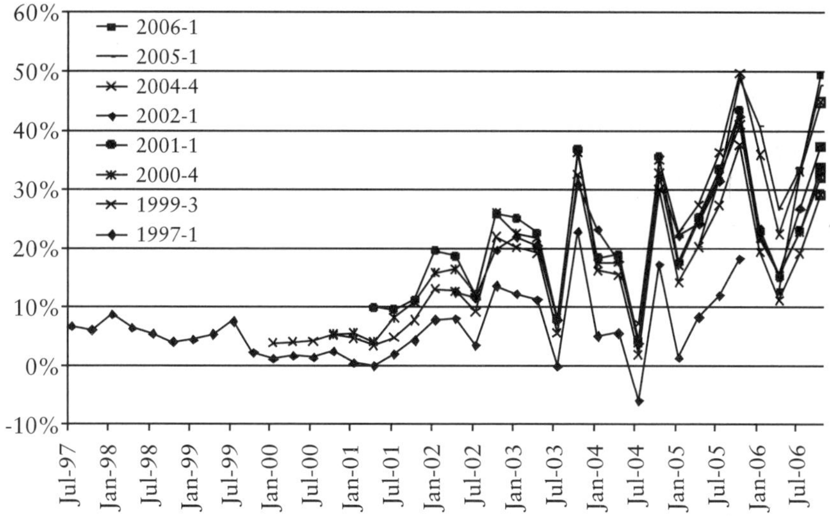

Source: Sallie Mae and Wachovia Capital Markets, LLC.

ISSUANCE

Student loan ABS issuance has increased substantially as can be seen in Exhibit 6.10. The most significant increase occurred from 2001 to 2002 when it more than doubled. The following year, growth slowed to a still-impressive 74% before slowing further in 2004 to 14%.

Sallie Mae is the leading issuer of student loan ABS. Exhibit 6.11 shows the top 20 issuers by 2005 new issue volume. Following Sallie Mae is Nelnet. Both of these issuers have FFELP, consolidation and private student loan transactions. Because Sallie Mae and Nelnet are the largest issuers of student loan ABS, we use data from their servicer reports to show examples throughout this chapter.

The largest issuers for private credit are Sallie Mae, Keycorp, First Marblehead (National Collegiate shelf) and Access Group. We show yearly issuance for these programs in Exhibit 6.12. Private credit experienced the most growth in 2003 with issuance jumping 147% from the previous year.

Versus auto and card ABS, outstanding debt for student loans has seen the most growth since the mid to late 1990s. While both auto and cards have been on the decline since 2003, student loans increased 16% and 33% in 2004 and 2005, respectively. (See Exhibit 6.13.)

EXHIBIT 6.10   Yearly Student Loan ABS Issuance

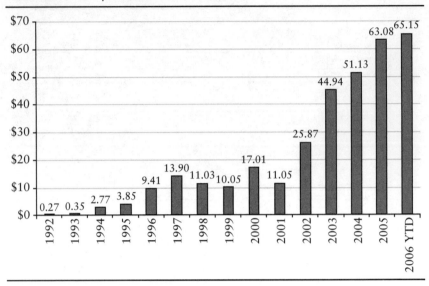

Source: Created from data obtained from *Asset Backed Alert.*

TYPICAL BOND STRUCTURES

Generic structures for student loan ABS differ depending on the underlying collateral. We examine recent transactions for FFELP, consolidation FFELP and private credit separately. While some features of the structures are the same, each varies to compensate for the unique characteristics of the underlying student loans.

Nonconsolidation FFELP transactions (see Exhibit 6.14) are generally structured as senior-subordinated with five or more A class notes and one subordinated B class note. The A class notes receive a triple-A rating, whereas the B class typically gets a single- or double-A rating. Payments of principal are sequential with the balance of the first note reducing to zero before the next note receives any principal. Class B note payments of interest are subordinate to the Class A's interest payments and, in addition, B notes' principal payments are subordinate to both interest and principal on the A class notes.

Private credit and consolidation FFELP transactions are also structured as sequential-pay senior-subordinate. However, subordinate notes receive principal payments starting on the step-down date, provided the trust student loans have not realized cumulative losses exceeding specified levels.

EXHIBIT 6.11   Top 20 Issuers of Student Loan ABS in 2005

	2005	2006 YTD
Sallie Mae	$26,990	$33,752
Nelnet Student Loan	$6,540	$5,313
SLC Student Loan Trust	$4,350	$4,912
Brazos Higher Education Authority Inc.	$3,717	$243
National Collegiate	$3,487	$4,724
College Loan Corporatin Trust	$2,700	$1,700
Collegiate Funding Services Education Loan Trust	$2,700	
Access Group Inc.	$2,074	$1,007
Wachovia Student Loan Trust	$1,800	$1,611
GCO Education Loan Finding Trust	$1,130	$2,643
Northstar Education Finance Inc.	$1,000	$653
Goal Capital Funding Trust	$1,000	$2,017
Higher Education Funding I	$1,000	
CIT Education Loan Trust	$1,000	
Keycorp Student Loan Trust	$963	$1,035
Education Loans Inc.	$821	
PHEAA Student Loan Trust I	$800	$500
Iowa Student Loan Liquidity Corp.	$700	
K2 Student Loan Trust I	$130	$325
Edinvest Company	$112	

Source: Created from data obtained from *Asset Backed Alert* and Wachovia Capital Markets, LLC.

Exhibit 6.15 shows a recent Nelnet consolidation transaction. Note the original *weighted average life* (WAL) of the subordinate tranche (B) in this transaction is less than that of the last-pay-priority A class.

Expected losses for private credit tend to be higher as they do not receive the federal government's reinsurance guarantee. These transactions command wider spreads. In Exhibit 6.16, a recent Sallie Mae private transaction is compared to a consolidation FFELP transaction to show the spread pickup.

In addition to spread, private transactions have higher subordination levels. Sallie Mae 2006-C, shown in Exhibit 6.17, has two subordinated tranches in contrast to the FFELP and consolidation transactions that only have one. Subordination of the A classes is 7.8% for the private deal shown below versus the consolidation and FFELP transactions, which only have 3%.

EXHIBIT 6.12   Largest Issuers of Private Student Loan ABS

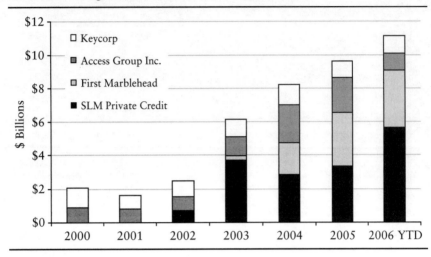

Source: Created from data obtained from *Asset Backed Alert.*

EXHIBIT 6.13   Outstanding ABS by Sector

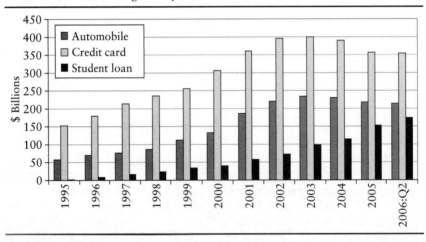

Source: Created from data obtained from the Securities Industry and Financial Markets Association.

EXHIBIT 6.14 FFELP Transaction, Sallie Mae 2006-3

Class	Original Principal Amount ($ million)	Original WAL	Moody's	S&P	Fitch	Interest Rate
A1	687.000	1.00	Aaa	AAA	AAA	3-month LIBOR minus 0.02%
A2	825.000	3.00	Aaa	AAA	AAA	3-month LIBOR plus 0.00%
A3	335.000	5.00	Aaa	AAA	AAA	3-month LIBOR plus 0.04%
A4	483.000	7.00	Aaa	AAA	AAA	3-month LIBOR plus 0.08%
A5	162.293	8.38	Aaa	AAA	AAA	3-month LIBOR plus 0.10%
B	77.082	8.38	Aa2	AA	AA+	3-month LIBOR plus 0.20%

Source: Bloomberg LP and Sallie Mae Prospectus.

EXHIBIT 6.15 Consolidation FFELP Transaction, Nelnet 2006-3

Class	Original Principal Amount ($ million)	Original WAL	Moody's	S&P	Fitch	Interest Rate
A-1	199.000	1.00	Aaa	AAA	AAA	3-month LIBOR minus 0.02%
A-2	384.000	3.00	Aaa	AAA	AAA	3-month LIBOR plus 0.01%
A-3	245.000	5.00	Aaa	AAA	AAA	3-month LIBOR plus 0.03%
A-4	384.000	7.00	Aaa	AAA	AAA	3-month LIBOR plus 0.07%
A-5	465.000	10.00	Aaa	AAA	AAA	3-month LIBOR plus 0.10%
A-6	469.500	14.43	Aaa	AAA	AAA	3-month LIBOR plus 0.14%
B	66.500	10.95	Aa1	AA+	AA+	3-month LIBOR plus 0.25%

Source: Bloomberg LP and Nelnet Prospectus.

EXHIBIT 6.16   Private versus Consolidation FFELP Student Loan Spreads

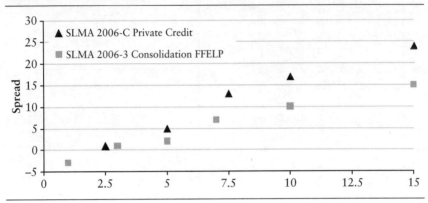

Source: Sallie Mae Prospectus, Bloomberg LP.

EXHIBIT 6.17   Private Credit—Sallie Mae 2006-C

Class	Original Principal Amount ($ million)	Original WAL	Moody's	S&P	Fitch	Interest Rate
A1	157.000	2.50	Aaa	AAA	AAA	3-month LIBOR plus 0.01%
A2	268.000	5.00	Aaa	AAA	AAA	3-month LIBOR plus 0.05%
A3	110.000	7.50	Aaa	AAA	AAA	3-month LIBOR plus 0.13%
A4	215.000	10.00	Aaa	AAA	AAA	3-month LIBOR plus 0.17%
A5	356.017	14.16	Aaa	AAA	AAA	3-month LIBOR plus 0.24%
B	39.177	11.54	Aa2	AA–	AA	3-month LIBOR plus 0.31%
C	54.245	10.50	A2	A	A	3-month LIBOR plus 0.39%

Source: Bloomberg LP and Sallie Mae Prospectus.

In addition to subordination, credit enhancement for student loan ABS includes excess interest, overcollateralization, reserve accounts and capitalized interest accounts. Reserve accounts receive an initial deposit from the net proceeds of the sale of the notes and are available to cover shortfalls. At issuance, reserve accounts are generally 25 bps of the note balance. As the notes pay down, target reserves are typically set to 25 bps of the remaining pool balance with a floor at 15 bps of original. Similarly, capitalized interest accounts cover shortfalls; however, they are not replenished like reserve accounts.

Most recent student loan ABS issues have floating interest rates that are typically indexed to three-month LIBOR, with the rate reset occurring quarterly. The auction rate market, which was once popular, suffered from controversy[6] leading to a Securities and Exchange Commission (SEC) investigation in 2004. The decline in issuance that followed bounced back as the matters of concern have since been resolved.

RISKS

The subordinated notes of student loan ABS are most at risk of not receiving the expected return of investment. They support the higher classes, and the sequential pay structure causes them to have a longer weighted average life. Both of these conditions put them at greater risk of suffering a loss.

Basis Risk

While the note's interest rate is determined on the basis of a specified index, the underlying loans adjust on the basis of different indices. This mismatch could lead to interest shortfalls. To hedge this risk, the trust may enter into an interest rate swap agreement. It is important to note that the swap agreements mitigate the risk but do not eliminate it completely.

Payments by the DOE somewhat compensate for basis risk for FFELP loans. Lenders receive a quarterly *special allowance payment* (SAP) to bring the interest rate up to equal three-month commercial paper plus a margin that depends on the loan type. Recent amendments to the HEA require lenders to repay excess interest over the special allowance support level.

Prepayment and Extension Risk

The borrower's right to prepay a loan at any time can shorten the length of time interest is accrued. This is particularly risky for transactions where the initial principal balance of the notes exceeds the outstanding pool balance. In this case, noteholders are relying on interest payments to reduce the note balance to the pool balance.

Conversely, the life of the loan can extend due to lower-than-expected prepayments or periods of grace, deferment and forbearance. Investors' securities are then outstanding longer and accruing interest for a longer period as well.

---

[6] Broker-dealer firms engaged in practices such as submitting or changing orders after auction deadlines, intervening to prevent failed auctions, and activities favoring certain customers and not others.

Servicer Risk

FFELP loans that are guaranteed and reinsured by the DOE are at risk of losing this guarantee if they do not comply with set servicing standards. Default claims that are rejected due to noncompliance pass through to the trust as a loss.

The July 1, 2006 HEA amendment reduces government guarantee levels by 100 bps to 97% from 98%. In addition, servicers who previously received 100% guarantee for "Exceptional Performance"[7] are now only 99% guaranteed.

Decreasing the government guarantee affects the loss severity for these loan types. Recovery rates drop for the defaulted loans by 100 bps for both undesignated and Exceptional Performer designated servicers.

CHARACTERISTICS OF STUDENT LOAN ABS

FFELP transactions consist of a mix of PLUS, Stafford loans and SLS loans. Exhibit 6.18 shows the weighted average loan types for Sallie Mae FFELP transactions. Subsidized Stafford loans make up the largest part, followed by unsubsidized Stafford loans, PLUS and SLS loans.

EXHIBIT 6.18   Weighted Average Loan Types for Sallie Mae FFELP Securitizations

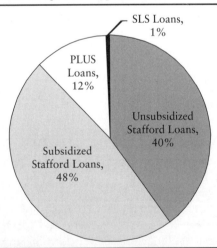

Source: Sallie Mae and Wachovia Capital Markets, LLC.

[7] Lenders and servicers who meet and maintain an overall compliance performance rating of 97% or higher for servicing requirements set by the DOE are given an Exceptional Performer designation.

Cash flows for student loans are dependent on the loan type and status. Loans in periods other than repayment are accruing interest, which is either paid to the trust or capitalized. Interest that is paid to the trust comes from government subsidies or the borrower. Interest that is capitalized increases the principal balance of the loan but, in turn, reduces the current cash flow.

Exhibit 6.19 shows the loan status for a Sallie Mae FFELP transaction. The percentage of loans in repayment increases as the issue seasons, because students graduate and their loans move from in-school status to repayment.

For consolidation securitizations, the percentage in repayment starts high and remains relatively constant throughout the life of the transaction. Exhibit 6.20 shows that the percentage of loans in repayment hovers around 72%. This should come as no surprise, as loans begin repayment schedules immediately following consolidation.

Loan types for private credit transactions differ among lenders. The following are some examples of loan types that are offered:

- Supplemental loans for undergraduate and graduate students
- Consolidation
- Business school students
- Law school students
- Medical school students
- K-12
- Parent

EXHIBIT 6.19 Loan Status for FFELP SLMA 2003-3

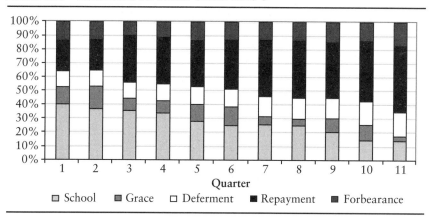

Source: Sallie Mae Servicer Reports and Wachovia Capital Markets, LLC.

EXHIBIT 6.20   Loan Status for Consolidation FFELP SLMA 2003-5

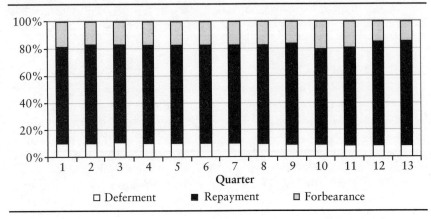

Source: Sallie Mae Servicer Reports and Wachovia Capital Markets, LLC.

EXHIBIT 6.21   Weighted Average Loan Types for Sallie Mae Private Securitizations

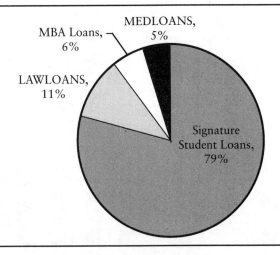

Source: Sallie Mae and Wachovia Capital Markets, LLC.

Sallie Mae's Signature loans provide supplemental funds for undergraduate and graduate students. These loans dominate private credit transactions at a weighted average of 79% (Exhibit 6.21). The remaining portion consists of other loan types from their private loan program. LAWLOANS, MBA Loans and MEDLOANS make up a weighted average of 11%, 6% and 5%, respectively, of private credit transactions.

EXHIBIT 6.22   Weighted Average Loan Types for Sallie Mae Private Securitizations

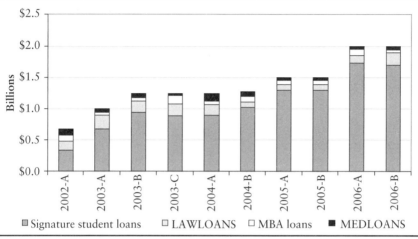

Source: Sallie Mae and Wachovia Capital Markets, LLC.

EXHIBIT 6.23   Loan Status for Private Credit SLMA 2003-A

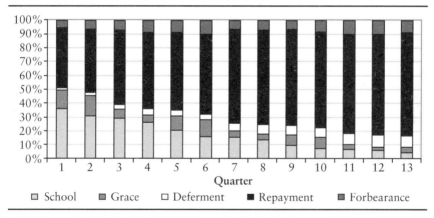

Source: Sallie Mae Servicer Reports and Wachovia Capital Markets, LLC.

As the demand to fill the funding gap has increased, so have private loan originations and transaction size. In Exhibit 6.22, the original pool characteristics are shown for Sallie Mae's private deals.

Loan status trends for private credit act similar to those for FFELP loans with the percentage in repayment increasing as the transaction ages. The overall loans in repayment, however, start at a higher percentage for private versus FFELP transactions. (See Exhibit 6.23.)

EXHIBIT 6.24   Weighted Average FICO for Private Credit Deals

| Transaction | Weighted Average FICO Score for Loans | |
	Cosigner	No Cosigner
NCSLT 2004-1	724	701
NCSLT 2004-2	721	697
NCSLT 2005-1	726	703
NCSLT 2005-2	726	700
NCSLT 2005-3	724	701
NCSLT 2006-1	727	699
NCSLT 2006-2	715	698
NCSLT 2006-3	713	705
SLMA 2002-A	735	703
SLMA 2003-A	731	694
SLMA 2003-B	736	695
SLMA2003-C	736	701
SLMA 2004-A	736	695
SLMA 2004-B	738	698
SLMA 2005-A	740	696
SLMA 2005-B	742	697
SLMA 2006-A	739	698
SLMA 2006-B	733	697

Source: Sallie Mae Servicer Reports, First Marblehead Servicer Reports.

Private credit loans often employ a cosigner to mitigate default risk. Borrowers and cosigners are typically prime credit quality with FICO scores in the high 600s to mid 700s. The weighted average FICO scores for loans with cosigners are higher than those for loans without cosigners (Exhibit 6.24).

SUMMARY

In this chapter we explain the investment characteristics of student loan ABS. We expect issuance of student loan ABS to grow at a steady rate as the costs of education and enrollments continue to rise. While the July 1, 2007 increase on FFELP loan limits should assist as a source of funding, the increase amount is modest. Demand to fill the funding gap will likely continue to spur growth in the private credit sector.

The July 1, 2006 amendment of the HEA takes away the reconsolidation option and changes FFELP loans originated on or after July 1, 2006, to a fixed interest rate. Prepayments will likely revert back to levels seen prior to the historically high levels of 2005.

Both private and FFELP transactions benefit from high credit quality of underlying loans. For FFELP loan transactions, the government guarantee of 97% to 100%, depending on the loan, substantially mitigates losses upon default. Private loans exhibit high FICO scores and often have cosigners. In addition to the high quality of the underlying collateral, excess spread, over-collateralization, reserve accounts and subordination provide transactions with substantial credit enhancement should losses occur.

CHAPTER 7

Small Business Loan ABS

Erin K. Walsh
Associate Analyst
Wachovia Capital Markets, LLC

There are approximately 25.8 million businesses in the United States. The Small Business Administration (SBA) Office of Advocacy defines a small business as an independent business having less than 500 employees. Small firms make up 99.7% of all employer firms and employ about half of all private-sector employees.

Small businesses can be viewed as one of the fundamental contributors to the growth and success of this country. The significance is apparent when looking at the role small businesses have played in job growth, entrepreneurialism and innovation. Over the past decade, small businesses have generated 60% to 80% of net new jobs annually. Some well-known brands we use every day started out as small businesses and have grown into large enterprises and household names.

Obtaining financing is probably the most important prerequisite for starting up a small business. While some borrowers can obtain conventional business loans for financing, often borrowers will lack the credit worthiness to secure these loans. The SBA's financial assistance is especially important for those borrowers who could not otherwise secure financing. The SBA programs offer several different loan types, but the most common are 7(a) loans, which are originated by private lenders with a portion guaranteed by the SBA. In 1992, securitization of the unguaranteed portion of loans was approved by the SBA.

Yearly issuance for small business loan securitizations is shown in Exhibit 7.1. Issuance more than doubled from 2002 to 2003 and, since,

The author would like to thank Michael Libman of BancLab LLC for his comments. The credit loss performance statistics in this chapter were provided by BancLab LLC.

EXHIBIT 7.1   Yearly Small Business Loan Securitization Issuance

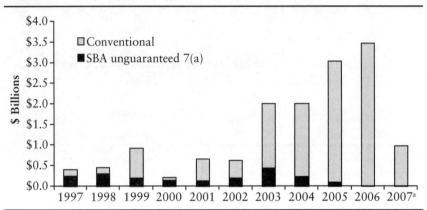

^a As of 8/27/2007.
Source: Intex Solutions, Inc.

has shown steady growth in conventional but a decline in SBA transactions. Because of accounting rules, securitization of 7(a) loans has lost its appeal to the largest underwriters, banks.

This chapter provides a guide to understanding the securitization of the unguaranteed portion of loans originated under section 7(a) as well as conventional small business loan securitizations.

SMALL BUSINESS ADMINISTRATION

On July 30, 1953, the federal government established the U.S. Small Business Administration with the purpose of aiding, counseling, assisting and protecting small businesses. SBA financial assistance is vital to the growth and startup of small businesses. Over the years, the SBA has grown in its total assistance provided and also the types of programs offered. Almost 20 million small businesses have received assistance through one or more of the SBA's programs.

In addition to financial assistance, the SBA also offers tools to manage a business from start to finish and has made improvements to its own business processes. Following the hurricanes of 2005 (Katrina, Rita and Wilma), the SBA experienced an overwhelming number of loan applications from disaster victims. Lacking the capacity to process all of the loans, the SBA established the framework for a recovery plan to deal with future disasters.

SBA 7(a) LOAN GUARANTEE PROGRAM

7(a) loans gain their name from section 7(a) of the Small Business Act, which provides a guarantee to lenders that make loans to American small businesses. Lenders that provide 7(a) loans are considered participants, and the SBA and participant share the risk of the loan as only a portion of the loan is guaranteed by the SBA.

For a borrower to qualify for a 7(a) loan, it must be shown that the borrower cannot obtain credit elsewhere. Additional eligibility requirements for these loans include the ability of repayment from the cash flow of the business and owners of 20% or more personally guaranteeing the loan.

The process for loan approval requires applicants to submit necessary documentation to lenders who then forward it to the SBA for loan approval. The decision for approving a loan for the SBA guarantee is solely dependent on the SBA. This process can be rather slow, taking approximately 20 calendar days for turnaround. Certified and preferred lender programs were introduced to speed up the process of loan approval.

In 1979, the certified lender program was introduced, which allowed a more rapid turnaround of the approval process. Under this program, the SBA strives to have applicants approved in approximately three business days. Lenders in this program are expected to have a solid understanding of the SBA's lending policies and procedures as well as a successful SBA-lending track record.

An even speedier process for approval, the preferred lender program, was introduced in 1983. Obtaining preferred lender status allows a lender the authority to approve loans and obtain the SBA guarantee without submitting the credit review application to the SBA prior to originating a loan. However, following origination, lenders in this program still must submit required documents and notify the SBA of the loan. This process offers the fastest service to the loan applicant. Lenders that demonstrate a proficiency in processing and servicing SBA loans are nominated by an SBA field office to participate. If a lender isn't nominated, it can request to be considered for this program if it meets the required standards of performance set forth by the SBA.

SBA loans are charged a fee to offset the cost to taxpayers. Lenders are required to pay a servicing fee and a guarantee fee, although the guarantee fee can be charged upfront to the borrower after the first disbursement of the loan. Guarantee fees range from 2.0% to 3.5%, depending on the deferred participation share of the total loan amount.

SBA 7(a) LOAN CHARACTERISTICS

Eligibility requirements for 7(a) loans are designed to be broad to allow funding to many small businesses of diverse types. The SBA specifies requirements for the following factors:

- Availability of funds from other sources
- Size
- Type of business
- Use of proceeds

First, to qualify for an SBA loan, the applicant must show a need for financing. Applicants with ample business and personal financial resources will be required to use those funds prior to being eligible for a loan.

For loans with amounts below $150,000, an 85% guarantee is extended. Loans above $150,000 only receive a 75% guarantee, and the maximum loan amount is $2 million, with a maximum SBA guarantee of $1.5 million.

If a payment default occurs, the government reimburses the lender for its loss up to the percentage of the SBA's guarantee. However, the SBA and lender share the risk as only a portion of the loan is guaranteed. Moreover, the guarantee is against borrower payment default and not faulty loans stemming from either misrepresentation by the borrower or imprudent lending.

The types of businesses that are eligible include the vast majority as long as the business operates for profit, has reasonable owner equity to invest and does business in the United States. Some restrictions apply to certain types of businesses; therefore, additional considerations are needed for specific businesses to determine whether applicants are eligible.

Eligible use of loan proceeds may include purchasing land or buildings, the cost of new construction, acquiring equipment or supplies, and short- or long-term working capital. Essentially, loan proceeds are required to be used for funding a new business or the operation, acquisition or expansion of an existing business subject to certain restrictions. Examples of ineligible use of proceeds include nonsound business purposes or refinancing existing debt where the lender would incur a loss.

Maturity terms for SBA loan programs are dependent on the purpose of the proceeds, ability to repay and the useful life of financed assets. For equipment and real estate, the maximum loan maturity is 25 years and, for working capital, the maximum is seven years. For loan proceeds that are used for mixed purposes, the maximum maturity can be either a weighted average or separate maturities for each purpose.

Interest rates are either fixed or variable and are negotiated between the lender and borrower but subject to maximums set forth by the SBA. Equal

EXHIBIT 7.2   Maximum Interest Rates by Loan Amount and Maturity

Maturity	≤ $25,000	$25,000–$50,000	≥ $50,000
< 7 Years	Prime + 4.25	Prime + 3.25	Prime + 2.25
> 7 Years	Prime + 4.75	Prime + 3.75	Prime + 2.75

Source: U.S. Small Business Administration.

to the prime rate plus a margin, the maximum rates are dependent on both the loan size and the maturity. Exhibit 7.2 details the maximum allowable interest rates.

Most SBA loans carry a variable interest rate indexed to the prime rate, but some are indexed to the SBA's *optional peg rate*. This rate is calculated on a quarterly basis by the SBA and is equal to a weighted average cost the government pays for loans with similar maturities to loans from the SBA.

Loans will be subject to penalties for prepayments but only under certain conditions set forth by the SBA. The penalties apply to loans that have a maturity of 15 years or more where the borrower is voluntarily prepaying 25% or more of the outstanding balance. In addition, prepayment penalties apply only during the first three years after the date of the first disbursement. The fee for prepayment is calculated as a percentage of the amount of prepayment and is dependent on the year the prepayment occurs with 5% for the first year, 3% the second year and 1% for the third year after disbursement.

It is important to note that the prepayment fees are not retained by the lender. All fees from prepayments are passed on to the SBA; therefore, the lender has no incentive to refinance loans to borrowers based on collection of prepayment fees.

SECURITIZATION OF UNGUARANTEED PORTIONS OF SBA 7(a) LOANS

In 1992, the SBA approved the securitization of the unguaranteed portions of the loans originated under the SBA 7(a) program. Typically, after a loan is originated under the SBA 7(a) program, the guaranteed portion is sold as either whole loan sales, or as part of a pool of loans. The retained unguaranteed portions can then be securitized. The seller/servicer of the loan remains responsible for servicing the entire loan amount.

Credit enhancement for securitizations is in the form of excess spread, reserve accounts, overcollateralization and subordination. A unique feature of 7(a) transactions is the excess spread that is used to support the deal. While only the unguaranteed portions of loans are included in a securitization, excess spread from the entire loan is used as credit enhancement for the transaction. Recall, the guaranteed portion makes up a greater part of the loan, typically 75% to 85%. Therefore, the ratio of excess spread from the entire loan to just the unguaranteed portion of the loan becomes quite significant.

Excess spread is used to absorb losses and to pay interest and principal shortfalls. In addition, excess spread can be used to build and/or maintain cash reserve accounts to specified levels. Reserve accounts are established when a transaction closes and are typically funded equal to a certain percentage of the original loan balance. In addition, reserve accounts can include target amounts and, if not funded in full initially, then excess spread is used to build up to the specified level.

For some transactions, the reserve account requirements are percentages of the outstanding balance and will vary as the pool amortizes. The reserve account can also be subject to floors, which are typically percentages of the original pool balance. Another characteristic of reserve accounts is to capture excess spread for loans that are delinquent 90 to 180 days or more, depending on the transaction.

Overcollateralization is a form of credit enhancement in which the collateral pool balance exceeds that of the bond balance. This not only allows a cushion for loan defaults, it also provides additional leverage for excess spread.

In general, transactions are structured with a senior AAA rated bond subordinated with a single-A rated bond. Subordination supports the higher-rated bond by allocating losses first to the lower-rated bond. The first line of defense against losses, however, is excess spread. In addition, the reserve account is available for principal and interest shortfalls.

SECURITIZATION OF CONVENTIONAL SMALL BUSINESS LOANS

While there are a few differences, the structures for conventional small business loan transactions are similar to those of the unguaranteed portions of SBA 7(a) loans. One distinction is the excess spread available. Note, for 7(a) transactions, excess spread from the entire loan is available with only the unguaranteed portion being securitized, where for conventional business loans the entire loan is in the transaction.

Conventional small business loans are also made to "qualifying borrowers," whereas the eligibility requirement of SBA loans is for borrowers that cannot obtain this financing. Therefore, the quality of conventional small business loans is generally better than SBA loans.

The average loan balance for conventional business loans for the most part will be higher than the SBA due to a lack of SBA limits on loan size.

Also recall that SBA loans are typically floaters indexed to the prime rate. Conventional loans tend to be indexed to three-month LIBOR because the investment community prefers LIBOR floating rate bonds. Indexing the underlying collateral to the same index mitigates basis risk. SBA transactions have basis risk; however, the rating agencies take this into consideration when specifying levels of credit enhancement for deals.

Large portions of conventional loans are secured by first liens on real commercial property. Transactions will often consist of pools of loans backed almost completely by real estate collateral. When the loan is not backed by real estate, losses on defaulted loans will typically be higher due to the lack of real estate collateral, which is generally an appreciating asset, versus collateral such as equipment, which is a depreciating asset.

Prepayment penalties for conventional loans tend to be more severe than the SBA. Penalties are set by the lender and will likely start at 5% and step down one percentage point per year for the first five years following disbursements.

SBA transactions are generally more geographically diverse than conventional transactions. Forty-eight states could be represented in an SBA transaction where conventional transactions may contain only eight with around 70% of loan concentration in one state. Small business performance is negatively affected by downturns in economic cycles; the geographic diversity of SBA transactions lessens some of this risk.

SMALL BUSINESS LOAN LOSS PERFORMANCE ON SBA 7(a) LOANS—BancLab LLC DATA

SBA performance is often used as a proxy for conventional small business loans. However, because SBA lending is considered to be lending of last resort, the historical loss experience should be considered the worst-case scenario for the small business loan sector.

SBA 7(a) small business loans originated over the past two decades have demonstrated a predictable credit loss curve even through different business cycles. The data in Exhibits 7.3, 7.4, and 7.5 show weighted average historical charge-offs and cumulative loss rates on nearly 800,000 SBA 7(a) loans.

BancLab LLC provided the data used in these exhibits from its proprietary small business lending credit risk database.[1] BancLab provides customized credit risk measurement tools to enhance the profitability of originating, servicing and securitizing small business loans. By analyzing loans with common underwriting standards nationwide over one or more

---

[1] www.BancLab.com.

full business cycles, BancLab is able to offer clients insight into small business loan performance.

Exhibit 7.3 provides a weighted average static pool analysis of the annual charge-offs experienced on SBA 7(a) loans originated from 1983 through 2006. Charge-offs are expressed as a percentage of the outstanding balance at origination.[2] SBA 7(a) loans exhibit a clear aging pattern, with credit losses peaking in years 4 through 6 (Exhibit 7.3). BancLab's underlying analyses of individual cohorts confirm that this pattern remains generally consistent regardless of the economic environment, but the actual peak in default rates is affected by the maturity of the assets within each cohort. Exhibit 7.4 portrays the cumulative weighted average net charge-off rate across all cohorts over the past 24 years, which is approximately 7.6%. As illustrated in Exhibit 7.5, which shows four-year cumulative loss rates by cohort year, individual cohorts can vary significantly in net charge-off rates.

The four-year cumulative loss rates initially depict a marked downward trend in losses after the 1990–1991 recession, later followed by increased loss rates related to macroeconomic conditions. For example, the average four-year loss rate was 1.6% for the 1992–1999 cohorts, spiked to 2.7% in the wake of the 2000–2001 economic downturn, and then declined to 1.1% for the 2002–2003 cohorts as the economy improved.

EXHIBIT 7.3   Weighted Average Static Pool Net Charge-Offs

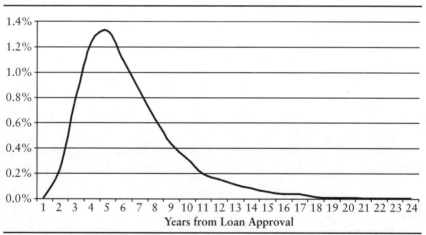

Source: BancLab LLC.

---

[2] To make this analysis consistent with previous publications on SBA performance experience, cohorts are defined by approval year, rather than disbursement year. Thus, this vintage analysis modestly overstates the time between origination and credit loss. In this analysis, charge-offs serve as a proxy for credit loss.

EXHIBIT 7.4   Cumulative Weighted Average Static Pool Net Charge-Offs

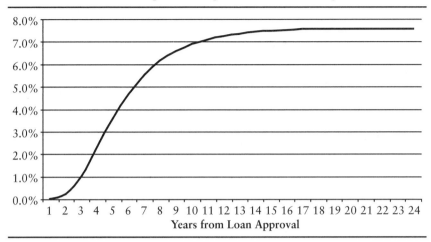

Source: BancLab LLC.

EXHIBIT 7.5   SBA Static Pool Charge-Offs Cumulative 4-Year Loss Rates by Cohort

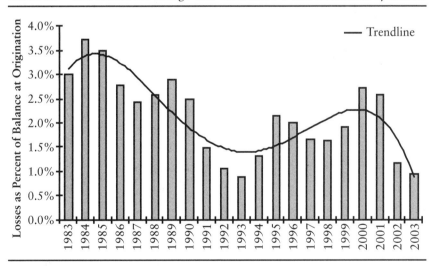

Source: BancLab LLC.

Analyzing small business loan performance on a national basis masks key differences in credit performance (i.e., defaults, loss-given default and prepayments) by risk factors such as borrower industry, collateral type and geographic location. For example, small business loans secured by real estate have lower default rates and greater recoveries on defaulted loans compared to loans not secured by real estate, resulting in lower net losses on real estate-secured loans.

In summary, small business loans exhibit fairly stable and predictable credit loss curves. Granular analyses based on key risk factors and macroeconomic conditions offer even greater transparency and confidence in these loans' historical performance and credit risks.

SUMMARY

Issuance volume in the small business loan sector is light in comparison to other structured asset classes. However, the importance of these loan types to the small business owner and the U.S. economy is nothing to be ignored. With the establishment of the SBA and the 7(a) loan program, lenders were able to offer loans to borrowers that they may not have otherwise.

While the underlying loans and structures of SBA and conventional small business transactions are generally the same, it is important to keep in mind some key differences. Geographic diversity, loan size, excess spread and basis risk are likely the most notable differences and should be taken into context when assessing risk. While the timing of losses of small business loans is relatively consistent, severity of losses is typically dependent on macroeconomic cycles.

CHAPTER 8

Valuation of Subprime ABS Credit Default Swaps

Shane Whitworth, CFA
Associate Analyst
Wachovia Capital Markets, LLC.

Credit derivatives in recent years have dramatically increased the size and liquidity of the debt markets. *Credit default swap* (CDS) contracts are now available on a wide variety of financial products, including subprime ABS. The subprime ABS market includes structured bonds that are backed by first- and second-lien subprime mortgages. The central focus of this chapter is to provide a solid understanding of CDS valuation techniques as they pertain to the subprime ABS market. The CDS contracts discussed in this chapter are *single-name CDS*, which means that we are discussing a credit default swap on a single bond rather than a portfolio of bonds. In Chapter 11, credit default swaps as they are used to created synthetic collateralized debt obligations are discussed.

CREDIT DEFAULT SWAPS

Credit default swap contracts are designed to allow one to trade in just the credit risk of a financial product. If, for instance, you owned a bond and you wanted to hedge out all of the credit risk related to that bond, you could do so with a CDS contract. The process of buying the hedge is called *buying protection*, as you would be buying protection against a credit event on the bond. Likewise, the counterparty that is insuring you against losses on the bond is *selling protection* to you. When a party sells protection, it is going long the credit risk. The buyer of protection is short the credit risk.

PAY-AS-YOU-GO CDS STRUCTURE FOR SUBPRIME ABS

Subprime ABS CDS contracts are standardized by the International Swaps and Dealers Association (ISDA). The *pay-as-you-go* (PAUG) forms were designed to closely mimic the relevant cash flows of the reference bonds. The resulting forms compensate the protection buyer for principal write-downs and shortfalls as well as any interest shortfalls just as a holder of the bond would not receive the relevant payments. Any write-downs or shortfalls that are recovered later are paid back to the protection seller with compounded interest. Notional amounts decline in a subprime ABS CDS just as the principal balance declines on the reference obligation. The protection seller receives a periodic fixed percentage of the outstanding notional balance of the reference bond from the protection buyer. This periodic payment is comparable to an insurance premium. (See Exhibit 8.1.)

INTEREST SHORTFALL CONSIDERATIONS

PAUG CDS contracts might or might not mimic the interest shortfalls exactly. There are three options for choosing how to handle the interest shortfalls.

1. *Fixed cap applicable.* Interest rate shortfalls are covered up to a fixed-rate × notional. The protection buyer has interest rate shortfall exposure of actual interest rate shortfall – (fixed rate × notional).
2. *Variable cap applicable.* Interest rate shortfalls are covered up to (LIBOR + a fixed rate) × notional. The protection buyer has interest rate shortfall exposure of actual interest rate shortfall – ((LIBOR + a fixed rate) × notional).

EXHIBIT 8.1 CDS Cash Flows on Subprime ABS "Pay as You Go" Contracts

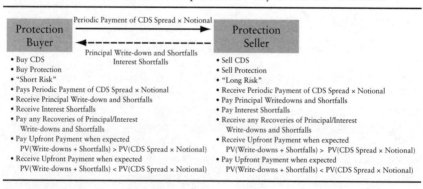

Source: Wachovia Capital Markets, LLC.

3. *Cap not applicable.* There is no cap on the interest shortfall amounts for which the protection seller is responsible. This option mimics the interest shortfalls of the reference bond.

STEPPING UP

In addition, there is an option in the PAUG form to handle coupon step-up of the reference bond. When step-up provisions are elected in the CDS contract, the protection buyer has the option to either break the contract when step-up begins on the reference entity or to increase the CDS spread by the amount of the coupon step-up. If step-up provisions are not applicable, the CDS spread will not step up even when the coupon of the reference bond steps up. Subprime ABS CDS usually trades with step-up provisions elected.

PHYSICAL SETTLEMENT

Protection buyers have the option to terminate the contract by delivering the actual reference obligation (the physical). This option is typically triggered by write-downs, downgrades to the distressed debt or the failure to pay the principal.

HEDGING WITH CREDIT DEFAULT SWAPS

In our previous example, once the hedge against the bond is purchased, you are essentially left with a risk-free investment on the principal balance of the bond. To understand CDS valuation, it is important to have a firm understanding of bond valuation. For instance, the purchase of a risky, floating-rate bond can be thought of as being equivalent to a purchase of two investments: (1) a risk-free bond and (2) the sell protection side of a CDS contract on a risky bond for the same par as value as the risk-free bond.

Bonds are valued with a risk-neutral methodology. It might surprise some bond investors to know that, theoretically, you are only expected to earn a risk-free return on the bond purchase. The expected net present value (NPV) of the entire bond trade is zero even though each counterparty feels it is receiving more than it is giving in the trade. So, assuming that PV(x) is the present value of x discounted at the risk-free rate (one-month LIBOR for our purposes), then what you pay for is what you get. At least, what you pay for now is the PV(what you get later). Therefore,

$$\text{Price of the bond} = \text{PV of the bond's cash flows} \qquad (8.1)$$

Assuming a \$100 par bond:

$$100 - \text{Up-front loss discount} = \text{PV}(100) + \text{PV}(\text{Coupon payments}) \\ - \text{PV}(\text{Expected losses}) \qquad (8.2)$$

We are discussing a floating rate bond that pays a coupon of LIBOR + a fixed credit spread. We therefore break the coupon into its two components, and our equation becomes

$$100 - \text{Up-front loss discount} \\ = \text{PV}(100) + \text{PV}(\text{LIBOR coupon payment}) \\ + \text{PV}(\text{Fixed credit spread coupon payment}) \\ - \text{PV}(\text{Expected losses}) \qquad (8.3)$$

Rearranging equation (8.3), we get

$$\text{NPV of the trade} = 0 = \text{PV}(100) + \text{PV}(\text{LIBOR coupon payment}) \\ + \text{PV}(\text{Fixed credit spread coupon payment}) \\ - \text{PV}(\text{Expected losses}) - 100 \\ + \text{Up front loss discount} \qquad (8.4)$$

Keep in mind that $\text{PV}(x)$ is the present value at the risk-free rate.
Similarly, a CDS on a bond is valued in a risk-neutral manner.

$$\text{PV}(\text{Expected payments to protection seller}) \\ = \text{PV}(\text{Expected payments to protection buyer}) \qquad (8.5)$$

In fact, to get to the equation that represents the position of the CDS agreement, just remove the par terms from equation (8.4) and rearrange the equation. Recall that we said a risky bond position is equivalent to a risk-free bond plus the sell protection side of a CDS contract. The "par terms" that we are about to remove constitute the risk-free bond component. Notice that the following terms from equation (8.4) sum to zero. $\text{PV}(100) + \text{PV}(\text{LIBOR coupon payment}) - 100$. These terms represent the risk-free bond that we want to remove. Also, the Fixed Credit Spread Coupon Payment is equivalent to CDS spread × Notional. After removing the par component, rearranging and substituting in the CDS spread × Notional and based on the principle that what the seller of protection pays for is what he gets, we obtain

$$
\begin{aligned}
\text{PV(Expected losses)} = \text{Up-front loss discount} \\
+ \text{PV(CDS spread} \times \text{Notional)}
\end{aligned}
\tag{8.6}
$$

What the buyer of protection pays for is what he gets and therefore

$$
\begin{aligned}
\text{Up-front loss discount} + \text{PV(CDS spread} \times \text{Notional)} \\
= \text{PV(Expected losses)}
\end{aligned}
\tag{8.7}
$$

The up-front loss discount can be negative (a premium) when

$$
\text{PV(Expected losses)} < \text{PV(CDS spread} \times \text{Notional)}
\tag{8.8}
$$

ZERO MONEY DOWN!

Notice how the protection seller receives the upfront loss discount at contract initiation when the floating reference bond is trading with a loss discount. The protection seller would have to pay the discount if the upfront loss discount were negative. What if the protection buyer wanted to buy protection with no money up front? Single-name CDS on subprime ABS can trade this way. In this case, all you need to do is solve for a new fixed credit spread coupon such that PV(New fixed credit spread coupon) = PV(Expected losses). This would be similar to buying the reference bond at par by requiring the debtor to increase the coupon enough to offset all the expected losses.

CDS PRICES VERSUS CASH BOND PRICES

CDS positions are referred to as *synthetic bonds*, and real bonds are referred to as "cash bonds." The price quoting convention for a CDS contract is done in such a way to allow you to compare it to the reference cash bond. The price is thus quoted as 100 – Upfront loss discount even though the par bond part has been removed. When we assume that the CDS contract cash flows exactly mimic the coupon spread and losses of the cash bond, the theoretical prices are equivalent between cash and CDS. As mentioned previously, the standardized PAUG form for subprime ABS single-name CDS might or might not mimic the relevant cash flows on the cash bond. The valuation within this article assumes that the CDS cash flows mimic the cash bond unless otherwise stated. In reality, CDS will not usually trade at the same price as cash because of the differing nature of the two instruments. Factors such as liquidity, the ease of shorting in the CDS market and funding differences affect the actual prices.

PRICING WHEN THE CDS SPREAD EQUALS THE REFERENCE COUPON SPREAD

Theoretical prices between a CDS contract and the reference bond are the same when the applicable CDS cash flows mimic those of the reference bond. In this case, we just need to know how to value the bond itself to get to a CDS price. One of the most accurate ways to value a bond, or virtually any investment for that matter, is to model the possible outcomes and weight the outcomes by their probabilities. Each outcome will give you a price of the bond, and you simply need to compute the expected value from the prices and probabilities. Expected value is just a weighted average price where the weights are the probabilities.

To illustrate this point, we will consider a bond issued by a toy store before we delve into subprime ABS bond and CDS valuation. Assume this fictional toy store, Danger Toys Inc., issued a monthly paying floating rate bond that will mature at year-end. There are two class-action lawsuits against the company for marketing spring-propelled lawn darts to young children. The company is awash with cash, and the bond can be assumed to be virtually risk free with the exception of the two lawsuits. The company will default immediately on the bond and pay no further principal or interest payments if it loses either of the lawsuits. The court hearings are in April and July. In addition, Danger Toys can call the bond for par in September. Our bond therefore has four possible outcomes with the following probabilities.

Default in April: 10% probability
Default in July: 20% probability
Prepay in September: 40% probability
Mature at year-end: 30% probability
The bond coupon is LIBOR + 2%

Exhibit 8.2 illustrates the equivalence between the CDS price and the reference bond price when the CDS spread equals the reference bond coupon spread and the CDS losses equal the reference bond losses. Numbers are given for the price of a $100 par amount bond. The risk-neutral price of both the CDS and the reference bond is 71.98.

EXHIBIT 8.2 Danger Toys Bond and CDS Pricing

Fixed Coupon Spread (or CDS Spread) = 2%

Interest Rate Forecasts	Jan	Feb	Mar	Apr	May	Jun	Jul	Aug	Sep	Oct	Nov	Dec
1 month LIBOR (forward rates)	4%	4%	4%	5%	5%	5%	6%	6%	6%	7%	7%	7%
Actual days in month	31	28	31	30	31	30	31	31	30	31	30	31
1 month LIBOR × Act/360	0.34%	0.31%	0.34%	0.42%	0.43%	0.42%	0.52%	0.52%	0.50%	0.60%	0.58%	0.60%
Risk-free discount factor	0.9966	0.9935	0.9901	0.9860	0.9817	0.9777	0.9726	0.9676	0.9628	0.9571	0.9515	0.9458
Fixed coupon spread × Act/360	0.172%	0.156%	0.172%	0.167%	0.172%	0.167%	0.172%	0.172%	0.167%	0.172%	0.167%	0.172%

EXHIBIT 8.2 (Continued)

Reference "Cash" Bond Valuation

Bond Cash Flow Scenarios	Jan	Feb	Mar	Apr	May	Jun	Jul	Aug	Sep	Oct	Nov	Dec
Default in April	0.5167	0.4667	0.5167									
Default in July	0.5167	0.4667	0.5167	0.5833	0.6028	0.5833						
Prepay in September	0.5167	0.4667	0.5167	0.5833	0.6028	0.5833	0.6889	0.6889	100.6667			
Mature at year-end	0.5167	0.4667	0.5167	0.5833	0.6028	0.5833	0.6889	0.6889	0.6667	0.7750	0.7500	100.7750

Discounted Bond Cash Flow Scenarios	Bond Price (Total)	Jan	Feb	Mar	Apr	May	Jun	Jul	Aug	Sep	Oct	Nov	Dec
Default in April	1.49	0.5149	0.4636	0.5115									
Default in July	3.23	0.5149	0.4636	0.5115	0.5751	0.5918	0.5703						
Prepay in September	101.49	0.5149	0.4636	0.5115	0.5751	0.5918	0.5703	0.6700	0.6666	96.9238			
Mature at year-end	101.97	0.5149	0.4636	0.5115	0.5751	0.5918	0.5703	0.6700	0.6666	0.6419	0.7417	0.7136	95.3128

Bond Prices and Scenario Probabilities	Bond Price	Probability
Default in April	1.49	10%
Default in July	3.23	20%
Prepay in September	101.49	40%
Mature at year-end	101.97	30%
Expected bond price	71.98	

EXHIBIT 8.2 (Continued)

CDS Valuation

CDS Protection Seller Cash Flows	Jan	Feb	Mar	Apr	May	Jun	Jul	Aug	Sep	Oct	Nov	Dec
Default in April	0.1722	0.1556	0.1722	−100.4167								
Default in July	0.1722	0.1556	0.1722	0.1667	0.1722	0.1667	−100.5167					
Prepay in September	0.1722	0.1556	0.1722	0.1667	0.1722	0.1667	0.1722	0.1722	0.1667			
Mature at year-end	0.1722	0.1556	0.1722	0.1667	0.1722	0.1667	0.1722	0.1722	0.1667	0.1722	0.1667	0.1722

Discounted CDS Protection Seller Cash Flows	CDS Price (Total + 100)	Jan	Feb	Mar	Apr	May	Jun	Jul	Aug	Sep	Oct	Nov	Dec
Default in April	1.49	0.1716	0.1545	0.1705	−99.0066								
Default in July	3.23	0.1716	0.1545	0.1705	0.1643	0.1691	0.1629	−97.7658					
Prepay in September	101.49	0.1716	0.1545	0.1705	0.1643	0.1691	0.1629	0.1675	0.1666	0.1605			
Mature at year-end	101.97	0.1716	0.1545	0.1705	0.1643	0.1691	0.1629	0.1675	0.1666	0.1605	0.1648	0.1586	0.1629

CDS Prices and Scenario Probabilities	CDS Price	Probability
Default in April	1.49	10%
Default in July	3.23	20%
Prepay in September	101.49	40%
Mature at year-end	101.97	30%
Expected CDS price	71.98	

Note: Up-front loss discount of 100 − 71.98 = 28.02 should be paid to the protection seller at settlement.
Source: Wachovia Capital Markets, LLC.

HEDGING WITH NO MONEY DOWN

In the previous example, the CDS spread matched the reference bond coupon spread. This case could be unlikely. A CDS contract can have virtually any spread as long as the upfront payment plus the spread payments compensate appropriately for the expected losses. Given a specific upfront payment, you can solve for the CDS spread. Likewise, given any arbitrary CDS spread, you can solve for an upfront payment (and thus price). Recall that the CDS price = 100 – Upfront loss discount. If we wanted to buy the Danger Toys bond at the price of 71.98 and then buy protection on the credit risk with no money upfront (a CDS price of 100), we could just solve for a new CDS spread that would allow us to do that. To get this spread, we iteratively try new spreads until we can get the CDS price to become 100. The zero-money-down CDS spread in this case is 41.04%. Exhibit 8.3 illustrates this example. This iterative process can quickly be accomplished in software by using the secant method, which is a numerical approximation to Newton's method. The secant method algorithm is beyond the scope of this chapter.

THE VALUE OF SCENARIO ANALYSIS

The key to valuing a structured bond such as subprime ABS is to understand that the expected collateral (mortgage) performance will not give you the expected bond or CDS price. For instance, assume that you performed collateral analysis on the mortgage pool backing a subprime ABS bond and you were able to compute the expected *conditional default rate* (CDR), *conditional prepayment rate* (CPR), and delinquency curves for that deal given the implied forward interest rates. You take these curves and you run this one scenario through the deal model and try to value the AA bond in the structure. What you are likely to find is that the bond experiences zero losses because it is so senior in the waterfall. Said another way, your averaged collateral scenario just told you that the bond experiences no losses and is therefore risk free under that scenario! However, you know this bond is not risk free because it is backed by risky subprime mortgages. What if you took the bond cash flows from that single scenario and discounted them at LIBOR + a discount spread? Would that not give you the right price? The answer is that yes it would ... IF you knew what discount spread use. The discount spread that should be used is actually a function of the expected losses of the bond. To determine the expected losses of the bond, you need to know the probability of the bond defaulting, and so far you only have one scenario, and it does not default the bond.

EXHIBIT 8.3 Solving for the CDS Spread

Fixed Coupon Spread (or CDS spread) = 41.04%

Interest Rate Forecasts	Jan	Feb	Mar	Apr	May	Jun	Jul	Aug	Sep	Oct	Nov	Dec
1 month LIBOR (forward rates)	4%	4%	4%	5%	5%	5%	6%	6%	6%	7%	7%	7%
Actual days in month	31	28	31	30	31	30	31	31	30	31	30	31
1 month LIBOR × Act/360	0.34%	0.31%	0.34%	0.42%	0.43%	0.42%	0.52%	0.52%	0.50%	0.60%	0.58%	0.60%
Risk-free discount factor	0.9966	0.9935	0.9901	0.9860	0.9817	0.9777	0.9726	0.9676	0.9628	0.9571	0.9515	0.9458
Fixed coupon spread × Act/360	3.534%	3.192%	3.534%	3.420%	3.534%	3.420%	3.534%	3.534%	3.420%	3.534%	3.420%	3.534%

CDS Valuation

CDS Protection Seller Cash Flows	Jan	Feb	Mar	Apr	May	Jun	Jul	Aug	Sep	Oct	Nov	Dec
Default in April	3.5336	3.1917	3.5336	−100.4167								
Default in July	3.5336	3.1917	3.5336	3.4196	3.5336	3.4196	−100.5167					
Prepay in September	3.5336	3.1917	3.5336	3.4196	3.5336	3.4196	3.5336	3.5336	3.4196			
Mature at year-end	3.5336	3.1917	3.5336	3.4196	3.5336	3.4196	3.5336	3.5336	3.4196	3.5336	3.4196	3.5336

EXHIBIT 8.3 (Continued)

Discounted CDS Protection Seller Cash Flows	CDS Price (Total + 100)	Jan	Feb	Mar	Apr	May	Jun	Jul	Aug	Sep	Oct	Nov	Dec
Default in April	11.18	3.5215	3.1708	3.4985	−99.0066								
Default in July	22.61	3.5215	3.1708	3.4985	3.3716	3.4691	3.3432	−97.7658					
Prepay in September	130.52	3.5215	3.1708	3.4985	3.3716	3.4691	3.3432	3.4369	3.4193	3.2925			
Mature at year-end	140.50	3.5215	3.1708	3.4985	3.3716	3.4691	3.3432	3.4369	3.4193	3.2925	3.3819	3.2538	3.3421

CDS Prices and Scenario Probabilities	CDS Price	Probability
Default in April	11.18	10%
Default in July	22.61	20%
Prepay in September	130.52	40%
Mature at year-end	140.50	30%
Expected CDS Price	100.00	

Note: Upfront loss discount of 100 − 100 = 0 should be paid to the protection seller at settlement.
Source: Wachovia Capital Markets, LLC.

To value the bond properly, multiple scenarios are needed. You need to know the distribution of the mortgage performance and how that distribution affects the bond performance distribution. The AA bond will likely default when you run some of the more stressful scenarios in the tail of the mortgage performance distribution. Once hundreds or thousands of scenarios are run through the subprime ABS deal structure, you can compute the average price of the bond and CDS contract in the same way that was demonstrated for the toy store. With 1,000 equally probable scenarios, the expected bond price is just a straight average of the bond prices from each scenario. Likewise, given a CDS contract spread, we can compute the CDS price for each scenario and average to get the expected CDS price. Given a CDS price, we can solve for the CDS spread using the secant method. One reason you might want to solve for the CDS spread is to be able to enter into a CDS contract with no money upfront, a CDS price of 100.

HOW ARE MORTGAGE POOL SCENARIOS CREATED?

Mortgage pool models may take as input:

1. A predicted future economic environment.
2. Mortgage pool characteristics (preferably loan level).

The models then output mortgage pool level forecasts such as CDR, CPR, delinquency and default severity curves. Together with the forecasted interest rates from the economic model, these curves define one scenario and can be used to price a subprime ABS bond or CDS under that scenario. To get multiple mortgage pool scenarios, you can use stochastic econometric models to create multiple economic scenarios of interest rates, home price appreciation, unemployment, and the like. Each economic scenario can be used to generate one mortgage pool scenario by passing it into the mortgage model along with the pool information. One subprime ABS bond price or CDS price can be generated for each scenario by the deal model and then averaged together to determine the expected price. This is summarized in Exhibit 8.4.

SUMMARY

Single-name CDS on subprime ABS can be valued using scenario analysis in a risk-neutral framework. The theoretical price between a CDS and the reference entity is the same when the relevant cash flows match between

EXHIBIT 8.4   Valuation of Subprime CDS

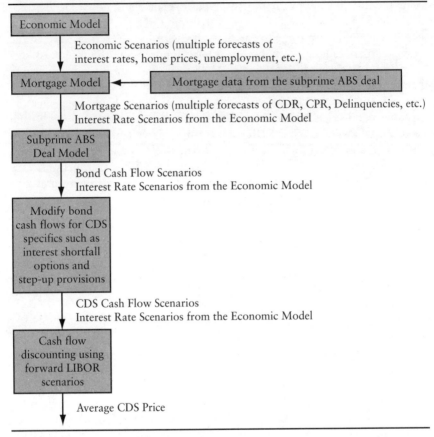

Source: Wachovia Capital Markets, LLC.

the CDS and the cash bond. PAUG options for the CDS contract can make the CDS cash flows deviate from those of the cash bond, and this should be taken into account when valuing a CDS contract. CDS prices are obtained by averaging the price of the CDS under various economic forecast scenarios. The important thing to remember is that bond prices are based on the bond performance distribution, which could look vastly different from the mortgage pool performance distribution. The average of the mortgage pool performance will not give an accurate representation of the bond cash flow performance. The full distribution of the mortgage performance is needed to generate the full distribution of the bond or CDS cash flows.

Three

Collateralized Debt Obligations

CHAPTER 9

Basics of CDOs

Brian McManus
Senior CDO Analyst
Wachovia Capital Markets, LLC

Dave Preston, CFA
Associate CDO Analyst
Wachovia Capital Markets, LLC

Anik Ray
Associate CDO Analyst
Wachovia Capital Markets, LLC

Steven Todd, Ph.D.
CDO Analyst
Wachovia Capital Markets, LLC

ollateralized debt obligations, or CDOs, are an evolving and growing
presence in today's capital markets. According to CreditFlux, the volume
of outstanding cash CDOs stood at $986 billion at the start of 2007, and
U.S. cash CDO issuance approached $400 billion in 2006.

While many investors still consider CDOs an esoteric asset class, CDOs
have had a profound and far-reaching impact on global markets. Since 2003,
CDOs have fueled two major market trends: (1) the growth of the private
equity market—leveraged loans formed by leveraged buyouts (LBOs) that
often reside in *collateralized loan obligations* (CLOs); and (2) the growth
of the subprime mortgage market. In addition, CDOs have helped drive the
rapid growth in the *credit default swap* (CDS) markets.

CDOs offer investors several advantages, including diversification
opportunities, varying risk/return profiles, and exposure to asset classes that
are often difficult to invest in directly. Investors should understand CDOs

as a technology or a security structure, rather than as an asset class. As investments, CDOs' performance can vary greatly, depending on the collateral, the structure, the manager, and the specific CDO note's position in the capital structure.

The importance of understanding the collateral performance in addition to structural characteristics of a CDO cannot be underestimated. When the collateral performs well, the CDO market works like a well-oiled machine as it distributes the underlying asset risk around the globe. When the collateral performs poorly, investors (particularly of the subordinated notes) feel the stress. It is during these periods that misinformation about CDOs tends to proliferate. In this chapter and those that follow in this part of the book, we provide the basics of CDOs and hopefully limit the misconceptions about this dynamic market.

A BRIEF HISTORY OF CDOs

The first CDO was structured in 1988 and was backed by a collateral pool consisting of high-yield (speculative-grade) bonds—a collateralized bond obligation, or CBO. Corporate loans became the second major CDO collateral asset class with issuance of CLOs (collateralized loan obligations) gaining momentum in the late 1990s. As an asset class, speculative-grade bonds fell out of favor following the last period of high collateral defaults and downgrades.[1] By 2002, cash CBO issuance had fallen to a trickle. The end of the high-yield CBO, however, did not halt CLO growth. Broadly syndicated loans proved to be less volatile and more resilient during tough times. From 2005 to 2007, CLOs constituted almost 30% of CDO issuance.

Corporate bonds, however, did not completely evaporate as CDO collateral. Synthetic structures arrived to satisfy investors wishing to gain exposure to senior unsecured corporate debt. These CDOs did not purchase corporate bonds, but sold protection on a group of corporate credits via a CDS.

The other major collateral sector is structured products, such as *asset-backed securities* (ABS), *commercial mortgage-backed securities* (CMBS), and other CDOs. When ABS CDOs[2] first arrived, the collateral consisted of a variety of asset classes to achieve high levels of diversification. The poor performance of collateral sectors such as manufactured housing and aircraft drove managers to return to their specialty in real estate products.

---

[1] The sell-off of the high-yield bond market in 1998 following the Russian default crisis and the collapse of Long-Term Capital did not halt CBO issuance, but the surge in default rates and low recoveries that followed did.

[2] Also referred to as *structured finance* CDOs or *resecuritization CDOs*. The latter is Moody's term for the sector.

Other collateral sectors include middle-market loans, *trust-preferred securities* (TruPS), subordinated CMBS notes, and the rare municipal bond CDO. There have even been CDOs linked to commodities. In fact, any type of security that offers a sufficient yield over the cost of CDO liabilities is potential collateral. More and more, CDOs are using synthetic markets to gain credit exposure, as opposed to purchasing cash assets. CDO managers can now sell protection on other CDOs, loans, ABS, and corporate debt.

CDO BASICS

The term *collateralized debt obligation* (CDO) refers to a particular class of securities for which the return is linked to the performance of a specific pool of assets. A CDO is sliced into several notes that are the structure's liabilities. A note's position in this capital structure determines its priority of claims on the collateral cash flows, which in turn determines the rating. Ratings can range from triple-A for the senior classes to unrated for the first loss coverage. A graphical depiction of a CDO is provided in Exhibit 9.1.

A CDO only redistributes the total credit risk associated with the pool of assets among the newly created securities. The structure itself neither increases nor reduces the total credit risk associated with the initial pool of assets. The manager, however, reinvests maturing collateral and is allowed a degree of

EXHIBIT 9.1 Graphical Depiction of a CDO

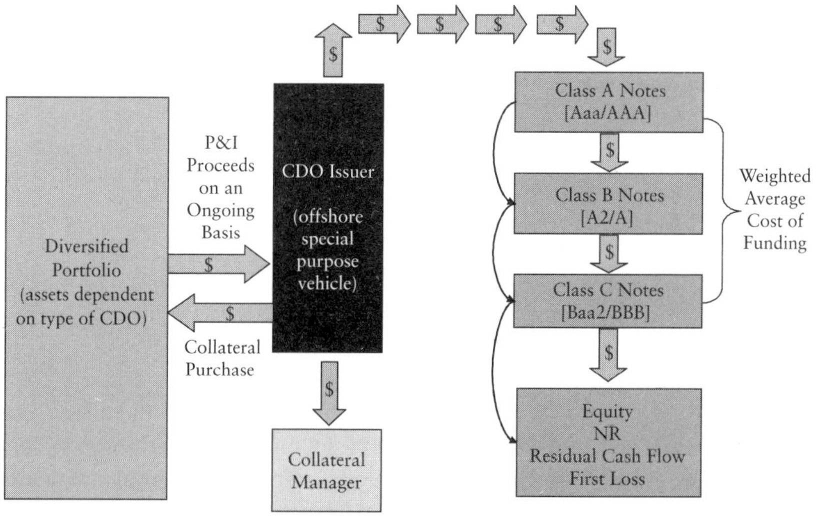

Source: Wachovia Capital Markets, LLC.

discretionary trading. A CDO's many quality covenants are designed to prevent managers from deviating too far from the original collateral risk profile.

The legal structure of a CDO can be a trust or *special purpose vehicle* (SPV). The proceeds raised from selling the SPV's liabilities (also referred to as *tranches, classes,* or *notes*) are used to purchase a portfolio of assets. The collateral pool (assets) consists of a diversified group of debt securities. The most common assets of new-issue CDOs are residential mortgage-backed securities (RMBS), bank loans, commercial mortgage-backed securities (CMBS), other CDOs or trust-preferred securities.

The coupons for CDO liabilities typically float above LIBOR, but may also be fixed. The method of distributing cash flows beginning at the top of the capital structure and flowing down to the bottom is referred to as the *waterfall*. The most senior tranche pays the lowest coupon by virtue of having the highest claim on the cash flows. Next in line are the mezzanine notes, which pay higher coupons and have lower ratings. The least senior, or *equity* tranche is the most risky, and does not have a set coupon; rather it represents a claim on all residual cash flows. The equity tranche is often structured as preferred shares for accounting purposes.

The senior notes are ideal for a low-risk, fixed income portfolio. The investment-grade-rated mezzanine classes are well suited for a credit-risk portfolio. The speculative-grade notes and equity interest compete with alternative investments and private equity funds for customers willing to risk capital for high returns.

PARTICIPANTS IN A CDO TRANSACTION

The major actors in a CDO transaction are the investors, but other players perform important roles. This section describes these roles in greater detail.

Manager

The manager runs the collateral portfolio, buying and selling assets. The manager uses his discretion, within prescribed limits, to maximize the returns of equity investors and note holders.

Underwriter

The responsibility of the underwriting bank is to structure and place the transaction. This involves several undertakings, including determining the precise architecture of the CDO (i.e., the composition of the capital structure, the hedge strategy and waterfall provisions), finding levels where the dealer can place the notes and entice equity investors, negotiating the requirements or characteristics that are set by the rating agencies to achieve particular ratings for the notes issued and providing (in many cases) a warehouse facility to help with the collateral acquisition process (before closing).

Often times, there is more than one underwriter for the transaction. Additional investment banks are named *co-lead underwriters* or *co-underwriters*, depending on the roles they play in the process.

Lawyer

The lawyer works with the investment bank in creating the deal documents, including the offering memorandum and indenture, which specify deal details.

Rating Agencies

There are three active agencies in the structured-finance arena: Moody's Investors Service, Inc., Standard & Poor's Corp. (S&P) and Fitch Ratings. The rating agencies perform collateral manager due diligence, review the legal documents governing the transactions and, most important, run several quantitative analyses. These quantitative analyses are designed to evaluate the performance of each class of notes under several asset pool default scenarios. In addition, the rating agencies participate actively in negotiating certain aspects of the legal documents with the bankers, sometimes imposing specific provisions aimed at protecting the note holders. Finally, the rating ultimately assigned to a tranche is a reflection of the credit risk associated with that tranche based on all of the factors mentioned previously.

Trustee

The role of the trustee is to "safe-keep" the assets and monitor the manager's trading activities. The CDO indenture spells out some specific rules regarding trading, and the trustee should monitor compliance with these rules. In addition, the trustee is responsible for issuing periodic reports describing the status of the CDO, including a description of the collateral pool securities, compliance with the coverage and collateral quality tests, cash payments allocated to each tranche and expenses incurred by the CDO.

Swap Counterparty

As explained before, a CDO might enter into a swap for interest rate hedging, currency hedging or the other side of a synthetic swap. The hedge counterparty is just the other leg of the swap. Occasionally, a CDO might enter into a basis swap to "smooth" the timing of the cash flows generated by the collateral (suppose, for instance, that the assets make semiannual payments and the liabilities receive quarterly coupons) or a currency swap.

Monoline Insurer

Some CDO transactions, in which the strength of the collateral pool is not sufficient (or is perceived to be insufficient by certain investors or the rating agencies), must enlist the help of a third party to provide certain investors (normally the senior bondholders) extra assurance that their cash flows will not be impaired. These third parties are the monoline insurers (e.g., AM-BAC, MBIA, XL, and FSA). These institutions, after reviewing in detail all of the aspects of a CDO, agree, in exchange for a fee, to step in should the collateral pool fail to generate enough cash to pay the tranche afforded this protection. Obviously, to be an effective participant in this market the monolines themselves must maintain a high credit rating (generally AAA/Aaa or, at least, AA/Aa2) because their insurance policies are only as good as their own financial strength. Hence, the monolines are constantly monitored by the rating agencies. In addition, an extra advantage of having a monoline in the transaction is the extra level of due diligence that this brings to the CDO (in addition to the oversight provided by the rating agencies).

CDO PURPOSES

A CDO can be viewed as a leveraged fund when issued by a fund management team or a financing tool when issued by a collateral originator. The former is sometimes referred to as an *arbitrage* CDO and the latter as a *balance sheet* CDO.

Arbitrage CDO

An arbitrage CDO uses the proceeds from the sale of the notes to purchase collateral in the primary and secondary markets. Actually, "arbitrage" CDO is a misnomer, as there is no true riskless profit. The equity investor merely exploits the difference between the assets' expected yield and the cost of funding the purchase. This difference could be considered a funding gap. Since asset yields vary depending on credit gains and losses, the realized return on equity can vary greatly from the initial estimate. A rough estimate of the funding gap is

> Funding gap = Asset weighted average spread
>
>   − All expenses, taxes, and fees − Losses due to default
>
>   − Liability weighted average spread

Balance Sheet CDO

Issuers (usually banks or specialty finance companies) tap the CDO market as a financing tool and as a means to provide the institution with capital relief. The issuing institution retains the assets on the balance sheet, but segregates or earmarks these assets as the CDO collateral. Balance sheet CDOs are primarily static, not managed, transactions. Balance sheet CDOs typically use only loans originated by the bank issuing the CDO. The issuer often retains the first loss piece. Ideally, CDOs provide a cheaper long-term funding structure for lower-rated issuers. Consider, for example, a BBB rated issuer. Since the senior tranche, typically AAA rated, has the lowest coupon and the largest notional amount, the cost of funding the CLO should fall below the issuer's BBB rated bond issues.

CDO STRUCTURES

A CDO collateral portfolio can be either a managed portfolio or a static pool. The assets can be cash, synthetic or a mixture, which is called a *hybrid transaction*. The covenants can be par based overcollateralization (OC) tests[3] (the cash flow structure) or market-value triggers (the market-value CDOs.) Triggerless deals are also possible. Finally, the liabilities may be distributed in the cash market or issued via CDSs to create a synthetic structure.

Managed Cash Flow CDO

The managed CDO is the most common cash flow structure. A portfolio manager actively trades the assets, within prescribed constraints. The CDO issuer is paid management fees, which include a flat fee and a performance-based fee. Managers traditionally retain some equity to show they have some "skin in the game." The amount retained (if any) can vary from a small sliver to 49%. Managers are careful not to purchase more than 50% of the equity, as this would lead to accounting treatment that would require the assets to be held on the balance sheet.

Static CDO

Static CDOs are not actively managed, and therefore do not have a reinvestment period. Credit risk substitutions are allowed, but the assets may not be traded. While most static cash CDOs are financings, some arbitrage

---

[3] Overcollateralization tests are based on overcollateralization ratios, which measure the collateral par amount divided by the note par amount.

transactions are static as well. These issues are popular among investors who wish to avoid manager risk and have increased transparency of the asset pool. Static deals amortize immediately, and therefore have a much shorter expected average life than an actively managed CDO. The liabilities of static CDOs have historically traded inside of managed CDOs due to the notes' shorter average lives.

Market-Value CDO

Market-value CDOs use the market value of the underlying portfolio, rather than stated par value, when calculating collateralization ratios. Therefore, the covenants require the marking-to-market of the assets. In addition, discount factors based on the asset liquidity and price or return volatility, called "advance rates," are applied to the asset pool for collateralization test purposes. The rating agencies calculate advance rates specific to each tranche and asset, and the rates are based on the portfolio's diversification, asset types, and asset compositions. The collateral market value (multiplied by the advance rate) must be greater than the liability par value. If the collateral balance falls below the limit, the manager must sell assets and pay off liabilities until the trigger is not breached. Market-value CDOs allow unlimited trading activity by the manager. The structures are traditionally less levered; that is, the equity tranche represents a greater portion of the capital structure.

Synthetic CDO

Synthetic CDOs combine the basic concept of CDO tranching with CDS technology. Unlike a cash flow deal, in which assets must be bought and placed in a trust, a synthetic CDO references a portfolio using CDS contracts. In this scenario, there are two parties: a protection buyer, who is insuring against default on the reference portfolio; and a protection seller, who gets paid a regular, periodic premium. In the event of default, the latter would have to pay the former the notional amount of default. Synthetic structures do not always have a waterfall. When defaults occur, the notional amount of the loss is written down from the bottom of the capital structure. A particular note can be defined by its attachment and detachment points. The amount of credit support is referred to as the tranche's attachment point. The detachment point is equivalent to the credit support for all notes senior to the tranche.

Exhibit 9.2 shows a typical funded synthetic CDO. The CDS market allows for greater structuring flexibility than the cash market. As such, not all synthetic structures issue an entire capital structure. An investor could

EXHIBIT 9.2   Synthetic CDO

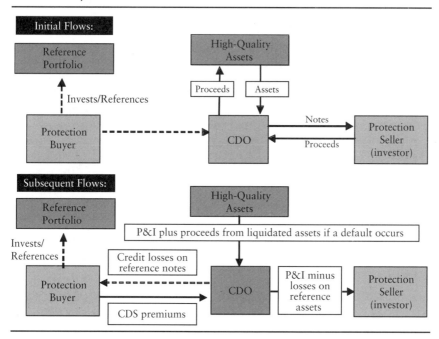

Source: Wachovia Capital Markets, LLC.

approach a dealer to design a tranche based strictly on attachment and detachment points for losses to a reference pool. For example, an investor could select a reference portfolio and sell protection on the 5% to 10% tranche. She would receive the initial cost of protection as long as the cumulative loss on the reference portfolio remains below 5%. She would have to compensate the buyer of protection for all losses above 5% but limited to 10% of the portfolio. This transaction is referred to as a *bespoke issue* with an attachment point of 5% and detachment at 10%.

Triggerless CDOs

Some cash-flow CDOs do not contain triggers (coverage tests). These CDOs are structured like synthetic CDOs with attachment and detachment points based on different risk levels. The lack of a cash trapping mechanism could hurt the senior classes should a default occur early in the structure's life. Issuers therefore provide greater credit support at all levels of the capital structure, making the transaction less levered than comparable deals with OC triggers.

CDO LIFE CYCLE

Ramping Up

The first phase of the CDO life cycle is the *ramp-up period*, during which the manager, otherwise known as the issuer, buys the portfolio collateral. A bank (usually the underwriter) provides a *warehouse facility* as financing to the CDO manager. The warehouse, coupled with a credit line, allows the manager to purchase the assets prior to note issuance. During the ramp-up period, the warehouse provider and the manager must agree on which assets to buy, as the former is long the collateral risk. The underwriter and manager begin marketing and eventually price the CDO while the manager is purchasing the assets. At *closing*, the CDO issues the notes and repays the warehouse provider. The ramp-up period can last from zero to nine months. An extended ramp-up period allows the manager to better time the market and take advantage of changing supply and demand technicals.

Reinvestment

After the ramp-up period comes the *reinvestment period*, which varies in length by deal. The original CBOs contained a five-year reinvestment period, but for some structures today, this period can last seven years. During this phase, the manager monitors and trades the portfolio, subject to the constraints laid out in the indenture. A manager may trade to exit credit-impaired or improved positions, and is allowed limited discretionary trading. The manager has a fiduciary responsibility to ensure the portfolio remains in compliance with the various collateral-quality tests (weighted average spread, weighted average rating, issuer concentration, etc.).

Amortization Period

The final phase of a CDO's life is the *amortization period*, which may be as short as one to two years, or as long as it takes to reach the stated maturity. During this period, the manager does not replace prepaying or maturing assets. As such, principal proceeds are used to retire the notes sequentially. There are two kinds of call options designed to limit the life of the deal (discussed below): an auction call and a cleanup call. Subordinate CDO notes typically have long, stated legal maturities (15 to 40 years), but have average lives ranging from four to 12 years due to the callable nature of the notes, and the amortization of the collateral.

EMBEDDED CALLS

CDOs typically have both investor-driven and event-driven calls. Event-driven calls are based on time or collateral amortization.

Optional Redemption Call

After a noncall period of typically three to six years, equity holders have the right to redeem the notes following a two-thirds majority vote. Equity holders may choose to redeem the notes if the *net asset value* (NAV)[4] minus transaction costs is greater than the secondary bid for the CDO equity position.

Auction Calls

The auction call acts to limit the final maturity of the transaction and is more common when the collateral includes long-dated assets typically found in the real estate markets. The terms of the auction call state that after a prescribed time horizon (e.g., 10 years), the trustee may liquidate the collateral if the proceeds are sufficient to make all investors whole, as well as to achieve the targeted *return on equity* (ROE) for equity investors. The collateral sale must produce enough to pay all outstanding expenses, rated notes, and preferred shares.

Cleanup Calls

Most deals contain a cleanup call provision, which allows for the sale of all assets should the collateral pool par value fall below a prescribed level (often 10% of the original balance). The cleanup call would occur only if the proceeds are sufficient to make investors whole.

COVERAGE TESTS

Most cash flow CDOs have a minimum of two sets of coverage tests: *over-collateralization* (OC) tests and *interest coverage* (IC) tests. The rating agencies determine appropriate levels for the tests. The tests are structured to protect the senior classes in the event of default or poor management. The test level is dependent on the quality of the portfolio and the amount of leverage in the deal. These triggers act as covenants and, when tripped, re-direct the equity cash flows to pay down the principal of the most senior outstanding notes.

---

[4] NAV is the aggregate market value of the collateral pool minus the par amount of the notes.

Overcollateralization Tests

The OC test is defined in terms of the OC ratio. Imagining a hypothetical two-tranche CDO, we can distinguish between at least two OC ratios: the Class A (or senior) OC ratio and the Class B (or mezzanine) OC ratio. For all ratios, we need to know the adjusted collateral par value, which equals:

Performing collateral par value (minus haircuts if applicable) + Cash
+ [(Defaulted collateral par value) × (Recovery rate)]

For the Class A test, we divide the result of this equation by the Class A par value, whereas for the Class B test, we divide the result by the sum of the Class A and Class B par amounts. In other words, for any Class X, we divide by the sum of the Class X par amount and the outstanding balance of notes ahead of Class X in the capital structure. This test compares the collateral par amount to the par amount of the notes and all notes senior to the note in question.

If the OC ratio is higher than the OC trigger, the test is considered "in compliance" and no cash flows are diverted. If the trigger is tripped, however, excess interest is diverted from the subordinated notes and is captured to reduce the principal amount of the senior notes. This action results in a smaller denominator and therefore a higher ratio. Excess spread is diverted until the note's OC test has risen back into compliance. Once the failing test is cured, interest payments may resume through the waterfall.

The triggers are determined by taking into consideration the values of the ratios at closing. A tight trigger provides little to no leeway, or "cushion" for collateral pool deterioration, whereas a loose trigger does the opposite. For instance, if the initial senior OC ratio has a value of 1.4, a tight trigger could be set at 1.35, but a more common loose trigger might be set at 1.2.

Many deals have haircuts, or discounts, for specified collateral security types (CCC rated assets, defaulted issues, etc.). Some deals also have a purchase-price haircut designed to discourage managers from buying discounted collateral in order to build par. This discount is multiplied by the collateral par amount, and the discounted par amount is used for test-ratio calculations. As previously mentioned, market-value structures have market risk discounts applied to collateral.

Interest Coverage Tests

IC tests are similar to OC tests, but measure the available excess spread. The IC ratio merely divides interest income by interest expense (for the appropriate note and any senior notes). Continuing with the two-tranche example, the Class A IC ratio is defined as:

$$[(\text{Performing collateral par amount}) \times (\text{Collateral weighted average coupon})]$$
$$[(\text{Class A par value}) \times (\text{Class A coupon})]$$

The Class B IC ratio is the same as above, with (Class B par value) × (Class B coupon) added to the denominator.

If the IC ratio is higher than the IC trigger, the test is in compliance and no cash flows are diverted. If the ratio is below the test threshold, cash is diverted until the note passes the test.

PIK

Many CDO tranches can *pay-in-kind* (PIK). When a "PIKable" bond is unable to pay interest, the buyer is compensated with more bonds. That is, the interest is paid by increasing the principal amount of the bond by the amount of unpaid interest. The PIK provision is used to prevent or at least delay a tranche's default. In the standard CDS contract, the "PIKing" of a CDO note is not considered an event of default if interest payments resume within a year.

SPECIAL TRIGGERS: PAR PRESERVATION AND TURBO FEATURES

Par preservation and turbo features are designed to better align the interests of the noteholders with those of the equity investors. These triggers can trip before conditions become severe enough to cause a classic OC test to fail.

If the par preservation test is not satisfied, a portion of available excess interest (that otherwise would go to equity) after paying interest on the notes is used to purchase additional collateral.

Par preservation tests (also called interest diversion tests) can vary from one structure to the next. Some are based on market values, while some are based on par values. The test is usually performed on the lowest investment-grade tranche and often includes a market-value haircut. When the interest diversion test is not in compliance, cash flows are diverted from the equity tranche to purchase more collateral.

APEX Structure

Wachovia's APEX structure is an example of a CDO structure that employs par preservation. When principal losses occur, the manager draws on a revolving credit line to purchase additional collateral. Excess cash flows, after interest is paid on rated notes, are used to repay the revolver.

The revolver is unfunded at closing (the revolver is not drawn unless a principal loss occurs), and is a credit line issued from the underwriting investment bank to the CDO issuer. If any principal losses occur during the reinvestment period, the issuer would tap the revolver to purchase additional collateral up to the amount of the principal loss. *Principal losses* are defined as realized losses resulting from the sale of a credit risk or defaulted asset, and mark-to-market losses on any defaulted assets not sold. If the CDO's actual asset par amount is greater than the target asset par amount, a draw on the revolver is not required.

For example, if the manager sells a credit-impaired asset at 75% of par (with a par value of $1 million), and if the principal reserve account[5] is zero at this time, the manager would be required to draw on the revolver. The APEX revolver would provide $250,000 for the manager to reinvest to cover the losses. These purchases help preserve the portfolio's initial par amount. On the next distribution date, excess cash flows in the interest waterfall available after payment of interest on the rated notes would be diverted to repay the outstanding revolver balance (with interest).

The revolver balance is repaid after the rated notes and prior to the equity in the interest waterfall. If the CDO fails an OC test, then excess interest is diverted to pay the APEX revolver balance prior to paying down the rated notes until the OC test is cured. The APEX revolver can only be tapped during the reinvestment period. Any outstanding revolver balance moves to the top of the principal waterfall after the reinvestment period ends.

In the case of default, the manager might not wish to sell the asset immediately (due to low liquidity, a workout period, etc.). The revolver can be used to cover these mark-to-market losses. In addition, if the revolver is drawn to cover the first month's mark-to-market loss, the revolver may be drawn on again to cover the next month's mark-to-market loss if the price of the defaulted asset continues to slide. For example, an asset defaults and is marked at 80% of par the first month. The revolver would pay the CDO the loss amount (20% of par). The next month, the asset is marked at 70%; the revolver again would pay the CDO the additional loss amount (now 10% of par). If, on the third month, the asset is sold for 75%, this gain (5%) can be used to repay the revolver.

The *APEX threshold utilization ratio* is equal to the revolver's balance at any point in time, divided by the revolver's limit. For example, if $5 million is drawn from a $20 million revolver, the threshold utilization ratio is

---

[5] The APEX revolver may not be drawn until the principal reserve account is zero. The principal reserve account is established using proceeds from the sale of notes. Funds are withdrawn from the account to cover the first principal losses; often, after a prescribed date (such as one year after closing), the reserve account is paid into the deal via the principal waterfall, allowing for reinvestment.

25%. If the threshold utilization test is tripped, the deal immediately ends the reinvestment period and begins amortization. Reinvestment may be reinstated once the test is cured and other conditions are met.

Since equity cash flows are diverted to repay the revolver, some investors believe the APEX feature benefits note investors at the short-term expense of equity investors. However, the APEX could benefit the equity holder in the long run, provided the manager wisely reinvests to build par. The revolver is most likely to be drawn on during periods of high systemic risk and presumably wider spreads. As such, the diverted equity cash flows could be used to buy higher-yielding collateral while protecting the funding structure and portfolio par balance. In addition, the APEX feature generally allows for greater leverage, giving equity investors potentially higher returns in a low-default environment.

Turbo Features

Some deals issue subordinated notes that contain a *turbo trigger*. Like the par preservation tests, the turbo trigger is designed to trip before the classic OC tests would. Typically the feature applies to the triple-B and double-B notes. In one form, when the turbo test fails and senior OC tests are passing, equity cash flow is used to amortize the note with the trigger. This achieves two goals: (1) it reduces the par amount of the notes that are failing the test; and (2) it pays down the most expensive debt. A second type of trigger trips when a specified equity return hurdle is met. In this case, a prescribed percentage of surplus spread is diverted to amortize the junior notes. A third trigger is tripped after a performing structure reaches a certain age, at which time the junior notes are amortized in order to boost equity returns.

Some senior investors contend that the par preservation and turbo features favor mezzanine note holders at their expense. It should be noted, however, that the tests become irrelevant if any OC tests are failing. As we stated earlier, the triggers are designed to align the interests of equity and note holders and discourage a manager from buying the cheapest bonds for the highest rating. The triggers favor the mezzanine holders because their investment is most at risk if the manager does "game the system" in this manner. Exhibit 9.3 below summarizes the pros and cons to investors at three different points on the capital structure of par preservation and turbo features.

CASH FLOW CDO WATERFALL

As the collateral kicks off *principal and interest* (P&I), these proceeds flow to CDO investors. This cash distribution is referred to as the *waterfall* of

EXHIBIT 9.3 Par Preservation and Turbo

	Par Preservation	Turbo
Description	Some or all of the equity cash flows are diverted to purchase additional collateral; the trigger may be based on OC or MV ratios.	Equity cash flows are used to accelerate the repayment of the most subordinated notes.
Senior Notes		
Pros	Impedes manager's ability to game the OC tests.	Net neutral
Cons	Less initial credit support; places greater faith in manager.	
Mezzanine		
Pros	Reduces manager's ability to game the OC tests, decreasing the likelihood of a downgrade.	For nonturbo tranches, see pros and cons of senior note holders above; for turbo tranche, early amortization reduces the likelihood of ratings transition.
Cons	Less initial credit support.	
Equity Investors		
Pros	Increased leverage; increases manager's ability to preserve funding structure.	Reduces cost of funding by paying off the most expensive tranche.
Cons	Increases the probability equity cash flows are withheld, relative to a traditional structure.	Reduces equity cash flows and delevers structure.

Source: Wachovia Capital Markets, LLC.

the CDO. Technically, there are two waterfalls, the interest waterfall and the principal waterfall. We can illustrate this trickle-down mechanism by using a simple three-tranche (Class A, Class B, and Equity) structure.

Interest Waterfall

Exhibit 9.4 shows the interest waterfall. Interest proceeds are used first to pay taxes, trustee/administrative fees and hedge payments. Next come the *senior management fees*, often 10 to 20 bps. Once the obligations to the above parties have been satisfied, interest proceeds flow to Class A current interest.

After paying current interest, the first hurdle is encountered, in the form of the Class A OC test and IC tests. If the CDO fails the Class A test, interest

EXHIBIT 9.4 Interest Waterfall

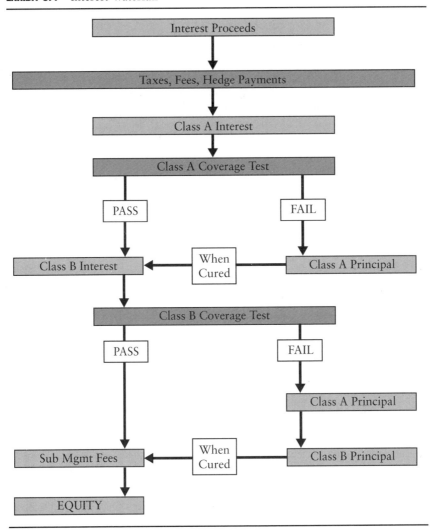

Source: Wachovia Capital Markets, LLC.

proceeds are used to pay Class A note principal. When enough notes have been retired to cure the test, interest is no longer trapped to pay down the tranche and may therefore move from Class A interest to pay Class B's current and deferred (if any) interest. The interest payments encounter another coverage test at each class.

After all current and deferred interest on the notes has been settled, the *subordinated management fee* (typically 20 to 40 bps) is paid. The subordinated management fee is paid after the notes but is senior to equity, thereby aligning the managerial interests with the debt-holder interests. Any remaining proceeds flow to the equity holders. Many deals contain *incentive performance fees* for the manager, such as 20% of residual cash flow after the Equity IRR surpasses a hurdle rate, or residual cash flows, after the equity holders have been made whole. This incentive fee is intended to better align the manager's interests with those of the equity holders.

Principal payments have two different waterfalls, one during the reinvestment period and the other during the amortization period. After the reinvestment phase, principal proceeds cover any interest shortfalls and are then used to amortize the notes sequentially. During the reinvestment period, principal payments are needed to maintain par. Principal proceeds first pay taxes and fees, then any unpaid interest on the notes. If coverage tests are violated, principal payments retire senior notes to bring the tranche into compliance. After paying unpaid interest, principal is used to purchase new collateral.

QUALITY TESTS

Collateral quality tests provide standards for the aggregate portfolio; the manager has a fiduciary responsibility to ensure that the portfolio remains in compliance with these tests throughout the life of the transaction. Should the CDO breach a quality test, the manager may not trade, except to improve the noncompliant test. For example, the manager may sell lower-rated assets and replace them with higher-rated ones. Quality tests reference the portfolio's rating, diversity, spread, coupon, and average life.

Weighted Average Rating Factor

Moody's and Fitch *weighted average rating factor* (WARF) metrics measure the weighted-average rating of the portfolio, based on the rating factors seen in Exhibit 9.5 (along with the equivalent S&P ratings).

Diversity Score

The higher the *diversity score* (DIV), the more diversified the collateral pool is deemed to be. The rating agencies calculate diversity scores based on asset default correlations.

EXHIBIT 9.5 WARF Table

S&P/ Fitch Rating	Moody's Rating	Moody's Rating Factor	Fitch Rating Factor
AAA	Aaa	1	0.19
AA+	Aa1	10	0.57
AA	Aa2	20	0.89
AA-	Aa3	40	1.15
A+	A1	70	1.65
A	A2	120	1.85
A-	A3	180	2.44
BBB+	Baa1	260	3.13
BBB	Baa2	360	3.74
BBB-	Baa3	610	7.26
BB+	Ba1	940	10.18
BB	Ba2	1,350	13.53
BB-	Ba3	1,766	18.46
B+	B1	2,220	22.84
B	B2	2,720	27.67
B-	B3	3,490	34.98
CCC+	Caa1	4,770	43.46
CCC	Caa2	6,500	48.52
CCC-	Caa3	8,070	48.52
CC	Ca	10,000	77.00

Source: S&P, Fitch, and Moody's.

Weighted Average Spread and Weighted Average Life Tests

The *weighed average spread* (WAS) and *weighted average life* (WAL) tests mandate that the collateral's weighted average spread and average life pass a specific hurdle rate.

Weighted Average Recovery Rate Test

CDOs often have two or three recovery rate tests based on different rating agencies.

EXHIBIT 9.6   Investment Criteria

Common CDO Portfolio Covenants	
% Rated below BB (for mortgage collateral)	% Second lien
% Rated CCC+ or below	% High-yield bond
% Non-U.S. issuer/Non-USD	% Debtor in possession loans
% Single issuer/Obligor	% Revolving credit facilities
% PIKable securities	% Delayed funding term loans
% Synthetic securities	% Current pay obligations
% Fixed rate securities	% Zero coupon securities
% CDO	% Same industry category

Source: Wachovia Capital Markets, LLC.

Investment Criteria

CDOs have many collateral covenants that limit how much of a specific type of asset the manager may purchase, including, but not limited to, those listed in Exhibit 9.6.

SPECIAL RIGHTS FOR THE CONTROLLING CLASS

The controlling class or the senior-most class has special rights relative to other classes in the event of default. The definition of default (as outlined in the indenture) varies from deal to deal. Some deals have stringent default conditions, such as tripping the OC test of a non-PIKable class. Other deals have looser default definitions, such as a missed interest payment on a non-PIKable class. It is important for investors to clearly understand the CDO's default language, as a current pay deal could be in technical default, depending on the specific definition. When a default event occurs, the controlling class is allowed to vote for the redemption of the deal, provided there is enough collateral to make some or all (again, depending on the deal) of the debt holders whole. In deals with a super-senior tranche or a wrapped senior class, one party typically purchases the entire class and thus has majority control over the vote.

The controlling class may also vote to fire the manager. The legally acceptable reasons for firing a manager would be spelled out in the indenture and offering memorandum. The most common reasons include fraud; a default event; the loss of a key person at the manager's firm; and breaking deal covenants. The right to fire a manager is at times shared with the equity holders and requires a two-thirds majority vote to be implemented. A new manager would then be hired and the deal would continue its life cycle according to the offering memorandum.

CDO CASH SOURCES AND USES

Once an investor understands the waterfall and covenant tests, there is one other piece of homework to be done before committing capital. All investors, from the top to the bottom of the capital structure, should take care to examine the CDO's sources and uses of cash (see Exhibit 9.7). The sources and uses table details exactly where the cash comes from (primarily proceeds from note sales, but may include payment from a swap), and how this cash is used (e.g., purchase of the collateral, underwriting fees, management fees,

EXHIBIT 9.7   Sources and Uses of Cash

Class	Rating	Note Par Value
Sources of Cash: Proceeds from Sale		
A-1	Aaa/AAA	$200,000,000
A-2	Aaa/AAA	$140,000,000
B	Aa2/AA	$30,000,000
C	A2/A	$35,000,000
D	Baa2/BBB	$35,000,000
E	Ba2/BB	$35,000,000
EQ	NR	$40,000,000
Total sources:		$515,000,000
Uses of Cash:		
Collateral purchase	500,000,000 @ 100.25	$501,250,000
Interest reserve		$2,530,000
Underwriting fees		$7,725,000
Manager upfront fees		$2,060,000
Rating agency fees		$767,000
Legal fees		$515,000
Administrative expenses		$153,000
Total uses		$515,000,000

Source: Wachovia Capital Markets, LLC.

legal fees, reserve account payments, etc.). The sources and uses information protects investors against a dealer's inadvertent (or possibly unscrupulous) omission of detail. If the sources and uses do not equal the same figure, investors should quickly question the manager and underwriter.

CDO TRUTHS, HALF-TRUTHS, AND MYTHS

The somewhat esoteric nature of CDOs has contributed to a number of popular misconceptions, especially among investors with limited investment experience with CDOs. We should remember that in times of crisis (such as the 1998 collapse of Long Term Capital), popular opinion may be quick to accuse any new or seemingly complicated asset of hiding the next financial cataclysm. We conclude this chapter with a closer examination of the many half-truths and myths that permeate the market should help clear away some of the most common misconceptions.

- *True: It is difficult to track down all investors in a CDO.* Securitization of assets works to redistribute the risk throughout the global financial system, and CDOs represent the latest evolution of securitization. CDOs do such a good job of redistribution that it is difficult to know where all the parts of the original product reside. Take, for example, the concern about the possibility of a contagion caused by CDOs backed by residential mortgages. In the years before securitization, and long before CDOs, residential mortgage risk would have been concentrated in banks and savings and loan institutions (S&Ls). When a crisis erupted, it may have been far easier to trace which institutions were at risk. However, that fact alone did not lessen the impact (in fact, it may have exaggerated it) of such a crisis on the U.S. economy.
- *Half-True: CDOs are opaque.* Journalists, academics, and even some investors argue that there is a lack of transparency to CLOs. Admittedly, there is some truth to this statement, as the synthetic markets have become increasingly private. Nonetheless, at least as far as cash flow CDOs are concerned, there is plenty of transparency for those willing to scratch beneath the surface.

As CDOs are 144a issues, there are established limitations on how much information managers and underwriters may disseminate publicly. For a particular transaction, potential investors receive a large amount of disclosure regarding covenants, collateral composition, and manager performance. Furthermore, deal information is readily available to investors via road shows, offering memoranda, and debentures. Once a deal has closed, investors receive monthly trustee reports, which list trigger and covenant status, cash flow distributions, trading activity, and detailed collateral information. Most dealers summarize these reports in periodic surveillance reports.

For those who are not investors (and who do not plan on becoming investors), rating agencies and third-party software vendors provide data and reports (for a fee) that summarize the sector's risk. In Chapter 12, we list a handful of such publications.

- *Half-true: CDOs are complex.* While there are nuances from one structure to the next, most CDOs follow a fairly standard cash-flow distribution mechanism that we have outlined in this chapter.
- *Myth: Falling asset values lead to forced sales, which, in turn, exacerbate a bear market.* The vast majority of CDOs lock in term funding with no forced sales of nondefaulted assets. A mere 5% of CDOs have market-value triggers, and these structures tend to be the least levered. The language of some CDOs, however, allow for conditions in which the controlling class can liquidate the collateral in the event of default on the CDO notes.
- *True for a few but not for all: CDOs are dumping grounds or "buyers of last resort."* This belief is rooted in the notion of the late 1990s of a "good CBO bond"—a bond that offered the highest spread for its rating. Frequently, this was due to rating agency inertia, as the bonds were downgraded shortly after purchase. Note holders, however, believed that the manager was "gaming the system" to extract higher-equity dividends. In many cases, however, the equity investors lost out as well.

While there have been a few bells and whistles added to some structures to discourage this practice, there are more powerful and natural self-regulating forces in the market. As with all investments, informed investors use their purchasing power as a vote of confidence for managers and should theoretically weed out the managers responsible for the most egregious practices. Managers who utilize these methods will likely be disciplined by their next deal's poor reception by the market, leading to unsold notes and equity.

CHAPTER 10

CDOs by Asset Type

Brian McManus
Senior CDO Analyst
Wachovia Capital Markets, LLC

Dave Preston, CFA
Associate CDO Analyst
Wachovia Capital Markets, LLC

Anik Ray
Associate CDO Analyst
Wachovia Capital Markets, LLC

Steven Todd, Ph.D.
CDO Analyst
Wachovia Capital Markets, LLC

All types of debt securities have been used as CDO collateral, and the options for collateral continue to expand. The most popular CDO assets are corporate leveraged loans, subprime and nonconforming *residential mortgage-backed securities* (RMBS), *commercial real estate* (CRE), *trust preferred securities* (TruPS), other CDO notes, investment-grade corporate bonds, and high-yield corporate bonds. In addition, many CDOs now contain a bucket for *credit default swaps* (CDS) that reference the aforementioned assets (see Exhibit 10.1). As explained in the previous chapter, a pure synthetic structure uses only CDS to gain exposure to its collateral. Investment-grade *collateralized bond obligations* (CBOs) have evolved from a cash structure to a pure synthetic structure.

This chapter highlights the special risks and consideration for various asset classes. We choose to focus on the most prominent CDO sectors found in the primary market in the summer of 2007. The new issue mix,

EXHIBIT 10.1   Collateral Composition of 2006 New Issue Cash Flow CDOs

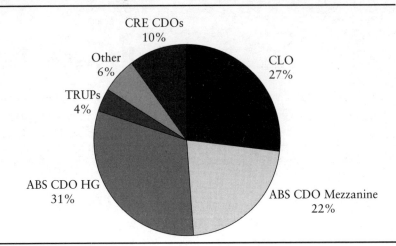

Source: Wachovia Capital Markets, LLC, IFR, MCM, Bloomberg, and LCD.

however, can change significantly over time. As an example, high-yield bonds were the most prevalent assets of new issue CDOs in the 1990s, while by 2006 *asset-backed securities* (ABS) were the most prominent collateral.

Investors must strike a balance between the higher yield they will be offered for an emerging asset class or innovative structure with the risk that the product will remain illiquid and possibly obsolete. Liquidity premiums are difficult to measure and can quickly change. During periods of high issuance and market stability the most liquid CDO notes—triple-A *collateralized loan* (CLO) notes, for example—can have a bid/ask spread as tight as bonds of a high-grade issuer. A major market disruption, such as the experiences of the fall of 1998 or summer of 2007, however, can sorely test dealers' abilities to make a fair market for even the most liquid structured products.

Past experiences suggest that if an emerging CDO sector does proliferate, liquidity premiums should shrink along with the tightening of other market risk premiums. As we will detail with examples, lending standards tend to relax during these periods to the point where investors are not only paying more for the product, but are in fact buying a riskier investment. Market disruptions act as reality checks, which may not only test the product's liquidity but also lead to tighter lending standards. Certain collateral could then fall out of favor as the CDO may no longer offer the most competitive funding structure.

CONSTRUCTING THE CDO PORTFOLIO

CDO managers employ different strategies when choosing CDO collateral. Note holders generally prefer a conservative strategy, whereas equity investors often pressure managers to increase dividends. A manager can boost cash flows to the preferred shareholders by investing in collateral that yields significantly more than the collateral's average yield. This practice can be taken to the extreme by buying the highest-yielding collateral for the rating. However, sophisticated investors have caught on to this practice and, as a result, the notes of these structures tend to trade wide to other issues in the secondary market. The problem with this particular strategy from the rating agency's standpoint is that the assets fit perfectly within the CDO framework. Hence, it is difficult to build covenants or adjust subordination levels accordingly. It is therefore up to discriminating note investors to know how to price the risk correctly.

A more subtle means of increasing equity dividends, while still meeting all covenant levels, is through the use of specialty buckets. Since any limitations related to these specialty buckets would be spelled out in the indenture, investors can vote their approval with their dollars. During periods of uncertainty, note spreads tend to diverge between clean deals and structures with significant buckets. The divergence could be large enough to cause an asset class to fall out of favor. Shortly after Russia defaulted on its debt in 1998, investors snubbed CBOs with *emerging market* (EM) debt. Soon thereafter, EM buckets shrank and eventually disappeared from many deals. As it became evident that loans were superior to bonds as CDO collateral, bond buckets began to shrink in CLO structures. For structured finance CDOs, aircraft, manufactured housing and franchise loans have faded from the CDO stage. Given the 2007 storm in the subprime collateral space, it would not surprise us if some adjustments were made to the future composition of ABS CDOs. Indeed, many 1H2007 *structured finance* (SF) CDOs have been marketed with claims of lower subprime buckets, no early 2007 vintage RMBS or limited Alt-A Collateral.

When discriminating, however, investors may not always be correct, and they may act prematurely. As an asset class, emerging market CDOs ended up outperforming high-yield bond CBOs. Furthermore, while bond buckets have been blamed for the demise of old-vintage CLOs, top managers have used the bucket to save the structure. Based on conversations we had with one such collateral manager, the 15% bond bucket in one of his deals helped preserve par during a period of rising defaults. The manager purchased discounted bonds, not of distressed companies, but rather of investment-grade companies and fallen angels (downgraded investment-grade bonds). In this case, the manager sacrificed coupon for par, or, in other words, traded *interest coverage* (IC) for *overcollateralization* (OC). The equity holders still achieved an 8% return through a period of historically high defaults, and the note investments turned out to be rock solid as well. This strategy is worthy of consideration. In a rising interest rate environment, a manager can increase par by sacrificing interest coverage without incurring additional credit risk. In an environment of high systemic credit risk, a manager can increase par and WARF by buying recently downgraded investment-grade debt.

In the end, the more CDO investors penalize managers for specialty buckets, the more it amounts to a vote of no confidence. The more constraints placed on a poor manager, the more predictable the underlying collateral should be. Carried to the extreme, this trend can lead to a return of static deals. At the other end, the more flexibility good managers have, the easier it is for them to use their better judgment. The "kiss of death" for CDO structures can occur when managers venture into a high-yielding asset class in which they have no expertise.

COLLATERALIZED LOAN OBLIGATIONS AND SPECULATIVE-GRADE CORPORATE COLLATERAL

CDOs backed by leveraged loans are referred to as *collateralized loan obligations* (CLOs), and represent approximately 30% of 2005 and 2006 cash CDO issuance.

In one sense, CLOs are an offshoot of the original high-yield CBO. As CBOs evolved, managers began to include a loan bucket in their transactions. Loans offer several advantages over bonds to CDO investors: (1) superior risk/return profiles; (2) higher recoveries (due to higher placement in the capital structure); and (3) the collateral's floating rate coupon obviates the need for an interest-rate swap.

CLO collateral is almost exclusively senior secured loans, but many deals contain buckets for high-yield bonds and second-lien loan collateral. Middle-market loans are also a popular collateral choice for boosting yields. Bonds and second-lien loans have lower and more volatile recovery rates. Middle-market loans are less liquid and more relationship-based than broadly syndicated loans.

While a bond bucket can be included in a CLO, pure CBOs are almost always synthetic. The use of CDSs eliminates the need for an interest-rate swap for fixed rate assets because a CDS can be combined with a low-risk floating rate asset to create a synthetic floating rate security.

EXHIBIT 10.2   Total Leveraged Loan Issuance

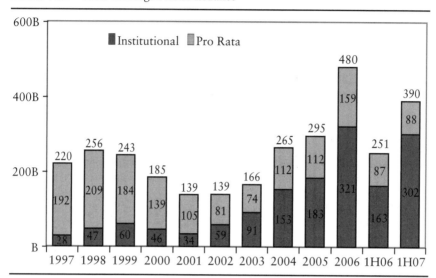

Note: These numbers comprise U.S. dollar denominated loans and are subject to revision as LCD collects additional data.

Source: LCD Quaterly 2007Q2, p. 230, US Dollar Denominated Quarterly New-Issue Leveraged Loan Volume. This material reproduced with permission of Standard & Poor's, a division of The McGraw-Hill Companies, Inc.

LEVERAGED LOANS AS COLLATERAL

Leveraged loan issuance has been steadily rising since credit spreads began tightening in 2003 (see Exhibit 10.2). In 2006, issuance rose 63% above the 2005 level. While credit easing and low interest rates have certainly helped to increase underwriting, CLOs, and hedge funds have also helped drive up issuance. In fact, as Exhibit 10.3 demonstrates, by 2000, CLOs had replaced prime rate funds as the primary buyer of new issue loans.

Leveraged loans are broadly syndicated term loans issued to firms rated below investment grade. Syndicated loans are originated by a group of lenders and sold to institutions. Each lender's credit exposure is limited to its share of the loan. Leveraged loans are generally callable at par (though prepayment penalties are possible), with a coupon that floats above LIBOR. The leveraged loan market includes first- and second-lien senior-secured, as well as mezzanine positions. As previously stated, first-lien senior secured loans dominate the CLO collateral field. The investment limitation on nonfirst-lien loans (including bonds) varies by structure but is often less than 10%.

EXHIBIT 10.3   Primary Institutional Loan Market by Investor Type

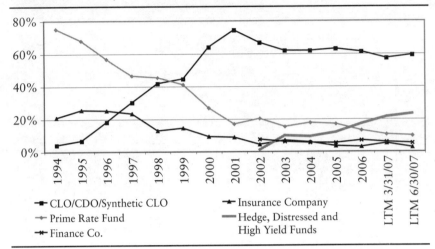

Legend:
- CLO/CDO/Synthetic CLO
- Prime Rate Fund
- Finance Co.
- Insurance Company
- Hedge, Distressed and High Yield Funds

LTM 3/31/07
LTM 6/30/07

Note: To provide a more realistic view of institutional buying habits in today's market, we add to the CLO tally the institutional commitments held by the arranger at close. For tax purposes of course, CLOs tend to participate as primary assignees and therefore are often left off the "at close" allocation list. In addition, beginning in 2002, we have made a better effort to track hedge funds and other investors in this analysis. As a result, we can only provide data for finance companies and hedge distressed & high-yield funds starting in 2002.

Source: LCD Quaterly 2007Q2, p. 138, Primary Institutional Market by Investor Type. This material reproduced with permission of Standard & Poor's, a division of The McGraw-Hill Companies, Inc.

There are two types of leveraged loan tranches: the pro rata tranche and the institutional tranche. The pro rata tranches are traditional bank syndications and comprise a revolver and a term loan (Term Loan A). Institutional tranches typically do not contain revolvers and are placed with nonbanking institutions and CLOs.

The loans are usually rated in the BB/B area; consequently, the initial WARF of a CLO collateral pool typically ranges from 2,100 to 2,700. CLOs' equity is generally levered 10 to 15 times (the equity interest amounts to 6.66% to 10% of the capital structure). Higher leverage is achieved by issuing speculative-grade notes (usually double-B rated). The dollar size of a CLO can vary from $300 million to $1 billion.

While CLOs and hedge funds have been increasing the demand for leveraged loans, *private equity groups* (PEGs) and *leveraged buyout* (LBO) firms have been driving the supply of new issue loans. From 2005 to 2007, the CLO market and LBO firms have had a symbiotic relationship. As long

EXHIBIT 10.4   LBO Volume and LBO Loan Volume

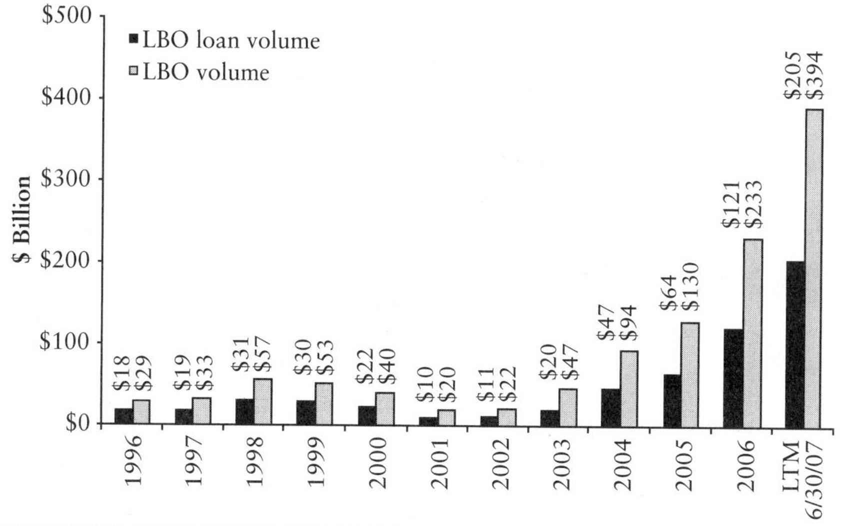

Source: Created from data obtained from LCD.

as CLOs continue to bid for leveraged loans, LBO firms can continue to take firms private. Exhibit 10.4 shows the rise in LBO activity, and the amount of loans issued by LBO firms for their deals.

Leveraging Statistics as a Measure of Default Risk

One negative consequence of this relationship has been an increase in the overall leverage of the loan market. High debt multiples are an indication of an increase in default risk. Total debt/EBITDA (earnings before interest, taxes, and depreciation and amortization) is a commonly used leverage ratio. LBO transactions have, on average, leverage multiples well above the market mean.

Leveraging statistics tend to move inversely to defaults. That is, as defaults rise, lending standards generally tighten, and issuance and debt multiples fall. As seen in Exhibit 10.5, leveraged loan total debt/EBITDA multiples bottomed in 2001. As defaults have slowed post-2004, leverage multiples have returned to 1999's level. Second-lien issuance has also contributed to higher debt multiples. The trailing 12-month leveraged loan default rate reached new lows in early 2007. As the credit environment improves, investors are generally more willing to reach for yield and take on more risk.

EXHIBIT 10.5 Average Debt Multiples of Highly Leveraged Loans

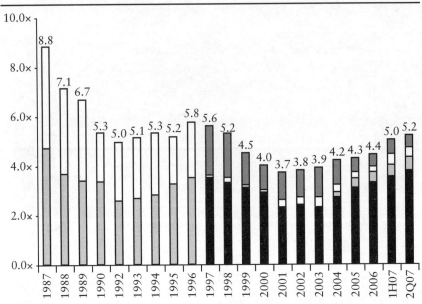

■ FLD/EBITDA ▨ SLD/EBITDA ☐ Other Sr Debt/EBITDA ▨ Sub Debt/EBITDA

Note: For years 1987–1996, breakouts of first-lien debt & second-lien debt were not available, therefore the lower portion of the column reflects Bank Debt/EBITDA and top reflects all Non Bank Debt/EBITDA

Source: LCD Quaterly 2007Q2, p. 17, Average Debt Multiples of Highly Leveraged Loans. This material reproduced with permission of Standard & Poor's, a division of The McGraw-Hill Companies, Inc.

Default and Recovery Rates

Leveraging statistics would not have increased had the risk of default not declined. In early 2007, the most recent 12-month trailing default rates on loans fell below 0.5% while recoveries remained above the historical mean.

The rating of a CDO (see Chapter 12) is based in large part on the ratings of the underlying assets and their historical performance. For cash flow transactions, however, the rating methodology does not consider market value volatility. Historically, leveraged loans have had lower default rates and higher recoveries than high-yield bonds with the same ratings. As a result, CLO equity may be levered 10 to 15 times, whereas CBO equity is levered 7 to 10 times.

When it comes to corporate credit risk, there is far more data on bonds than on loans. The growth of the syndicated loan market did not accelerate until the 1990s, whereas Moody's began rating bonds before the Great Depression. Exhibit 10.6 shows the default rate for speculative-grade bonds from 1970 through 2007. The average default rate for this 37-year period is 3.78%.

Some investors would argue that the speculative-grade bond market prior to the 1980s was a market of fallen angels (downgraded investment grade bonds), as the new issue speculative-grade market did not take off until the late 1980s. Indeed, the high-yield default rate from 1987 to 2006 averaged a much higher 4.85%.

Exhibit 10.6 shows three complete credit cycles. Most CDO issuance occurred after the 2001–2002 peak in defaults. While default rates did not reach a historical peak during the recession of 2001–2002, the market endured the longest stretch of above-average default rates to date.

For default rates on leveraged loans, we graph data since 1998 in Exhibit 10.7. Loan default rates have averaged 3.5% during this period, which is less than the 1970–2007 high-yield bond default rate of 3.78%

Default rates tell only part of the story, however. The ultimate recovery rate determines the loss-given default on an asset. Fortunately, there is a secondary market for most distressed assets that provides useful data regarding the price at which a manager can sell a defaulted security. Exhibit 10.8 shows Moody's estimate of the issuer-weighted recovery rates from 1990 to the 2006. Senior secured loans have averaged a 70.8% recovery, compared to a 43.8%

EXHIBIT 10.6　Global Speculative Default Rate (trailing 12-month)

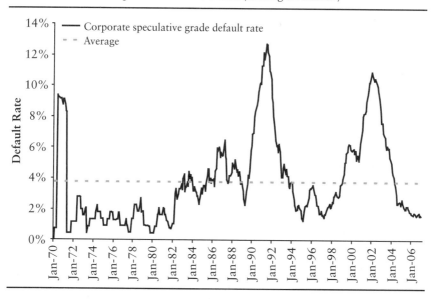

Source: Created from data obtained from Moody's Investor Service.

EXHIBIT 10.7   Lagging 12 Month Default Rate (by Principal Amount)

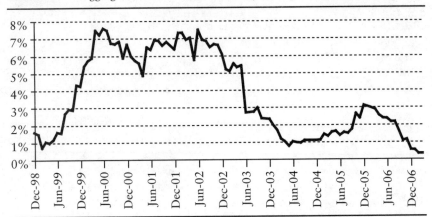

Source: LCD Quaterly 2007Q2, p. 17, Lagging Twelve-Month Default Rate by Principal Amount & Rolling Twelve-Month Principal Amount of Index Defaults. This material reproduced with permission of Standard & Poor's, a division of The McGraw-Hill Companies, Inc.

recovery for senior unsecured bonds. Thus, the average loss-given default for senior secured loans (29.2%) is less than half that of senior unsecured bonds (66.2%). We expect the increase in second-lien issuance to drive down senior secured recovery rates and would therefore advise investors to track recoveries on first-lien senior-secured loans separately from second liens.

The Collateral's Market Value Volatility

In general, the rating agencies do not consider the collateral's market value except in certain OC haircuts. As previously stated, there are no forced sales resulting from changes in market value for a cash flow structure. Nevertheless, we believe determining the correct amount of leveraging given an asset's volatility plays an important part in the stability of a structure. During periods in which risk premiums decline, managers could overpay for collateral, thereby increasing the downside risk. When the market hits bottom, the collateral has far more upside and could accelerate the curing for failed tests. The experience of CBOs and CLOs from 1997 to 2007 is a case in point.

CDOs that buy high-yield bonds have fixed rate assets and floating rate liabilities, and therefore must enter into a swap to hedge this risk. Defaults typically rise when the economy worsens. A bad economy pushes long-term rates down, but any benefit a CBO might gain from falling yields is lost to the swap. For this reason, in many CBOs embedded swaps exacerbated the damage caused by the credit downturn of 2000–2001.

EXHIBIT 10.8 Issuer Weighted Recovery Rates per Moody's

Year	Sec. Bank Loans	Sr. Sec. Bonds	Sr. Unsec. Bonds	Sr. Sub. Bonds	Sub. Bonds	Jr. Sub. Bonds	All Bonds
1982	NA	72.5	34.4	48.1	32.3	NA	35.6
1983	NA	40.0	52.7	43.5	41.4	NA	44.8
1984	NA	NA	49.4	67.9	44.3	NA	46.3
1985	NA	83.6	60.2	30.9	42.7	48.5	44.2
1986	NA	59.2	52.6	50.2	43.7	NA	47.9
1987	NA	71.0	62.7	49.6	46.2	NA	52.9
1988	NA	55.3	45.2	33.4	33.8	36.5	38.5
1989	NA	46.5	46.2	34.6	26.4	16.9	32.3
1990	76.1	35.7	37.0	26.8	20.5	10.7	26.1
1991	70.6	49.5	38.9	43.4	25.3	7.8	35.1
1992	50.0	62.7	45.9	47.9	37.8	13.5	44.2
1993	47.3	NA	44.7	51.9	43.7	NA	46.0
1994	61.0	69.3	53.7	29.6	33.7	NA	44.1
1995	82.8	63.6	47.6	34.3	39.4	NA	44.5
1996	89.1	47.6	62.8	42.8	24.3	NA	41.5
1997	83.1	76.0	55.1	44.7	41.3	30.6	51.1
1998	59.3	53.7	38.6	42.7	13.3	62.0	38.7
1999	68.3	43.3	38.0	29.1	35.5	NA	35.9
2000	71.6	41.7	23.2	20.3	32.9	15.5	25.5
2001	67.0	41.7	21.8	20.9	15.9	47.0	23.8
2002	55.8	46.9	30.3	25.3	24.5	NA	31.2
2003	77.9	63.5	40.5	38.9	12.3	NA	41.6
2004	86.1	78.7	53.2	47.5	82.9	NA	59.9
2005	82.1	69.2	55.5	31.0	51.3	NA	55.8
2006	76.0	74.6	58.3	43.6	56.1	NA	58.0
Avg	70.8	57.4	43.8	36.5	34.8	26.7	41.3

Avg is Average since 1990
Source: Moody's Corporate Default and Recovery Rates, 1920 -2006, 2/27/07 (EX 19) Corporate Default Study 2006.pdf

Granted, CBOs were structured with less leverage than CLOs. Prior to the rise in default rates in 2000, a typical triple-B CLO note had 10% credit support, whereas a triple-B CBO tranche had 14% credit support. The extra 4% support is little comfort when the collateral's volatility is three times higher.

We cannot blame the embedded swaps for everything, nor do we recommend writing off bonds as a collateral class. While the average recovery of a defaulted bond is roughly $0.44 per dollar of par, many bonds contain a call schedule that allows the investment to rise as high as $110 per $100 par. Most loans, by contrast, can be called at par.

A small unhedged bond bucket can be a valuable tool for an experienced CDO manager.[1] During a period of widening credit spreads, a new issue loan or bond often trades at a discount in the secondary market. In this environment, a nondistressed bond could not only be purchased at a greater discount than a nondistressed loan but, if credit spreads were to tighten back, it could rise to a higher price. The high upside of bonds have helped save some CBOs. Whereas CBOs were downgraded at a far greater rate than CLOs during the last downturn, many tranches were upgraded back to the original rating when the credit markets recovered.

ABS CDOs

As stated earlier, the ABS CDO product, also referred to as structured finance CDOs and RESEC CDOs, has evolved from its debut in 1999. Early in the sector's life, diversity score requirements caused managers specializing in mortgage risk to purchase esoteric ABS, including aircraft ABS, mutual fund 12b-1 funds, franchise loans, and, worst of all, manufactured housing. Post 2003, the primary asset classes backing ABS CDOs are tranches of ABS backed by subprime and nonconforming RMBS, and tranches of other CDOs. In general, the market differentiates by the quality of the underlying assets. Mezzanine ABS CDOs refer to structures with an average credit risk equivalent to triple-B. *High-grade* (HG) ABS CDOs buy mostly double-A and some single-A rated collateral.

Mezzanine ABS CDOs

Mezzanine (mezz) ABS CDOs are collateralized by the mezzanine tranches of subprime and nonconforming RMBS, and other structured products. The collateral rating distribution generally shows a 70% to 80% BBB stack, and a 20% to 30% A stack. Mezz ABS CDOs often contain a below-investment-grade

---

[1] The rating agencies allow for unhedged bonds as collateral as long as the amount is not large enough to threaten the structure during a sharp rise in interest rates.

limit of 5%. The structures are typically smaller than HG ABS CDOs, with deal sizes ranging from $300 million to $1.5 billion. Due to the higher spread and lower-rated collateral, mezz ABS CDOs are less levered than their high-grade counterparts; leverage on mezz ABS CDOs ranges from 10 to 30 times.

The liabilities can include an unfunded super senior swap that accounts for the top 65% to 70% of the capital structure. Prior to the third quarter of 2006, the triple-B Mezz ABS CDO tranche had only 4% subordination. Subordination levels subsequently rose, with late 2006 and 2007 issues supported by a 6% to 8% equity interest.

Unfortunately, there is far less historical data available for structured products than for corporate credits. Moreover, the performance of one structured product can vary greatly from another. Mezzanine tranches of manufactured housing structures are among the worst performers, whereas triple-A credit cards have a very clean history.

Exhibit 10.9 shows the estimated five-year cumulative loss rates by sector and initial credit rating for various structured products. U.S. HEL structures comprise mostly subprime loans, while U.S. RMBS are nonconforming prime loans. Exhibit 10.9 illustrates that, prior to 2005, it historically outperformed the greater ABS sector.

EXHIBIT 10.9   Five-Year Cumulative Loss Rates by Sector and Cohort

	Estimated 5-yr. Cumulative Loss Rates by Sector and Cohort Rating 1993–2005					
	U.S. CMBS	U.S. RMBS	U.S. HEL	Global CDOs ex. HY CBOs	ABS ex. MH & HEL	Global Corporate
Aaa	0.00%	0.03%	0.00%	0.00%	0.03%	0.00%
Aa	0.00%	0.06%	0.00%	0.92%	2.69%	0.08%
A	0.09%	0.34%	0.47%	2.47%	1.31%	0.23%
Baa	0.36%	2.17%	3.42%	10.28%	6.31%	1.24%
Ba	1.40%	3.26%	10.25%	12.60%	21.46%	7.04%
B	9.06%	5.82%	22.44%	27.63%	28.04%	18.61%
Caa	14.88%	19.77%	n/a	n/a	n/a	37.70%
Inv. grade	0.14%	0.51%	0.95%	3.73%	1.67%	0.77%
Spec. grade	5.70%	4.42%	14.19%	17.07%	25.71%	26.97%
All ratings	1.46%	1.00%	2.03%	5.67%	2.69%	6.97%

Source: Default & Loss Rates of Structured Finance Securities: 1993–2005, Jian Hsu, April 2006, pg 23 Figure 36 "Estimated Five-Year Cumulative Loss rates by Sector and Cohort Rating, 1993-2005", © Moody's Investors Service, Inc. and/or its affiliates. Reprinted with permission. All Rights Reserved.

Many investors, however, are wary that historical data do not adequately reflect the risks of the 2006–2007 HEL vintages. The growth of the subprime market from 2003 to 2007 is unprecedented.

High-Grade ABS CDOs

High-grade ABS CDOs are backed by highly rated subprime and nonconforming RMBS bonds, as well as tranches of other CDOs. Most of the collateral is rated AA or A, and deals have strict limits on the percentage of AAA and BBB collateral. Accordingly, these CDOs have a WARF ranging from 40 to 70, implying a portfolio credit quality of A to AA–. Because such highly rated collateral does not provide much spread, HG ABS CDOs are extremely leveraged transactions, with leverage ranging from 50 to 250 times. Due to the tighter funding gap, large deal sizes—generally $1 billion to $3 billion—are required to produce a profitable economy of scale. HG ABS CDOs often contain a privately placed super senior tranche that accounts for 70% to 90% of the structure.

Because of the commonly held belief was that the risk of default for high grade collateral was close to zero, the credit support for a triple-B note can be less than 1%. Such a highly levered structure, however, leaves little room for error, not only for default risk, but also for the timing of cash flows.

With few exceptions, it is impossible to precisely predict portfolio cash flows even when losses follow expectations, as would be the case with high-quality assets. As such, the equity interest of all CDO structures bears some degree of risk unrelated to credit losses. This risk increases with leveraging.

The volatility of interest coverage under various scenarios is an easy way to measure this risk. It should be noted, however, that while the interest rate risk of HG CDOs increases the possibility of an IC trigger tripping, a note failing IC triggers is far more likely to be cured than a note tripping the OC limit.

When the first HG CDOs came to market in 2003, the funding gap was significantly wider than it is now. As the gap narrowed, leveraging increased, putting more pressure on IC coverage. Many of the risks detailed below were exacerbated by the narrow spreads of RMBS collateral. Conversely, HG ABS spreads began to widen in early 2007. Access to cheaper collateral should not only mitigate interest coverage risk but, under certain scenarios, could possibly lead to higher equity dividends.

Nondefault Risks for HG CDOs include the following:

- *High prepayments in a credit tightening environment.* This risk is one very good reason 2004 structures were pushing up against IC tests in mid to late 2006. The average cost of funding a CDO fell to 38 bps in the summer of 2006 from 46 bps in 2004, but collateral spreads tightened even more rapidly. The challenge for 2005 transactions was finding a product that yielded enough to create a funding gap. As a result, the WARF for high-grade deals began to shift higher.

■ *Extension and prepayment risk of fixed rate notes.* ABS notes typically contain buckets of fixed rate assets, which are then hedged with a swap. The length of the swap is determined by the average life of the liabilities. As mortgage assets are prepayable, predicting the amortization schedule can be one of life's great challenges. Given a base-case prepayment rate, the rating agencies require the structure be stressed by doubling the speed and then running half the speed.

■ *LIBOR basis risk.* This risk is less significant but could contribute to IC test failure. Most CDOs are funded with quarterly pay liabilities, but often the assets are paying monthly. This mismatch can affect CDOs due to either a large rise in the basis between one- and three-month LIBOR, or a substantial and sudden rate shock.

Commercial Real Estate CDOs

The first *commercial real estate* (CRE) CDOs were mostly static financing deals, but many CRE CDOs are now managed, arbitrage structures (Exhibit 10.10). CRE CDOs buy CMBS and real estate investment trust (REIT) debt, as well as non-CUSIP'ed collateral such as commercial real estate mezzanine debt, preferred equity and B notes. CRE CDOs traditionally have many more tranches than other CDOs due to commercial real estate investors' desire to buy at many different ratings. CRE CDOs are discussed further in Chapters 15 and 17.

MIDDLE-MARKET CLOs

Somewhere between broadly syndicated leveraged loans and small business loans lies a middle-market (MM) sector of growing importance to CLO investors. The traditional middle-market CLOs were, and sometimes still are, structured as financings with 100% of the equity retained. Some of these lenders have begun to develop platforms to increase assets under management and are offering equity participation in their issues. Many *broadly syndicated loan* (BSL) CLO managers began adding, or increasing the size of, middle-market buckets. During periods of tightening loan spreads, the less liquid middle-market sector offered a nice alternative to lower quality BSL loans as a means of boasting equity dividends.

EXHIBIT 10.10   CRE CDO Volume

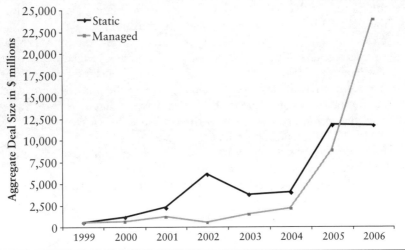

Source: Wachovia Capital Markets, LLC.

What Is a Middle-Market Loan (MML)?

Not surprisingly, the middle-market sector is much smaller than high-yield bonds or leveraged loans (Exhibit 10.11), and is primarily backed by traditional cash flow loans, although some deals are asset-backed loans collateralized by accounts receivable and inventory. As we will explore further, the market's size has been growing, helped by the resources of the CLO market.

The data above represent only one sector of what could be defined as middle market. The loans behind the data are syndicated and are often rated. The data do not include unrated middle-market loans that never leave originator's balance sheets, nor do they include loans sold through what is often referred to as a *club syndication*—a small group of originators formed to coinvest in an issue.

EXHIBIT 10.11   Debt Issuance ($ billion)

	2005	2006
Middle-market loans (inst.)	25	23
Leveraged loans (inst.)	183	321
High-yield bonds	83	130

Source: S&P's LCD and Wachovia Capital Markets, LLC.

Investors can divide middle-market players into two groups: banks and nonbanks. Bank loans are traditionally syndicated and finance the working capital needs of the borrower, while nonbank loans are often used for *private equity group* (PEG) activities such as LBOs, acquisitions and recapitalizations. Nonbank players include specialty finance companies, hedge funds, and asset managers.

The origination process of the loans varies depending on the motivation of the lender, the size of the company, and the size of the loan. The simplest origination arrangement is the *bilateral loan*, in which a single lender originates the loan and retains it on the balance sheet. Bilateral loans are smaller in size, as many lenders do not have the balance sheet required to absorb larger loans. One-stop lenders are those that service all parts of the capital structure, issuing senior-secured loans (first and second lien), mezzanine debt, subordinated loans and growth equity. The *club transaction* is similar to the bilateral loan, but the lender chooses not to retain the entire loan and instead sells the remaining portion to other club members. Often, the club is a group of firms with like-minded strategies concerning risk and investing.

The bank syndication market focuses on originating the largest middle-market loans. This type of MM loan overlaps with the BSL market, and it is not always clear where one market stops and the other begins. *Leveraged Commentary and Data* (LCD) defines middle-market products as loans to companies with EBITDA under $50 million. As we explain next, the sector could also be defined by loan size or company size. The definition of middle market becomes extremely vague when one tries to distinguish between a small, broadly syndicated loan and a sizable middle-market syndication. In contrast, the line between small business and middle-market loans is more definitively drawn. Small business loans are less than $5 million in size and are collateralized by assets, often real estate. The main difference is that small business loans often provide for recourse from the personal assets of the proprietor.

The market offers several different definitions of a middle-market loan. Some participants use company size (based on EBITDA or revenue), while others use loan size. The market sets $50 million in EBITDA as the upper end of the middle market, while the lower bound falls at $5 million. Others in the market use facility size, defining traditional middle-market loans as less than $125 million, large middle-market loans between $125 million and $250 million and broadly syndicated loans as greater than $250 million. These definitions are used to show the market's liquidity levels, as well as the level of investor involvement in setting the loan terms.

Structures

The vagueness of terminology applies not only to the collateral but to the structures as well. At one end of the market, we find the original balance-sheet CLOs sponsored by middle-market originators. The balance-sheet deals are initiated primarily by specialty lenders, and the assets remain on the issuer's balance sheet. The lender uses the CLO as a source of financing. The originator/servicer retains 100% of the equity position. These CLOs do not have OC triggers, and equity cash flows are locked out after the first delinquency. Initially, these structures were passive with no revolving period. As one would expect with static structures, the average lives of the early MM CLOs were very short, often less than three years. As of 2007, most contain a three to five year revolving period, and amortization has changed from sequential to pro rata with sequential triggers.

At the other end lie the traditional (arbitrage) managed CLO structures with a large middle-market bucket. These deals are mainly issued by asset managers looking to increase *assets under management* (AUM) and receive management and performance fees. These structures have a three to five year noncall period and a five to seven year reinvestment period and contain triggers familiar to CLO investors such as OC and IC tests. The manager traditionally retains 15%–25% of the equity and markets the remainder.

There is a fuzzy middle ground between these two ends that is forever changing. Some of the sponsors that have, in the past, retained all of the equity are looking at setting up a platform that would allow them to sell a portion. The movement from the original static, sequential, short-term financing structure toward pro rata, managed, arbitrage deals highlighted in Exhibit 10.12 has created new opportunities for equity investors.

The best way we can find to analyze CLOs with MML exposure is to step through the data we have for the MM syndicated market first, and then take a close look at the traditional lenders. The arbitrage MM CLO is a more diversified structure, and investors can gain comfort in its similarity to the traditional CLO.

As for the CLOs from traditional MML lenders, the differences among these deals are far greater than what we would expect among BSL CLOs. Traditional middle-market lenders usually specialize in a few industries, which explains the CLO's lower diversity score. We therefore recommend investors diversify among managers, being aware of what industry concentrations they carry.

Prepays, Default and Recovery Data (or Lack Thereof)

With more CLO managers trying to tap the middle market for yield, coupled with rising issuance from traditional middle-market managers, comes

EXHIBIT 10.12   Managed versus Static Deals (per Moody's)

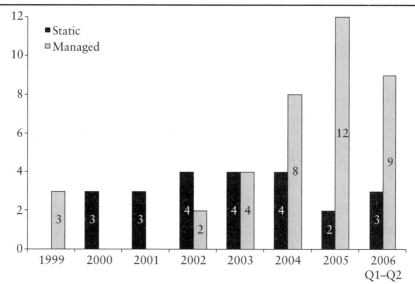

Source: Created from data obtained from Moody's Investors Service, Inc.

a litany of questions concerning the performance of these loans. This information, to put it bluntly, is almost nonexistent. We cannot pull up pretty charts comparing the default rates of these loans to their broadly syndicated cousins. Without default rates, it is hard to know what recovery rates would be, nor do we have any comprehensive data on prepayments.

Given the lack of publicly available data, competing opinions exist regarding the expected prepayment rates of middle-market loans. One camp argues that middle-market loans should prepay at a slower rate than broadly syndicated loans due to the nature of the market. This theory holds that middle-market borrowers are more relationship based and less likely to come back to the lender to save a few basis points on the loan. In addition, traditional middle-market borrowers do not have fee-seeking investment bankers offering better terms, as large public loan issuers do. In contrast, middle market issuance is the domain of specialty lenders. The counterargument is that MMLs have historically prepaid faster than BSLs based on data provided by some of the earlier lenders. Investors should consider the context of this data. During the tight credit market of 2001 to 2004, MM issuers had far less competition than exists today. With increased competition came tighter spreads and faster prepayments. What investors will probably find is that prepayments vary greatly from one sponsor to the next, depending on the industries and the points on the capital structure to which the issuer lends.

Investors can scrape together pieces of information concerning default and recovery rates from issuers and the syndicated market for the larger middle-market loans. Investors may have heard or already seen numbers kicked around by investment bankers or sell-side analysts. The figures are typically extracted from rating agency data. Although none of the major agencies have published an official study on the defaults and recoveries of middle-market loans, one can segregate smaller loans from a particular study and calculate defaults, recoveries and prepayments for this sector.

An S&P publication suggested little difference in cumulative default rates when segregated by either EBITDA (provided EBITDA is positive) or facility size. The agency calculated the 1995–2006 cumulative institutional loan default rates for public loan issuers.[2] The cumulative rate breaks down as follows: 28.1% for companies with negative EBITDA, 5.7% when EBITDA is less than $50 million and 5.5% for all loans in the sample. By loan size, the agency calculated a cumulative rate of 4.1% for loans under $100 million, 4.8% from $100 million to $250 million, 5.1% from $250 million to $499 million and 6.2% above $500 million.

The cumulative rates underestimate what we should expect on an annualized basis, as the surge in loan issuance in 2006–2007 weights the results toward lower-defaulting, less-seasoned issues. A cohort study from the same publication found that cumulative default rates for *all* loans issued between 1997 and 2000 averaged 18.58%, whereas for all other vintages, the average was only 2.39%.

As for recovery rates, selecting defaulted loans between 1987 and 2005 from S&P's U.S. LossStats Database, for example, would find that the facilities under $250 million had recovered, on average, more than 85% compared with not quite 70% for facilities more than $250 million.

A recovery rate of more than 85% clearly refers to first lien senior secured loans. Many balance sheet MML transactions invest heavily in non-senior debt. In an August 2006 publication, Moody's stated that the average recovery of three frequent issuers was 40%.[3] This extremely low number is explained by the fact that the debt was not first lien but a mix across the capital structure. The low recovery rates of mezzanine and subordinated debt can easily drag down a pool's average.

Adding MMLs to the BSL Mix

The rearview mirror analysis above highlights an important fact: MMLs, like BSLs, have experienced few defaults in 2006 and 2007. Moreover,

---

[2] *Standard & Poor's: Q4 06 Institutional Loan Default Review.*
[3] David Burger and Shan Lai, *Update on the Market for U.S. SME CLOs*, Moody's Investors Service, August 25, 2006.

BSL recoveries are running near a historic high. In 2006 and early 2007, investors became increasingly concerned with rising leverage and weaker covenants for large LBOs. They felt the flood of CLO money feeding the BSL syndicated markets had only encouraged this trend. In the summer of 2007, market liquidity began to fall and with it, many high-profile BSL issues failed as investors demanded more covenants.

The barrier to entry is far greater for middle-market lending, so we would expect change to occur more slowly than it does in the BSL market. Logically, the syndicated middle market is the first place excess capital from the BSL markets will go. Indeed, the whole trend toward adding MML buckets was a result of tighter BSL spreads.

While the BSL market was overheating, MML companies also began to increase leveraging and tried dropping covenant. The MML market, however, had only a brief flirtation with covenant-lite issuance before the faucet ran dry.

LCD tracks statistics for syndicated loans from companies with an EBITDA under $50 million. Again, the data embodies a small percentage of the MML universe, but it captures the larger end of the market and is a good representation of the loans found in MML buckets of hybrid and "arbitrage" deals.

Exhibit 10.13 compares the average debt multiples of companies with EBITDA inside of $50 million to companies with EBITDA exceeding this amount. The more times debt is levered to EBITDA, the higher the risk of default. Higher leveraging through the loan's position on the capital structure implies a lower recovery in the event of a default. With the exception of 2005 and 2006, this debt multiple for BSL companies (EBITDA more than $50 million) was consistently higher than for MM companies (EBITDA less than $50 million). In both cases, the average debt multiple has climbed significantly since hitting bottom during the 2000–2003 period of historically high default rates.

The average middle-market multiple through first-lien debt (FLD) is consistently higher than the comparable figure for broadly syndicated notes. For both sectors, the debt multiples bottomed in 2001 and by 2006 returned to 1997 levels.

When we discuss the LCD debt multiples for the broadly syndicated market with loan managers, many have expressed the belief that the multiples understate the leveraging of the new issue market. According to LCD, the multiples represent an average of all transactions they track, including many transactions that are refinancing. The latter dilute the trend toward higher levered LBO transactions, which worries many seasoned managers.

Exhibit 10.14 compares the BSL multiples for the LBO transactions with the MM LBO multiples. As with the market as a whole, total leverag-

EXHIBIT 10.13   Average Debt Multiples of Large Loans versus Middle-Market
Loans

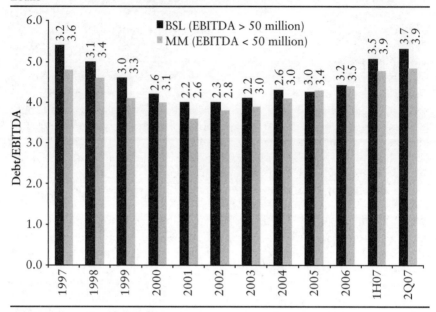

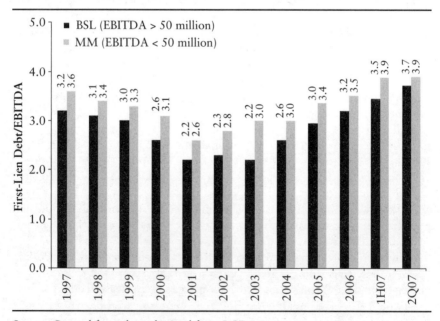

Source: Created from data obtained from LCD..

EXHIBIT 10.14   Average Debt Multiples of Large LBO Loans versus Middle-Market LBO Loans

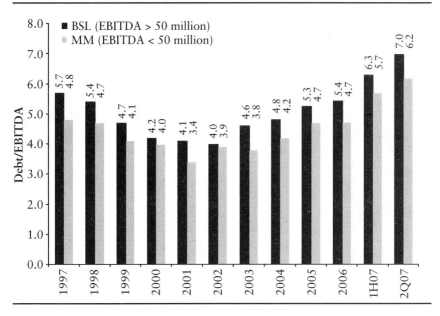

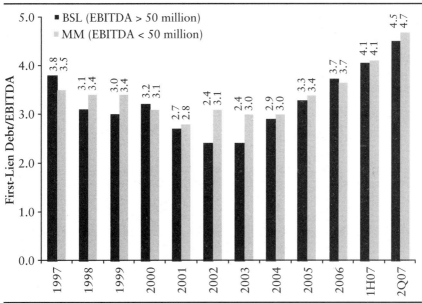

Source: Created from data obtained from LCD.

ing is consistently higher for BSL than MML, but the difference in multiples is significant. Unlike the market as a whole, LBO leveraging through the first lien has been nearly the same for BSLs as MMLs from 2004 to 2007.

The data support a belief that middle-market proponents hold, and we are inclined to agree. The BSL lending standards are more vulnerable to swings in capital flows. In late 2006 and early 2007 money was pouring into the private equity market, leading to a surge in LBO activity in both the United States and Europe. With default rates running below 1%, LBO lending standards slipped more for BSLs than MMLs. When easy money leaves a market, however, the weakest borrowers are the first to default, leading to the surge in bankruptcies we saw from 2000 to 2002.

Liquidity

The growth of private equity and hedge fund industries coincided with an impressive increase in secondary market liquidity for BSLs. As for MMLs, many would argue that the secondary market is still in its infancy. A CLO manager can easily trade out of a credit risk BSL while, for MMLs, the manager should expect to proceed through the normal bankruptcy channels to recover lost capital. As more CLO managers clamor onto the middle-market bandwagon, investors should be asking which ones will do best when credit conditions reverse. Clearly, having an intimate understanding of the borrowers comes in handy when they get behind on their debt payments.

The poor liquidity also makes it difficult for the new kid on the block. The loan market, be it broadly or narrowly syndicated, is in general a clubby network. Many new managers have a hard time getting allocations on the best deals, making it difficult for neophyte CLO managers to compete with established ones. For middle-market lending, this effect is even more exaggerated. New entrants will find it easier to buy the riskier mezzanine debt than the often oversubscribed FLD. As the managers build their relationships, they may be granted more access to the top of the capital structure.

Adding MMLs to a BSL CLO is a trend that developed in 2006. As discussed previously, the lack of transparency leaves many questions about default and prepayment rates unanswered. It also makes it difficult for some new investors to eagerly embrace these opportunities, particularly for a CLO of a debutante manager.

Still, where there's a yield, there's a way. By adding middle-market loans to a portfolio, a CLO manager can boost equity dividends substantially. For this reason, the top BSL CLO managers who had the foresight to build middle-market platforms while many banks were withdrawing from the business posted some impressive CLO equity returns.

The Grass Root Lenders

The bulk of middle-market loans originate and mature on the balance sheet of the lender. As previously mentioned, even with BSL syndicated loans it is difficult for a neophyte manager to gain access to the best deals. For syndicated middle-market loans, it is even more difficult.

Many note investors value the long-term commitment the veteran crop of lenders has made to the middle-market business and could be a bit wary of a Johnny-come-lately whose only business model is rotating assets. The mortgage business has its share of such lenders and, indeed, investors prefer originators who invest in their deals.

Diversification versus Specialization

Traditionally, MML managers specialize in only a few select industries. Consequently, when using the CLO market as a source of financing, they achieved lower diversity scores and, therefore, less levered structures than their BSL counterparts. MML investors should determine in which industries a manager specializes, and whether exposure to these industries is desired. Investors should also determine the points on the capital structure that the manager prefers.

While it may be unwise for MML managers to begin originating loans in industries for which they have no expertise, a move to a more diversified platform by hiring people with the expertise could make sense in the long run. As more MML managers use the CLO market either as a source of financing or to increase assets under management, we expect such a trend to occur.

The Performance of Middle-Market Lending

Tracking the performance of BSL CLOs has come a long way. Investors have 10 years of data on rating transition risk. Moody's has standardized several reports that track performance by vintage and sector. If that is not enough, investors have ample information on the long-term collateral performance.

On the one hand, the MM CLO financing structure exaggerates equity returns because of the very different way of accounting for a credit risk security. Although there have been few substitutions, given the benign credit environment, the practice of substituting a delinquent security at par creates tremendous stability for noteholders. Such a practice, however, would be a high price to pay had the issuer sold rather than retained the equity interest. Under these circumstances, the issuer would be essentially granting the equity investor a free put to sell a credit back to the sponsor at par. In a typical CLO, an issue rated triple-C or below would receive a haircut that would lower to the OC ratio. The OC ratio would also decline if the manager were to sell the loan at a discount and replace it with one at par. As traditional MM managers begin implementing a business model that allows for an increase in assets under management through CLO issuance, we expect more MML structures to resemble the traditional arbitrage deal.

On the other hand, certain features of the financing structures were more punitive to equity holders. Before cash was released to the preferred shares, the typical structure required at least two months of interest due to noteholders be placed in a reserve account. If any loans were delinquent more than 60 days, the interest due on these loans would also be placed in reserves. These provisions had the effect of curtailing equity cash flow more readily than a traditional CLO. A final point worth mentioning is the difference in structures. The early MML CLOs paid sequentially, thereby amortizing the cheapest funding first. The market is now embracing the pro rata pay structure, or, alternatively, the conditional pro rata structure. Conditional pro rata deals transform into sequential-paying structures after a specific event, primarily a credit event or breaching a pool factor trigger (often 50%). Pro rata payments produce a longer-lived asset, allowing for better deal economics. The structure payments benefit equity investors by paying down the more costly junior notes along with the senior notes, and by maintaining credit enhancement levels. The sequential trigger is in place to protect noteholders against the rise in idiosyncratic risk as the number of loans dwindles.

TruPS

TruPS CDOs debuted in 2000, and have seen a steady increase in issuance ever since. The sector was dominated by bank and thrift issues in its earliest stages, but has since seen a rise in REIT and insurance collateral. Insurance TruPS are usually included as a minority portion of Bank TruPS CDOs, while REIT TruPS CDOs are primarily comprised of only REIT collateral. TruPS CDO tranches, middle-market loans and REIT debt are all beginning to appear as collateral in TruPS CDOs, but on a limited basis.

What Are Trust Preferred Securities?

Trust preferred securities are typically 30-year bullet securities with floating rate coupons. TruPS usually have five-year call protection and dividend deferral rights of 20 quarters—that is, the security is not in default during a dividend deferral of up to five years. TruPS are considered debt for tax purposes, allowing for tax deduction of interest payments, but are considered equity by the regulatory entities. For this reason, the securities are especially attractive to firms in heavily regulated industries, such as banks, insurance companies and REITs. To qualify as Tier 1 capital, the securities must have a maturity of at least 30 years, no step-up provisions, five-year dividend deferral, and five-year call protection. This allows firms to raise capital that is cheaper than common equity but with the tax advantages of debt. Trust preferreds are also not dilutive to ownership, as they do not carry voting rights.

TruPS collateral is not always rated by a rating agency. The shadow rating equates to the triple-B or triple-B minus area. While the default risk may be low, the loss-given default should be expected to be close to 100%. Moody's assumes a 10% recovery rate[4] for bank trust preferred securities when rating the structures. The security's position in the capital structure is just a hair above equity.

TruPS Structure

TruPS are issued by a wholly owned special purpose vehicle (the "trust"). The trust then lends the proceeds from the TruPS to the holding company and receives a junior subordinated note. This note is below debt in the holding company's capital structure, and is senior only to common and preferred equity. The interest paid to the trust by the parent company largely parallels the required dividend payments owed to TruPS purchasers.

Bank Trust Preferreds

The Federal Reserve defines Tier 1 capital as "the sum of core capital elements (capital stock, surplus, undivided profits, qualifying noncumulative perpetual preferred stock and minority interest in the equity accounts of consolidated subsidiaries) less goodwill and other intangible assets."[5] Tier 1 capital is important for banks, as they must maintain adequate capital to asset ratios. Starting in 1989, the Federal Reserve allowed "qualifying cumulative perpetual preferred securities" (traditional preferred stock) to comprise 25% of the Tier 1 capital. In 1996, the Fed expanded this to allow minority interest (in the form of TruPS) to be included in the 25% of core capital requirements. In 2005, the regulators affirmed this level for TruPS, adding the constraint that trust preferreds can count for 25% of core capital, *net of goodwill less any associated deferred tax liability.*

TruPS are obviously beneficial to banks that wish to find cheaper funding that still satisfies regulatory capital requirements. However, high issu-

---

[4] James Brennan, *Moody's Approach to Rating U.S. REIT CDOs*, Moody's Investors Service, April 4, 2006.
[5] St. Louis Federal Reserve Bank, http://www.stlouisfed.org/col/director/Materials/alco_capitaladequacy_ratios.htm.

EXHIBIT 10.15 TruPS CDO Collateral Statistics

Year	No. of Deals	Total Assets Backing TruPS CDOs	Bank/ Thrift	Insurance	REIT	Approx. Avg. Spread to LIBOR
2000	2	541	100%	0%	0%	3.80%
2001	6	3,227	100%	0%	0%	3.70%
2002	9	4,346	100%	0%	0%	3.45%
2003	15	6,302	87%	13%	0%	3.15%
2004	19	7,454	81%	19%	0%	2.80%
2005	15	8,440	58%	16%	26%	2.30%
1H 2006	9	6,465	47%	19%	34%	2.20%
Totals	75	36,775	75%	13%	12%	2.90%

Source: Moody's Update on the US Trust Preferred CDO Sector, James Brennan, Aug 2006, pg 2, Fig. 1, "Assets Backing Moody's-Rated TRUPS CDOs by Year", © Moody's Investors Service, Inc. and/or its affiliates. Reprinted with permission. All Rights Reserved.

ance costs closed the trust preferred market to smaller banks until 2000. In that year, pooled trust preferreds hit the market and found their way into TruPS CDOs. The proliferation of this structure opened the trust preferred market to many of the bank holding companies that previously had no practical access to the capital markets. According to the Federal Reserve, approximately 800 bank holding companies have more than $85 billion trust preferred securities outstanding.[6]

Bank TruPS were the first TruPS to be securitized into CDOs, and made up the majority of TruPS CDO Collateral (Exhibit 10.15) until 2006. A stable economy for banking, combined with healthy spreads, led to CDOs purchasing more and more bank TruPS, driving the spreads down. Investors still favor bank securities because of the healthy banking environment, and a perception that a floundering bank will be rescued by an opportunistic buyer. However, investors would be wise to remember that often the M&A bid disappears at precisely the moment it is most needed.

Insurance Trust Preferreds and Surplus Notes

The insurance industry entered the TruPS game in 2002. Smaller insurance companies were attracted to the trust preferred market for the same reason as small banks and thrifts: these securities provided access to capital

---

[6] Federal Reserve System, *Risk Based Capital Standards: Trust Preferred Securities and the Definition of Capital*, 12 CFR Parts 208 and 225, March 4, 2005.

markets and regulatory equity capital while allowing for tax deductibility of interest. In addition to TruPS, another insurance security found in trust preferred CDOs is the surplus note. Surplus notes are unsecured obligations, subordinate to other debt and to policyholders, and add to the issuer's surplus while providing tax deductible interest payments. Each payment of principal or interest is subject to prior approval of the issuer's state insurance regulatory body.[7]

As spreads on bank-issued TruPS tightened, CDO managers turned to insurance TruPS and surplus notes as a way to increase spread (Exhibit 10.15). Managers were attracted by the similarities between the banking and insurance industries: highly regulated industries enjoying a healthy economic outlook.

One only has to look at the Gulf Coast in 2005 to see the potential hazards for insurance firms, especially smaller regional insurers. While equity investors were generally enjoying higher dividends and excellent performance, note investors were spooked by a series of natural disasters. TruPS CDOs with insurance exposure had to be offered at a discount to pure bank deals.

REIT Trust Preferreds

Because REITs are not able to retain earnings, funding growth is a major concern. As issuers shy away from secondary equity offerings and may not have access to debt capital markets, trust preferred stock offers an attractive source of capital. Many REITs have limited operating histories, no credit rating and tight margins, and wish to avoid onerous covenants required by lenders. CDOs backed by REIT trust preferreds debuted in 2005,[8] allowing smaller REITs access to pooled capital, thus reducing issuance costs.

As Exhibit 10.15 shows, REIT TruPS quickly became an investor favorite. REIT TruPS CDOs provide exposure to sectors such as homebuilders' debt, CMBS, equity REITs, and residential and commercial mortgage REITs. Investors certainly enjoyed this exposure during 2005 and early 2006, but as these sectors headed south in early 2007, the enthusiasm has been replaced by concern. Close to 20% of REIT TruPS CDO assets are in residential REIT TruPS and subordinated debt. According to a March 2007 Moody's publication, however, only one deal among those it has rated has subprime exposure greater than 5%.[9] Another contributing factor to the pressure on notes spreads is the homebuilder debt exposure, which Moody's estimated

---

[7] Emmanuel Modu, *Rating Surplus Note and Insurance Trust Preferred CDOs*, A.M. Best, July 25, 2005.

[8] TruPS in REITs, Fitch Ratings, Dec. 21, 2005

[9] James Brennan, *Subprime Real Estate Distress Likely to Have Minimal Direct Impact on Moody's TruPS CDO Ratings*, Moody's Investors Services, March 22, 2007.

to be around 14%. Investors would therefore be wise to fully understand their exposure before committing to buy.

EUROPEAN CDOs

The European CDO market is primarily made up of corporate debt, as opposed to structured finance assets. European investors and bankers have led the way in synthetic structures. Synthetic corporate products are prevalent in Europe, but are primarily high-grade assets, as the European high-yield market is less developed than in the United States. The European CLO market was originally more focused on middle-market lenders and balance sheet deals than in the United States. However, BSL managers have become more common since 2005 and the issuance of European BSL-CLOs has soared. A Europeans CRE CDO market has also begun to take hold as the market for the underlying CMBS collateral emerges.

European CLOs began as balance sheet financings to achieve capital relief, and the synthetic structure quickly became the preferred risk-transfer method. European balance sheet issuance soon outpaced American financing issues. This structure was most easily adapted to the cozy relationship that European lenders have with their customers. In fact, the balance sheet CLO allowed the lenders to retain their relationships while limiting their risk. In general, European borrowers have been more reliant on banks and less on capital market than their U.S. counterparts.

The European debt markets have been rapidly changing. As European nations gradually liberalized economic policies, and LBOs become more common in the Eurozone, the pound sterling, and euro-leveraged loan market took hold (Exhibit 10.16). Not coincidentally, the rise in leveraged loan issuance has been coupled with surge in BSL-CLO issuance volume. (Exhibit 10.17).

Investors comparing the European and U.S. loan markets often observe the higher average leverage of the former. Indeed, Exhibit 10.18 appears to support this argument. It should be noted, however, that the European market is dominated by LBO debt. A more appropriate comparison would be to the average debt/EBITDA multiple for large U.S. LBO issues. Here we note that while in Europe the average debt/EBITDA ratio rose in 2007, it did not keep pace with the surge in the average U.S. LBO debt/EBITDA multiple.

Not all metrics of risk and U.S. technology can be blindly applied to the European CLO market. American CDO investors entering the European market can take comfort in an understanding of the basic deal structure, but must be mindful of a few key differences. In particular, European loans originate from a variety of nations with different regulations and bankruptcy provisions. An American CLO backed by loans issued in 20 states is far different from a

EXHIBIT 10.16 European Senior Loan Issuance

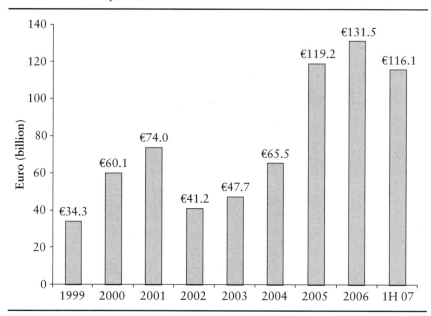

Source: Created from data obtained from LCD..

EXHIBIT 10.17 European Arbitrage CLO Volume

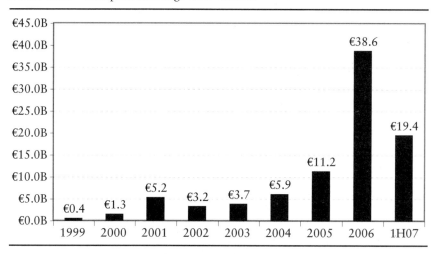

Source: LCD European Quaterly 2007Q2, pg 140, Annual Arbitrage CLO Volume Based on Transaction Size, this material reproduced with permission of Standard & Poor's, a division of The McGraw-Hill Companies, Inc.

EXHIBIT 10.18   European versusU.S. Leverage

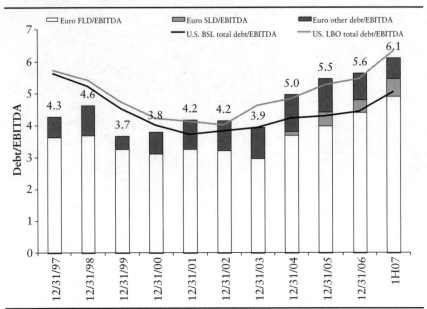

Source: Created from data obtained from LCD.

European CLO with loan collateral originated in five different nations. One could argue that the European CLO will generate a more diversified portfolio, as the different bankruptcy domains should produce differing default and recovery rates. However, these differences could conversely lead to less transparency and greater modeling challenges. Also, as the European loan market is less developed, there is a smaller universe of credits. Finally, investors must note varying accounting standards, legal frameworks, and regulations.

Then there is the question of the manager's competence. Some American mangers have tried to enter the Eurozone but quickly discover their disadvantage relative to the tighter customer relationship European managers hold. In this sense European managers are similar to the U.S, middle market manager. Not to be shut out, American managers have formed partners with European managers to create U.S./euro hybrid deals.

SUMMARY

The wide variety of collateral used in CDOs illustrates why CDOs cannot be treated as an asset class, but as a technology. Over time, assets fall in and out of favor as CDO collateral, and we have focused on the assets used as collateral for CDOs in mid-2007. Investors may be suspicious of the new asset class, or conversely, may be attracted to the higher yields offered by the novel CDO types. Buyers should be wary that innovative products can be the first to suffer during market disruptions, as an untested product could be more vulnerable to illiquidity and headline risk. Just as CDO types and structures evolve, underlying collateral asset types may change over time. This transformation is driven primarily by changes in lending standards which coincide with the credit cycle. For example, the lending standards for subprime RMBS issued in 2003 were far stricter than in 2006. Similarly, CLOs have weathered a full credit cycle, with loan defaults peaking in 2000, and reaching historical lows in 2007. Consequently, the lending standards in the years 2001 and 2002 were far stricter than either 1996 or 2007. One could argue that during a credit cycle the CDO becomes a victim of its own success. By allowing investors with varying degrees of risk tolerance access to new asset classes it is a highly effective means of raising capital. It does not, however, guarantee that the capital will be wisely spent.

CHAPTER 11

Credit Derivatives and Synthetic CDOs

Brian McManus
Senior CDO Analyst
Wachovia Capital Markets, LLC

Steven Todd, Ph.D.
CDO Analyst
Wachovia Capital Markets, LLC

Dave Preston, CFA
Associate CDO Analyst
Wachovia Capital Markets, LLC

Anik Ray
Associate CDO Analyst
Wachovia Capital Markets, LLC

A credit derivative is a financial instrument whose value derives from the creditworthiness of an underlying asset, issuer or portfolio of assets. Examples include single-name *credit default swaps* (CDS), CDS indexes, CDS index tranches, and synthetic collateralized debt obligations (CDOs). These products are an evolving and growing presence in today's capital markets. According to the International Swaps and Derivatives Association (ISDA), as of April, 2007, the total notional amount of outstanding credit derivatives exceeded $35 trillion. Growth has been explosive; as recently as 1997 the market was tiny.

Credit derivatives are distinct from the cash assets issued in the primary markets by corporations, individuals and governments in need of cash. Like other derivatives, credit derivatives allow investors to hedge against or speculate on fairly nuanced financial outcomes. Investors can efficiently express macroviews and make relative value (convergence) trades across the capital structure, sectors, geographical regions and vintages. CDO issuers can use credit derivatives to hedge the ramp-up risk of a cash CDO or as collateral for a synthetic CDO. Investors and dealers may also use CDS indexes and tranches to hedge assets in inventory against spread movements and defaults.

This chapter contains five sections, which build on each other, and provide basic information for new investors as well as more detailed analysis for experienced investors. The first section examines the terminology and mechanics of credit default swaps on corporate entities, asset-backed securities, and CDOs. In the second section we investigate the most actively traded CDS indexes and tranches of these indexes. We explore tranche trading strategies and market dynamics in the third section. In the fourth section, we build upon our description of credit default swaps to explain the dynamics of synthetic CDOs. We conclude with a section where we discuss correlation. Correlation is the term used to describe the degree to which defaults are synchronized among collateral names and tranche trading strategies are often called *correlation trades*.

SINGLE-NAME CREDIT DEFAULT SWAPS

Single-name *credit default swaps* (CDS) lie at the heart of all synthetic transactions, from index correlation trades to synthetic *collateralized debt obligations* (CDOs). A CDS is similar to an insurance contract between two parties, a *protection buyer* (insured) and a *protection seller* (insurer). The protection buyer seeks to insure an asset against a loss of principal. The protection seller agrees to provide insurance for a fee. We say that the protection seller is *long* the underlying credit risk and the protection buyer is *short* the underlying credit risk. The underlying asset, known as the *reference obligation*, could be the bonds or leveraged loans of a corporate issuer, sovereign debt, a basket of bonds or loans, an *asset-backed security* (ABS) or a tranche from a CDO. The buyer of protection makes periodic *fixed payments* to the protection seller, until the contract expires, or in the case of corporate CDS, until the earlier of contract expiration or a *credit event*. See Exhibit 11.1.

When the underlying asset is a corporate debt, credit events include issuer *bankruptcy*, *failure to pay principal* and sometimes *debt restructure* (for European obligors and North American investment grade entities). For structured finance assets and CDOs, the definition of a credit event is expanded to include *interest shortfalls* and *principal write-downs or implied write-downs*. CDS contracts can be settled via a cash payment or with the

EXHIBIT 11.1 What is a Credit Default Swap?

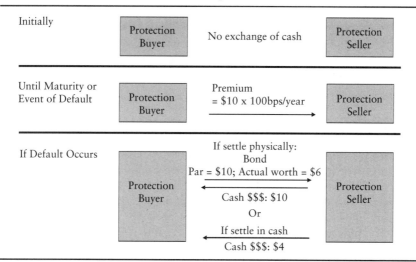

Source: Wachovia Capital Markets, LLC.

physical delivery of the underlying asset. With *cash settlement*, the protection buyer receives a cash payment equal to the difference between the par amount of the underlying asset and its recovery value. With *physical settlement*, the protection buyer delivers the reference obligation to the protection seller in exchange for a par payment.

Corporate CDS

Corporate debt CDS first appeared in the mid-1990s. These were later followed by CDS on structured finance securities, including *residential mortgage-backed securities* (RMBS) and *commercial mortgage-backed securities* (CMBS). CDS on CDOs are a more recent innovation. According to the Bank for International Settlement (BIS), the market for CDS has experienced dramatic growth, from a *notional* amount of $180 billion in 1997 to more than $35 trillion as of April, 2007. Most of the outstanding contracts reference corporate entities. The International Swaps and Derivatives Association (ISDA), a trade organization of participants in the market for *over-the-counter* (OTC) derivatives, has been influential in standardizing CDS contracts.

For CDS on corporate debt, credit events are typically limited to bankruptcy of the referenced entity and failure to pay principal on the debt. CDS written on European corporate entities, sovereigns and North American investment grade corporate entities generally expand the list of credit events to include *"restructuring"* events. Restructuring events encompass efforts by corporate entities to preempt formal insolvency (bankruptcy) proceedings by negotiating changes in debt terms with creditors. In response to problems arising from Conseco's restructuring in 2000, North American high-yield corporate entities generally exclude restructuring events from the list of credit events.

Most corporate CDS contracts reference the senior unsecured debt of issuers. The most liquid contracts *terminate* 3, 5, 7, or 10 years after the *effective date*, although almost any maturity is possible since the contracts are negotiated privately. In the case of physical settlement, deliverable securities are typically restricted to loans or senior unsecured bonds maturing in 30 years or less, denominated in a standard currency and not subject to some contingency before becoming due. Obviously, protection buyers will favor *the cheapest to deliver* asset. Physical settlements are adversely affected by operational problems when the notional amount of synthetic assets exceeds that of eligible deliverable assets. For this reason, CDS contracts allow for cash settlements. Cash settlements present an additional set of challenges in the case of illiquid, distressed assets with wide bid-ask spreads.

ABS CDS

Unlike corporate CDS that can reference multiple bonds or loans of a corporation, ABS CDS reference specific tranches of asset-backed securities. The first credit default swaps on ABS tranches made use of the cash/physical settlement template of corporate CDS, terminating when a credit event triggered a payment from the protection seller to the protection buyer. This proved unsatisfactory because ABS cash flows differ from those of a corporate bond. For ABS and other structured finance securities, interest shortfalls do not result in default and tranche write-downs may be reversed with subsequent write-ups. Moreover, ABS securities rarely default before their legal maturities.

In an effort to replicate ABS cash flows more closely, ISDA introduced a pay-as-you-go (PAUG) template in June 2005. Instead of a single credit event triggering a payment, PAUG provides for two-way payments between protection sellers and buyers over the life of the CDS contract. Each period, the protection buyer (*fixed rate payer*) pays the protection seller (*floating rate payer*) a *fixed payment* equal to the product of the CDS *fixed rate* (*premium*), the average notional balance of the CDS and the actual number of days in the calculation period, divided by 360.

Interest shortfalls, principal shortfalls and write-downs result in *floating-rate payments* from the protection seller to the protection buyer. For example, if an ABS tranche experiences an interest shortfall, the protection seller compensates the protection buyer for the interest shortfall. If the shortfall is later reversed, the protection buyer repays the protection seller a one-time *additional fixed payment* equal to the amount she received. The PAUG template allows for multiple trigger events, called *floating amount events*. In addition to interest shortfalls, floating amount events include principal write-downs and principal shortfalls.

Interest shortfalls are reimbursed in one of three ways, depending on which "toggle" feature the CDS contract employs. Under the *no cap* option, the protection seller covers the full amount of the interest shortfall, even if it exceeds the protection buyer's fixed payment. With a *variable cap* basis, the protection seller reimburses interest shortfalls up to the amount of the fixed payment plus LIBOR. Hence, the maximum out of pocket payment that the protection seller makes is LIBOR. In contrast, the *fixed cap* basis limits the shortfall amount to the fixed payment only. Hence, the protection seller never makes a net cash payment to the buyer. Protection buyers enjoy the greatest protection under a no cap basis; the fixed cap option offers the least protection to the insured counterparty.

The physical settlement option can be triggered by principal write-downs, failure to pay principal or if the underlying asset is downgraded to Caa2/CCC or below (or if the rating is withdrawn by one or more rating agencies). These events are called *credit events*, in contrast to the floating amount events that trigger two-way payments. If a credit event occurs, the protection buyer has the option to effect full or partial settlement or to continue the contract. Cash settlements are not allowed. If the protection buyer delivers the reference bond for a *portion* of the CDS notional, the PAUG contract remains in force for the remaining notional amount.

Home equity ABS often employ a cleanup call provision that allows the issue to be called if the loan balance falls below a targeted level (e.g., 10% of the original balance). When this call is not exercised, interest payments on the tranches of the ABS may be raised, an event known as *coupon step-up*. If the CDS contract employs a step-up provision, the protection buyer may terminate the contract if coupon step-up occurs on the underlying ABS. If the protection buyer chooses not to exercise his termination option, the CDS contract will continue and the premium will be raised by the same amount as the coupon step-up. If the CDS contract does not include the step-up provision, the CDS premium will not change, even if the cleanup call is not exercised and the coupon steps-up on the underlying ABS. Hence, protection sellers prefer contracts with step-up provisions.

CDS contracts on ABS tranches typically have long maturities, matching those of the reference entities. The standard template also adjusts the notional amount of the reference entity to account for amortized principal, prepayments, write-downs, and defaults.

CDO CDS

The CDO CDS template is based on the standardized template for ABS CDS, but adjustments are made to account for *payment-in-kind* (PIK) events and *implied write-downs*. Although actual write-downs are common in ABS transactions, CDOs rely on a waterfall mechanism to reallocate cash flows when the collateral deteriorates. A failed coverage test results in interest cash flow being redeployed to amortize the principal of more senior notes until test compliance is achieved. Some mezzanine tranches may PIK; for these notes, unpaid interest accrues as principal. Because of PIK events and implied write-downs, the risk profile of a CDO CDS contract may diverge from that of a cash bond.

The CDO CDS template lists failure to pay interest as both a credit event and a floating payment event. Similar to ABS CDS, if a credit event (including failure to pay interest) occurs, the protection buyer has the option to continue receiving floating payments or to effect physical settlement. For non-PIKable tranches, failure to pay interest immediately triggers a floating payment/credit event, subject to a $10,000 minimum interest shortfall for the tranche. If a tranche is PIKable, then the interest shortfall must persist and remain unreimbursed for a grace period of 360 calendar days before a credit event is triggered, again subject to the $10,000 minimum interest shortfall.[1]

Whereas ABS CDS list both actual and implied write-downs as credit/floating payment events, CDO CDS employ a toggle option for implied write-downs based on overcollateralization (OC) ratios provided by the trustee.[2] Generally, when collateral is downgraded below a minimum rating, its par value receives a *haircut*, reflecting the possibility of a future loss in principal. Protection buyers find the implied write-down toggle appealing because it capitalizes the losses from a deteriorating collateral pool early, rather than at the note's legal final maturity.

In Exhibit 11.2, we compare the key features of CDS on ABS and CDOs. In both markets, settlement is pay-as-you-go, and the underlying asset is a specific tranche or obligation. Protection buyers pay sellers an amount equal to the product of the protection premium and the notional principal. The

---

[1] During the PIK grace period, the protection seller makes floating payments to the protection buyer. If physical settlement occurs at the end of the grace period, the protection buyer delivers bonds in an amount equal to the PIK-ed interest plus the notional amount on the CDO CDS. The seller excludes the capitalized interest from his payment.

[2] If the trustee does not provide an OC ratio for the reference tranche, then the implied write-down calculation is based on the OC ratio for the next most senior tranche, or, the next most junior tranche, if the former is unavailable. If both ratios are not available, the calculation agent provides a fallback.

EXHIBIT 11.2 CDS on CDO and ABS

CDS on CDO	
Reference obligation	Specific tranche of specific CDO (CUSIP specific)
Deliverable obligation	Specific tranche of specific CDO (CUSIP specific)
Maturity	Usually matches maturity of reference obligation
Settlement	PAUG Physical
Credit Events—Lead to Physical Settlement: One-Time Events	
Failure to pay principal	CDO does not pay tranche principal by effective maturity of CDO (earlier of liquidation/amortization or legal final)
Failure to pay interest, non-PIKable	Credit event immediately upon shortfall
Failure to pay interest, PIKable	Triggered if interest shortfall (deferral) > 360 (720) days
Distressed rating downgrade	Rating on Reference CUSIP falls to CCC/Caa2 or below
Floating Amount Events—Lead to PAUG settlement: Reversible	
Failure to pay principal	Technically classified as *floating amount event* so that protection buyer can receive a payment despite not owning CDO tranche At deal wrapup, protection buyer receives notional amount
Write-down/implied write-down	■ Triggered by OC under 100 ■ OC as calculated by deal indenture ■ Protection seller pays amount of write-down to buyer ■ Implied write-down benefits protection buyer
Interest shortfall	
Fixed cap	■ Protection seller pays amount of shortfall to buyer ■ Shortfall covered up to certain amount ■ Buyer payment reduced by shortfall amount. ■ Better for taking view on credit risk ■ Benefits protection seller
Variable cap	■ Reference rate (LIBOR) included in shortfall payment ■ Better replicates cash ■ Better for hedging ■ Benefit to protection buyer
No cap	■ Seller must cover entire amount of shortfall ■ Most benefit to protection buyer
Most Common Structures	
Variable cap with no implied writedown Fixed cap with implied write-down *Note:* These two structures balance benefits to seller and buyer.	

EXHIBIT 11.2 (Continued)

CDS on ABS	
Reference obligation	Specific tranche of specific ABS bond (CUSIP specific)
Deliverable obligation	Specific tranche of specific ABS bond (CUSIP specific)
Maturity	Usually matches final maturity of reference obligation
Settlement	PAUG Physical

Credit Events—Lead to Physical Settlement: One-Time Events	
Physical Settlement Option—Triggered by Three Events:	
Writedown	Buyer can deliver reference obligation
Failure to pay principal	■ Buyer may deliver for full or partial notional amount ■ If partial notional amount is delivered, PAUG remains in place for remainder of notional
Distressed rating down-grade	Rating withdrawn by one of three rating agencies or below CCC/Caa2

Floating Amount Events—Lead to PAUG Settlement: Reversible	
Failure to pay principal/write-down	Protection seller pays amount of writedown/shortfall to buyer
Implied write-down	Reference bond is under collateralized or shortfall between pool balance and aggregate balance of other securities (equal or higher obligations) backed by pool
Interest shortfall	
Fixed cap	■ Protection seller pays amount of shortfall to buyer ■ Shortfall covered up to certain amount ■ Buyer payment reduced by shortfall amount up to cap ■ Benefits Protection Seller
Variable cap	■ Reference rate (LIBOR) included in shortfall payment ■ Better protection for available-funds cap risk ■ Benefit to protection buyer
No cap	■ Seller must cover entire amount of shortfall ■ Most benefit to protection buyer

Step-Up Provision	
If applicable	■ If exercised, buyer has option to terminate contract ■ If not exercised, premium rises by amout of step-up
If not applicable	■ Premium remains unchanged after step-up ■ Protection seller loses by receiving below market premium

Source: Wachovia Capital Markets, LLC.

notional principal amortizes in concert with the ABS or CDO tranche. A credit event occurs if there is a failure to pay principal or interest on the reference obligation, or if the underlying asset is downgraded to a distressed rating level. For PIKable CDOs, the interest shortfall must persist for 360 consecutive days for a credit event to be deemed to have occurred. When a credit event occurs, protection payments are made in exchange for physical delivery of the reference.

A floating amount event, which triggers a payment from protection sellers to buyers, occurs if there is an actual or implied write-down, or if there is an interest shortfall. With an implied write-down (the most common), the protection seller makes a payment when the current period write-down exceeds that of the prior period. This payment is reimbursed if in a subsequent period, the current write-down amount falls below that of the prior period. Write-down amounts are not paid if the OC ratio exceeds 100%. Interest shortfalls lead to different cash flows under the three possible cap options. An interest shortfall compounding option is available which requires protection sellers to pay buyers accrued interest on previously unpaid interest. In general, the obligations of protection sellers are minimized with a fixed cap option, where there are no interest shortfall compounding and there is also no implied write-down. Protection buyers fare best with a no-cap (or variable cap) option, with interest shortfall compounding and implied write-downs.

The no implied write-down toggle is usually paired with a variable cap basis for CDS referencing mezzanine tranches, which are typically PIKable. Protection buyers, who are often hedging their cash positions prefer the variable cap option, which provides compensation for interest shortfalls of up to LIBOR plus the CDS premium. The implied write-down toggle is usually paired with a fixed cap basis for CDS referencing senior notes, which are not PIKable. In general, toggle options reduce the liquidity of CDO CDS.

For a given CDO tranche, which toggle pairing should command a higher premium, fixed cap with implied write-down or, variable cap with no implied write-down? The answer depends on the likelihood that a tranche will PIK before it becomes undercollateralized. For those tranches that are more likely to face write-downs before they PIK, the benefits of the implied write-down option will likely exceed the costs of the fixed cap option (relative to the variable cap option) for protection buyers. This is generally the case for the mezzanine tranches of mezzanine-ABS CDOs. In contrast, for those tranches that are more likely to PIK before they face write-downs, the benefits of the variable cap option may exceed the costs of the no implied write-down option (relative to the implied write-down option) for protection buyers. This is generally the case for the mezzanine tranches of high-grade ABS CDOs.

ISDA is currently considering a modification to the implied write-down convention that would require protection buyers to pay sellers LIBOR on the cumulative implied write-down, provided the tranche is still paying interest. This modification would obviously lower the value of the implied write-down option.

The Basis

In theory, the spread on a CDS contract should track the spread paid on the underlying cash asset. In reality CDS and cash spreads often diverge. The difference between the CDS premium and the reference entity's asset-swap spread defines the *basis*. When the CDS spread is greater (less) than the asset-swap spread the basis is said to be positive (negative). A negative or positive basis is possible if the risk profile of a CDS contract diverges from that of the cash asset. The basis is also influenced by a host of fundamental and technical factors such as the supply of and demand for liquidity, hedging activities, dealer pricing power, and financing costs and conditions.[3] Because many cash investors are buy-and-hold accounts and CDS contracts offer investors an efficient means of leveraging a short or long credit position, the synthetic markets serve as marginal providers of liquidity and synthetic spreads generally lead cash spreads.

Theoretically, a highly negative basis should encourage *negative basis* trades. Here an investors takes a long credit position in the cash market while simultaneously buying protection on his position. At its best, this trade swaps the reference entity's risk for CDS counterparty risk. In order for a clean swap to occur, the CDS contract must perfectly mimic the cash asset. PAUG contracts are better suited for this trade; in contrast, corporate CDS must consider the risk of the underlying reference entity being called or the contract being cancelled due to a debt restructuring event.

CDS INDEXES

A CDS index is a basket of single-name CDS, usually equally weighted. The basket may be formed by combining CDS on corporate bonds (e.g., CDX, iTraxx), leveraged loans (e.g., LCDX) or structured product securities (e.g., ABX or CMBX). Currently, there is no CDS index of CDOs. Unlike many CDOs, which are managed, CDS indexes are static. As with other credit

---

[3] Investors who wish to lever a long credit risk position will consider both the spread differential between cash and synthetic markets and the financing terms (margins, haircuts, etc.) that are available in both markets. Cash and synthetic spreads may be equivalent, but the financing terms may favor one market over the other.

default swaps, a protection buyer makes periodic payments to a protection seller. The contract remains in effect until maturity.

When a credit event occurs on any of the basket corporate entities, the protection buyer has the right to sell the defaulted security at par to the protection seller. The defaulted corporate entity is then removed from the index and the contract continues with a reduced notional for its remaining term.

The asset-backed indexes do not allow for physical settlement and instead use PAUG settlements that mirror the standard ABS CDS templates, with some exceptions.[4] Generally, the notional amount of an asset-backed security index adjusts as any of the reference entities amortize, prepay, default, or incur write-downs or write-ups. Index attributes for the most actively traded indexes are summarized in Exhibit 11.3. Eligibility rules are presented in Appendix A to this chapter.

The corporate indexes have the option of physical settlement or cash settlement of the underlying credits based on an auction price. Physical settlement may suffer from operational problems if the notional amount of synthetic assets exceeds that of eligible deliverable assets. A *short squeeze* is then possible. To avoid a short squeeze, corporate CDS index contracts allow for cash settlement. Cash settlement presents an additional set of challenges in the case of illiquid, distressed assets with wide bid-ask spreads. To overcome these challenges, Creditex/Markit administers an auction of the senior, unsecured debt of defaulted issuers. The mechanics of Delphi's cash settlement on November 4, 2005 are described in Appendix B.

The first CDS indexes were launched in 2003. In 2004, they merged to form a new set of indexes called *CDX* (North American and Emerging Markets) and *iTraxx* (Europe, Australia and Asia). The indexes are divided into subindexes, based on geography, rating and sector. So, for example, CDX. NA.IG specializes in North American investment grade entities, whereas iTraxx Europe TMT specializes in European investment grade entities from the telecom, media and technology sectors. Under normal market conditions, some of these indexes and subindexes are very liquid, with tight bid-ask spreads, averaging less than one-half of a basis point. These bid-ask spreads widened significantly during the credit turmoil experienced during the summer of 2007.

The contents of an index are determined by polling a global group of broker-dealers, who serve as market makers. Every six months the index *rolls*. On the *roll date* a new *on-the-run* index is created; we say the index *rolls*. The on-the-run index generally combines the most liquid single-name

---

[4] For example, ABX.HE excludes maturity extension and rating downgrades from its list of credit events. Hence, an ABX.HE contract will not terminate before the underlying cash ABS issues mature. Also, unlike single-name ABS CDS, ABX.HE does not include step-up provisions.

EXHIBIT 11.3 Actively Traded Indexes

	CDX.NA.IG	CDX.NA.HVOL	CDX.NA.XO	CDX.NA.HY	iTraxx Europe
Asset type	Investment-grade entities	Investment grade (most volatile)	Crossover rating entities	Noninvestment grade entities	European CDS
Number of entities	125	30	35	100	125
Ratings	Investment grade	Investment grade	Crossover 4B, 5B	Noninvestment grade	Investment grade
Inception date	10/21/03	10/21/03	9/21/05	10/21/03	June 2004[a]
Reference entity	Point in capital structure	Point in capital structure	Point in capital structure	Point in capital structure	
Quote type	Spread	Spread	Spread	Spread	Price
Weighting	Equal weighting	Equal weighting	Equal weighting	Equal weighting	Equal weighting
Settlement	Physical	Physical	Physical	Physical	Pay as you go
Subindexes	Industrial Financial HVOL index Telecom			BB index B index	DJ iTraxx Europe HiVol DJ iTraxx Europe Crossover Nonfinancials Financials (sr & sub) TMT Industrials Auto Energy Consumer
Tranche attachments	3%, 7%, 10%, 15%, 30%				3%, 6%, 9%, 12%, 22%

[a] iTraxx was formed by the merger of two indexes; these indexes began in 2003

Source: Markit.

EXHIBIT 11.3 (Continued)

	ABX.HE	TABX.BBB	TABX.BBB–	LCDX.NA.8	CMBX.NA
Asset type	Subprime home equity	ABX BBB tranches	ABX BBB– tranches	Loan credit default swaps	CMBS
Number of entities	20	40	40	100	25
Ratings	Investment grade	BBB	BBB–	BB, B	AAA, AA, A, BBB, BBB+, BB
Inception date	1/19/06	2/14/07	2/14/07	5/22/07	3/7/06
Reference entity	Specific note	ABX subindex	ABX subindex	First-lien, syndicated secured loans	Specific note
Quote type	Dollar price	Dollar price	Dollar price	Dollar price	Spread
Weighting	Equal weighting Weightings may change as assets amortize	Equal weighting Weightings may change as assets amortize	Equal weighting Weightings may change as assets amortize	Equal weighting	Equal weighting
Settlement	Pay as you go	Pay as you go	Pay as you go	Physical/Cash	Pay as you go
Subindexes/tranches	Aaa subindex Aa2 subindex A2 subindex Baa2 subindex Baa3 subindex	0%–3% 3%–7% 7%–12% 12%–20% 20%–35% 35%–100%	0%–5% 5%–10% 10%–15% 15%–25% 25%–40% 40%–100%		AAA AA A BBB BBB– BB[b]

[b] BB Tranche added after CMBX.1

Source: Created from data obtained from Markit.

CDS contracts.[5] Once the list of single-name obligors is chosen, the *fixed spread* on the index is calculated by averaging the quotes from participating dealers, with the outliers removed. Off-the-run index series continue to trade, but with reduced liquidity. The indexes use standardized maturities (5, 7, and 10 years are most liquid) and regular payment dates, for example the 20th of March, June, September, and December of each year.

At issuance, the fixed spread on the index (the premium that protection buyers pay) represents the spread that generates a zero net present value for the contract's expected cash flows. As the market reassesses individual single-name CDS risks, the spread changes. If a CDS trade is initiated after the index is first priced, then an *upfront payment* (discount) is applied. The protection buyer pays premiums every quarter on the fixed payment dates and a prorated partial payment if the contract is initiated between payment dates. If one of the underlying assets defaults on a nonpayment date, the protection buyer also makes an accrued premium payment.

CDS indexes trade in both *funded* and *unfunded* forms. No down payment is required in the purely unfunded form, although margin requirements may apply. In the fully funded form, the protection seller holds the trade's notional in a portfolio of low-risk (typically AAA) securities. The portfolio is then used as collateral by the protection buyer, eliminating counterparty risk.

The U.S. and European CDS indexes differ in their treatment of corporate debt restructuring events. The U.S. indexes consider bankruptcy and failure-to-pay to be credit events that trigger default on any single-name obligor. Restructuring is not deemed a credit event, even though most underlying single name CDS contracts trade with modified restructuring as a credit event. The European indexes trade with the same credit events as the underlying CDS contracts, including bankruptcy, failure to pay, and modified restructuring.

ABX.HE is an index of asset-backed securities collateralized by subprime *home equity loans* (HEL). The index comprises five subindexes created by pooling like-rated tranches rated AAA, AA, A, BBB, and BBB–. The first series, 06-01, was launched in January, 2006 and new series are introduced every six months, in January and July. Each series includes 20 HEL ABS reference obligations, chosen by polling a group of global broker-dealers. The index notional amount adjusts as any of the reference entities amortize, prepay, default, or incur write-downs or write-ups. Due to a dearth of subprime issuance in late 2007, the ABX roll scheduled for January 2008 was suspended.

ABX.HE indexes trade with the standardized PAUG template which allows for three floating amount events: write-downs (implied write-downs);

---

[5] Dealers have a vested interest in maintaining some degree of continuity among the series. Hence, many names remain unchanged when an index rolls. Defaulted securities in all indexes and fallen angels in the IG indexes are replaced by new names.

principal shortfalls and interest shortfalls (fixed cap only). Write-downs and principal shortfall events trigger a payment from the protection seller to the protection buyer.

Unlike its investment grade cousins, but similar to the high yield and LCDX—a corporate index of leverage loan CDS—indexes, ABX.HE market quotes are priced based, rather than spread based. At each roll, an initial coupon and price are determined. Because the initial coupon is capped at 5%, the initial price may be set below par. As the market reassesses individual single-name CDS risks, the price deviates from its initial value. When the quoted price is below par, the protection buyer makes an upfront payment of par, minus the index price to the protection seller; if the quoted price is above par, the protection seller makes an upfront payment equal to the index price, minus par to the protection buyer. Over the life of a contract, the protection buyer pays the fixed rate amount established on the roll date to the protection seller, based on the current notional amount of the index. Protection buyers make monthly fixed rate payments on ABX.HE, in contrast to the quarterly payments required on the corporate indexes.

LCDX was launched in May 2007. The term of the index is five years and the market quote convention is price based. The index defines two credit events only, bankruptcy and failure to pay. Copying recent protocols for senior unsecured CDS settlements, the index uses cash settlement via an auction procedure. Provided the LCDX market develops solid liquidity, we expect an increase in the demand for synthetic *collateralized loan obligations* (CLOs). The index was sorely tested as it debuted during the market turmoil of 2007. Like the major investment grade indexes, the LCDX continued to trade but with significantly less liquidity.

New CDS indexes routinely appear. Some succeed, others fail. The most successful indexes are those that are generic enough to appeal to a wide investment audience, yet specific enough to allow for good two-way order flow from hedgers and speculators. In general, indexes that are not representative of the cash market fail as hedging instruments. The broker-dealer community derives significant benefits from successful indexes that are actively traded, because such indexes can be used to hedge inventory.

For single-name CDS, the basis measures the difference between the CDS premium and the reference entity's asset-swap spread. For CDS indexes, the basis measures the difference between the CDS index premium and the (equally) weighted average of the CDS spreads on the underlying reference entities. Arbitrage activities should minimize the basis for an index, but a nonzero basis is possible because of differences in liquidity between the single-name and index CDS markets. A CDS index will head into a self-destructive slide if the basis becomes particularly wide.

Tranches of CDS Indexes

Some CDS indexes (e.g., CDX, iTraxx and ABX) are sliced into *tranches*, replicating a synthetic CDO with the index's reference entities acting as collateral. Index tranches allow broker dealers to offset the risks they incur when they structure transactions for investors who target a particular credit strategy to a specific point in the capital structure. A tranche is defined by *attachment* and *detachment* points. The attachment point defines the amount of subordination the tranche enjoys. The tranche *thickness*, measured by subtracting the attachment point from the detachment point, represents the maximum loss that can be sustained. For example, consider a 3%–7% tranche. This tranche first experiences losses when the index suffers losses in excess of 3% of the notional. The tranche can then withstand losses of an additional 4% (the tranche thickness). As with any standard CDS index, a tranche can be traded after an initial transaction by unwinding the contract or by assigning it to a new counterparty.

Credit events and tranche characteristics such as maturity, payment dates and premium accruals, follow the conventions of the CDS index in question. In general, protection buyers pay sellers either a full running spread or a combination of a *running spread* and an *upfront payment*. The latter convention is commonly used for tranches that are more likely to incur losses, such as the first loss, 0%–3% tranche of an entity the market believes is at risk of bankruptcy. Protection sellers compensate buyers for any losses in the index portfolio that breach the tranche's attachment point. Losses that exceed this attachment point reduce the notional amount of the tranche on which the spread is paid.

As an example, consider the 3%–7% tranche of CDX.IG. The attachment point is 3%, the detachment point is 7% and the tranche width is 4%. Assume the index notional is $1 billion. The tranche would have an initial notional of $40 million. It would start to sustain losses when portfolio losses exceed $30 million (3% of $1 billion). The tranche's notional would be reduced to zero at $70 million losses (7% of $1 billion). It is obvious that tranches with lower attachment points are more likely to sustain losses. To compensate for this risk, spreads tend to be higher on tranches that are lower in the capital structure. For two tranches with the same attachment point but different detachment points, the thinner tranche (i.e., the one with the lower detachment point) faces a higher probability of a complete write-down and is therefore more levered. See Exhibit 11.4.

The distinction between losses and defaults is critical and illustrative of the difference between the ratings of S&P and Moody's. The former rates to the first dollar loss, while the latter rates to expected loss. Tranche attachment and detachment points refer to portfolio losses, not defaults.

EXHIBIT 11.4 Tranche Loss Given Collateral Loss for 3%–7% and 3%–5% Tranches

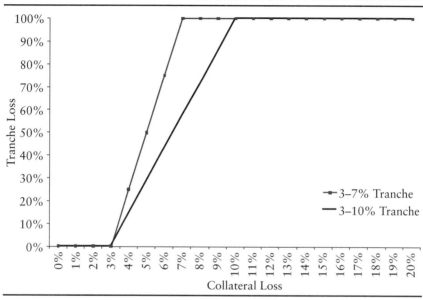

Source: Wachovia Capital Markets.

Assuming a loss given default of 50%, the 3%–7% tranche can withstand defaults of up to 6% of the portfolio (6% × 50% = 3%, the attachment point) before it sustains losses. Since the underlying CDX index aggregates 125 corporate entities, the tranche would experience no cash flow losses for the first seven defaults, though its credit support would shrink from 3% to 0.2% (3% – 50% × 7/125). The eighth default would cause the tranche to lose 5% of its notional [((50% × 8/125) – 3%)/4%]. If 18 defaults occur, the tranche's notional would be entirely wiped out, and the note above the 3%–7% tranche would incur its first dollar loss.

These results are based on a static recovery rate of 50%. In reality, recovery rates tend to be highest during periods of low default and lowest when defaults reach historical peaks (see Chapter 9). The results also offer little information about returns or price volatility. Additional information on the timing of defaults is needed to compute these metrics. Clearly, if all the defaults occur near the end of a contract's life, the protection seller would fare better because she would receive premiums for a longer period of time. For this reason, investors need to consider not only loss expectations, but also the timing of defaults. Correlation is the term used to describe the degree to which defaults are synchronized among collateral names and tranche trading strategies are often called *correlation trades*. We address correlation issues in the final section of this chapter.

EXHIBIT 11.5 Standardized Tranches

	CDX. NA.IG	iTraxx Europe	ABX. HE	TABX.BBB	TABX. BBB–	CMBX. NA
	0%–3%	0%–3%	AAA	0%–3%	0%–5%	AAA
	3%–7%	3%–6%	AA	3%–7%	5%–10%	AA
	7%–10%	6%–9%	A	7%–12%	10%–15%	A
	10%–15%	9%–12%	BBB	12%–20%	15%–25%	BBB
	15%–30%	1%2–22%	BBB–	20%–35%	25%–40%	BBB–
	30%–100%	22%–100%		35%–100%	40%–100%	BB[a]

(Row label: TRANCHES)

[a] BB Tranche added after CMBX.1.
Source: Created from data obtained from Markit.

The most liquid tranches are those on CDX and iTraxx. A list of standard tranches on actively traded indexes is presented in Exhibit 11.5.

Synthetic ABS and CMBS indexes were launched in early 2006. Standardized tranches for these indexes appeared soon after. Thus far, these indexes and tranches have not garnered the same success as their corporate cousins, at least when liquidity is our metric for performance. Although the ABX had a fighting chance for liquidity before the subprime crisis of 2007, there are several reasons why we should expect CDS on structured products to be less liquid, even in the best of times. First, the underlying cash markets are smaller and less liquid than for corporate bonds. Second, the PAUG template necessitates a cash flow model for structured products.

Vendor software is available, but cash flows are extremely sensitive to model assumptions about prepayments. The dealer community was enthusiastic about TABX, a tranched version of ABX, launched in February, 2007. However, TABX has not lived up to expectations, due to its limited diversification and lack of liquidity.

INDEX TRANCHES, SWAPS, SYNTHETIC EQUITY, AND CDOs

A cash flow triggerless CDO resembles a synthetic transaction, but there is at least one major difference when impairments arise. The principal of a synthetic note is written down when collateral losses exceed the attachment point. The protection seller then receives payments on a lower notional amount. In most CDOs (with or without triggers), there is no explicit writedown of principal until the deal matures or is called. Instead, equity gets cut-off from receiving cash flow until the notes above it are made solvent.

The index market is fully aware of this difference and pays the protection seller a higher premium for going long equity (0%–3%) as a pure swap versus selling protection on the index and buying protection above 3% (a synthetic equity position). In our example, the initial full running dividend is 20%, the reference spread is 70 bps and the cost of protection above 3% is 29.9 basis points. The initial dividend for synthetic equity is $13.67 per $100 (100 × 0.70 – 97 × 0.299)/3. Assuming a 45% recovery rate, we see that after seven defaults the equity swap no longer receives a payment. Synthetic equity continues to receive cash flow even after the notes becomes impaired. In contrast, cash flows to the equity tranche of a cash flow CDO (with or without triggers) would cease. See Exhibit 11.6. It follows that the spread between the 0%–3% premium and the synthetic equity premium should decrease with a decline and increase with a rise in default expectation.

Trading Strategies Using Synthetics

Synthetic assets such as single-name CDS (on corporate debt, ABS and CDOs), CDS indexes and CDS index tranches theoretically add to market completeness, allowing investors to hedge against or speculate on fairly nuanced outcomes. Using synthetics, investors can efficiently express macroviews and make relative value (convergence) trades across the capital structure, sectors, geographical regions and vintages. CDO issuers can use synthetics to hedge the ramp-up risk of a cash CDO or as collateral for a synthetic CDO. Investors and dealers may tap the synthetic markets to hedge assets in inventory against spread movements and defaults. We provide a few examples:

- *Express a macroview.* An investor who is bullish on corporate credit spreads can sell protection on CDX; an investor who is bearish on subprime housing risk can buy protection on ABX.
- *Relative value trades across the capital structure (i.e., a correlation trade).* If an investor believes corporate credit risks will shift from equity to mezzanine tranches then he could initiate what is referred to as a correlation trade. For example, he could sell protection on the 0%–3% tranche of CDX and buy protection on the 3%–7% tranche of CDX. The trade could be made indifferent to small changes in reference spread by neutralizing the delta (i.e., by sizing the relative positions so that the net position has a delta equal to zero).[6]
- *Relative value trades across sectors.* An investor who believes senior, secured loans are expensive relative to high-yield (senior, unsecured)

---

[6] In this case, delta measures the sensitivity of a tranche's value to small changes in the spread of the underlying portfolio.

EXHIBIT 11.6 Synthetic Equity versus Pure Swap Equity

Reference Spread 70
Cost of Protection 29.9
Synthetic Equity 13.67
Full Running 20

Defaults	Losses	Reference Notional	Equity Notional	Notes Notional	Note Impairment	Synthetic Equity Dividend	Full Running Dividend
0	0.0%	100.0%	3.0%	97.00%	0.00%	13.67	20.00
1	0.4%	99.6%	2.6%	97.00%	0.00%	13.56	17.07
2	0.9%	99.1%	2.1%	97.00%	0.00%	13.46	14.13
3	1.3%	98.7%	1.7%	97.00%	0.00%	13.36	11.20
4	1.8%	98.2%	1.2%	97.00%	0.00%	13.26	8.27
5	2.2%	97.8%	0.8%	97.00%	0.00%	13.15	5.33
6	2.6%	97.4%	0.4%	97.00%	0.00%	13.05	2.40
7	3.1%	96.9%	0.0%	96.92%	0.08%	12.96	0.00
8	3.5%	96.5%	0.0%	96.48%	0.52%	12.90	0.00
9	4.0%	96.0%	0.0%	96.04%	0.96%	12.84	0.00
10	4.4%	95.6%	0.0%	95.60%	1.40%	12.78	0.00
11	4.8%	95.2%	0.0%	95.16%	1.84%	12.72	0.00
12	5.3%	94.7%	0.0%	94.72%	2.28%	12.66	0.00
13	5.7%	94.3%	0.0%	94.28%	2.72%	12.60	0.00

Source: Wachovia Capital Markets, LLC.

bonds could sell protection on the HY.NA.CDX index while simultaneously buying protection on the LCDX.

- *Relative value trades across geographical sectors.* An investor who believes European growth will be stronger and more stable than U.S. growth could sell protection on iTraxx Europe and buy protection on CDX.NA.IG. A more levered, but less liquid trade would involve going long LEVX and short LCDX.
- *Relative value trades across vintages.* Since structured product indexes reference specific assets that were originated usually within six months of the roll date, it is possible to pit one vintage's performance against another. If an investor believes subprime assets originated in the second half of 2005 are superior to those originated in the second half of 2006, then she could sell protection on ABX 06-01 and buy protection on ABX 07-01.
- *Ramp a CDO.* A CLO manager could quickly gain exposure to a basket of leveraged loans by selling protection on LCDX.
- *Hedge assets against spread movements or default.* An investor who is long an A rated tranche of a mezzanine-ABS CDO could buy protection on that tranche in the single-name CDO CDS market.

Market Dynamics: CDS and CDOs

New-issue CDO spreads are influenced by the demands of long-term investors and the activities of at least three distinct groups: *speculators, hedgers, and arbitrageurs.* Speculators (often hedge funds) may choose to express a bullish (bearish) view on an asset class by selling (buying) protection on a CDS index. Dealers and CDO issuers often hedge their pipelines by taking a short position on a CDS index. Some long-term investors (insurance companies, pension and mutual funds) may be concerned enough about specific issues or systemic risks that they seek to hedge their CDO holdings with a CDS index or single-name CDS.

Meanwhile, arbitrageurs (often dealers and CDO managers) attempt to exploit the price differences between the cash and synthetic markets. However, the "arbitrage" opportunities in structured products markets are never without risk; markets can freeze, bid-ask spreads can widen and basis risk cannot be completely eliminated. See Exhibit 11.7.

It is common to fixate on one dominant group that seems to be moving the market. In reality, every trade involves two parties, often with opposing views. In general, when bearish sentiment is strong, CDS spreads trade wide to cash and synthetic bid-ask spreads widen. When bullish sentiment dominates, CDS spreads trade tight to cash and the bid-ask spread narrows. CDO cash spreads are stickier than CDS spreads or index prices because it

EXHIBIT 11.7   Market Participants

Group	Dominant Members	Position
Hedgers	Dealers, CDO issuers; long-term investors	Short CDS and CDS indexes
Speculators	Hedge funds and other short-term investors	Long (short) CDS indexes
Arbitrageurs	Dealers, CDO managers	Short (long) CDS indexes; long cash

Source: Wachovia Capital Markets, LLC.

is not possible to take a short position in the cash market. Hence, CDO cash spreads tend to lag the synthetic markets.

SYNTHETIC CDOs

A synthetic CDO is created by marrying CDO technology to a basket of CDS contracts. The first synthetic CDOs appeared around 1997. The structures quickly gained favor as a means to manage bank lending activities and "cleanup" a bank's balance sheet. Issuers could free up capital by selling to investors the risk of default on a portfolio of loans. Many of the original synthetic issues were *blind pools*, meaning investors were only given limited information on the portfolio's attributes. Several downgrades later, investors insisted on full disclosure. The market soon evolved from supply-driven balance sheet transactions to demand-driven "arbitrage" issues, in which the collateral exposure was achieved via secondary or syndicated market purchases, rather than through primary market issuance.

In a synthetic CDO, a *special purpose vehicle* (SPV) serves as the intermediary between buyers and sellers of credit risk. In contrast to cash CDOs, the SPV acquires risk via CDS contracts instead of cash assets.[7] The SPV sells protection on a reference basket of assets to a *sponsor* (or *arranger*) and receives a premium for the risk it assumes. The SPV then distributes the credit risk to different tranches, which receive a portion of the premium based on how much risk they assume.

In a *fully funded* transaction, the sponsor raises capital from note investors and purchases eligible floating rate collateral such as cash, government securities or *guaranteed investment contracts* (GICs) issued by highly rated insurance companies or structured products. Cash flows from the collateral and the default swap premiums are then distributed to CDO investors, either

---

[7] Cash flow CDOs often allow synthetic collateral buckets of 20% to 30%; some cash flow issues contain an unfunded super senior tranche. In hybrid transactions, CDS buckets can be much larger, up to 60% of the collateral pool.

sequentially, from the top of the capital structure to the bottom, or on a pro-rated basis. Equity investors are essentially selling protection on a collateral pool and simultaneously buying protection above a particular detachment level from note investors. Note investors are entering into a swap agreement which pays them LIBOR plus a fixed premium on a notional amount. That notional amount is reduced to zero if losses exceed the detachment point. See Exhibit 11.8.

When a credit event occurs for any asset in the collateral pool, the SPV pays the protection buyer an amount linked to the loss incurred on the asset. The loss is then passed on to investors in reverse order of seniority, with the junior most tranche absorbing the first loss. A tranche's risk profile is a function of its attachment and detachment points. As with index tranches such as CDX, the attachment point defines the amount of subordination a tranche enjoys before it is subject to its first dollar loss. A tranche's notional amount declines with each dollar loss above its attachment point. The detachment point defines the total collateral losses that need to occur for a tranche to incur a complete loss of principal. Tranche thickness, the difference between the detachment and attachment points, defines the total losses a tranche can

EXHIBIT 11.8 A Synthetic CDO

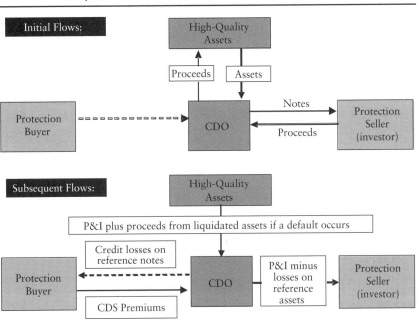

Source: Wachovia Capital Markets, LLC.

withstand. As previously stated, given the same attachment points, the thinner a tranche, the more levered it is.

In a fully funded transaction, investors may be exposed to dealer counterparty risk (if the collateral securitizing a transaction is held by the dealer), or monoline counterparty risk (if funds are invested in a GIC issued by a monoline). Some transactions are structured as *total return swaps* (TRS), in which dealers may gain or lose with a positive or negative total return. Most funded synthetic CDOs are actually partially funded. The interest income received by investing the proceeds, plus the premium income from the CDS contracts that are written, form the money available to pay interest to the funded note holders and premiums to the unfunded tranches.

Compared to cash CDOs, synthetic CDOs enjoy many advantages. First, ramp-up is instantaneous and originators are not limited to assets that can be physically sourced. Hence, synthetic CDOs can select securities from the entire universe of assets. Second, sourcing assets synthetically delivers efficiencies, such as cheaper funding costs for super-senior tranches. Third, investors can take short positions in CDS contracts and these short buckets can be used to mitigate systemic credit risks. Fourth, synthetic assets eliminate the interest-rate and prepayment risks of cash assets and can therefore simplify a foreign investor's efforts to hedge currency risks with swaps. Fifth, synthetic CDOs enjoy simplified structures with no complex waterfalls or triggers.

Synthetic CDOs may pose additional challenges. First, synthetic tranches are classified as derivatives and most investors must mark-to-market these transactions. High volatility can result in dramatic marks and decreased liquidity, which can discourage certain investors from participating in synthetic CDOs. Second, compared to cash CDOs, synthetic CDOs may be penalized by the more liberal credit event definitions used in PAUG templates for ABS and CDOs. Write-downs, distressed rating triggers and certain PIK events may result in losses that are front-loaded compared to cash assets.

Bespoke Transactions

The creation of a liquid market for index tranches facilitated the development of *bespokes*. These are synthetic CDOs in which an investor chooses the names in the reference portfolio, as well as the attachment and detachment points.[8] The simplicity of determining tranche losses, given collateral losses, has contributed to popularity of bespoke investing. We would go one step further and say that simplicity gives transparency a fighting chance.

---

[8] Strictly speaking, the term bespoke can be used to differentiate single tranche CDOs from full capital structure deals; it can also be used to distinguish CDO tranches from index tranches or managed deals, which use standard portfolios.

Cash CDOs, which rely on a waterfall mechanism and various quality and coverage tests, require elaborate models to determine note cash flows.[9]

A bespoke transaction can be structured as a swap between an investor and an arranger (dealer). The arranger does not need to raise proceeds to purchase the collateral portfolio. In theory, the investor chooses the credits and decides on the attachment and detachment points. In reality, the dealer has a good deal of input when it comes to credit selection. Most dealers offset their risks with short positions in CDX indexes and they have limited interest in buying protection on illiquid names not found in an index.

Initially, most bespoke CDOs were *static* (the collateral pool was fixed). Now, investors are looking to managers to not only do the credit selection but to trade in and out of the underlying credits in order to exploit opportunities or avoid downgrades.

CORRELATION

Consider an index portfolio of 100 investment-grade corporate bonds. Assume the underlying average spread on the bonds is 100 basis points over LIBOR. Suppose we tranche the index into three slices: equity, mezzanine and senior notes, with attachment/detachments points of 0%–10%, 10%–30%, and 30%–100%, respectively. Note that the 100 basis point spread on the collateral is shared unequally among the tranches, with equity receiving the lion's share of the spread (53 basis points), mezzanine notes receiving a smaller share (26 basis points), and the senior notes receiving the smallest share (21 basis points).

The average spread tells us something about the expected number of defaults for the portfolio. The tranche spreads tell us something about the degree to which individual bond defaults are synchronized. In this example, risk is concentrated in the equity tranche, so the underlying individual bonds are not terribly likely to default en masse. See Exhibit 11.9.

Correlation measures the degree to which cross-sectional defaults are synchronized.[10] With high correlations, defaults are synchronized; con-

---

[9] Most cash flow CDOs have a minimum of two sets of coverage tests: *overcollateralization* (OC) tests and *interest coverage* (IC) tests. The tests are structured to protect the senior classes in the event of default or poor management. Generally the test trigger levels depend on the quality of the portfolio and the amount of leverage in an issue. These triggers act as covenants and, when tripped, redirect equity cash flow to pay down the principal of the most senior outstanding notes.

[10] Strictly speaking, correlation measures the relationship between pairs of random variables, such as corporate bond default times. Most CDO and synthetic pricing models assume a common correlation value for all pairs of assets within a sector. Hence, we speak of one correlation metric for a portfolio of like assets.

EXHIBIT 11.9   Tranche Spreads

Attach – Detach Point	0%–10%	10%–30%	30%–100%	Total[a]
Spread	530	130	30	
Spread × Thickness	53	26	21	100

[a] Total spread equals the sum of the products of the spreads and the tranche thicknesses.
Source: Wachovia Capital Markets, LLC.

ditional on one default, other defaults are likely. With low correlations, defaults are not synchronized. Correlation says nothing about the probability of default; it is entirely possible to have low default rates and high correlations. Correlation is an indication of market sentiment on the distribution of risk across the capital structure. Portfolios with low correlation will have risk concentrated in equity tranches, whereas portfolios with high correlations allocate more risk to mezzanine and senior notes.

Assume that each of 100 corporate bonds in our index has a 5% probability of defaulting over the next year. Suppose the bonds are essentially identical. Then, they are perfectly correlated, and there are only two possible outcomes: either all 100 bonds default or none default. With perfect correlation, the probability of 100 defaults is 5% and the probability of 0 defaults is 95%. Note that the expected number of default is five $[(100 \times 0.05) + (0 \times 0.95)]$, but the average fails to capture the extreme dispersion in outcomes. With 100% correlation, the outcome is highly variable (or volatile).

Now assume each bond is unique and default behavior is independent. With zero correlation, the probability of 100 defaults is 0.05^{100} and the probability of 0 defaults is 0.95^{100}, both low probability events. Most of the probability distribution is in fact centered around the mean number of defaults, which is still five.[11] With 0% correlation, the outcome has low dispersion, or low volatility. See Exhibit 11.10.

Default correlations are usually positive for most pairs of assets because systemic risks, such as the risk of a liquidity crisis, recession, or inflationary spike, impact most assets similarly (in the same direction). Continuing with our example, suppose investors reassess the financial landscape and conclude that default correlations will increase going forward. Assume total risk does not change; hence there is no change in the average spread of the index. Then, what we have is a repricing of risk across the capital structure. With higher correlations, there is an increased chance that senior notes will incur a loss. There is also an increased chance that equity will be spared

---

[11] The total number of defaults follows a binomial distribution, with p, the probability of default equal to 5% and n, the number of trials, equal to 100.

EXHIBIT 11.10   Probability Distribution for Total Defaults

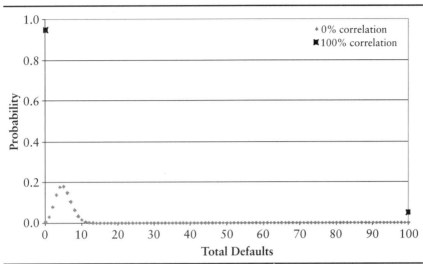

Source: Wachovia Capital Markets, LLC.

a poor outcome. In our example, spreads on equity could fall to 390 and spreads on senior notes could rise to 50.

Holding total spreads (or average risk) constant, an increase in correlation is a positive outcome for a long equity position (i.e., spreads fall and prices rise) and a negative outcome for a long senior note position (i.e., spreads rise). In our example, the mezzanine tranche faces no price change, but this outcome is by design.

Now assume we move in the opposite direction and investors conclude that default correlations will decline going forward. If total risk remains unchanged, then risk is reallocated across the capital structure, with spreads on equity rising to 600 and spreads on senior notes falling to 20. Holding total spreads (or average risk) constant, a decrease in correlation would lower the value of a long equity position (i.e., spreads rise) and raise the value of a long senior note position (i.e., spreads fall). Again, in our example, we have arbitrarily assumed no change in the risk of mezzanine tranches. See Exhibit 11.11.

Default correlations are not static. They rise and fall with the economic cycle. During good times, *idiosyncratic risks* tend to dominate *systemic risks* and correlations are low. During bad times, systemic risks dominate and correlations tend to rise. In general, we don't see large correlation moves without coincident large moves in spreads. This is because the macroeconomic factors that affect correlation also affect credit spread. However,

EXHIBIT 11.11 Tranche Spreads under Different Correlation Assumptions

Attach–Detach Point	0%–10%	10%–30%	30%–100%	Total[a]
Base-case spread	530	130	30	100
High-correlation spread	390	130	50	100
Low-correlation spread	600	130	20	100

[a] Total spread equals the sum of the products of the spreads and the tranche thicknesses.
Source: Wachovia Capital Markets, LLC.

due to technical factors related to bespoke issuance and hedging activities, CDOs may occasionally experience a significant repricing of correlation. On the whole, equity tranches provide investors exposure to idiosyncratic risks and senior tranches provide exposure to marketwide systemic risks.

In our contrived example, the mezzanine tranche is correlation independent. Generally, this tends to be true for small moves in correlation. For larger correlation shifts, the mezzanine tranche resembles a chameleon. When spreads widen dramatically, the mezzanine tranche behaves as equity; when spreads tighten dramatically, the mezzanine tranche behaves as senior notes.

Option valuation models such as the Black-Scholes model allow us to solve for an implied volatility, given an option price. In CDO pricing, default correlation functions in a similar way.[12] For equity options, volatility is directly observable and hedgeable. In contrast, default correlation is neither observable nor hedgeable in single tranche CDOs. Moreover, correlation risk can be quite significant.

A *term structure of correlation* can be estimated by fixing the tranche (attachment and detachment point combination) and solving for base correlation values for different maturities. The term structure tells us something about the expected timing of defaults. If the term structure is upward sloping, then defaults are expected to be more clustered for longer maturities. In other words, conditional on a no-default outcome at a point in time, the probability of default increases with time. If the term structure of credit spreads is flat, and the term structure of equity correlation is upward sloping, then equity's share of the reference spread will decline with maturity.

---

[12] A distinction is made between tranche (compound) correlation and *base correlation*. With base correlation pricing, correlations are computed for contiguous segments, from the bottom tranche up. In our example, we could compute correlations for three segments: 0%–10%, 0%–30% and 0%–100%. In general, the curve of correlations obtained by calibrating to the first loss tranche is more stable than that obtained by computing correlations for detached segments.

SUMMARY

Several forces have combined to fuel the growth of credit derivatives. These include capital market integration, deregulation, increased cross-border flows of capital and dramatic wealth creation. Though liquidity crises, protectionist measures and concerns about counterparty risk may inhibit growth and lead to temporary market shutdowns, derivative assets are here to stay.

Credit derivatives serve a need. They make it easier for investors to target specific investment or risk-reduction strategies. Going forward, we can expect a flurry of innovation and the creation of many new products. Some products will succeed and others will likely fail. Investors should strive to keep abreast of credit derivative markets as these assets increasingly influence the pricing and trading behavior of fixed-income cash assets.

APPENDIX A: INDEX ELIGIBILITY RULES

CDX.NA.IG

125 entities domiciled in North America.

Senior unsecured debt rated investment grade by two of S&P, Fitch, and Moody's.

Outstanding debt and CDS contract must remain liquid.

Entity must not have a merger or corporate action that makes it no longer eligible.

Guaranteed affiliates of a CDX.NA.IG entity are NOT eligible.

CDX.NA.XO

35 entities either domiciled in North America or with a majority of outstanding bonds and loans denominated in US$.

Outstanding debt and CDS contract must remain liquid.

Entity must not have a merger or corporate action that makes it no longer eligible.

An eligible rating defined as follows:

1. A crossover (7B) rating: BBB/Baa by S&P, Fitch, and Moody's, and BB/Ba by the other two agencies.
2. A 6B Rating: BB/Ba rating by S&P, Fitch, and Moody's.
3. BB/Ba rating by one or two of S&P, Fitch, and Moody's, and no rating by the other(s).

CDX.NA.HVOL

30 entities within DJ CDX.NA.IG that voting members consider the most volatile.

CDX.NA.HY

100 entities rated below investment grade by two or more of S&P, Fitch, and Moody's.
North America domiciled entities.
Entity must not be defaulted.
Guaranteed affiliates of a CDX.NA.HY entity are not eligible.
Outstanding debt and CDS contract must remain liquid.
Entity must not have a merger or corporate action that makes it no longer eligible.

LCDX.NA

100 syndicated secured first-lien loans, as defined by ISDA.
Guaranteed affiliates of a LCDX.NA entity are not eligible.
Outstanding loans and LCDS contract must remain liquid.
Entity must not have a merger or corporate action that makes it no longer eligible.

ABX.HE

20 residential MBS bonds that include tranches with ratings of AAA, AA, A, BBB, and BBB–.
Issued and settled within six months of the roll date.
Deal size (at issuance) must be at least $500 million.
At least 90% of the assets backing the transaction must be first lien.
Weighted average obligor FICO score can not exceed 660 at issuance.
Payment dates must be the 25th calendar day of the month.
AAA tranche must have WAL greater than five years (at issuance) and must have longest WAL of all tranches with the same priority.
Other tranches must have WAL greater than four years, based on pricing speed at issuance.
AAA tranche must have principal amount of $15 million at issuance.
No tranche may be insured or guaranteed by a third party.
Max of five deals per originator/six deals per master servicer.
Floating rate, with reference rate as one-month LIBOR.
Identity and principal economic terms must be listed on Bloomberg.
Be rated by Moody's and S&P; lesser of rating applies.

TABX

Two subindexes: TABX.BBB and TABX.BBB–.

40 Entities consisting of BBB (or BBB–) rated reference obligations in BBB or (BBB–) tranche of the ABX.HE for the roll date, and the ABX.HE for the roll date immediately prior.

CMBX.NA

25 reference entities that are CMBS offerings and include tranches of AAA, AA, A, BBB, BBB—and BB (as rated by two of the three rating agencies, S&P, Fitch, and Moody's).

Must be publicly rated by two of S&P, Fitch, and Moody's.

Required tranche at each rating will be tranche with the most credit support at that rating, and with the longest WAL of similarly rated tranches with equal credit support.

Collateral can not be credit-linked notes or synthetic obligations.

Issue must be more than $700 million.

Triple-A class must be greater than $100 million and have a WAL between 8 to 12 years, using 0% CPY as of solicitation date.

Reference entity must contain at least 50 separate mortgages that are obligations of at least 10 nonaffiliated borrowers.

One state can not represent more than 40% of aggregate value of underlying properties.

No single real estate type can represent more than 60% of aggregate value of the underlying properties.

No tranche may be insured or guaranteed by a third party.

Identity and principal economic terms must be listed on Bloomberg.

Current factor of one as of roll date.

USD-denominated and fixed-rate obligations.

iTraxx Europe

Selects the top-125 European entities by CDS volume for the six months prior to roll date, subject to sector weightings.

Must be rated investment grade by S&P, Fitch, or Moody's. If reference obligation is rated by two or more agencies, lowest rating is considered.

Excludes entities rated Baa3/BBB– with negative outlook.

Guaranteed affiliates of an iTraxx entity are not eligible.

Final portfolio selected by choosing entities with highest trading volume, as broken down by sector:

10 Auto
30 Consumer
20 Energy
20 Industrials
20 TMT
25 Financial

iTraxx Crossover

50 nonfinancial European entities with > €100 million in publicly traded debt.

Reference obligations rated BBB—with stable outlook or higher are ineligible. If reference obligation is rated by two or more agencies, lowest rating is considered.

Guaranteed affiliates of an iTraxx Crossover entity are not eligible.

Eligible entities have five-year CDS spreads equal to or greater than twice the average spread of the iTraxx Non-Financial Index underlying entities on the last trading day of the month prior to index roll.

50 most traded entities meeting spread requirements are selected.

Source: Markit.

APPENDIX B: THE MECHANICS OF CASH SETTLEMENT

Calpine Price Auction from 17 Jan 06, administered by Creditex/Markit

Step 1. Dealers submit bids and offers.

Dealer	Bid	Offer	Dealer
Banc of America Securities, LLC	19.500	21.500	Banc of America Securities, LLC
Bear, Stearns & Co., Inc.	18.250	20.250	Bear, Stearns & Co., Inc.
Credit Suisse First Boston, LLC	19.500	21.500	Credit Suisse First Boston, LLC
Citigroup Global Markets, Inc.	19.125	21.125	Citigroup Global Markets, Inc.
Deutsche Bank Securities, Inc.	18.750	20.750	Deutsche Bank Securities, Inc.
Goldman, Sachs & Co.	19.000	21.000	Goldman, Sachs & Co.
J.P. Morgan Securities, Inc.	18.250	20.250	J.P. Morgan Securities, Inc.
Lehman Brothers, Inc.	19.000	21.000	Lehman Brothers, Inc.
Merrill Lynch, Pierce, Fenner & Smith, Inc.	20.125	22.125	Merrill Lynch, Pierce, Fenner & Smith, Inc.
Morgan Stanley & Co. Inc.	18.250	20.250	Morgan Stanley & Co., Inc.
UBS Securities, LLC	20.250	22.250	UBS Securities, LLC

Step 2. Bids are sorted highest to lowest. Offers are sorted lowest to highest.

Dealer	Bid	Offer	Dealer
UBS Securities, LLC	20.250	20.250	JPMorgan Securities, Inc.
Merrill Lynch, Pierce, Fenner & Smith, Inc.	20.125	20.250	Bear, Stearns & Co., Inc.
Credit Suisse First Boston, LLC	19.500	20.250	Morgan Stanley & Co., Inc.
Banc of America Securities, LLC	19.500	20.750	Deutsche Bank Securities, Inc.
Citigroup Global Markets, Inc.	19.125	21.000	Goldman, Sachs & Co.
Lehman Brothers, Inc.	19.000	21.000	Lehman Brothers, Inc.
Goldman, Sachs & Co.	19.000	21.125	Citigroup Global Markets, Inc.
Deutsche Bank Securities, Inc.	18.750	21.500	Banc of America Securities, LLC
Morgan Stanley & Co., Inc.	18.250	21.500	Credit Suisse First Boston, LLC
JPMorgan Securities, Inc.	18.250	22.125	Merrill Lynch, Pierce, Fenner & Smith, Inc.
Bear, Stearns & Co., Inc.	18.250	22.250	UBS Securities, LLC

Step 3. Tradeable markets (Bid $\geq$ Offer) are identified.

Dealer	Bid	Offer	Dealer
UBS Securities, LLC	20.250	20.250	JPMorgan Securities. Inc.

Step 4. Trade is executed.

Dealer	Bid	Offer	Dealer
UBS Securities, LLC	20.250	20.250	JPMorgan Securities. Inc.

Step 5. Best pairs are averaged. Midpoint of average is inside market midpoint.

Dealer	Bid	Offer	Dealer
Merrill Lynch, Pierce, Fenner & Smith, Inc.	20.125	20.250	Bear, Stearns & Co., Inc.
Credit Suisse First Boston, LLC	19.500	20.250	Morgan Stanley & Co., Inc.
Banc of America Securities, LLC	19.500	20.750	Deutsche Bank Securities, Inc.
Citigroup Global Markets, Inc.	19.125	21.000	Goldman, Sachs & Co.
Lehman Brothers, Inc.	19.000	21.000	Lehman Brothers, Inc.
Goldman, Sachs & Co.	19.000	21.125	Citigroup Global Markets, Inc.
Deutsche Bank Securities, Inc.	18.750	21.500	Banc of America Securities, LLC
Morgan Stanley & Co., Inc.	18.250	21.500	Credit Suisse First Boston, LLC
JPMorgan Securities, Inc.	18.250	22.125	Merrill Lynch, Pierce, Fenner & Smith, Inc.
Bear, Stearns & Co., Inc.	18.250	22.250	UBS Securities, LLC
Average =	19.450	20.650	
Inside market midpoint =	20.050		

Note: Inside market midpoint is used as final price only under these conditions :
a) No unmatched market orders (zero open interest).
b) Open interest is on offer side, and last matched limit BID > Inside market midpoint.
c) Open interest is on bid side, and last matched limit Offer < Inside market midpoint.
Additionally, limit orders more than 15% of par from inside market midpoint are disregarded.

Step 6. Open interest is calculated

Market order bids = $16 million

Market order offers = $61 million

Open interest = $45 million (on the offer side)

Step 7. Open interest is matched with submitted limit order bids.

Dealer	Limit Bid	Quote Amount ($ millions)	
UBS Securities, LLC[a]	20.25	10	
Merrill Lynch, Pierce, Fenner & Smith, Inc.[b]	20.125	10	
Goldman, Sachs & Co.	20	2	Total = $44 millions
Credit Suisse First Boston, LLC[a]	19.5	10	
Banc of America Securities, LLC[a]	19.5	10	
Goldman, Sachs & Co.	19.25	2	
Citigroup Global Markets, Inc.[a]	19.125	10	$1 millions of the $10 millions bid is taken to sum to $45 millions
Goldman, Sachs & Co.[a]	19	10	
Lehman Brothers, Inc.[a]	19	10	

[a] These limit bids result from inside market submissions by the dealer.

Step 8. All limit orders are filled. Therefore, no second auction is needed. 19.125 is the final matched limit order bid and therefore is fixed as the final price.

Source: Markit.

CHAPTER 12

CDO Performance

Steven Todd, Ph.D.
CDO Analyst
Wachovia Capital Markets, LLC

Brian McManus
Senior CDO Analyst
Wachovia Capital Markets, LLC

Anik Ray
Associate CDO Analyst
Wachovia Capital Markets, LLC

Dave Preston, CFA
Associate CDO Analyst
Wachovia Capital Markets, LLC

nvestors in *collateralized debt obligations* (CDOs) routinely ask research analysts to evaluate asset managers. However, it is difficult for any Wall Street analyst to produce a comprehensive report on asset managers. Analysts generally have limited access to data on CDO issues that were not underwritten in-house. In fact, investors themselves often have more complete return data, albeit manager supplied and therefore subject to spin.

Even if comprehensive data were available, there would be little consensus on how managers should be ranked. Note holders view manager performance very differently than do equity investors. Moreover, managers' track records are subject to a vintage bias. Managers who entered the market in 2003 probably have fewer problems with downgrades or poor equity cash flows than do those who began before 1999. Yet these later-entry managers often lack the experience of more seasoned ones who have survived one of the worst periods of credit defaults in history.

This chapter aims to examine the issue of how CDO managers can be evaluated. Along the way, we provide investors a toolkit to appraise CDOs as potential or current investments. We examine some of the challenges in comparing managers, including timing biases and the lack of benchmarks. Investors should also be aware of the conflicting interests of note and equity holders, and how a manager's interest can be aligned with a particular investor class. By using historical rating transition data, and equity cash flow studies, we hope to provide a more complete picture of investor concerns when examining CDOs. Finally, we detail the rating agencies' various reports and research, and how these materials can aid portfolio managers in assessing their CDO investments.

UPGRADE/DOWNGRADE STATISTICS SUFFER FROM A VINTAGE BIAS

When the first structures began showing problems, the investor community reacted by evaluating managers based on the downgrades experienced by note holders. Exhibit 12.1 shows the number of S&P rating actions by vintage, as of March 30, 2007. Since S&P downgraded no collateralized loan

EXHIBIT 12.1   Downgrades by Vintage

	Cash Flow HY CBO		Cash Flow HY CLO		ABS CDO		Corporate Synthetics	
Vintage	UG	DG	UG	DG	UG	DG	UG	DG
1996	0	6	1	1	0	0	0	0
1997	6	43	4	1	0	0	0	0
1998	28	75	12	6	0	6	0	12
1999	76	195	24	0	0	0	14	22
2000	54	99	9	0	3	44	17	36
2001	5	29	4	0	29	96	54	159
2002	2	0	0	0	57	87	94	48
2003	0	0	0	0	36	15	126	100
2004	0	0	0	0	53	1	82	105
2005	0	0	0	0	1	1	52	167
2006	0	0	4	0	23	0	24	251
2007	0	0	0	0	0	0	0	6
Total	171	447	58	8	202	250	450	904

Note: UG–upgrade, DG–downgrade.
Source: Standard & Poor's.

obligations notes issued after 1998, it is clear that managers who entered the market post 1998 have enjoyed impressive records.

Some managers may attempt to defend their inexperience by claiming they did not see value in an asset. According to *Moody's Equity Score Report, CDO Deal Summary Performance,* February 2007 (May 8, 2007) every 1997 vintage *collateralized bond obligation* (CBO) covered has ceased paying equity holders; the top-performing issue generated only 81.1% of the original investment. Moreover, of the high-yield CBO tranches S&P rated in 1997, downgrades were seven times as prevalent as upgrades. Was it bad luck or poor judgment to have issued a high-yield CBO in 1997? In hindsight, it may seem far-fetched that the market could have gobbled up all of the business-plan telecom bond deals of the late 1990s. It was, nonetheless, a revolutionary time in technology growth, and it was easy to be seduced by the latest fad.

Measuring manager performance is a bit like comparing college ball teams that play in different leagues. Is the undefeated team the best, or should we consider the strength of schedule? A team with a strong tradition but a weak schedule will typically command more respect than a newcomer with anything but a strong schedule.

RETURN PERFORMANCE DATA MAY NOT BE INFORMATIVE

What is a reasonable strategy for selecting managers? We might focus on past performance, if we believe past performance is useful in predicting future performance. It turns out that assessing past performance is no easy matter. First, access to return data is limited. Second, which performance should we measure—equity returns, note returns or upgrade/downgrade ratios? Even if we are able to assess past performance, we may still find that past performance is useless when it comes to predicting future performance. Winners may not repeat, either because the personnel of winning teams changes over time or because winning in the management game may come down to luck, rather than skill.

WHAT DOES THE MARKET TELL US ABOUT MANAGERS?

Differences in new issue spreads on similarly rated CLO notes offered around the same time suggest that there are some signs of either manager or structural tiering at the subordinated note level. One might assume that poor-performing or inexperienced managers would be priced out of the market because they would face higher funding costs (and consequently lower equity returns). During volatile times, tiering increases, whereas during stable periods, it decreases. Thus, it is during stable periods that the number of first-time managers increases. In 2006, the market for CDO managers grew rapidly, with Fitch reporting nearly 200 management teams, some completely new to the market.[1] Focusing on new-issue spreads alone may not convey the true degree of manager tiering for several reasons:

1. Although a CDO is subject to quality and coverage tests and has other covenants restricting investment choices, there is still plenty of wiggle room when it comes to reaching for asset yield. A naïve equity investor may overlook this detail when comparing one expected yield to another.
2. An aggressive underwriter may subsidize the transaction by holding inventory that could jeopardize a portion of its banking fees. New-issue spreads are derived from initial coupons, yet poorly received deals could sit in a dealer's inventory and end up selling at a discount. This is the same risk any underwriter willing to issue a CDO in a soft market must assume, be it with a tier-one or tier-three manager. Of course, dealers want to avoid this fate, so they do their best to determine the fair market value during price talk.
3. Some debutante managers are willing to take down all of the equity and, in some cases, the lower-rated mezzanine notes as well. High demand for senior notes can still create an attractive leveraged investment.

Ultimately, funding costs may not differ all that much across managers because most of the spread-widening attributable to manager tiering occurs at the BBB level and below, and these tranches represent a small portion of the capital structure.

Manager tiering would seem to be consistent with managerial skill. Yet, even if all market players agreed that performance is driven by luck, rather than skill, we would argue that price differences across managers would still persist. Investors are paying not just for a manager's credit-picking skills but also for a manager's trading muscle. Bigger or more experienced fund managers may enjoy better execution, lower bid-ask spreads, better access to information, and size discounts.

The largest managers often enjoy better allocations in hot deals. If a sponsor has too many deals in the market, however, some investors complain that the manager is forced to "buy the market." Tiering might also be related to experience. Investors might expect experienced managers to perform better than inexperienced managers during periods of transition. The experience of

---

[1] See "CDO Managers Are Proliferating at Breakneck Pace," *Structured Finance Weekly*, July 17, 2006. Notwithstanding the explosive growth in CDO manager rosters, the CDO market has spawned more than a few one-trick ponies—those managers who do one transaction and then exit, stage left, because of poor performance. In rare cases, a management team is replaced.

having lived through a significant increase in corporate defaults might provide valuable knowledge that managers can use in subsequent credit downturns. Finally, tiering could be a proxy for infrastructure investments. Managing a CDO requires at least a minimum investment in infrastructure, including technology, communications, data, credit analysis expertise, and the like.

If CDO managers added no value, they could be replaced by computers. The fact that we have not seen this outcome in the marketplace suggests that managers do add value. Unlike computers, managers can strategize and learn. Moreover, the movement toward managed synthetic transactions suggests that investors are willing to pay managers for their credit-picking skills.

SOME CASE STUDIES

Absent a metric for precisely ranking managers or structures, investors can learn a great deal from anecdotal evidence. Exhibit 12.2 illustrates the dangers of ignoring vintage effects. Here, we chart cumulative cash flow returns to equity based on Intex cash flows for all outstanding 2002–2005 vintage CLOs reported in the January 2007 Moody's CDO Index report.[2] Equity cash flow data quickly becomes outdated, and this analysis is an attempt to show vintage effects, as well as illustrating a method for examining performance. The horizontal axis measures the number of quarters that have elapsed since an issue closed. The exhibit clearly demonstrates that cash-on-cash returns vary by vintage. Controlling for aging effects, CLOs issued in 2002 generated higher equity returns than those issued in 2003 or 2004.[3]

Exhibits 12.3 and 12.4 display the equity cash flows for *asset-backed securities* (ABS) CDOs as of January 2007. As with Exhibit 12.2 which displays CLO equity cash flows, the cash flows are for all outstanding 2002–2005 vintage deals based on the Moody's CDO Index report. Exhibit 12.3 shows the equity cash flow for deals with a *weighted average rating factor* (WARF) greater than 100—primarily midgrade and *mezzanine* (Mezz) ABS CDOs. Exhibit 12.4 displays the equity cash flow for high-grade (HG) deals, which have a WARF below 100. In Mezz ABS CDOs, the 2004 vintage has shown higher equity returns than any other vintage, as of January 2007. In HG ABS CDOs, the cash flows for vintages are significantly more clustered, showing a smaller vintage bias than any other type of CDO. As of January 2007, the 2005 vintage shows the highest return, a result of being at the sweet

---

[2] Moody's Investors Service, *Collateralized Debt Obligations Indices: January 2007*, April 2, 2007.

[3] In fact, the 2000 and 2001 vintages outperformed CLOs issued in 2002. Those earlier vintages benefited from a wider funding gap. For additional information on CLO equity performance, see Moody's Investors Service, *Moody's Equity Score Report, CDO Deal Summary Performance.*

EXHIBIT 12.2 CLO Equity Cash Flows versus Vintage as of January 2007

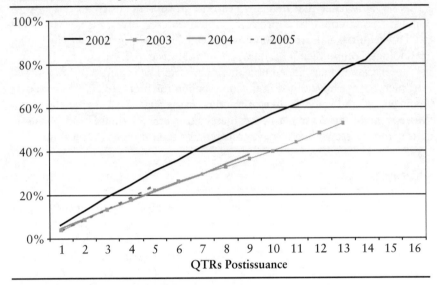

Source: Intex and Wachovia Capital Markets, LLC.

EXHIBIT 12.3 Mezz ABS CDO Equity Cash Flow versus Vintage as of January 2007

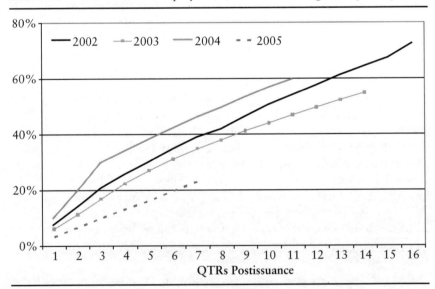

Source: Intex and Wachovia Capital Markets, LLC.

EXHIBIT 12.4   HG ABS CDO Equity Cash Flow versus Vintage as of January 2007

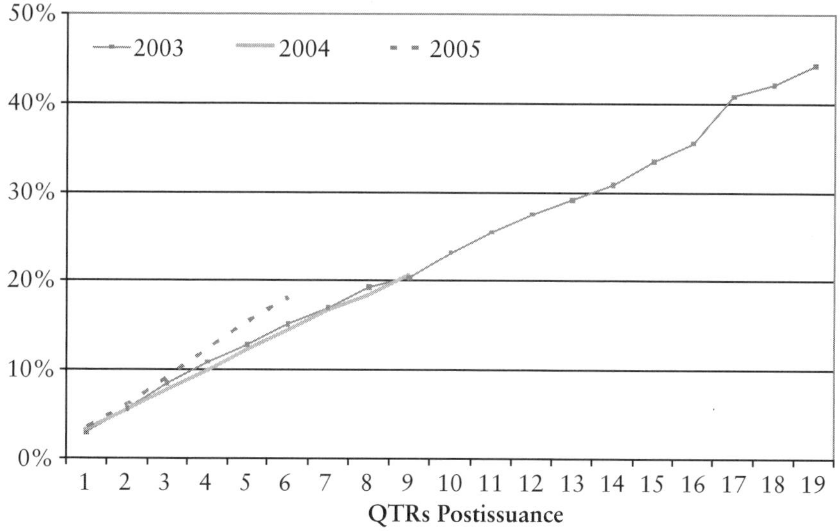

Source: Intex and Wachovia Capital Markets, LLC.

point for locking in a wide funding gap. Although collateral spreads tightened from 2004 to 2005, ABS CDO funding costs fell at a more rapid pace.

We attempt to isolate manager differences by focusing on the cross-sectional variation of CLO equity cash flows in Exhibit 12.5. Here we plot dividend yields based on the most recently reported equity cash flows, sorted by issue and deal closing date (horizontal axis) and grouped by CLO manager. We focus on the 10 largest CLO managers. Four points merit discussion. First, the exhibit clearly demonstrates that equity cash flows are front loaded.[4] As of 2007: 1Q, the earlier vintage deals (issued before 2004) were paying dividend yields of 6% to 17%, whereas later vintage deals (those issued in 2005) were currently paying dividend yields of 7% to 25%. All of the deals we analyzed were in their reinvestment periods, and deal expenses, which typically lower equity cash flows during the first two quarters after a deal closes, do not affect any of the deals we plot. Second, there is considerable variation in equity dividend yields across CLO issues grouped by closing date. For example, focusing on those CLOs that closed around Febuary 17, 2005, we find a range of equity dividend cash flows of 9% to

---

[4] This result comports with findings by Standard & Poor's that CLO equity cash flows typically peak one year after issuance. See Standard & Poor's *CDO Spotlight: First Study of U.S. CDO Equity Performance Highlights Payment Trends*, September 12, 2005.

EXHIBIT 12.5   CLO Equity Cash Flows as of 2007: 1Q

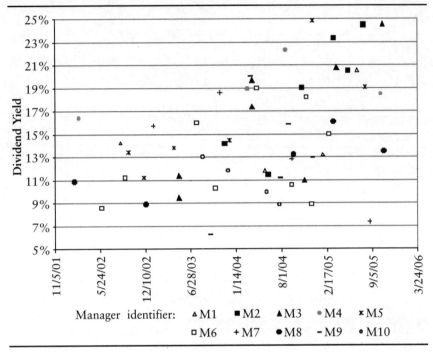

Source: Intex and Wachovia Capital Markets, LLC.

25%, as of 2007: 1Q. Clearly, collateral differences, structural variation, and manager discretion contribute to these differences. Third, there is some evidence of manager styles. M2 is an aggressive manager; its equity cash flows are generally near the top of a vintage; M8 is a cautious manager; its equity cash flows are generally near the bottom of a vintage. Finally, most managers have a mixed record of equity performance. For example, M3 has some issues near the top of a vintage and other issues near the bottom of a vintage. This is the case for most managers.

WHAT DO THE RATING AGENCIES HAVE TO SAY ABOUT MANAGERS?

The rating agencies have taken different approaches to evaluating CDOs and managers. Fitch ranks managers, Moody's computes deal scores, and S&P has examined the performance of equity.

Fitch focuses on qualitative issues when it evaluates managers. Using a five-point scale, with CAM 1 representing the highest rank and CAM 5 representing the lowest rank, Fitch reviews surveillance data, public information and information provided by asset managers. Managers are ranked within managerial peer groups formed by size, scale, portfolio composition and business strategy. Seven categories of information are considered, including company and management experience, staffing, procedures and controls, portfolio management, CDO administration, technology, and CDO performance.

Moody's makes no attempt to rate managers; instead, it computes a *Moody's deal score* (MDS) that represents a rate of growth in the expected losses on notes initially rated investment grade. A negative MDS value is consistent with an improving deal. MDS is computed as the natural log of the ratio of current to initial expected losses. Current expected losses are estimated based on changes in *overcollateralization* (OC) ratios since a deal closed. Unfortunately, Moody's deal score may provide conflicting signals to investors.

One CBO issued in October 1998 is an interesting case in point. The issue appeared to be perfectly timed. In the months before closing, high-yield spreads had widened considerably, responding to the Russian government debt default, the unwinding of the Long Term Capital Management hedge fund, and the global flight to quality. Assets were cheap, but liability spreads had not yet widened. In the years that followed, soaring default rates would destroy nearly all of the 1998 vintage CBOs. Yet Moody's assigned the CBO we examined a negative MDS (representing an improving deal). Upon further investigation, we found that the notes and the lowest-rated tranche had defaulted.

In 2005, S&P attempted to quantify equity performance by examining a limited set of CLOs and CBOs.[5] Focusing on dividend payments only, S&P found that returns were positively related to leverage, negatively related to downgrades, and not correlated with either CLO weighted average spreads or the percentage of CCC rated assets. Equity returns were higher for CLOs than for CBOs and generally lower for older vintages. CLO managers with multiple deals registered solid returns. S&P also found that no downgraded CBO was able to resume payments to equity, even if notes were subsequently upgraded. This has implications for newer vintage CLOs that use OC haircuts.

SHOULD EQUITY INVESTORS LOOK FOR MANAGERS WITH EQUITY STAKES?

CDO equity investors should expect managers to protect equity interests; however, the mutual fund industry has taught us that such alignment is not

---

[5] See Standard & Poor's, *CDO Spotlight: First study of U.S. CDO Equity Performance Highlights Payment Trends*, September 12, 2005.

always perfect. In 2003, investigators uncovered evidence of illegal mutual fund trading practices such as market-timing and aftermarket trades that benefited one class of investors at the expense of others, thus undermining the industry's basic tenet that each shareholder is given a fair and level playing field. As detailed in a 2006 paper, researchers have uncovered evidence that some fund managers who manage mutual funds and hedge funds use one fund to subsidize another.[6] Other research finds that if a manager's personal wealth is large relative to the incentive compensation he earns for managing a fund, then the manager may not take the appropriate amount of risk. Reputational risk can cause a manager to be overly conservative.[7] Alternatively, managers may choose to maximize short-term income to the detriment of long-term equity return.

Fortunately, CDOs have far more restrictive covenants preventing the worst of the aforementioned abuses. Nonetheless, during the 2001–2002 market downturn, note holders accused certain managers of "gaming" the system and leaking cash flows to equity investors. Consequently, the rating agencies and dealers have added additional covenants to limit these behaviors. Still, not all note holders are convinced that a manager's investment in equity benefits them. To appease both groups of investors, some managers are willing to buy a portion of the senior notes and the equity tranche. Other creative solutions to this potential conflict include placing the manager's fee at the same level as the interest on the notes (instead of being senior in terms of priority) or basing the fee on the performance of the mezzanine tranche.[8]

In most cases, equity investors' interests are better aligned with those of the manager if the latter has a personal stake in the issue. Nevertheless, a subtle conflict can occur with respect to the optional redemption clause. Consider the case in which a manager receives an incentive fee once she achieves a threshold internal rate of return. If the manager controls more than a third of the equity vote, she may delay the exercise of the optional redemption clause (a two-thirds majority vote is required). Such behavior is rational if reputational effects are not priced by the market. Thus, the manager's compensation structure can produce a slight misalignment between the manager's optimal strike price and that of other equity investors.

[6] See Gjergji Cici, Scott Gibson, and Robin Moussawi, "For Better or Worse? Mutual Funds in Side-by-Side Management Relationships with Hedge Funds," Working Paper, University of Pennsylvania, 2006.
[7] See Tom Nohel and Steven Todd, "Compensation for Managers with Career Concerns: The Role of Stock Options in Optimal Contracts," *Journal of Corporate Finance* 11 (2005), pp. 229–251.
[8] This feature is used in a 2006 synthetic CDO managed by MFS Investment Management.

IS GOOD PERFORMANCE THE RESULT OF LUCK OR SKILL?

Numerous studies have documented that, when it comes to equity and fixed-income mutual fund managers, there is little evidence of performance persistence, except in the case of particularly bad performance. These studies suggest good performance could be attributable to luck, rather than to skill, and bad performance can result from incompetence or excessive management fees.[9]

Of course, CDO and mutual fund managers differ in their job tasks and skill sets. A high-yield mutual fund credit analyst with a sterling performance record might wither as a CDO manager when faced with the task of managing a set of liabilities. In fact, during the late 1990s several mutual fund companies with strong high-yield performance records branched into CBOs and discovered the hard way that success in the flexible world of mutual fund management did not help them when managing the numerous constraints of CBOs.

MARKET EFFICIENCY AND MANAGER PERFORMANCE

Suppose we were to run a contest in which a group of 30 individuals were asked to predict the outcomes (heads or tails) on a series of coin flips. After each coin flip, some of the players would drop out because they made the wrong selection. If we continue the experiment until there is one person left, the winner, would he be skillful or simply lucky? In any contest, there are winners and losers. In sporting events, we attribute winning performances to skill. Does this make sense in other endeavors? If markets are completely efficient, there should be no reward for skill, so ex post abnormal performance can only be attributed to luck.

Another interpretation is that the market prices managerial skill at fair value. So, an exceptional manager who generates an alpha of 2% earns that 2% in the form of a management fee. After fees, that manager's performance looks identical to the average manager who generates an alpha of 0.25% and earns a 0.25% management fee.[10] The lack of variation in CDO manager-fee structures suggests that the marketplace does not currently price skill differences across managers.

---

[9] See Mark Carhart, "On Persistence in Mutual Fund Performance," *Journal of Finance* 52 (1977), pp. 57–82. See also Wayne Ferson, "The Timing Ability of Fixed Income Mutual Funds," Working Paper, Boston College, 2005.

[10] See Heber Farnsworth, Wayne Ferson, David Jackson, and Steven Todd, "Performance Evaluation with Stochastic Discount Factors," *Journal of Business* 75 (2002), pp. 473–503.

NO CDO BENCHMARKS

Analyzing CDO performance is challenging because there is no publicly available secondary market data. Furthermore, there are no readily available performance statistics or CDO indexes to gauge total returns. Certain proxies for CDO collateral performance exist, such as leveraged-loan closed funds (as a proxy for CLOs), synthetic residential MBS indexes, and leveraged-loan indexes, but due to structural and managerial differences, these are not always a good substitute for the various notes in the CDO structure.

Still, there is ample information available to investors to monitor their individual transactions. Most dealers publish surveillance reports. Moody's publishes a series of monthly reports (see the appendix to this chapter) that detail CDO performance, broken down by vintage and collateral type. These reports are the closest publication we have to a market performance matrix. Moody's even details CDO equity returns. The reports are extremely beneficial when examining macrotrends in the CDO market but, because names are not listed, the reports cannot be used to determine the performance of specific deals.

CDO RATINGS TRANSITIONS

All three major rating agencies publish reports detailing the rating transition of the CDOs they rate. Moody's goes one step further by providing impairment rates and loss-given default statistics. A list of the many useful publications for investors can be found in the appendix to this chapter.

Moody's published a special report in February 2007 on the rating migration of CDOs.[11] This data is dated, and is presented as an illustration on how readers can use rating agency data. The rating agency found historical rating transitions can vary greatly from one CDO asset class to another. CLO notes have had the most stable ratings by far. As previously discussed, the issuance in this sector has risen dramatically during the benign credit environment of 2003–2006. Meanwhile, CBO cash flow issuance has slowed to a trickle. The data for CBOs are therefore heavily weighted toward the weaker vintages. Nevertheless, CLOs outlasted CBOs during the 2001–2002 credit downturn by virtue of a more robust structure. Upon closer examination, Moody's showed that the weaker-vintage CLO notes had far greater rating stability than comparable CBO notes (Exhibit 12.6).

As for residential securitization (RESEC) or ABS CDOs, through early 2007, the higher-rated notes were more stable than comparable corporate bonds or CDOs as a whole. For notes in this sector rated below Baa3, the

---

[11] Danielle Nazarian, "Credit Migration of CDO Notes, 1996–2006 for US and European Transactions," *Moody's Special Report*, Febuary 28, 2007.

results have been mixed. The rating transition of RESEC CDOs improved significantly from 2003–2006 as managers shifted from the earlier multisector platform to the more recent residential mortgage platform.

Commercial real estate (CRE CDOs), the subject of Chapter 15, have very favorable historical upgrade/downgrade ratios (see Exhibit 12.7). Most issues, however, have yet to experience a full credit cycle. CRE-CDO performance was boosted in 2006 by numerous CMBS upgrades as rising property values led to the defeasance of many loans.

EXHIBIT 12.6 Historical Average One-Year Downgrade Risk, as of February 2007

	ACF CBO	ACF CLO	RESEC	Synth Arb ($US)	Synth Arb (non-US$)	CDOs	Corporate
Aaa	5.20%	0.10%	1.80%	4.90%	6.80%	2.91%	3.50%
Aa2	15.70%	1.50%	4.40%	11.20%	16.30%	8.00%	7.10%
A2	13.11%	0.00%	3.49%	14.18%	11.76%	7.04%	10.40%
Baa2	20.40%	1.20%	7.70%	12.20%	17.20%	10.30%	12.00%
Baa3	19.80%	11.20%	16.30%	8.20%	25.80%	15.10%	12.00%
Ba2	27.10%	2.40%	10.00%	18.80%	25.90%	13.20%	18.10%
Ba3	23.90%	5.60%	12.50%	10.70%	20.00%	13.70%	18.90%

Source: Danielle Nazarian, *Credit Migration of CDO Notes, 1996–2006, for US and European Transactions*, Figure 6: Historical Avg One Year Downgrade Risk, p. 12. © Moody's Investors Service, Inc. and/or its affiliates. Reprinted with permission. All Rights Reserved.

EXHIBIT 12.7 CRE CDO Rating Actions

Action Year	Moody's Up	Moody's Down	Fitch Up	Fitch Down	S&P Up	S&P Down	Totals Up	Totals Down	Ratio
2000	0	0	0	0	0	0	0	0	—
2001	0	0	0	0	0	0	0	0	—
2002	0	0	0	0	0	0	0	0	—
2003	0	0	0	0	0	0	0	0	—
2004	0	0	4	3	0	0	4	3	1.3
2005	11	0	55	2	4	0	70	2	35.0
2006	98	0	171	1	33	11	302	12	25.2
1Q 2007	28	0	0	3	32	4	60	7	8.6
Totals	137	0	230	9	69	15	436	24	18.2

Source: Wachovia Capital Markets, LLC; Fitch; Moody's; and Standard & Poor's.

Other CDOs not listed above which have had exceptionally stable ratings are middle-market CLOs and emerging-market CBOs. While issuance of the latter is a rare event, middle-market and CRE CDOs are rapidly growing sectors.

LIQUIDITY CONSIDERATIONS

CDOs gained a bad reputation of being extremely illiquid when the product was first introduced. Therefore, it should come as no surprise that new investors question the depth of the secondary markets. When the credit markets hit bottom in 2002, secondary trading in CDOs began to proliferate. Most dealers now have secondary trading desks and make markets in each others' transactions. As a result, bid-ask spreads have narrowed substantially since early 2000.

Clearly, the narrowest bid-ask spreads are found at the top of the capital structure. In 2006, however, even equity bid-ask spreads (particularly for CLO equity) narrowed. As with all financial products, liquidity evaporates during periods of high volatility.

We believe equity investors should assume they are buying to hold, and any liquidity they receive should be viewed as a bonus. As for note investors, the key to avoiding a liquidity crunch is to stick to straightforward, easy-to-model CDOs. Third-party software has been instrumental in helping secondary trading desks make a market in each others' deals. If the structure is too esoteric, however, it may not make it into the vender's database. In that case, an investor would most likely only have the underwriter to turn to when it comes time to sell.

The growth of the *credit default CDO* (CDCDO) market should, in the long run, continue the trend toward a more liquid secondary market. It could also lead to a few traffic bumps in the short term. A CDS contract requires one party to go long the risk, while another is effectively short. This fact alone opens the door to speculators who help provide liquidity, but who also increase market volatility. Higher market volatility leads to wider bid-ask spreads.

SO WHAT SHOULD INVESTORS DO?

Unfortunately, there is no single metric that investors can use to choose CDOs or managers. In general, senior investors should focus on structures, more than on managers; mezzanine and equity investors should give equal weight to structures and managers. All investors should consider the following points:

1. *Keep the manager's track record in perspective.* Most newer-entry managers have unblemished records due to the benign credit environment we enjoyed from 2003 to 2006. Seasoned managers may have valuable experience; their track records may suffer from a vintage bias. Moreover, personnel changes at the manager level may render performance records meaningless. Finally, prior performance may have no predictive power when it comes to future performance.

2. *Perform due diligence on management teams.* Reward experience, infrastructure investments, like technology, and controls and administrative procedures. Track Fitch's CAM rankings.

3. *Focus on the manager's strategy.* Look for managers who say and do things with which you agree. Examine how the manager's WARF, IC and OC scores evolve through time, after a CDO is issued. Ask managers about their appetites for second-lien, middle-market, and covenant-light loans. Most important, check for consistency. A manager professing one style and adopting another can damage investors' confidence.

4. *Assess whether the manager's interests are aligned with yours.* Does the manager have an equity stake? Does the manager have a debt stake? How is the manager compensated?

5. *Examine how much discretion the manager has.* What limits are placed on the portfolio holdings of corporate bonds, second-lien loans and unsecured loans? In general, do not eschew transactions with flexible investment parameters if you have confidence in the manager's abilities.

6. *Analyze the structure.* Does the CDO contain par preservation or turbo mechanisms? How much leverage is there? If you are an equity investor, do not automatically penalize transactions with par preservation mechanisms. If you are a senior note investor, do not robotically avoid transactions with a turbo class. How restrictive are the OC and *interest coverage* (IC) triggers? Perform stress tests and examine the solvency of particular tranches under reasonable default and recovery scenarios. Do not fixate on diversification scores as a proxy for solvency.

7. *Diversify across managers and across CDOs.* With so many moving parts, it is impossible to predetermine the optimal manager or structure. We have found the most experienced CDO investors can list the managers they prefer. These managers employ varying styles and structures.

CONCLUSION

Ignorance is never bliss when it comes to CDO investing. Performance can vary greatly from one position to the next depending on the collateral, structure and manager, as well as the asset's position in the capital structure. Investors who paint the sector with a broad brush could not only miss out on opportunities during volatile times but could also retain a false sense of confidence during more stable periods.

A well-constructed portfolio of CDO assets offers access to, and diversification benefits from, a myriad of asset classes. As banking reforms converge and securitization technology spreads, the menu of assets that collateralize CDOs will likely expand. Currently, most CDOs are tied to U.S. or European assets, but collateral from Asian countries may soon follow.

While the CDO structure offers an extremely efficient means of raising capital, it does not guarantee that money will be put to good use. It is therefore important that investors gain some familiarity with the underlying assets, particularly when buying lower-rated notes. We are not suggesting that investors analyze each and every asset backing a CDO. Instead, buyers should gain a solid understanding of the risks and rewards of the various collateral sectors. A good CDO portfolio manager is neither a fundamental nor a technical analyst, but rather a global strategist.

APPENDIX: RATING AGENCY REPORTS

In addition to providing ratings for CDOs, the three major rating agencies produce special topical research, often concerning whatever fear or belief is gripping the structured products world. These research reports are very useful to investors and provide a quality view of different sectors. The rating agencies also produce regular reports on the entire market, as well as specific reports concerning a particular transaction or manager.

Moody's

Ratings Methodology

Moody's has three methods of rating CDOs. The original methodology was known as the Binomial Expansion Method, detailed in the 1996 report. The newer methodology is known as the correlated binomial, and is used for highly correlated cash flow CDOs; that is, ABS CDOs. This methodology is detailed in Moody's *Correlated Binomial Default Distribution*, published August 10, 2004. Moody's utilizes CDOROM v2.0 to rate synthetic CDOs;

changes from CDORom v1.0 can be found in the presentation: *Moody's Releases Update Synthetic CDO Models,* on November 30, 2004.

For more details on Moody's rating methodology, please refer to the following reports:

- Arturo Cifuentes and Gerard O'Connor, "The Binomial Expansion Method Applied to CBO/CLO Analysis," *Moody's Special Reports,* December 13, 1996.
- Yuri Yoshizawa, "Moody's Approach to Rating Synthetic CDOs," *Moody's Special Reports,* July 29, 2003.
- Gary Witt, "Moody's Correlated Binomial Default Distribution," *Moody's Special Reports,* August 10, 2004.

CDO Asset Exposure Report

The *Asset Exposure Report* breaks down the collateral portfolios by CDO type and vintage. For each type and vintage, the report includes the following items: Top Holdings, Top Holdings on Up/Downgrade Watch, Top Holdings Purchased/Sold, Top Industries, Top Industries Bought/Sold, Top Issuers with Caa or Lower Rating (but still performing), and Top Defaulted Issuers. For example, an investor can see the defaulted issuers most prevalent in the collateral of 2005 CLOs, or how much of 2005 RESEC Collateral is high-yield CDOs.

CDO Index Report

Moody's has a series of CDO indexes, divided by asset type and vintage. The indexes are made up of more than 800 deals and contain deals going back to 1996. The CDO Index report details aggregate covenant status and collateral composition, and the report includes the following items: the mean, max, min, standard deviation and 80th and 20th percentiles for each stratum. For example, an investor can use the CDO Index report to find the mean amount of investment-grade collateral in all CBOs (that are in Moody's CDO Index), or to determine what is the highest WARF of all 2002 CLOs. In addition, the CDO Index report lists OC and IC test levels, and by how much the deals are exceeding their triggers. This can be useful for investors to see that, on average, the 2001 RESECs are within x% of the Mezzanine OC test levels, or to see which asset types and vintages are, on average, failing their tests.

Deal Score Report

Moody's *Deal Score Report* is unique in that it lists the deals by actual name, rather than using aggregate data or proxy serial numbers. The *Deal*

Score Report lists the following information: the deal name, number of tranches, whether the deal has a monoline insurer credit wrap, whether the CDO is on up/downgrade watchlist, vintage, WARF compliance (violation) level, average annual loss/gain of OC, adjusted average annual OC loss/gain and Moody's Deal Score. The report also provides scatter plots of deal data compared to the market averages for OC loss/gain and WARF levels. The Moody's Deal Score is the average of the natural log values of the ratios of current to initial expected loss for all notes initially rated investment grade. Expected loss is measured by Moody's rating. Moody's also reports a tranche score for each tranche initially rated investment grade.

Equity Score Report

The Moody's *Equity Score Report* breaks down results by vintage and asset type, and further into terminated and nonterminated deals. This report lists each deal (with a nine-digit number as the Moody's Equity Score Report Deal ID), and then lists the following information: the total cash return, dividend yield, previous dividend yield, cash-on-cash return, XIRR and payoff date (if applicable). Total cash return is the nondiscounted sum of all payments to equity from closing to the most recent payment date, divided by initial equity balance. Dividend yield is the most recent payment to equity, divided by initial equity balance, multiplied by the payment frequency. Nonpayments are treated as zero for dividend yield calculations. Cash-on-cash return is the nondiscounted sum of the equity payments over the previous year, divided by the initial equity balance. Deals with less than one year of equity payments do not have the cash-on-cash return calculated. XIRR is the internal rate of return for equity cash flows, adjusted for the timing of these payments. The Moody's XIRR assumes equity is purchased at par, and that the equity has zero liquidation value. This last assumption is problematic, as it is highly doubtful that the collateral pool has zero value, and leads to large negative XIRRs for deals in which the equity holder has not yet been made whole.

The *Equity Score Report* shows investors how the equity of different deals is performing. Moody's disguises the deal names, but investors still can use the report to look at trends in equity performance. For example, the investor can examine how many 2001 RESECs are currently paying double-digit dividends, or how many CBOs terminated without making whole equity holders.

CDO Performance Overview

The *Performance Overview* is a detailed, deal-by-deal list. Moody's gives each tranche's current balance and rating, along with monthly collateral characteristics, such as collateral principal and interest, WARF, diversity score, WAC, WAS, WAM, Caa-C assets, and defaulted assets. The *Performance Overview* also lists the OC and IC test levels, with the deal's current OC and IC levels. This report is helpful in tracking the portfolio's changing composition over time. An investor looking to buy a certain CDO could use this report to examine how much the WARF has increased in the past six months, or whether the percentage of Caa assets held is decreasing.

Presale Reports

Moody's issues presale reports on transactions, with a provisional rating; this provisional rating is based on the information presented to Moody's at that time. For this reason, the provisional ratings may not always equal the final ratings. The report provides a summary of the deal, to include size, capital structure, ramp-up period, maturity and covenants (WAL, WARF, Diversity Score, WARR, WAS, etc.). Moody's lists the strengths, weaknesses and mitigants and examines the principal and interest waterfalls. The analysis studies the deal's managers, as well as hedges and coverage tests, plus any possible call features. Moody's describes how the provisional ratings were determined, and notes the sensitivity of the ratings.

Ratings Actions

Moody's issues ratings action reports when a CDO is issued, or when a change in the transaction occurs that is significant enough to cause an upgrade or downgrade.

Fitch

Ratings Methodology

Fitch's methodology is explained in

> *Criteria for Cash Flow Collateralized Debt Obligations*, Fitch, October 11, 2006.

CAM Profile

The *CDO Asset Manager Profile* is a two or three page, quick reference report on the manager. Fitch gives a brief history of the manager, and describes the assets under management, and any previous CDOs issued. The report summarizes strengths and challenges/mitigants for the manager.

Fitch issues a score to each manager; on a scale of 1 to 5 (1 is the best score). The ratings are relative to peer groups based on size, strategy and asset type. The score is based on an assessment of the manager in the following categories: Company/Management Experience, Staffing, Procedures and Controls, Portfolio Management Analysis, CDO Administration, Technology, and CDO Performance. Fitch publishes the score (again, on a 1 to 5 scale) for each category. Fitch uses a five-phase process, featuring an onsite review by its analysts, along with monthly surveillance, annual manager reviews, and rating updates in issuing or changing the CAM score.

Presale Reports

Fitch issues presale reports with preliminary ratings. After a summary description of the transaction (capital structure, deal type, ramp-up period, maturity, expected close, size, payment dates, expected WAS and WAL, noncall period, and reinvestment period), these presale reports cover the strengths, concerns, and mitigants of the transaction, along with an analysis of the collateral, manager trading flexibility, and structure (to include IC/OC tests). Additionally, sector outlooks are provided for the collateral assets. The Fitch CAM profile is also included in the presale report.

New-Issue Report

The new-issue report is similar to the presale report, but has the advantage of having actual final data, as opposed to expected or tentative details.

Rating Actions Report

Fitch issues rating actions reports to describe any change in the rating status of a tranche, along with the motive for the change.

Standard & Poor's

Ratings Methodology

CDO Evaluator is the model S&P uses to rate CDOs. The latest version of the evaluator is 3.2. Information on the latest methodology can be found in Standard & Poor's *Modifies Structured Finance Default Assumptions in CDO Evaluator and the CDO Evaluator* Version 3.0: Technical Document

> Erkan Ertuk and Calvin Wong, *Standard & Poor's Modifies Structured Finance Default Assumptions in CDO Evaluator,* Standard and Poor's, June 19, 2006.

CDO Manager Magnifier

The *CDO Manager Magnifier* is a quick reference guide for investors looking at a particular manager. The report summarizes the manager by listing assets under management, asset focus, background, team members, credit philosophy, operations and technology, and any deals outstanding.

CDO Manager Focus

The *CDO Manager Focus* is a detailed summary of the CDOs from a manager. S&P lists the manager's CDOs, along with summary statistics for each deal. The summary statistics include a collateral breakdown, and trigger ratios and current levels. The report details the management team, investment approach/style, and provides an overview of the operations. This report is useful in providing investors with an in-depth look at all the CDOs by manager, and deal performance. The report also shows historical and current levels for top-three holdings, top-three industries held, sector and geographic breakdown, default and ratings breakdown, OC, IC, WAS and WAC, and par erosion.

Rated Overcollateralization Report

The *Rated Overcollateralization* (ROC) report lists several benchmarks for more than 80 CDOs. The benchmarks are as follows: *weighted average rating* (WAR), *default measure* (DM), variability measure, and correlation measure. The default measure describes the portfolio's annualized expected default rate, per S&P. It is the annualized, weighted average of the collateral assets' default probability. The variability measure is the annualized standard deviation of the default rates. This describes the possible variation of actual and expected portfolio default rates. The correlation measure is the ratio of the default rate standard deviation (calculated with correlation) to the default rate standard deviation (calculated without correlation). This measure shows the effect of correlation on the default rate standard deviation.

Additionally, S&P lists the ROC, which "calculates the effective overcollateralization of the tranche at its credit rating." ROC is calculated as:

Principal amount of debt supportable at tranche rating/Outstanding principal amount of debt at the tranche rating or higher

According to S&P

ROC is a dynamic point in time measure of the capacity of a CDO portfolio to support a tranche of CDO debt at its current rating.

Unlike traditional overcollateralization tests, ROC estimates the "effective" overcollateralization of a tranche of CDO debt by explicitly taking into account three of the most important components of support:

- The credit quality of the collateral;
- The projected recovery rates on collateral assumed to default in the future; and
- The net excess interest available to support additional principal.

Rating Actions

S&P issues rating action reports to describe an upgrade or downgrade, along with the rationale for the action.

Presale Reports

The presale reports details the transaction, and the preliminary rating given by S&P. The report lists the recommended subordination for each tranche, and gives the output of S&P's CDO evaluator model. Like other presale and rating reports, the S&P presale report lists the strengths, concerns and mitigating factors. S&P gives a collateral breakdown, along with the covenants specifying maximum levels. The report contains a waterfall analysis, and the results of the scenario analysis.

New-Issue Reports

S&P produces new-issue reports to accompany any rating issued to new deals. These reports include: ratings rationale, IC/OC triggers and current levels, call information, interest rate risks, a summary of the scenario analysis, a brief description of the manager, and a synopsis of the trading restrictions.

CHAPTER 13

CDO Equity

Brian McManus
Senior CDO Analyst
Wachovia Capital Markets, LLC

Steven Todd, Ph.D.
CDO Analyst
Wachovia Capital Markets, LLC

Anik Ray
Associate CDO Analyst
Wachovia Capital Markets, LLC

Dave Preston, CFA
Associate CDO Analyst
Wachovia Capital Markets, LLC

The equity of a *collateralized debt obligation* (CDO) represents a residual claim on the cash flows from the assets collateralizing a CDO. By providing access to assets that investors cannot easily gain exposure to, CDOs deliver diversification benefits that expand the efficient frontier. Although CDO equity returns are closely linked to the performance of the underlying assets, returns will not be perfectly correlated due to structural provisions that affect the way collateral cash flows are distributed.

CDO equity investors can earn high dividend payments that are typically front-loaded. Moreover, compared with private equity and hedge fund investments, CDO equity offers greater transparency. Like the former, CDO equity is also risky and illiquid and investors could lose part of their original investment. We recommend investors thoroughly understand this product before investing.

We believe CDO equity investors should stress-test issues using vector analysis. By using vector analysis, investors can determine how equity will perform if defaults are front-loaded (worst case) or back-loaded (best case). Potential buyers often request CDO equity performance statistics, but these are not easily summarized due to data deficiencies and aggregation problems.

In this chapter, we first discuss the general investment characteristics of CDO equity and then examine the equity returns on actual transactions and look at other data sources for insights on how equity has performed. Readers should note that equity cash flow data changes on every payment data, and the figures presented are meant only as an illustration of how to measure equity performance, not to be indicative of future performance.

WHAT IS CDO EQUITY?

CDOs are privately placed securities backed by pools of financial assets. CDO equity represents a residual claim on the cash flows from the assets collateralizing a CDO. Those assets could be leveraged loans, corporate bonds, residential mortgage loans, commercial mortgage loans, or something else (e.g., emerging market debt and trust-preferred securities).

A CDO redistributes cash flows from a set of assets to a series of notes. The *cash flow* structure is the most common type of CDO and will receive the bulk of this report's attention. With this structure, cash flow coverage tests are based on asset par amounts. With the less common *market value* structure, coverage tests are based on asset market values. Synthetic structures, many of which forego coverage tests, are also quite common. In funded synthetic CDOs, the collateral is a combination of *credit default swaps* (CDS) and high-quality assets.

In cash flow structures, the mechanism that determines the allocation of cash flows is called a *waterfall*. Equity payments are last in priority, after liability payments, management fees and taxes. The residual cash flows available to pay equity can be diverted if interest and par coverage ratios fall below prescribed limits. Collateral losses due to default and trading losses will result in equity principal losses. A typical waterfall appears in Exhibit 13.1.

Because a CDO is collateralized by a pool of assets, a long equity position is similar in risk to a long position in the collateral and a short position in the senior notes. The senior note investors typically receive a fixed spread above LIBOR. Hence, equity is a matched funded position when the collateral is floating rate.[1] The term funding structure implies that equity is also a nonrecourse, leveraged investment. *Nonrecourse* means the investment does not require additional funding other than what is originally tendered, regardless of how poorly the assets perform. *Leveraged* means the investor

---

[1] With fixed rate collateral in excess of a prescribed notional amount, the rating agencies typically require an interest rate hedge via caps or swaps.

EXHIBIT 13.1   CDO Waterfall

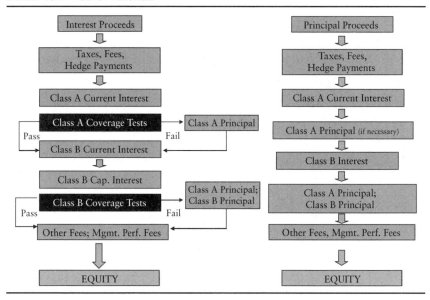

Source: Wachovia Capital Markets, LLC.

borrows money to purchase the security, presumably at a lower interest rate than the expected return on the investment. This allows investors to increase the potential return (but also the risk) of their investment.

WHAT ARE THE ADVANTAGES OF CDO EQUITY?

CDOs provide access to a host of assets that investors cannot easily gain exposure to, either because of liquidity or rating constraints. As previously mentioned, these assets include leveraged loans, noninvestment-grade bonds, residential subprime mortgages, and commercial real estate loans. By providing access to these assets, CDOs deliver diversification benefits that expand the efficient frontier. In cases where the pool of financial assets is not static, but rather managed by a portfolio manager, CDO equity gives investors access to a manager's expertise.

CDO structures do not manufacture diversification. CDO equity returns are closely linked to the performance of the underlying assets. They will not be perfectly correlated with the underlying asset performance because of structural provisions that affect the way the collateral cash flows are distributed to equity.

CDO equity offers high dividend payments that are typically front-loaded. The investment typically competes for capital with private equity and hedge funds. CDO equity offers far greater transparency than either of these two asset classes. With CDOs, the funding costs and cash flow allocation rules are known. Moreover, there is a trustee and regular surveillance through which investors can know the contents of a manager's portfolio. In addition, the rating agencies closely monitor the CDO market and publish regular reports.

WHAT ARE THE RISKS OF CDO EQUITY?

CDO equity does not offer high dividends without significant risk. Investors could lose part of their original investment if cash flow coverage tests are tripped early in the CDO's life. Moreover, there is no guarantee that high dividends will persist, as investors are exposed to significant reinvestment risks. In short, returns are volatile and sensitive to the credit cycle.

CDO equity is illiquid. Although the secondary market is expanding, trading CDO equity is not like trading a blue chip stock. Wide bid-ask spreads are common, particularly during distressed times. Trying to sell equity in the secondary market soon after an issue closes is especially costly because a significant portion of the CDO's upfront expenses are typically deducted from the equity's market value.

HOW CAN INVESTORS GAIN EXPOSURE TO CDO EQUITY?

Investors can purchase CDO equity directly or through a fund-of-funds. Purchasing directly results in lower management fees but forces investors to develop their own diversification, reinvestment and surveillance strategies. We advise investors who directly purchase CDO equity to diversify across asset classes and managers.

Investors who purchase equity via a fund-of-funds pay higher management fees, however, a well-managed fund earns it management fee in the form of superior surveillance, trade execution, and access to the secondary market. Funds-of-funds are typically diversified across asset classes, vintages and managers.

WHAT ARE THE SOURCES OF EQUITY CASH FLOWS?

The source of equity cash flows in a CDO is the excess spread between the assets and liabilities. This funding gap is simply the difference between the average collateral yield and the weighted average funding cost. We measure the latter quantity as the average cost of the CDO notes.

EXHIBIT 13.2 Funding Gap Example

CDO Structure and Funding Costs			
Rating	Percent of Issue	Spread	Weighted Average Funding Cost
AAA	75	23	75% × LIBOR + 23
AA	7	32	7% × LIBOR + 32
A–	4	55	4% × LIBOR + 55
BBB	4	125	4% × LIBOR + 125
BB	2	325	2% × LIBOR + 325
Equity	8		8% × LIBOR + 0
Total	100		LIBOR + 33.19

	LIBOR +
Collateral yield	250.0
Weighted average funding cost	33.2
Funding gap	216.8

Source: Wachovia Capital Markets, LLC.

In Exhibit 13.2, the floating rate collateral pays LIBOR + 250 bps. The notes pay spreads of 23 to 325 bps above LIBOR. As is typical with most CDOs, the AAA notes form the bulk of the transaction, and these notes have the lowest funding cost (i.e., the lowest spread over LIBOR). If we compute the average spread on the notes where we weight the tranches by their respective sizes, we obtain a weighted average funding cost of LIBOR + 33.2 bps. Subtracting the funding cost from the weighted average spread, we obtain a funding gap of 216.8 bps.

To compute a base case dividend yield for equity, we take the funding gap and net out the CDO expenses. These include manager fees, taxes, trustee fees and hedge costs. Continuing with our example, we assume that manager, trustee and rating agency fees are 50 bps, 5 bps and 7 bps per year, respectively. Origination fees of 1.5% amortized over seven years (the expected average life of the issue) equate to approximately 26 bps per year.

Subtracting the CDO expenses from the funding gap, we obtain the adjusted funding gap:

	Funding gap	216.8 bps
–	Annualized fees	88.0 bps
=	Adjusted funding gap	128.8 bps

The remaining spread can now be multiplied by the leverage factor to obtain a base case dividend yield on CDO equity. The leverage factor is simply the ratio of the collateral notional to the equity notional, in this case 100/8, or 12.5.

	Adjusted funding gap	128.8 bps
×	Leverage multiple	12.5
=	Base case dividend yield on CDO equity	LIBOR + 16.10%

This base case dividend yield could be construed as the expected return on equity under the assumption that there are no defaults on the collateral and no changes in the composition of the assets. If we assume defaults occur at a constant annual rate and net these out of the funding gap, we can compute adjustments to the base case yield under the assumption of constant defaults. These appear in Exhibit 13.3.

We use the word *construed* because this simple analysis is riddled with problems. First, defaults, prepayments and recoveries are cyclical and therefore do not propagate at constant rates. Exhibit 13.4, which plots the default rates on leveraged loans, drives home this point. In general, front-loaded defaults (those occurring early in an issue's life) do more harm to equity returns than back-loaded defaults. When defaults are front-loaded, the excess spread generator is turned off early, resulting in less ongoing cash for equity at the start.

Second, in managed issues, the funding gap is not static, even if the notes are not amortizing. During the reinvestment period, the composition of the collateral portfolio is changing, as the manager purchases and sells assets in response to prepayments, downgrades and defaults. Spreads on new assets will differ from those originally purchased, reflecting changing risk assessments. Third, in both static and managed issues, the funding gap will change as the notes pay down. In most cases, funding costs rise as the most senior tranches, which generally receive the lowest spread, amortize.

EXHIBIT 13.3 Adjustments to Base Case IRRs

Default Rate	Recovery Rate	Loss Rate	Adjustment to Base Case IRR
1%	70%	0.30%	−3.75%
1%	50%	0.50%	−6.25%
2%	70%	0.60%	−7.50%
2%	50%	1.00%	−12.50%

Source: Wachovia Capital Markets, LLC.

EXHIBIT 13.4   Leveraged Loan Spreads and Default Rates

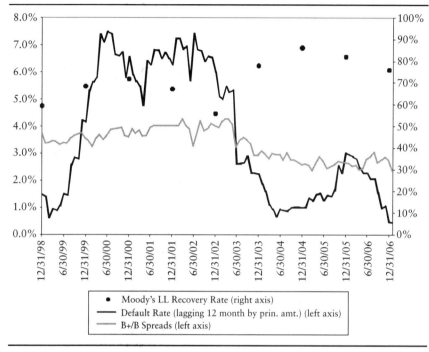

Source: Standard & Poor's and Moody's.

WHAT IS THE BEST TIME TO INVEST IN CDO EQUITY?

CDO equity generally offers the best value when the funding gap is large. The funding gap increases if funding costs fall or if the spreads on the assets collateralizing a CDO widen. Although cheaper assets are usually associated with wider funding gaps, the converse is not necessarily true. For CLOs, the funding gap did not change significantly between 2004 and most of 2006, although assets spreads tightened.

   If new-issue funding costs fall during a CDO's noncall period, equity will likely trade at a discount to *net asset value* (NAV). If the collateral backing a CDO is negatively convex, then, when spreads tighten, the price response is muted. Such is the case for leveraged loans. We see this effect in Exhibit 13.5, where we chart new issue CLO funding costs versus the *market value weighted average price* (MVWAP) of the CSFB leveraged loan index.

   Term funding cuts both ways; hence, negative convexity helps investors in a retreating market. Between late 1998 and October 31, 2003, leveraged

EXHIBIT 13.5   Funding Gap Analysis

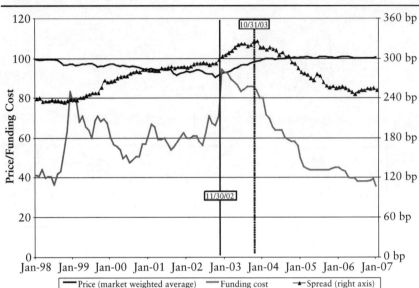

Source: Credit Suisse First Boston and Standard & Poor's.

loan spreads rose almost 100 bps; over the same period, the MVWAP slowly fell. Between November 30, 2002 and October 31, 2003, however, prices and spreads rose in tandem—negative convexity at its best.

When asset spreads widen, managers are able to reinvest in higher-yielding collateral, offsetting some of the mark-to-market loss on their holdings. In 2002, leveraged loan default rates peaked. However, spreads continued to rise until the end of 2003, even while default rates plummeted. During this period, CLO funding costs rose from LIBOR plus 56 bps in mid-2002 to nearly LIBOR plus 80 bps by the end of the year, and they did not fall back below 60 bps until early 2004. CLO managers who locked in relatively low funding costs in 2001 and 2002 were well positioned to buy cheap collateral in 2003.

Investors can use funding gap analysis to monitor market trends; but they should be very careful about inferring whether the equity of a specific issue is rich or cheap based on a static analysis of the funding gap. Most CLOs ramp up assets over a long horizon, sometimes as much as nine months. Skilled managers will try to buy more assets when collateral issuance is high (and spreads are generous) relative to CDO issuance. In 2006, leveraged loan (B+/B) spreads were as wide as 302 bps and as tight as 236 bps (according to LCD), while the cost of funding traded in a narrow range of 38 to 45 bps. A CLO coming to market when the funding gap is particularly narrow could have already purchased 80% of its assets.

WHAT IS THE TYPICAL LIFE CYCLE FOR EQUITY?

CDOs typically experience three distinct life stages: ramp-up, reinvestment, and amortization/maturity.[2] *Ramp-up* defines the time between the premarketing phase of an issue and the first cash flow distribution. For cash transactions, the ramp-up phase usually lasts one to nine months; for synthetic transactions, shorter ramp-ups are common. During the *reinvestment period*, the CDO manager adjusts the collateral portfolio by buying or selling securities, subject to a set of prescribed constraints. The reinvestment period can be as short as three years (for some middle-market CLOs) and as long as seven years.

Equity investors have the right to call the transaction following the noncall period subject to a 2/3 majority vote. This option is most likely exercised when funding costs have fallen and the collateral is trading at or above par. In many cases, equity investors can roll their investment into a new issue and save on underwriting fees. We have estimated this optional redemption clause was worth approximately 61 basis points over the period September 2003 through September 2006. (See the appendix to this chapter.) Alternatively, if funding costs rise, this option falls out of the money and has little value.

During the final life stage, the *amoritization/maturity* stage, a CDO distributes the principal payments from the collateral to the notes, amortizing the latter according to a prescribed schedule. Nearly all older vintage transactions had five-year reinvestment and three-year noncall periods; recent vintage issues typically have longer noncall and reinvestment periods. The final life stage of a CDO can be shortened via a cleanup call (exercised when the collateral's outstanding balance drops below 10% of its original par value).

HOW CAN WE MEASURE PERFORMANCE?

The ideal performance measure for CDO equity is a cash flow based yield or internal rate of return. For issues that have terminated, we can compute actual *internal rate of returns* (IRRs) under the assumption that an investor purchased the equity at par. An IRR calculation assumes an investor can reinvest intermediate cash flows at the computed internal rate of return. For nonterminated issues, we need the secondary market price to accurately cal-

---

[2] Static CDOs do not contain a reinvestment period.

culate a total return. Unfortunately, there is no reliable source for secondary market prices.

Investors should be cautious about using proxies such as the Credit Suisse First Boston (CSFB) Leveraged Loan Index to infer equity returns. We compared the returns on this index with the returns earned by closed-end funds. The low correlations we observed suggest the index is a poor proxy for CDO equity performance because it ignores the effects of structure and managers. Of course, a closed-end fund can trade at a discount or premium to the portfolio's NAV. To the extent that time-variation in this discount or premium captures the cost (value) of a manager's expertise, we should not be surprised by this result.

ISSUE PERFORMANCE

In this section, we examine the equity returns on transactions underwritten by Wachovia that have matured. We believe these transactions provide us with the best source of data because we track the underlying cash flows. As this relatively small sample might not reflect the entire market, this data is presented as an example of how to measure performance.

As of February 28, 2007, 17 Wachovia transactions have matured. Eight of these transactions were middle-market CLO financings in which the issuer retained the equity on its balance sheet. Another eight transactions were CLOs that produced a portfolio (value-weighted) annual yield of 15.7%.[3] The remaining transactions, backed by residential mortgage securities (RESEC), generated a 49% return. In Exhibit 13.6, we plot the distribution of equity returns on terminated Wachovia issues.

We monitor the performance of nonterminated Wachovia transactions in Exhibit 13.7, where we provide summary dividend yield statistics. Equity cash flow data changes as the deal seasons; therefore, this data should be treated as an example of how to measure returns. The CDO issues backed by *asset-backed securities* (ABS) are predominantly high-grade (AA and A) transactions, which are highly levered (up to 200 times). The dividend yield annualizes the sum of interest and principal cash flows paid to equity over the past quarter relative to notional principal. Though dividend yields are informative, they are not easily converted to IRRs unless we make gross assumptions about equity's current price.

In Exhibit 13.8, we provide aggregate measures of performance by sector for Wachovia nonterminated issues, as of February 28, 2007. The vertical axis measures the portfolio (value-weighted) IRR; the horizontal axis mea-

---

[3] The mean (equally weighted) yield on these eight transactions is about 100 bps lower. This is an inferior performance metric, as we argue below.

EXHIBIT 13.6 Terminated Wachovia CDO Return Histogram

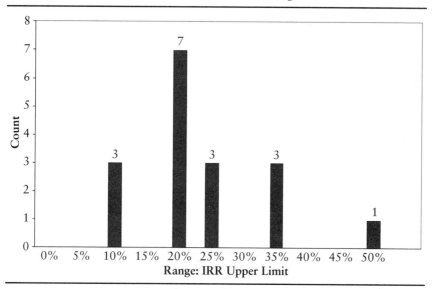

Source: Wachovia Capital Markets, LLC.

EXHIBIT 13.7 Wachovia Nonterminated CDO Dividends, as of February 28, 2007

	Dividend Yield			
	Max	Min	Mean	Median
ABS CDO	23.52%	0.00%	9.98%	9.55%
CRE CDO	37.94%	6.96%	17.93%	15.46%
CLO	26.58%	0.00%	18.29%	20.23%

Source: Wachovia Capital Markets, LLC.

sures the portfolio (value-weighted) liquidation price. At higher liquidation prices, the portfolio sector returns are higher. The relationship between IRR and liquidation price is steepest for *commercial real estate* (CRE) CDOs and flattest for CLOs. The slope differential confirms that our sample of CLO cash flows has a longer effective duration than our sample of CRE CDO cash flows.[4] The first CLO cash flows arrived in August 1999; in contrast, the first CRE CDO cash flows arrived in 2004. The duration differential drives home the obvious point that the longer an investor holds his equity position, the less sensitive his realized return is to the secondary market price.

---

[4] The effective duration measures the percentage change in price per unit change in yield; it is the reciprocal of the slope of the relation between liquidation price and IRR.

EXHIBIT 13.8   Wachovia Nonterminated CDO IRRs, as of February 28, 2007

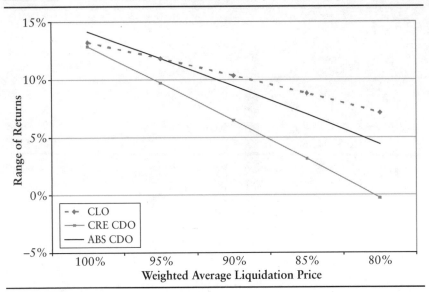

Source: Wachovia Capital Markets, LLC.

WHAT INSIGHTS DO OTHER DATA SOURCES SAY ABOUT EQUITY PERFORMANCE?

Since Wachovia transactions may not be representative of the market over-all, potential investors should inquire about fund-of-funds equity perfor-mance. We examined one experienced fund that posted annual returns of 6% to 40%, as of February 28, 2007. Managers who purchased distressed CDO notes and equity at deep discounts enjoyed the best performance.

Moody's publishes a monthly equity score report that summarizes the performance of terminated and nonterminated issues. The agency calculates the returns on nonterminated issues under the assumption that equity's mar-ket value is zero. For obvious reasons, we reject this performance metric because most equity investments are solvent, particularly recent vintages.

Historical Performance of Terminated Transactions

We will use data provided by Moody's to analyze the historical performance of transactions that have terminated, as of February 2007. Exhibit 13.9 shows the historical equity performance by sector (underlying collateral type) for terminated transactions. Transactions terminate either because they are

EXHIBIT 13.9   Terminated Deal Equity IRRs, as of February 2007

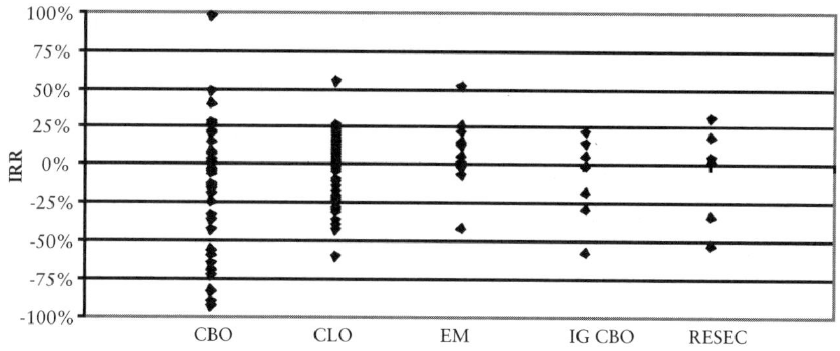

Data Source: Moody's February 2007 Equity Score Report, May 9, 2007.

EXHIBIT 13.10   Terminated CDO Equity Return Summary

	CBO	CLO	EM	IG CBO	RESEC
Sample	36	61	13	7	17
Mean	−14.08%	2.47%	9.52%	−8.27%	−3.65%
Median	−4.65%	8.35%	13.07%	−0.35%	5.72%
Min	−92.33%	−59.02%	−40.59%	−56.84%	−59.08%
Max	98.52%	55.60%	52.45%	22.60%	32.56%
StDev	43.50%	20.83%	21.17%	27.72%	29.78%
Number > 0	15	42	10	3	11

Data Source: Moody's February 2007 Equity Score Report, May 9, 2007.

redeemed (via an optional call) or because they have matured (possibly due to an early amortization event). Unlike the Wachovia sample, the Moody's data includes distressed deals. The scatter plot below summarizes performance for the two most active sectors, leveraged loans (CLOs) and residential loans (RESECs) and three currently inactive sectors, high-yield bonds (CBOs), emerging market debt (EM), and investment-grade bonds (IG CBOs).

Summary measures of performance on terminated transactions appear in Exhibit 13.10, as of February 2007. In each sector, the mean IRR sits below the median IRR, indicative of a skewed distribution with a fat left tail. The EM sector enjoys the best mean performance (9.52%), whereas CBOs suffer from the worst mean performance (−14.08%). CBOs were the most poorly timed structured product. Most CBO transactions closed before 2000, just before the credit cycle turned and defaults spiked. Issuance slowed to a trickle when the sector was at its cheapest. As of 2006, CBOs have been completely subsumed by synthetics.[5]

Emerging market CDOs were expected to sink alongside the CBO boat, so issuance in this sector dried up. Exhibit 13.9 shows that most terminated EM CDOs performed well. Only the earliest EM issues, which weathered the Russian debt default, suffered poor performance.

The data in Exhibits 13.9 and 13.10 are based on a Moody's Equity Score report from May 2007 (reflecting data as of February 2007), and are subject to a survivorship bias. Investors should be cautious about making equity return forecasts based on terminated transaction data alone. Currently, early terminations include many extreme performers. Most transactions have matured either as a result of an early amortization or because the optional redemption clause was exercised. In the former case, poor performance resulted. In the latter case, the NAV exceeded the present value of expected equity cash flows. This is usually good news for equity holders.

Investors might be tempted to use the data in Exhibit 13.10 to draw conclusions about average performance by sector. We recommend they resist this temptation. Individual IRRs are not easily aggregated into portfolios. We do not know the vintages of terminated issues, nor do we know the exact timing of each issue's equity cash flows. Finally, it is not obvious how we should weight individual issues. Should we consider an equally weighted portfolio of returns, or one weighted by issue size? The mean returns in Exhibit 13.10 are not actual, realized returns attributable to specific issues. The mean IRR is simply an *equally weighted* average of IRRs, without any regard for timing. The median IRR, on the other hand, is a real return, earned by an actual issue.

Forecasting future equity returns based on terminated transaction data alone is problematic if the product has changed substantially since its inception. Early RESEC issues were partly collateralized by loans on manufactured housing, aircraft, and franchises. CDO managers had little expertise to properly value these assets, which proved to have low recoveries. Post 2002 vintage RESECs are collateralized predominantly by residential and commercial mortgage loans only.

In Exhibit 13.11, we plot the distribution of equity returns on terminated CLOs (as of February 2007), the sector for which we have the most data. Note that the distribution is skewed, with a fat left tail. The 10% to 20% yield bucket enjoys the highest participation rate, but the mean and median returns are only 2.47% and 8.35%, respectively (see Exhibit 13.10).

---

[5] The rating agencies required CBOs to hedge the interest rate risk that resulted from using fixed rate assets to fund floating rate liabilities. This ultimately hurt performance, because interest rate and credit cycles are nonsynchronous. For speculative-grade credits, interest rate risk mitigates credit risk over long holding periods.

EXHIBIT 13.11   Terminated CLO-Equity IRRs, as of February 2007

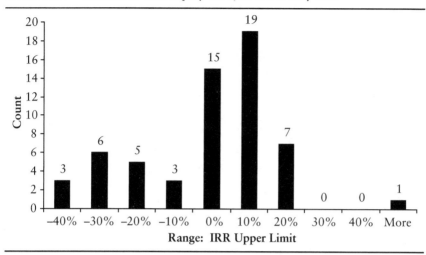

Data Source: Moody's February 2007 Equity Score Report, May 9, 2007.

It is our belief that the mean IRR likely understates the (value-weighted) portfolio yield, due to the outsized weight given to poor performing transactions (which tend to be smaller issues). As we do not have actual cash flows, we cannot confirm this hypothesis, although we did observe this pattern in Wachovia transactions.

How Nonterminated Transactions are Performing

Once again, we use data reported by Moody's as of February 2007 in our analysis of how nonterminated transactions are performing. In Exhibits 13.12 and 13.13, we examine the equity performance of nonterminated CLO and RESEC issues by sector and vintage (the year an issue closed). Total cash returns measure the nondiscounted sum of cash flows (interest and principal) paid thus far to equity, relative to notional principal. A 100% total cash return corresponds to an IRR of 0%, under the assumption that an investor purchases equity at par. When the total cash return exceeds 100%, we say the investor has been "made whole."

In the CLO sector, more than half of the 2000 and 2001 issues (16 out of 28) and a few issues from 2002 and 2003 have been made whole by February 2007 (see Exhibit 13.12). In contrast, fewer than two-fifths (10 out of 28) of the pre-2000 issues generated total cash returns above 100% by February 2007. Many of these issues had telecom exposure in their high-yield bond buckets. On closer inspection, only 11 out of 28 issues have paid a dividend over the four quarters preceding February 2007.

EXHIBIT 13.12   CLO Total Cash Returns by Vintage for Nonterminated Issues as of
February 2007

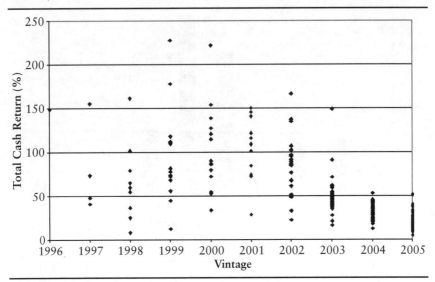

Data Source: Moody's February 2007 Equity Score Report, May 9, 2007.

EXHIBIT 13.13   RESEC Total Cash Returns by Vintage for Nonterminated Issues as
of February 2007

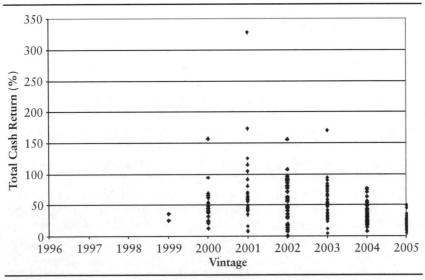

Data Source: Moody's February 2007 Equity Score Report, May 9, 2007.

As of February 2007, nonterminated RESEC issues have not performed as well as CLOs. Of the 255 issues Moody's tracks, only 10 had been made (see Exhibit 13.13). On closer inspection, roughly half (34 out of 64) of the 2001 and 2002 issues have paid dividends in the four quarters preceding February 2007. Many of these multisector issues will terminate with poor equity performance. The RESEC sector actually includes three very different species of CDOs: early vintage multisector issues, high-grade structured finance issues and mezzanine issues. These subsectors have posted very different performance numbers.

In Exhibit 13.14, we plot average total cash returns by vintage for CLOs, RESECs, and CBOs. Generally, as we would expect, the newer vintages have accumulated lower cash payments than early vintages, although early vintage CBOs defy that trend due to their very poor performance. The 2001–2002 RESECs have substantially underperformed similar vintage CBOs and CLOs. This result reverses the trend we saw earlier for terminated transactions (see Exhibit 13.10). As we mentioned previously, the RESEC sector is a motley crew of pure real estate and multisector issues. The latter issues, which included loans on manufactured housing, franchises and aircraft, have performed poorly. More recent vintage (post-2002) RESECs (most of which are pure real estate plays) have posted healthy total cash returns thus far.

EXHIBIT 13.14 Average Total Cash Returns by Vintage and Sector as of February 2007

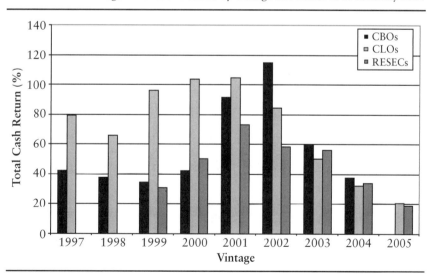

Data Source: Moody's February 2007 Equity Score Report, May 9, 2007.

We continue our analysis of the equity performance of nonterminated issues in Exhibit 13.15, where we plot median cash-on-cash returns by vintage for CLOs, RESECs and CBOs. Cash-on-cash returns measure the non-discounted sum of cash flows (interest and principal) paid to equity over the past four quarters relative to notional principal. A cash-on-cash return of zero usually signals that there is no excess spread available for equity. This can occur if the CDO locked in relatively high funding costs and collateral spreads have since fallen. It can also happen if defaults sufficiently erode the collateral par value.

Median returns probably capture the interest component of dividends better than mean returns, which can be biased upward due to the contribution of principal payments from amortizing issues that have lived beyond their reinvestment periods. Vintage 2002 CBOs have very high median cash-on-cash returns, probably due to the presence of significant principal payments. Most of these issues are past their reinvestment periods. The 2001–2005 CLOs were paying higher cash-on-cash returns than vintages 1999 and 2000. Newer vintage CLOs look particularly strong, especially the youngest vintage (2005). Compared with similar vintage RESECs, CLOs are posting superior cash returns.

We complete our analysis of equity performance in Exhibit 13.16, where we plot median dividend yields by vintage for CLOs, RESECs, and CBOs.

EXHIBIT 13.15   Median Cash-on-Cash Returns by Vintage and Sector for Nonterminated Issues as of February 2007

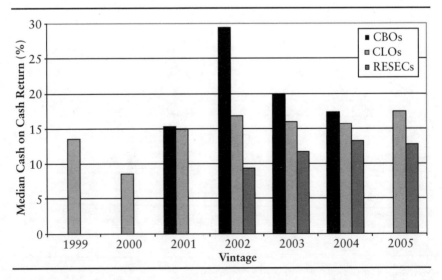

Data Source: Moody's February 2007 Equity Score Report, May 9, 2007.

EXHIBIT 13.16 Median Dividend Yields by Vintage and Sector for Nonterminated Issues as of February 2007

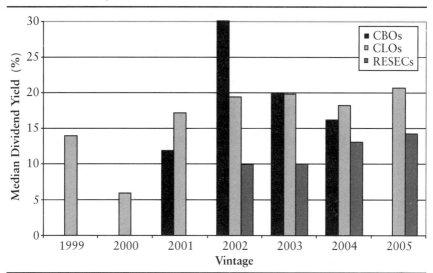

Data Source: Moody's February 2007 Equity Score Report, May 9, 2007.

The dividend yield measures the annualized sum of interest and principal paid to equity over the past quarter, relative to notional principal. According to a study conducted by S&P,[6] equity interest payments generally peak three or four quarters after an issue closes, once all deal expenses have been paid. In Exhibit 13.16, we see that vintage 2001 CBOs and CLOs are paying relatively high median dividends, most likely reflecting the effect of principal payments from amortizing issues. For vintages 2002–2005, CLOs were paying higher dividends than similar vintage RESECs, with vintage 2005 looking particularly robust.

Collectively, Exhibits 13.12 to 13.16 show that 2004 and 2005 vintage CLOs and RESECs were healthy, based on current dividend yields and cash flow returns to date. Nevertheless, equity returns are quite variable, even when we fix the sector and vintage.

CDO EQUITY PERFORMANCE DRIVERS

Differences in the three variables—collateral, structure, and manager—account for the large variation in equity performance across issues.

[6] See Standard & Poor's *CDO Spotlight: First Study of U.S. CDO Equity Performance Highlights Payment Trends*, September 12, 2005.

The pool of assets that collateralizes a CDO will vary from one issue to the next. Even issues from the same sector and vintage may have little collateral overlap. Each CDO places investment constraints on issuer, industry and geographic concentrations. Hence, each CDO exposes equity investors to a unique set of portfolio prepayment, default and recovery risks.

Structural differences account for much of the within-sector variation in equity performance. Waterfall nuances such as turbo, par preservation, and shifting interest rules result in differences in the way a CDO allocates cash flows to the tranches. Collateral quality and coverage tests vary from one issue to the next. Each CDO defines a unique set of *weighted average rating factor* (WARF) and *weighted average spread* (WAS) targets, as well as *interest coverage* (IC) and *overcollateralization* (OC) triggers.[7] Moreover, the length of the reinvestment period and the optional redemption features vary from issue to issue.

Differences in manager styles, skills and fortunes account for much of the within-sector variation in equity performance. Some managers are cautious, preferring to protect noteholders, fully expecting funding costs to rise. Other managers are more aggressive, intent on maximizing equity returns. These managers may eschew high-quality collateral in favor of lower-quality collateral with higher spreads. Each manager brings a unique set of experiences to the table. Moreover, there are significant differences in personnel, procedures, administration and technology across managers. Ex post, we know which managers were skilled (or lucky); ex ante, we may not know. For this reason, we recommend investors diversify across managers and sectors.

HOW SHOULD INVESTORS ANALYZE EQUITY RETURNS?

Because the funding gap is not static, investors should not rely solely on base-case IRRs when they evaluate equity investments. Instead, investors should stress-test issues using vector analysis. Ideally, investors should model defaults, recoveries, prepayments and reinvestment rates over a complete credit cycle. In general, when defaults rise, recoveries fall, credit spreads widen, prepayments fall and managers are able to invest at higher spreads.[8] By using vector analysis, investors can determine how equity will perform if defaults are front-loaded (worst case) or back-loaded (best case).

---

[7] See Brian McManus, Steven Todd, Anik Ray, and David Preston, *Structures and Managers: Risk or Reward?* Wachovia Capital Markets, LLC, August 15, 2006.

[8] In a recent study examining corporate issuers, Moody's found a high negative correlation between senior unsecured bond default and recovery rates. See Moody's Investors Service, *Corporate Default and Recovery Rates, 1920–2006*, February 2007.

CONCLUSION

In general, tightening collateral spreads pressure CDO funding costs and deal expenses lower, as equity investors try to offset the loss in dividend income. On the one hand, equity investors can increase leverage (via the issuance of double-B notes) and lock in cheaper funding costs. On the other hand, rich assets often lead CDO managers to search for yield by moving into riskier or less liquid collateral, such as second lien or middle-market loans. In this environment, the loan market becomes increasingly issuer friendly with fewer (or more liberal) deal covenants. In a strong collateral market, the average secondary price of CDO collateral rises above par. In this environment, the optional redemption clause comes in the money, contributing to higher returns on CDO equity.

Widening collateral spreads can be good or bad for equity investors. With a moderate spread widening, new issue CDOs can lock in a wider funding gap and existing CDO managers can reinvest in cheaper collateral. Extreme asset volatility, however, such as what we are currently experiencing in the subprime home equity loan market, can be particularly challenging for new and existing issues. Pricing a CDO becomes exceptionally challenging. Secondary market prices for equity and lower rated notes fall and the market becomes increasingly illiquid. It is in this environment that top-tier managers shine and bottom-tier managers go out of business.

The term funding structure of a CDO benefits equity investors in volatile times because it guarantees that there can be no forced liquidation. In theory, this helps managers focus on long-term fundamental value, even when short-term, mark-to-market risk and illiquidity premiums rise. Historical data suggest that most managers struggle to limit the damage, but some managers are capable of hitting home runs even during the worst markets.

APPENDIX: WHAT IS THE COST OF EARLY REDEMPTION?

CDOs have two options: an *optional redemption clause* (ORC) and a clean-up call. The former can be exercised after a stated noncall period; the latter is exercised when the outstanding balance of the transaction falls below a specified amount. In older deals, the noncall period is three years, the reinvestment period is five years and the issue matures in 10 years. In more recent deals, the noncall is four or five years and the maturity is 12.

In a sequential pay structure, the last maturing rated tranche is also the most junior (other than equity). If spreads tighten, this tranche has the most to lose if the ORC is exercised. Between March 2004 and March 2007, credit spreads tightened, shortening the average lives of CDOs and dampening the benefits of tighter spreads.

We can estimate how much the optional redemption clause has cost noteholders these past three years by using new issues spreads. Suppose we buy a double-B tranche each week and swap it for a new issue one week later. Assume we buy the new issue notes at par. In reality, under certain market conditions discounts are offered; however, these same market conditions diminish secondary market liquidity.

The secondary market price of the position we are selling should reflect the change in primary market spreads. Our credit duration depends on the issue's average life. For a BB rated CLO note, the original average life lies between 9 and 11 years and is related to the reinvestment period (which can range from five to seven years). If credit spreads tighten, pricing to the original average life overstates the price gains; if spreads widen, pricing to the call date understates price losses. In reality, investors will discover the secondary market price is the lower of two possible values. Therefore, when credit spreads tighten, we price the note to the call date, and when spreads widen, we price the note to its maturity.

Between March 2004 and March 2007, double-B spreads tightened fairly consistently. In Exhibit 13.7, we compare the returns on two double-B rated notes: one with a four-year noncall period (priced to the call), the other with no ORC (priced to maturity). We find the return differential is 7.61%. Though the noncallable note generates a higher return, its volatility is elevated. In fact, the callable note achieves a higher Sharpe ratio by virtue of its lower volatility.

It should come as no surprise that, as we move up the capital structure, higher-rated tranches have less to lose from early redemption. The cost to triple-A noteholders is only 37 bps (i.e., instead of earning LIBOR + 104 bps, triple-A investors earn LIBOR + 67 bps). On average, assuming the capital structure weights shown in Exhibit 13.7, the ORC costs noteholders 91 bps in yield.

The call option is not always in the money as quickly as secondary note investors might assume. Equity holders pay 2.0 to 2.5 points in upfront rating agency and origination fees. If they call the notes on the first callable date, they end up amortizing these costs over a shorter period, though underwriters may cut them a deal if all equity investors roll their investments into a new transaction. Two points upfront are worth about 30 bps more if amortized over four years instead of 10. Therefore, the ORC ends up saving equity investors about 61 bps.

Commercial Real Estate

CHAPTER 14

Commercial Mortgage-Backed Securities

Brian P. Lancaster
Senior Analyst
Wachovia Capital Markets, LLC

Anthony G. Butler, CFA
Senior CMBS Analyst
Wachovia Capital Markets, LLC

Greg Laughton
Analyst
Wachovia Capital Markets, LLC

C ommercial mortgage-backed securities (CMBS) came into existence in the late 1980s through private-placement transactions, but it was the Resolution Trust Corp. (RTC) in 1991–1992 that provided the initial jumpstart to the CMBS market as we now know it. CMBS are structured and rated bonds backed by commercial real estate mortgage loans. The RTC helped to create the first basic bond structures[1] backed by commercial real estate that were widely accepted by investors and traded in the capital markets. Since then, the CMBS market, driven by increasingly efficient bond structures from the borrower and investor perspectives, has experienced tremendous growth in absolute terms as shown in Exhibit 14.1 and had been increasingly taking market share from more traditional on-balance-sheet lenders, such as insurance companies and government-sponsored enterprises that lend in the multifamily space.

---

[1] By credit-enhancing commercial real estate deals with government guarantees and U.S. Treasuries to mitigate potential unknown losses and defaults.

EXHIBIT 14.1   History of the CMBS Market

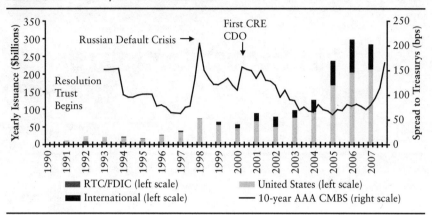

* Data as of November 2007.
Source: Wachovia Capital Markets, LLC, and Commercial Mortgage Alert.

After a slow but steady start, CMBS had a significant year in 1998. Experiencing average annual issuance growth of 37% up until 1998, CMBS issuance ballooned to about $80 billion. However, beginning in about August 1998, the Russian default crisis and the ensuing bond-market panic temporarily, but effectively, shut down the market. This caused CRIIMI Mae (one of the largest product buyers of the below-investment-grade tranches of CMBS) to file for bankruptcy protection. Losses incurred by such major market players as Nomura were reputed to be in the billions of dollars.

However, out of these problems, the market grew stronger with the advent of commercial real estate collateralized debt obligations (CRE CDOs), the subject of Chapter 15, which provided a more effective way to finance below-investment-grade CMBS, and bargain hunters began purchasing CMBS (which had never experienced a loss) at remarkably cheap levels. Soon the market was well on its way to achieving new issuance records, driven by declining interest rates in the wake of the dot-com crash and 9/11, as well as strong relative performance, more efficient rating agency credit-enhancement levels and wider investor distribution, making for better liquidity than even corporate bonds.

As of year-end 2006, there was $697 billion of CMBS outstanding (Exhibit 14.2), which is approximately 46% of the size of the U.S. asset-backed securities (ABS) market. Per the Federal Reserve, the total market size of multifamily residential and commercial loans in 2006 came to more than $2.9 trillion. Thus, the CMBS market accounts for approximately 23% of all commercial loans.

EXHIBIT 14.2   CMBS versus Other Securitized Markets

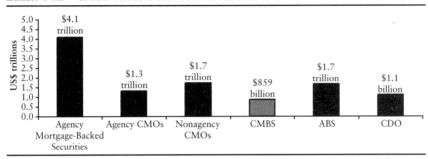

Note: Data as of August 2007. Reflects deal balances.
Source: Wachovia Capital Markets, LLC, Intex Solutions, Inc., and Federal Reserve Board.

WHAT ARE COMMERCIAL MORTGAGE-BACKED SECURITIES?

CMBS are securitizations of pools of mortgage loans on commercial properties. The following two primary features differentiate CMBS from *mortgage-backed securities* (MBS, or securitization of residential mortgages): (1) Call protection and (2) sequential-pay bond structures.

Call protection can take various forms, namely, lockout, defeasance, yield maintenance, and penalty points. Securitizing loans with call protection allows the creation of bonds with stable or more predictable cash flows. Call protection is discussed later in this section.

Sequential-pay means that as the principal from the underlying loans is paid, it is allocated to the top of the structure first (highest-rated tranche) and continues down through the bond structure in sequential order after each bond is paid off (Exhibit 14.3). In contrast, loan losses work from the other direction as they are applied to the lowest-rated tranche outstanding and continue upward through the structure. Sequential-pay bonds are typically rated by two agencies from AAA to nonrated (NR). Front-end bonds are exposed to "default-induced prepayment risk" as outstanding troubled loans are paid down at par first to these front-end bonds using the proceeds of the liquidated property(ies) backing the loan.

As shown in Exhibit 14.3, the AAA rated bonds have subordination levels of 11% to 30%. Exhibit 14.4 shows another schematic of a typical CMBS deal of 2005 vintage, which includes the *interest-only* (IO) bonds, X-P, and X-C.[2]

The X-P and X-C bonds are IO bonds. The cash flow to pay these bonds comes from the excess interest available in the structure—*weighted average*

---

[2] For greater detail regarding the characteristics of AAA CMBS securities see the Appendix.

EXHIBIT 14.3 CMBS Paydown and Loss Schedule

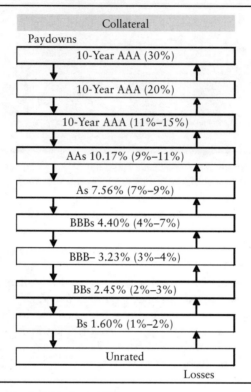

Source: Wachovia Capital Markets, LLC.

coupon (WAC) of the loans less the WAC of the bonds. The X-P is called a planned amortization class (PAC) IO bond, and the X-C is the support or levered IO bond. The name PAC is borrowed from the residential bond structure world and is meant to connote the stability of this stream of cash flow. This bond is typically structured to withstand prepayment rates of a 6% *constant default rate* (6 CDR). The support IO will lose cash flow when a loan prepays (default induced or not). Some deals have just one IO (the combination of X-P and X-C), which is called a *WAC IO*.

Exhibit 14.5 shows how subordination levels for all ratings have improved since 1995. As the CMBS asset class grew and performed well, the rating agencies continued to lower subordination levels across the bond structure. This was driven primarily by expectations (self-proclaimed by the agencies themselves) that a BBB-rated CMBS bond should have similar risk characteristics (probability of default as well as upgrades/downgrades) as a BBB corporate bond (or any other rated class).

EXHIBIT 14.4 Structural Overview

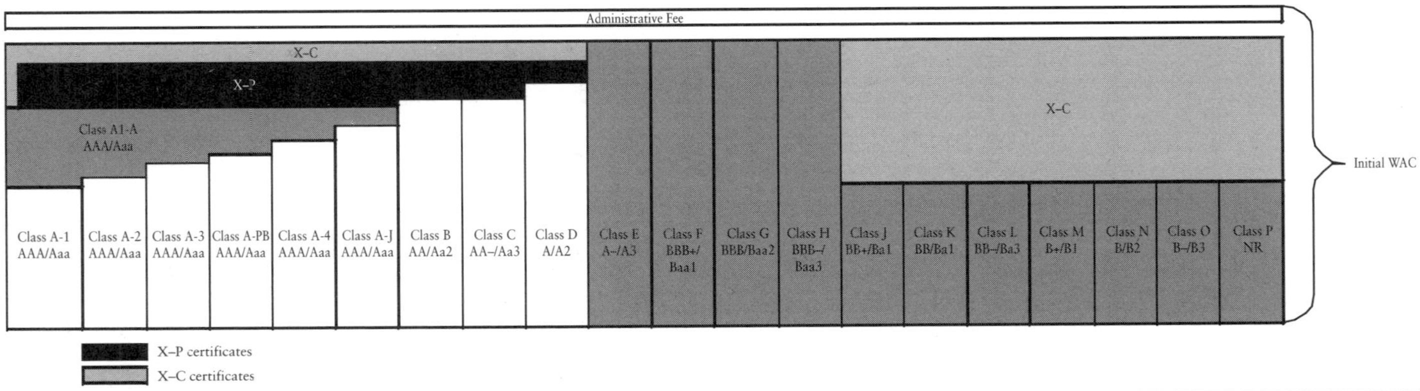

Note: Classes are not drawn to scale.
Source: Wachovia Capital Markets, LLC.

EXHIBIT 14.5   Trends in CMBS Subordination Levels: Fixed Rate Conduit Deals

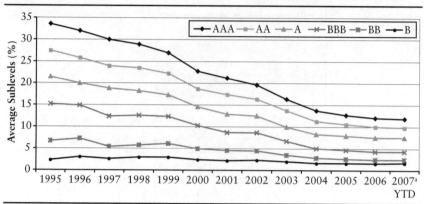

^a Data through September 2007.
Source: Wachovia Capital Markets, LLC, and Intex Solutions, Inc.

As illustrated in the following transition matrixes (Exhibits 14.6 and 14.7), CMBS has recorded a better performance profile than its corporate bond counterparts.

THE CHARACTERISTICS OF COMMERCIAL REAL ESTATE LOANS

The following four property types constitute the majority of CMBS collateral—apartment buildings, shopping or strip malls, office properties and industrial properties. Other asset types included in CMBS pools are hotels, manufactured housing, self-storage, and healthcare properties.

One appealing factor for borrowers is that the loans are nonrecourse (or limited recourse) to the borrower. Ultimate repayment comes solely from the collateral and not the borrower. There are exceptions for fraudulent borrower activities or representations, and the like. Borrowers typically make their borrowing decisions either on price (which conduit or other lender is offering the cheapest financing) and/or proceeds (which lender is willing to lend the largest amount of proceeds—that is, allowing the borrower the greatest leverage).

In exchange for nonrecourse and favorable rates, the loans come with prepayment restrictions, making it possible to create bonds that have excellent call protection and average life stability. Most loans amortize over a 25- to 30-year period. However, most loans also balloon at 10 years and must be paid in full. Since 2004, the amount of loans with IO periods (where no amortization is taking place) has been increasing. For many years, IO periods as a percentage of a loan's term has hovered around 5%. This percentage has grown to nearly 70% as shown in Exhibit 14.8.

EXHIBIT 14.6 Standard & Poor's Weighted-Average Multiyear U.S. CMBS Rating Transition, 1985–2006

From/To	AAA	AA	A	BBB	BB	B	CCC	CC	C	D	Upgrade/Stable	Downgrade
Weighted-Average Five-year rating transition												
AAA	97.6	2.0	0.2	0.2	0.0	0.0	0.0	0.0	0.0	0.00	97.6	2.4
AA	30.7	64.0	2.6	0.6	0.0	1.2	0.5	0.0	0.0	0.24	64.7	5.3
A	15.0	15.0	61.3	6.2	1.8	0.3	0.0	0.0	0.0	0.38	91.3	8.7
BBB	9.0	15.2	15.9	50.8	5.0	1.3	1.1	0.1	0.0	1.64	90.9	9.1
BB	2.0	2.4	5.4	16.1	52.4	7.6	3.6	0.7	0.5	9.45	78.3	21.7
B	0.4	0.4	0.9	3.3	11.2	53.4	11.4	0.0	0.0	19.02	69.6	30.4
CCC	0.0	0.0	4.8	0.0	0.0	2.4	53.0	0.0	0.0	39.76	60.2	39.8
CC	0.0	0.0	0.0	0.0	0.0	0.0	0.0	100.0	0.0	0.00	100.0	0.0

Note: AAA ratings from the same transaction are treated as a single rating in the calculation of this table. When ratings are withdrawn, the last rating before withdrawal is used in the transition rate calculation. Full rating categories are used when determining rating transitions for upgrades and downgrades. Each period's outstanding number of unique ratings is used for weighted average statistics.

Source: Eric Thompson, Larry Kay, and Erkan Erturk, *Transition Study: North American CMBS Ratings Achieve High Levels of Stability in 2006,* 29 January 2007, Table 9–Standard & Poor's Weighted Average Multiyear U.S. CMBS Rating Transition (1985–2006) (Weighted-Average five-year rating transition). This material is reproduced with permission of Standard & Poor's, a division of the McGraw-Hill Companies, Inc.

EXHIBIT 14.7 Standard & Poor's Weighted-Average Multiyear U.S. Corporate Rating Transition, 1985–2006

From/To	AAA	AA	A	BBB	BB	B	CCC/C	D	Upgrade/Stable	Downgrade
Weighted-Average Five-year rating transition										
AAA	71.41	22.11	5.67	0.29	0.15	0.07	0.07	0.22	71.4	28.6
AA	2.09	61.91	29.53	4.90	0.82	0.35	0.05	0.35	64.0	36.0
A	0.17	5.58	69.59	19.28	3.26	0.99	0.20	0.94	75.3	24.7
BBB	0.11	0.95	13.07	66.84	11.35	3.78	0.66	3.25	81.0	19.0
BB	0.05	0.18	2.08	19.95	43.70	17.47	2.21	14.36	66.0	34.0
B	0.00	0.12	0.85	3.01	16.57	34.27	5.17	40.01	54.8	45.2
CCC/C	0.00	0.00	0.66	1.33	3.76	10.84	4.42	78.98	21.0	79.0

Source: Eric Thompson, Larry Kay, and Erkan Erturk, *Transition Study: North American CMBS Ratings Achieve High Levels of Stability in 2006,* 29 January 2007, Table 10–Standard & Poor's Weighted Average Multiyear U.S. Corporate Rating Transition (1985–2006) (Weighted-Average Five-year rating transition). This material is reproduced with permission of Standard & Poor's, a division of the McGraw-Hill Companies, Inc.

EXHIBIT 14.8 Interest Only (IO) Percentage of Balance

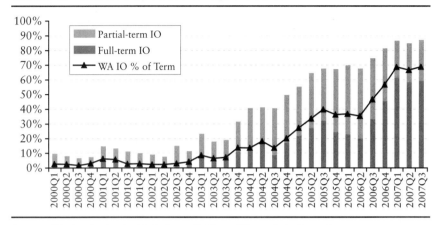

Source: Wachovia Capital Markets, LLC, and Intex Solutions, Inc.

The refinancing risk at the balloon date is critical. Some loans have five- or seven-year terms, and a few have greater than 10 years, though this is uncommon, as the CMBS deal structure is not necessarily the most efficient execution for longer-term paper.

Loans paying down at or before the balloon date can result in the deleveraging of a deal and a potential tranche upgrade. This is sometimes referred to as *credit convexity*.

ANALYZING AND VALUING CMBS

What to Look For: Two Key Credit Indicators Are DSCR and LTV

A loan's *debt service coverage ratio* (DSCR) is the most important credit-quality indicator (of default and loss risk). DSCR equals net operating income divided by the mortgage payment. This number helps to gauge the likelihood of a loan defaulting during the loan term.

Loan-to-value ratio (LTV) is closely related to DSCR as it is a function of a property's net cash flow (net operating income less estimated replacement reserves or tenant improvements and leasing commissions) and a capitalization rate. The cap rate can be thought of as the desired return an owner would require if the property were owned for cash. LTV is an important statistic but dependent on the capitalization rate, which is an assumed rate. Agencies focus on LTV as it has a strong relationship with the possible severity of loss experienced should the loan default.

EXHIBIT 14.9   A Quick Guide to CMBS Quality: DSCR and LTV Ratios

	Excellent	Very Good	Good	Fair	Poor
Average DSCR	> 1.50×	1.49×–1.35×	1.34×–1.25×	1.24×–1.20×	< 1.20×
Average LTV	< 65%	65%–69%	70%–74%	75%–80%	> 80%

Source: Wachovia Capital Markets, LLC.

The dispersion of DSCRs and LTVs is important to examine (see Exhibit 14.9) particularly if one is buying lower-rated CMBS subordinates or first-pay bonds as these bonds would be among the first affected in a deal should there be a problem with any one loan. For example, the percentage of the deal with an LTV greater than 75% is probably more important than the weighted average LTV. Interestingly in CMBS, unlike corporate bonds, the ratings of some tranches of a deal may be upgraded, whereas others may be downgraded when losses occur due to the paying down of troubled loans and deleveraging of the deal.

Some important qualitative factors to consider in judging the quality of commercial real estate include the following:

1. Can many different types of tenants use the property—i.e., can an office property be converted to apartments? (See Exhibits 14.10 and 14.11.)
2. What is the quality of the tenants?
3. Is the property diversified with different types of tenants. Sponsorship (the borrower and manager of the property) quality is also an important consideration.

What to Look for: Geographic and Property Diversification

Risk reduction is not only driven by the credit quality of the collateral but also the collateral's diversification. Therefore, concentration or lack of diversification by any measure is typically a negative. To mitigate this risk, a CMBS investor typically likes to see a geographic concentration of less than 25% in one geographic area and no more than 40% in one property type.

What to Look for: Property Types

- *Multifamily loans.* These loans are considered the most desirable: short-term leases; limited leasing risk; strong historical credit experience; relatively transparent financial reporting; large potential universe of new tenants; generally widely available financing, including FHLMC and FNMA; and 24.8% of outstanding commercial real estate loans. However, they are susceptible to economic downturns and generally have higher LTVs.

EXHIBIT 14.10   A Quick Guide to CMBS Quality: Property Type and Geographic Location

	Acceptable	High
Geographic concentration	< 25%	70%–75%
Property type concentration	< 40% in one property type	40% or greater in one property type

Source: Wachovia Capital Markets, LLC.

EXHIBIT 14.11   Breakdown of CMBS by Property Type: Percent of Current Balance

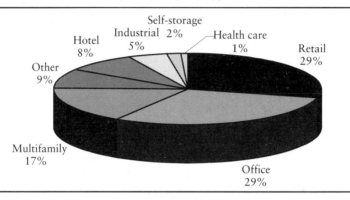

Note: Data as of September 2007.
Source: Intex Solutions, Inc., and Wachovia Capital Markets, LLC.

- *Retail properties.* Regional malls to community strip centers. The keys here are tenant quality, unanchored or anchored by the major tenant and the relationship of the lease rent to the market rent.
- *Office properties.* Central business district versus suburban, longer-term leases, the high cost of attracting new tenants and large office loans (many exceed $100 million) can diminish pool diversification.
- *Industrial properties.* Strong historical credit experience and short leases require underwriting expertise for specialized uses, potential limitations for alternative uses. Many lenders stick to warehouses and distribution facilities. Other factors include access to local labor, proximity to supply sources and customers and accessibility to transportation. The lease structure and rollover risk analysis are important.
- *Hospitality properties.* These properties are more like an operating business than commercial real estate. This requires a separate underwriting discipline. Limited service properties tend to be characterized by stiff competition and low barriers to entry. Luxury or destination properties may possess unique attributes. Potential cash flow volatility is another

possible drawback: leases last 24 hours, occupancy in certain areas can be volatile and dependent on the economy and consumer travel budgets—"the canary in the mine."

What to Look for: Loan Size/Concentration

The loan size varies from $1 million to, more recently, greater than $1.5 billion. Smaller loans allow for greater diversification and less credit risk, yet they are more difficult to analyze. Large-loan deals are typically purchased by buy-and-hold accounts, such as insurance companies and pension funds with real estate expertise, and often are preferred by these "real estate-savvy investors" as it is economical to spend the time analyzing the property. Smaller loan deals (conduit) are more liquid and are typically purchased by total-return, mark-to-market investors that, lacking real estate experience, are more apt to rely on diversification and the rating agencies' analysis and judgment.

Fusion deals, presently the most common type of CMBS deal, are "lumpy" conduit deals. Generally, a fusion deal has a few large loans that are typically shadow-rated investment-grade loans that are combined with a diverse pool of conduit loans. They grew in popularity after 9/11, which shut down the single-asset and large-loan type CMBS deals due to concerns that the risk of a terrorist act against one large property was too great. As a result, these large loans were split up and portions placed into various CMBS, thereby creating fusion deals. Much focus is placed on the top 10 and top 20 loans in any given deal as these can have a substantial influence on performance.

Concentration is important because it is sometimes difficult for the rating agencies to predict commercial loan defaults. The rating agencies use measures to score loan concentration and, accordingly, require more or less credit enhancement. For example, Moody's uses the Herfindahl index to determine the effective number of loans within a pool. A pool of 100 loans that had a Herfindahl index of 65 indicates that the pool has an effective diversity of 65 loans.[3]

What to Look for: Loan Types

Loan coupons may be fixed or floating. As of September 2007, about 94% of loan coupons were fixed rate. Medium- and long-term commercial mortgage loans (five-plus years) are generally fixed rate and have attractive investment features such as prepayment penalties described in greater detail below. Floating-rate loans can be more risky, as the DSCR changes with

---

[3] Moody's, *CMBS 1Q 99 Review and Outlook.*

interest rates (though LIBOR caps are required), and they usually have no amortization and the properties are often transitional properties. Transitional properties are those in which the borrower may be trying to renovate, retenant or improve in some other way. As such, the borrower typically prefers to finance the property at the cheapest level possible (floating rate debt) until the property's cash flow is stabilized, at which time the borrower pays down the floating rate loan and locks in longer-term fixed rate financing. Floating rate deals are more prone to adverse selection due to the few number of loans in a deal (typically 8 to 15) and the possibility that the best transitional properties will be paid off first as floating rate loans typically have no or limited prepayment penalties unlike fixed rate loans. Short-term or interim financing often is at an adjustable rate with low or no prepayment penalties (in the form of penalty points from 0.25% to 2.00%).

In addition, floating rate loans provide the borrower with the ability to extend the maturity of the loan to as much as five years, if necessary.

What to Look for: Prepayment Terms/Call Protection

Call protection and average life stability are key reasons investors buy CMBS. These two characteristics set CMBS apart from their residential MBS cousins.

Loans in CMBS deals can have several different types of call protection (see Exhibit 14.12).

- *Lockout.* The borrower is prohibited from prepaying. Many CMBS are locked out for the first two years (and sometimes longer). Lockout is often used in combination with other forms of prepayment protection.
- *Defeasance.* This is the most desirable. The borrower must purchase a basket of Treasury obligations (and, in some cases, agency debt is allowed) that replicate the scheduled future loan cash flow. There is no change in investor cash flow timing, plus higher-quality U.S. Treasuries replace commercial-loan cash flow, which can sometimes result in upgrades of deal tranches. A loan cannot be defeased until two years after securitization due to REMIC laws governing substitution of collateral. Thus, loans with defeasance call protection have lockout periods of at least two years.

EXHIBIT 14.12 A Quick Guide to CMBS Quality: Prepayment Protection

	Excellent	Very Good	Good	Fair
Geographic concentration	Defeasance/ lockout	Yield maintenance	Prepayment penalty points	

Source: Wachovia Capital Markets, LLC.

- *Yield maintenance.* This is designed to compensate the lender or security holder for early principal retirement. The yield maintenance penalty is calculated by taking the present value of the future commercial loan cash flows, discounted by the prevailing market yield of an equivalent average life Treasury equal to the remaining loan term. Formulas for calculating the discount yield to use and discounting methodology can and do vary. A key issue to consider is how the penalty gets allocated among the various tranches. It is quite possible, depending on the formula and other factors that all bonds may not be made whole.
- *Penalty points.* The penalty point premium is easily understood as it is the product of the current unpaid balance and a predetermined percentage. There are not many loans that use this call-protection approach alone.
- *Open.* The loan is free to prepay without any penalty.

It is not uncommon to have loans with various combinations of call protection, although, increasingly, lockout and Treasury defeasance have become the norm with penalty points less common.

HOW CMBS TRADE

CMBS, unlike some other fixed income products, are priced at spread-to-swap rates. Prior to May 1999, they were priced at a spread to U.S. Treasury rates. As shown in Exhibit 14.13, since the beginning of 1999 CMBS spreads versus swaps have been fairly stable, ranging from wides in late 2007 of 100+ bps versus swaps, to as tight as 20+ bps. In the fall of 1998,

EXHIBIT 14.13　　10-Year CMBS versus 10-Year Swap Spreads

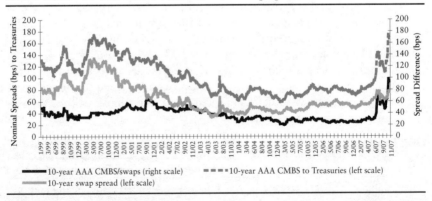

Note: Data as of August 2007.
Source: Wachovia Capital Markets, LLC.

these spreads widened out considerably due to the circumstances posed by the Russian default crisis mentioned earlier. In 2007, they widened in the market contagion brought on by the subprime crisis and general liquidity unwind. CMBS spreads have come in over time as the market has matured, performed well and attracted growing numbers of investors. That being said, CMBS's day-to-day or week-to-week spread movements often take their cue from the corporate market.

CMBS PERFORMANCE

CMBS has had a terrific track record from an upgrade-versus-downgrade perspective. As noted above, the CMBS industry was born out of the troubles of the early 1990s with the memory of the mid- to late-1980s not yet dimmed either. Therefore, the rating agencies were conservative in their approach to underwriting and subordination levels. Hence, we have observed the large upgrade-to-downgrade numbers as shown in Exhibit 14.14.

Losses have been contained as well. The 1996 vintage, thus far, is the poorest performing vintage with cumulative losses coming in at 3.05% (see Exhibit 14.15).

Exhibit 14.16 shows how far up in the capital stack the 1996 loss performance would reach in to current deal's subordination structure. Today's BBB– bonds would be able to withstand the 1996 performance average.

The greatest default rate experience in commercial real estate over the past 30-plus years came from loans originated in 1986 (before CMBS came into existence), which resulted from a one-time change in U.S. tax law that was unfavorable to U.S. commercial real estate investors. For this year (or vintage), the default rate hit 31.7% (weighted by balance or 17.7% by loan count) with ultimate estimated losses topping 8%.[4] Indeed, it is this set of life insurance company data upon which the rating agencies originally based their credit-enhancement levels for CMBS. In contrast, CMBS performance during the 1990s to present has been far superior—one of the reasons for the tight pricing in the sector and the wide acceptance of the product. Exhibit 14.17 illustrates the lifetime-to-date cumulative default rates for CMBS. Whether the commercial real estate backing CMBS will continue to outperform these earlier periods is unknown; however, we believe that performance will likely be considerably better. Loan underwriting has been better up until 2006 and 2007; CMBS loans in particular are underwritten three times—by the originator, the B-piece buyer and the rating agency. Another

---

[4] For a closer look at the loss study on life insurance company loans, see Howard Esaki, "Commercial Mortgage Defaults: 30 Years of History," *CMBS World*, Winter 2005.

EXHIBIT 14.14 CMBS Upgrades and Downgrade by Rating Agency

Year of Rating Action	Fitch			Moody's			Standard & Poor's		
	Upgrade	Downgrade	U/D Ratio	Upgrade	Downgrade	U/D Ratio	Upgrade	Downgrade	U/D Ratio
1997	—	—	—	25	3	8.3	9	7	1.3
1998	—	—	—	56	8	7.0	39	7	5.6
1999	149	10	14.9	98	12	8.2	64	5	12.8
2000	229	26	8.8	91	19	4.8	88	22	4.0
2001	345	15	23.0	134	35	3.8	174	62	2.8
2002	374	125	3.0	57	190	-3.3	132	178	-1.3
2003	441	142	3.1	183	172	1.1	301	215	1.4
2004	623	108	5.8	290	204	1.4	508	164	3.1
2005	677	32	21.2	675	143	4.7	957	117	8.2
2006	1781	52	34.3	1120	116	9.7	889	116	7.7
Total	4619	510	9.1	2729	902	3.0	3161	893	3.5

Source: Fitch, Standard & Poor's, and Moody's.

EXHIBIT 14.15 Cumulative Loss Rates by Origination Cohort

Cohort	Dec-99	Dec-00	Dec-01	Dec-02	Dec-03	Dec-04	Dec-05	Dec-06	Oct-07
1995	0.05%	0.12%	0.29%	0.85%	1.54%	2.43%	2.79%	2.79%	2.87%
1996	0.03%	0.05%	0.10%	0.44%	0.85%	1.93%	2.38%	2.75%	3.05%
1997	0.00%	0.03%	0.10%	0.38%	1.01%	1.45%	2.04%	2.42%	2.58%
1998	0.00%	0.02%	0.06%	0.25%	0.59%	1.09%	1.43%	1.66%	1.78%
1999	0.00%	0.00%	0.01%	0.09%	0.32%	0.59%	0.89%	1.18%	1.33%
2000		0.00%	0.00%	0.07%	0.32%	0.59%	1.06%	1.30%	1.41%
2001			0.00%	0.02%	0.08%	0.21%	0.47%	0.73%	0.86%
2002				0.00%	0.01%	0.05%	0.17%	0.23%	0.43%
2003					0.00%	0.00%	0.02%	0.03%	0.07%
2004						0.00%	0.00%	0.01%	0.05%
2005							0.00%	0.00%	0.01%
2006								0.00%	0.00%
2007									0.00%

Note: Cohort based on securitization date.
Source: Wachovia Capital Markets, LLC, and Intex Solutions, Inc.

EXHIBIT 14.16 CMBS Paydown and Loss Schedule versus the Worst CMBS Cohort

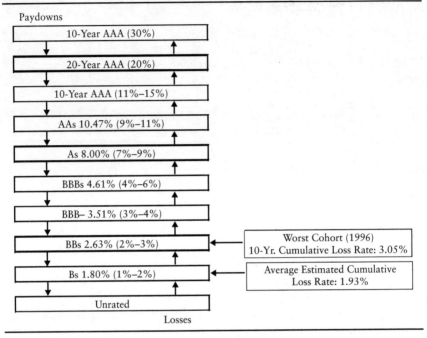

Source: Wachovia Capital Markets, LLC.

EXHIBIT 14.17 Cumulative Default Rates by Origination Cohort

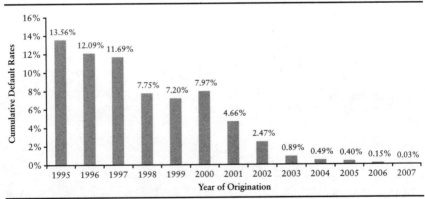

Source: Wachovia Capital Markets, LLC, and Intex Solutions, Inc.

reason is low interest rates and capitalization rates, as they are helping to maintain and, in some cases, boost property prices.

Wachovia has developed a historically based default and loss model that can be helpful in analyzing CMBS deals.[5] In addition, Wachovia has developed *Property Risk Monitor*, which provides a short-term (18 to 27 month) outlook on real estate investment risk and opportunities in the office, apartment, retail, and industrial sectors in the top U.S. markets (up to 55 metros) as well as a short-term outlook on the top 17 European office markets.

WHO SHOULD AND DOES INVEST IN CMBS?

Given the solid credit performance of CMBS and generally positive convexity, the number and types of investors that purchase CMBS and CMBS derivative products have grown considerably over the years to encompass just about every type of investor—at home and abroad. Investors include banks, corporate bond buyers, insurance companies, pension funds, state funds, credit unions, money managers who manage funds versus an index, hedge funds and real estate CDOs. International investors typically purchase floating-rate CMBS but have also been known to purchase fixed. Most international investors are in Europe (United Kingdom, Ireland and Germany), although a growing buyer base exists elsewhere in Europe, Asia, the Middle East, Australia, New Zealand and even South America.

CONCLUSION

The CMBS market has been coming of age. Now a meaningful part of many fixed income indices—it was added to the Lehman Aggregate index in 1999—it has grown to be about a $700 billion market with investors located throughout the world. Its excellent performance to date has made it one of the premier investments in the fixed income markets, even while it is increasingly garnering market share in commercial real estate finance. 2007 has brought challenges to this and other structured products markets. However, liquidity and stability should return and CMBS should continue to serve an important role in the real estate capital markets.

---

[5] For more information on Wachovia's default and loss model, see Brian L. Lancaster, Tony Butler, and Stephen Mayeux, *The Wachovia CMBS Loss Model*, December 1, 2006.

CHAPTER 15

Understanding Managed CRE CDOs

Brian P. Lancaster
Senior Analyst
Wachovia Capital Markets, LLC

Anthony G. Butler, CFA
Senior CMBS Analyst
Wachovia Capital Markets, LLC

Greg Laughton
Analyst
Wachovia Capital Markets, LLC

The nature of *commercial real estate collateralized debt obligations* (CRE CDOs) has changed significantly since their introduction in 1999. CRE CDOs were typically static transactions consisting primarily of fixed-rate collateral, specifically unsecured *real estate investment trust* (REIT) debt and conduit *commercial mortgage backed securities* (CMBS) bonds. These static deals allowed for the sale of collateral only for credit reasons (e.g., delinquency triggers, downgrades, and defaults). The ongoing involvement of the collateral manager was strictly limited to credit surveillance. Any return of principal during the life of the transaction was used to pay down issued liabilities in a straight sequential fashion.

In 2004, an entirely new type of CRE CDO was introduced and proliferated. Key features of these "managed" CDOs include the ability of the collateral manager to reinvest principal proceeds for a period of time, trade collateral assets for other than credit reasons, and include non-CUSIPed assets such as B-notes, rake bonds, mezzanine loans, and preferred equity. CDO technology has been applied to achieve new financing solutions. Just as the first generation of static CRE CDOs emerged in response to the permanent financing needs of CMBS B-piece buyers (with no mark-to-market risk), the new generation of managed CRE CDOs is providing similar term financing for managers of shorter-term floating rate assets. Several key driving forces were behind the evolution of managed CRE CDOs, specifically, the advancement of rating agency methodologies, the increased supply of floating rate, high-yield assets (B-notes and mezzanine), the finite repo funding capacity of the Street, and the maturation of CRE CDO buyers.

Whereas the evolution of the CRE CDO market may be viewed as a positive for commercial real estate finance as it allows for better match term funding for sponsors, increased manager flexibility, and a wider product offering for investors to consider, it also gives CDO managers an important role in influencing the credit quality and prepayment risk of CMBS transactions. As deals become more complex and include less liquid assets, it is incumbent upon both CMBS and CRE CDO investors to deepen their understanding of these structures and the underlying assets. This chapter attempts to provide insight into both.

EVOLUTION OF THE MARKET FOR B-NOTES, MEZZANINE LOANS, PREFERRED EQUITY, AND RAKE BONDS

From 2001 to 2005, adversity, technology, and strong real estate markets conspired to dramatically reshape the landscape of structured real estate finance. The tragic events of September 11, 2001 and subsequent legal and insurance disputes surrounding CMBS deals such as GMACC 2001-WTC-A and BALL 2001-WTC, deals backed by World Trade Center properties, effectively "shut down" the single-asset, large-loan market in CMBS. For many, the terrorist event risk (and insurance problems) associated with investment in a security backed by one large loan, usually that of a "trophy property," was either too great or too difficult to calculate. In the fixed-rate market, the response was (and is) to spread the risk relating to any one property by the splitting of large loans into senior investment-grade *pari passu* A-notes which are placed in different CMBS deals and subordinate, below investment grade, B-notes[1] that are either included in the trust as single-asset rake bonds[2] or sold outside of the trust as B-notes.

The placement of the senior A-notes or the investment-grade portion of these large loans in conduit deals helped alleviate investor concerns regard-

---

[1] For the purposes of this chapter unless otherwise mentioned, we use the common market term *B-notes* to refer to any junior portion of a fixed or floating rate mortgage loan, whether documented as a junior note or a junior "participation" of a single note.

[2] Rake bonds, which will be discussed in much greater detail, may now be either fixed or floating rate. A few years ago, they were primarily floating rate. They may also be credit tranched.

ing both the credit risk and concentration risk presented by the large, single asset. From the issuer's perspective, the impact of barbelling a CMBS deal with an investment-grade A-note(s) along with typical, full-leverage smaller conduit loans (the combination is referred to as a "fusion" deal) was positive in terms of required credit enhancement levels.[3] Benefiting both issuer and investor, these "fusion" deals have proliferated and now dominate the fixed-rate CMBS market.

In contrast, in the floating rate market, the entire A-note was (and is) usually contributed to a large-loan floating-rate CMBS deal (typically containing 10 to 20 loans) and the noninvestment-grade portions (i.e., B-notes, rake bonds, and mezzanine loans[4]) sold off as nonpooled instruments to third parties (such as the subsidiaries of life insurers, real estate investors, money managers and, more recently, CRE CDO managers).

The driving force behind the proliferation of B-notes, mezzanine loans, preferred equity and other forms of subordinate debt, such as rake bonds, whether fixed or floating, has been the divergence between market capitalization (cap) rates and the static cap rates that the rating agencies assume (see Exhibit 15.1).[5] Since 2002, commercial real estate property values have continued to rise and market cap rates[6] to decline. In short, real estate investors have been willing to pay higher prices and accept lower returns on their real estate investments given the low and often volatile returns available in other asset classes, such as corporate bonds or stocks, as well as the upside in commercial real estate due to the potential growth component of rents and, therefore, *net operating income* (NOI). In contrast, the rating agencies take a longer term "through the cycle view" of commercial real estate values and assume, by and large, unchanged or static cap rates.[7]

---

[3] Whereas market participants typically focus on these large loans in their discussions of deal credit quality, we suspect greater issues may lurk among the smaller, "fully leveraged" loans.

[4] Mezzanine loans, like B-notes, have payment and control rights that are subordinate to the first mortgage on the property, however, they are backed by a pledge of equity in the real estate owner or entity that controls/owns the property.

[5] We show market and rating agency cap rates for office because most of the subordinate debt discussed in this chapter is backed by office properties and so that the exhibit is not cluttered. However, apartments exhibit a similar dramatic divergence. There is also a significant divergence between retail and industrial rating agency and market cap rates but not as dramatic.

[6] Cap rates are similar to an internal rate of return concept, that is, they are the returns that real estate investors expect to earn on their real estate investment before leveraging the asset.

[7] For further discussion of this topic, see "CMBS: When Are Cap Rates Too High, Too Low, or Just Right? *Moody's Special Report,*" March 11, 2003.

The rating agencies view their cap rates, not as market driven, but as long-term sustainable levels.

The effect of the divergent views between rating agency static cap rates and market-driven cap rates is apparent in Exhibit 15.1. Indeed, it is no coincidence that the yawning gap between the rating agencies' view of cap rates and the commercial real estate market's view since 2000 has generally coincided with the issuance explosion of B-notes, mezzanine loans, rake bonds, preferred equity, and other extra layers of debt that investors/lenders are willing to provide to property owners (Exhibit 15.2).

EXHIBIT 15.1 Cap Rate Trends

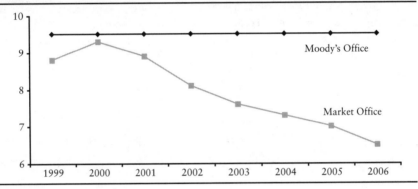

Source: NREI and Moody's.

EXHIBIT 15.2 B-Notes, Rake Bonds and Mezzanine Debt (dollar amount and number of loans)

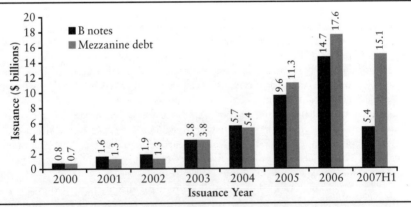

Note: The data set includes: (1) large-loan floating-rate deals, (2) fixed-rate conduit/fusion deals, and (3) single asset/single borrower transactions.
Source: Wachovia Capital Markets, LLC, Intex Solutions, Inc., and Trepp, LLC.

EXHIBIT 15.3 Real Estate Risk Premium by Sector (difference between cap rates and U.S. Treasuries)

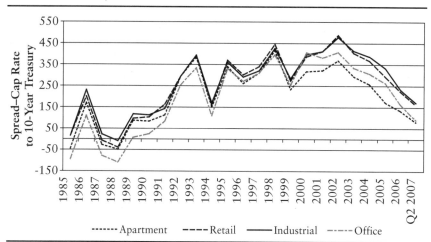

Source: NREI, Global Insight, Real Capital Analytics, and Wachovia Capital Markets, LLC.

Although the rating agencies' position on cap rates is understandable, so too is the position of many real estate investors. Market cap rates indicate and reflect the market's perception of risk. If instead of looking at the level of market cap rates but rather the difference between cap rate levels and the 10-year Treasury—a risk premium for owning real estate if you will—investors had been getting near-record wide incremental returns over alternative investments until recently (Exhibit 15.3).[8]

Regardless of which view you take, it is important to note that cap rates reflect returns before leverage is applied (i.e., the willingness of borrowers to accept these low levels is influenced by their current ability to leverage their returns higher with currently cheap money). As rates rise, this will influence investors' willingness to accept lower returns, the spread between market and rating agency cap rates and, hence, issuance of the kinds of debt and equity discussed in this chapter.

EVOLUTION OF COMMERCIAL REAL ESTATE CDOs

As the size of the market for B-notes, mezzanine loans, and other types of subordinate debt has grown (along with the number of buyers), investment

---

[8] Spreads are now near or somewhat wider than their 10-year average depending on the property type.

banks and the buyers (or lenders) of these types of debt have sought a more stable and appropriate way to finance them. Typically, buyers of B-notes or mezzanine loans have financed themselves via short-term repurchase agreements (repo debt). However, short-term repo debt for these types of non-investment-grade collateral carries several types of risks. Rarely is it match-term funded.[9] It is subject to mark-to-market risk as well as the risk that it may not be renewed each year. In addition, borrowing costs both in terms of high financing rates and *haircuts*[10] can make it expensive. Investment banks and other lenders of this repo debt have risk limits as to how much of this type of debt they are willing to finance and have in some cases hit limits as the size of the market has grown. Applying CDO technology to B-notes, mezzanine loans and other types of this debt is a logical extension of the commercial real estate securitization market as it eliminates most of the risk these types of investors face with repo debt, provides capital recycling for repo lenders and, equally important, potentially reduces funding costs.

The first generation of CRE CDOs was primarily backed by subordinate CMBS (B pieces)[11] and REIT debt and helped B-piece buyers, such as Allied Capital Corp., Anthracite Capital Inc., Arcap REIT Inc., GMAC Commercial Mortgage Corp. (GMACCM), and Lennar Corp. finance their business more cheaply and stably. These early CRE CDOs were always static (e.g., no trading except for credit reasons) and typically included just CMBS and REIT debt. Managed CRE CDOs fill a key need for mezzanine lenders, B-note investors and others, primarily because they are a nonmark-to-market, longer-term financing vehicle. Issues of margin calls, price volatility, and the mismatch of short-term financing are eliminated and financing costs significantly reduced. Indeed, it is no coincidence that the first few "managed CRE CDOs" have been issued by major B-note investors and mezzanine lenders such as Arbor Realty Trust, Brascan Real Estate Fund and Capital Trust. In addition, through the CDO vehicle and the creation of higher-rated investment-grade tranches from the collateral, a whole new investor base, both at home and abroad, is being created.

Clearly, static CRE CDOs would not be viable for B-note and mezzanine investments because their short average life (two to four years) would make

---

[9] Maturities of the asset being funded are the same as the repo liability incurred.

[10] A *haircut* is the amount of "margin" repo lenders require repo borrowers to maintain as a condition for lending money against an asset such as a mezzanine loan or B-note. For example, if a mezzanine loan were equal to $50 million at par, a repo lender might only lend $30 million against it to guard against fluctuations in the value of the mezzanine loan. The haircut would be $20 million.

[11] B-pieces as opposed to B-notes, which are discussed in this report, refer to below-investment-grade tranches of a fixed-rate CMBS deal. See Exhibit 15.7 for a diagram illustrating the difference between B-pieces and B-notes in the CMBS capital structure.

the deal economics unattractive. In addition, these assets are also floating rate, readily prepayable and have to be reinvested on prepayment The key to using CDOs to finance B-notes and mezzanine loans was for Wall Street banks with rating agency support to create a mechanism and process which would allow CRE CDOs to reinvest the return of principal during some defined early period of time (typically four to five years).

In addition, rating agency technology had to advance to a point where it would be able to handle "non-CUSIPed" collateral, an essential development as non-CUSIPed assets do not carry ratings. Non-CUSIPed assets, such as B-notes and mezzanine loans, are shadow rated pursuant to the same standards as conduit and large loan CMBS loans.

Like most new products and markets, the shift from older static CRE CDOs to the newer managed CRE CDO discussed here has been gradual (see Exhibit 15.4). Indeed, several transitional CRE CDOs, such as CREST Exeter Street Solar 04-1, emerged backed not only by subordinate CMBS and REIT debt but also by small amounts of B-notes and credit tenant leases. Most recently, this process has come to its logical conclusion with new milestones in the market, Brascan Real Estate CDO 2004-1 (79% B-notes), Arbor (62% mezzanine debt as well as preferred equity and B-notes) and CapTrust (65% B-notes and 19% mezzanine debt).

EXHIBIT 15.4   Evolution of the Commercial Real Estate CDO

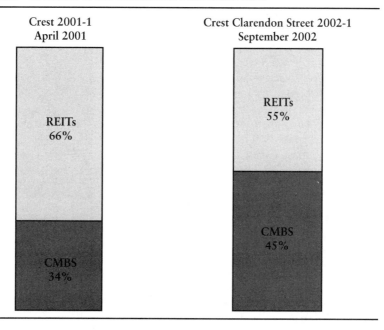

EXHIBIT 15.4 (Continued)

Crest Exeter Street Solar 2004-1
April 2004

Brascan Real Estate CDO 2004-1
October 2004

Arbor Realty Mortgage Securities Series 2004-1
January 2005

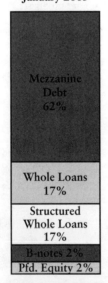

CapTrust RE CDO 2005-1
March 2005

Source: Wachovia Capital Markets, LLC.

ANATOMY OF THE NEW MANAGED CRE CDO STRUCTURES

Collateral Differences and a New Revolving Feature

One of the principal differences between this new generation of managed CRE CDOs and the older static CDOs is the introduction of a reinvestment or revolving period. (Exhibit 15.5) summarizes this and other key differences). The older generation of CRE CDOs were most often backed by noncallable REIT debt and the subordinate debt of fixed rate CMBS, which

EXHIBIT 15.5   Static CRE CDOs versus Managed CRE CDOs

	Static CRE CDOs	Managed CRE CDOs
Collateral type	Fixed	Fixed or floating rate (any combination)
Commercial real estate sectors	CMBS conduit REIT Fixed rate	CMBS conduit REIT Whole loan Large loan floating CMBS Credit tenant leases (CTLs) B-notes Rake bonds Mezzanine loans Preferred equity
Reinvestment of return of principal	None	4–5 years
Collateral quality tests (CQTs)	None	Yes (see below)
Sale of collateral	Credit risk • Default	Credit risk Default Credit improved Discretionary
Advancing agent on non-PIKable classes	No	Yes
Collateral manager fees	Senior fee: 10 bps Junior fee: 10 bps	Senior fee: 10–15 bps Junior fee: 15–20 bps
Balance sheet management	Repay liabilities (only straight sequential)	Either: (a) Reinvest in assets subject to collateral quality test; or (b) Repay liabilities
Surveillance	Pure surveillance	Surveillance and full balance-sheet management

Source: Wachovia Capital Markets, LLC.

have long maturities and strong call protection.[12] Hence, CRE CDOs tended to be structured as static pool CRE CDOs, and CDO managers often had no ability to reinvest returns of principal or trade underlying assets (except for credit risk or defaulted assets).

In contrast, this newer generation of CRE CDOs often contains shorter-maturity floating rate assets (e.g., B-notes, mezzanine loans, and rake bonds). Floating rate commercial real estate loans typically have short maturities of two to three years (plus two to three years of extension options) and are prepayable[13] after a minimal call protection period, often 6 to 18 months. The shorter maturities and "prepayability" of floating rate assets require that the new CRE CDO structures have a revolving or reinvestment period enabling the collateral to be reinvested by the CDO manager as paydowns occur. If this were not the case, the fixed costs associated with repeatedly doing a new deal would be prohibitive.

Collateral Quality Tests: A New Feature of Managed CRE CDOs

To maintain the credit quality of the managed CDO throughout its life as new collateral enters and exits, the rating agencies have a long list of *collateral quality tests* (CQTs) that the new collateral must meet. Although it is beyond the scope of this chapter to list all of them, Exhibit 15.6 summarizes most of them with highlights on the most important ones, such as maximum *weighted average rating factor* (WARF)—a measure of credit quality; minimum diversity score (e.g., Moody's Herfindahl score); minimum weighted average spread (floaters) and coupon (fixed rate assets) (mitigates the risk that the yield on the collateral will be insufficient to cover the cost of funding for the CDO liabilities and increases the likelihood that the deal will generate excess spread); and concentration limits on property type and geographic location. For those new to the sector, Exhibit 15.6 briefly describes why each CQT is important to the investor.

Sale of Collateral: Managed CRE CDO Managers Given Greater Leeway

Another important difference between the old and new structures noted in Exhibit 15.5, static CRE CDOs versus managed CRE CDOs, is that the col-

---

[12] Some common forms are lockouts, Treasury defeasance, and yield maintenance.
[13] Borrowers like this feature as it allows them to take advantage of temporary short-term low rates and, later on, refinance into long-term, fixed rate debt. This may be done either to "play the interest rate market" or because borrowers do not want to lock in fixed rate financing for a "transitional property" until after they increase the value of the property through retenanting, renovation or some other repositioning.

EXHIBIT 15.6 Typical Collateral Quality Tests for Managed CRE CDOs

Typical Collateral Quality Tests	Issue Addressed	Description
Maximum Geographic Concentration	Diversity	Limits concentration of properties in any one geographic region; mitigates exposure to local economic downturn that may negatively affect commercial real estate in that region.
Maximum Property Concentration	Diversity	Reduces event risk of single large property default or deterioration leading to sudden and substantial losses to the pool.
Minimum Weighted Average Fixed Coupon	Cash flow	**Mitigates risk that the yield on the collateral will be insufficient to cover the cost of funding for the CDO liabilities and increases the likelihood that the deal will generate excess spread.**
Minimum Weighted Average Floating Coupon or Spread	Cash flow	**Same as above but for floating rate collateral.**
Maximum Weighted Average Life (WAL)	Cash flow/ Credit quality	Reduces the likelihood of principal repayment on the underlying collateral extending beyond the maturity date(s) of the CDO's liabilities; also limits the average cumulative default probability of the pool.
Maximum Percentage of Floating Rate Assets	Hedging	Mitigates risk that fixed/floating asset mix will move outside the range for which the interest rate hedge (which may be a natural hedge) will be most effective.
Maximum Percentage of Fixed Rate Assets	Hedging	Same as above.
Maximum Issuer/Obligor Size	Diversity	Limits exposure to any one issuer/obligor, which reduces risk that credit deterioration of a single issuer/obligor will have significant impact on the pool.

343

EXHIBIT 15.6 (Continued)

Typical Collateral Quality Tests	Issue Addressed	Description
Rating Distribution of Collateral: Maximum Percentage of Collateral Below Ba3, B2, etc.	Credit barbelling	Limits concentration of low-rated assets in the portfolio to reduce the potential for "barbelled" credit quality (average credit quality may mask the inclusion of securities with very low ratings if there are sufficient securities with high ratings).
Maximum Weighted Average Rating Factor (WARF)	Credit quality	**Reduces the likelihood of the average probability of default of the pool rising above a given threshold (rating factor increases as credit quality decreases).**
Maximum Percentage of Different Types of Collateral Such as REIT Debt, CRE CDO, etc.	Diversity	Limits risk that collateral from the same asset class share certain characteristics (e.g. structural, legal, regulatory) that may lead to positively correlated deterioration.
Herfindahl Score (Minimum)	Diversity	**Reflects diversification as measured by the effective number of loans in a pool, which may be different from the actual number of loans in the pool depending on the range of loan sizes.**
Largest Single Origination Year	Diversity	Mitigages risk that collateral of the same "vintage" share characteristics (e.g., common underlying assets for structured products collateral, similar underwriting standards) that may lead to positively correlated credit deterioration.
Weighted Average Recovery Test	Credit quality	Ensures collateral quality of the pool.
S&P CDO Monitor Test Satisfied	Various	Ensures the original rated parameters of the pool are complied with over time.

Note: Bold text indicates a key collateral quality test. See N. Levidy, "CMBS: Moody's Approach to Revolving Facilities in CDOs Backed by Commercial Real Estate Securities," *Moody's Special Report,* July 29, 2004; and T. Phillipp, et al., "CMBS 1Q99 Review and Outlook: Smaller, But Still Solid Market For 1999 Holds Different Risks for Investors," *Moody's Special Report,* April 16, 1999.
Source: Created from data obtained from Moody's Investor Services, Inc., and Wachovia Capital Markets, LLC.

lateral manager is allowed far greater leeway in selling collateral. Under the old static structure, managers could only sell collateral when a default or other credit impairment had occurred or was likely. In addition to having this ability, CRE CDO managers of the new managed structures are also allowed to sell a piece (or pieces) of collateral if their credit has improved. In this case, the manager is typically limited to selling only credit improved "CUSIPed" collateral assets (e.g., CMBS, REITs or CRE CDOs). A key issue here is how realized capital gains (premiums above par) are treated in the CRE CDO waterfall. Are they included in the principal waterfall (conservative) and available for reinvestment in new collateral or the repayment of debt which builds overcollateralization? Or are they "leaked out" to the equity investor (aggressive)? An investor-friendly approach is to have capital gains treated as principal proceeds flowing through the principal waterfall rather than allowing it to "leak out" to the equity holder. Structural differences from deal to deal obviously have relative value implications for the investor.

Unlike the older static CRE CDOs, managed CRE CDOs also typically permit the manager discretionary authority to trade up to 10% of deal assets (usually limited to CUSIPed deal assets, such as CMBS, REITs, and CRE CDOs) per year. Whereas an individual's discretion is always a double-edged sword, this can be beneficial in the case of a CRE CDO backed by floating rate debt. One of the problems with floating rate CMBS is that adverse selection can occur over time. CMBS floaters may be backed by "transitional properties" that the respective borrowers may be trying to improve in various ways, such as renovating the property or leasing vacant space, after which the borrower prepays the short-term, floating rate loan and locks in a long-term, fixed rate loan. This tendency can result in the collateral quality of CMBS floaters deteriorating as better loans prepay out of the pool (adverse selection). By giving a manager discretionary authority, this impact can be mitigated through trading unlike with a conventional CMBS floater.

In addition to allowing the manager far greater leeway in selling the collateral, new revolving structures also allow the manager to reinvest the proceeds of these sales during the reinvestment period (subject to the collateral quality tests). Under the old static structure, proceeds from a sale could only be used to pay down liabilities (the CDO tranches) sequentially.

Advancing Agent Required on Non-PIKable CDO Liabilities

Another new feature common to these managed CRE CDOs is the presence of an advancing agent. An advancing agent is required by the rating agencies on the non-PIKable CDO liabilities (typically the AAA and AA classes) to ensure timely payment of interest. Non-PIKable liabilities are CDO bonds that do not allow for deferred payment of interest or in the event of interest shortfalls do not *pay-in-kind* (PIK). In the event of interest shortfalls, "PIKable" bonds make interest payments to investors in the form of additional bonds or an increase in the principal balance of the bonds, rather than with a cash payout. In other words, a security that is not allowed to capitalize its interest payments is non-PIKable.

In the event of interest shortfalls on a non-PIKable bond, the advancing agent would advance the shortfall to that class (subject to recoverability) or it would be an event of default of the entire CDO. By contrast, interest shortfalls on PIKable CDO classes are not events of default. PIKable CRE CDO bonds are similar to CMBS bonds in that the nonpayment of interest is not an event of default in either type of securitization. Specific mechanisms exist in both CMBS deals (master servicer advancing which is subject to the recoverability standard) and CRE CDOs (interest coverage tests which are automatic and not subject to the recoverability standard) to minimize the likelihood of interest shortfalls.

The rating agencies require an advancing agent on deals that contain substantial amounts of non-CUSIPed collateral that by its nature does not provide for master servicer advancing. Traditional static pool CRE CDOs consisted of CUSIPed collateral, and these, therefore, did not require an advancing agent. For example, a portion of the collateral of traditional static pool CDOs often consisted of subordinate CMBS debt, which because it was part of the original CMBS pool and trust, was entitled to servicer advancing. With these new structures, some collateral, such as B-notes, is not part of the trust or pool and, hence, not entitled to servicer advancing.[14] In the case of managed CDOs, the CDO manager typically serves as the advancing agent with the trustee acting as a backup.

Balance Sheet Management, Management Fees, and Surveillance

By now, it should be obvious that the role of the collateral manager of managed CRE CDOs is significantly greater than that of the older static pool CRE CDOs. Indeed, given the amount of leeway available for reinvesting in assets, paying down debt, trading (e.g., credit improved, discretionary and credit risk), the new manager is for all practical purposes engaged in balance sheet management. As such, their fees are greater, surveillance requirements are critical and the quality of the manager in terms of real estate experience and "deep pockets" is absolutely essential. We cannot emphasize this last point enough. As we shall see in our discussion of B-notes, mezzanine loans

---

[14] This is an important distinction between rake bonds and B-notes. Although rake bonds are similar to B-notes, they are part of the CMBS trust and, hence, entitled to servicer advancing whereas B-notes are not. For further information, see the later discussion on the key differences between B-notes and rake bonds.

and the other collateral types that make up these new CRE CDOs, CDO managers will be faced with making critical decisions in a timely manner should difficulties arise with the underlying commercial real estate.

UNDERSTANDING THE COLLATERAL: MEZZANINE DEBT, B-NOTES, RAKE BONDS, AND PREFERRED EQUITY

It is important for investors to understand the structural differences between mezzanine loans, B-notes, rake bonds and preferred equity, the collateral that supports each and the rights (both prior to a default and after) of each class of investor. Exhibit 15.7 provides a succinct hypothetical road map of the major types of debt[15] and equity backing this latest generation of CRE CDOs.

EXHIBIT 15.7 Deconstructing the Real Estate Finance Tower

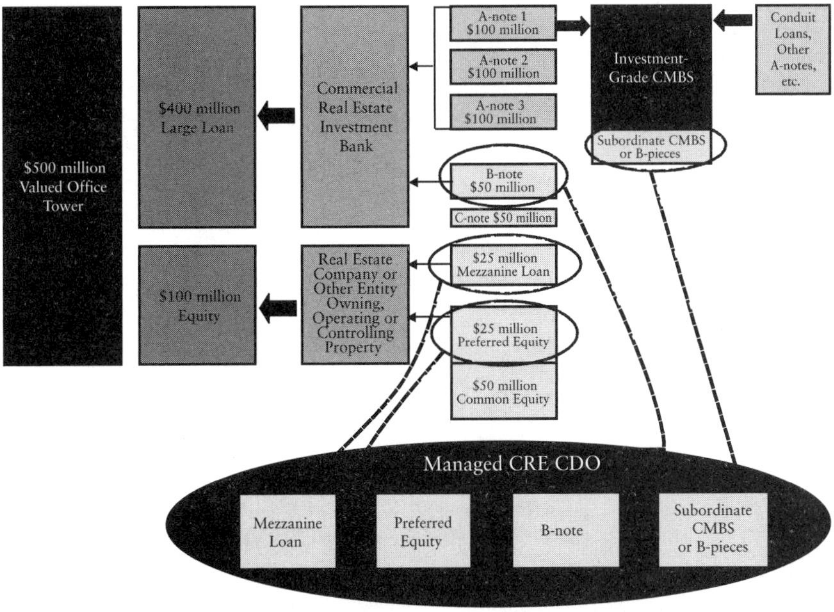

Source: Wachovia Capital Markets, LLC.

---

[15] Managed CRE CDOs are typically backed by floating rate debt. While most of the debt and equity represented in Exhibit 15.7 could be found in fixed or floating rate deals, as noted previously the A-note of floating-rate deals is typically not spilt, whereas the A-note of fixed rate deals can be.

As shown in the exhibit, the financing of a theoretical $500 million commercial real estate property today, such as an office tower, might consist of a $400 million "large" mortgage loan made by a Wall Street investment bank and $100 million of equity financing pledged by an entity which owns, operates and/or controls the property.

The $400 million "large," fixed rated mortgage loan is typically split into a lower-rated, subordinate B-note and several higher-rated (usually investment grade) *pari passu* A-notes,[16] each of which is typically placed in a different fixed rate CMBS deal. Up until the creation of these new CRE CDOs, these B-notes were typically placed outside the CMBS deal with a limited number of B-note and mezzanine buyers, such as insurance company subsidiaries and real estate operating companies.[17]

As mentioned earlier, a substantial purpose of the B-note[18] is to reduce the leverage of the A-notes as the B-note interest and principal payments are subordinate to those of the A-notes. This strategy of delevering and credit enhancing the A-note, as well as splitting it into several *pari passu* A-notes that are placed in different deals, is key as a large, low-rated loan, if not split in this way, would be detrimental to deal credit enhancement levels and the economics of a CMBS deal. The rating agencies would require greater subordination and credit enhancement for the deal because of the loan's low rating and because of the impact of its size on the diversification in the CMBS deal.

Although market participants often refer to B-notes and mezzanine loans in the same breath, it should be readily apparent from Exhibit 15.7 that mezzanine loans occupy a different position in the commercial real estate capital structure than B-notes. Where B-notes are collateralized by a subordinate interest in the first mortgage, mezzanine loans are backed by an equity interest in the real estate owner or entity that controls/owns the property, the proceeds of which may be used to finance the entity's or owner's "equity" in the property.

Mezzanine loans can increase the loan to value ratio on a property to as high as 90% or greater. The rating agencies are concerned that mezzanine loans further reduce the owner's equity in the property, thereby reducing the owner's commitment to the property during difficult times. As a result

---

[16] For further information regarding the risks and mitigants of *pari passu* A-notes, see Wachovia Securities' March 24, 2004, CMBS and Real Estate research report, *Pari Passu Notes in CMBS: Who's in Charge?*

[17] B-notes are also increasingly being included with the original CMBS trust as a directed pay class or property specific class. In this form, we refer to them as rake bonds.

[18] C-notes, D-notes, and so on, which are subordinate to B-notes, are also sometimes created as well as *pari passu* B-notes.

of this concern, the rating agencies assume higher default frequencies for these loans.[19]

Mezzanine lenders are usually seasoned, deep-pocketed real estate operators (or should be) who understand how to own, manage, and "turn around" a commercial real estate property if need be. As such, they often prefer the position of mezzanine lender as it is more straightforward for a mezzanine lender to seize control (foreclose) on a property from the original owning entity and "cure" the default than it would be for a B-note buyer in the case of a default. The rating agencies take some comfort in the fact that should the original borrower default, there is another seasoned, deep-pocketed real estate investor (the mezzanine lender) that can step in and take over the property (e.g., although default frequency may be higher and loss severity may be lower).[20]

In cases where borrowers are restricted, usually by the first mortgage, from arranging a mezzanine loan, they may sometimes issue preferred equity interests to a potential lender (Exhibit 15.7). Although preferred equity is legally equity, from the investor's perspective, it is similar to fixed income securities in that an investor's principal expected source of return is not capital appreciation but rather regular dividend or other payments, not unlike a bond. Preferred equity payments are subordinate to mezzanine loan payments.

A good "real life" example of how the capital structure of one office building purchased for $675 million with a $515 million first mortgage can be "sliced and diced" with the corresponding pieces placed in difference CMBS and CRE CDO deals is 11 Madison Ave.—a deal securitized in 2004 by Wachovia (see Exhibit 15.8). As shown, different pieces of this capital structure with varying risks and returns were placed in four different CMBS deals (four *pari passu* A-notes totaling $402.9 million), four different CRE CDOs (two nonpooled components in two CRE CDOs, a $10 million B-note in another CRE CDO and a C-note senior participation in yet another CRE CDO), one life insurance company (a junior C-note), one seasoned real estate operator (a $37.5 million D-note) and one real estate investor (the $160 million of equity). In this example, unlike the hypothetical one shown in Exhibit 15.8, the equity was not "sliced and diced," however, we show with dotted lines how this too would have been possible.

---

[19] For a good discussion of this issue, see "CMBS: Moody's Approach to A-B Notes and Other Forms of Subordinate Debt," *Moody's Special Report*, February 4, 2000.
[20] "CMBS: Moody's Approach to A-B Notes and Other Forms of Subordinate Debt," *Moody's Special Report*.

EXHIBIT 15.8 More Efficient Loan Structuring: 11 Madison Ave., New York, NY

11 Madison Ave. A-1 Pari Passu Note (S&P/Moody's) BBB/Baa2 Holder: WBCMT 2004-C10 $143,333,333	11 Madison Ave. A-2 Pari Passu Note (S&P/Moody's) BBB/Baa2 Holder: WBCMT 2004-C11 $95,555,556	11 Madison Ave. Pooled Component A-3 Pari Passu Note (S&P/Moody's) AAA/Aa3 Holder: WBCMT 2004-C12 $82,000,000 11 Madison Ave. Nonpooled Component $13,555,556 Holder: Fairfield St. Solar 2004-1	11 Madison Ave. Pooled Component A-4 Pari Passu Note (S&P/Moody's) AAA/Aa3 Holder: WBCMT 2004-C14 $82,000,000 11 Madison Ave. Nonpooled Component $13,555,556 Holder: Fairfield St. CREST 2004-1

First Mortgage—$515 million

11 Madison Ave. B-note/Holder: Newcastle CDO IV
$10,000,000

11 Madison Ave. C-note Senior Participation/Holder: Crest Exeter St. Solar 2004-1
$10,000,000

11 Madison Ave. C-note Junior Participation/Holder: Life Insurance Company
$27,500,000

11 Madison Ave. D-note/Holder: Seasoned Real Estate Operator
$37,500,000

Mezzanine Debt

Preferred Equity

Equity

Borrower Equity—$160 million

Source: Wachovia Capital Markets, LLC.

Mezzanine Loans

As mentioned earlier, mezzanine loans are usually secured by a pledge of ownership interests in the entity that directly or indirectly owns the property.[21] The mezzanine lender holds the most junior position in the debt "capital stack" for any given property. The mezzanine lender is senior only to the equity owner's position in the property. Given this position, if the property's cash flow is not sufficient to make the monthly payments required under the

---

[21] In some cases, the ownership interests backing a mezzanine loan may represent only a partial interest in the entity that owns the property. As such, they may not control either the property owner or the related underlying commercial property which may limit the ability of the holder of this type of mezzanine loan from fully realizing its ownership interests.

total financing (i.e., both the mortgage and mezzanine loan), the mezzanine lender will be the first lender to absorb the cash flow shortfall.

Postdefault Control Rights and Remedies

Upon a default under a mezzanine loan, but no default under the mortgage loan, the mezzanine lender's primary remedy is to take over ownership of the property and step in as the borrower on the senior mortgage loan. Upon defaults under both the mortgage loan and the mezzanine loan, the mezzanine lender's primary remedy is to either cure the mortgage loan or buy out the mortgage loan in accordance with the terms of the intercreditor agreement between the mezzanine lender and the mortgage lender, in addition to the mezzanine lender's right to take over ownership of the property.

These rights and remedies are more clearly illustrated through several examples. In the first case, assume that the borrower/owner entity defaults on the mezzanine loan but not on the senior mortgage loan. The mezzanine lender has the option to effectively take control of the property by foreclosing on (i.e., acquiring) 100% of the ownership interests in the legal entity that owns the property[22] using Uniform Commercial Code (UCC) foreclosure rights. As long as the mezzanine lender is not in violation of the intercreditor agreement, the lender becomes the sole owner of the mortgage borrower/property owner.

Some investors/lenders prefer being a mezzanine lender rather than a B-note holder since foreclosing on a pledge of equity through a UCC foreclosure auction is generally quicker and easier than a mortgage foreclosure on real estate. A UCC foreclosure is a nonjudicial foreclosure (i.e., no court or judge) in which the holder of the ownership pledge can hold a private auction, after posting notice for 60 to 90 days, to sell the ownership interest in the property owner. In most cases, any third-party bid would fall short of the mezzanine position, and the mezzanine lender would win the bid and the right to take over the ownership position. The mezzanine lender would then step in as the owner of the borrower with respect to the mortgage loan.

In our second scenario, the borrower/owner entity not only defaults on the mezzanine loan but also on the senior mortgage loan. In this case, the servicer under the mortgage loan gives notice of such default to all interested parties including the mortgage borrower, the mezzanine lender, and any B-note holder. If the mortgage lender were to foreclose and take over the property as a result of the mortgage default, the mezzanine lender would effectively lose all of its collateral as title to the property would be transferred to the mortgage lender or the successful bidder at the mortgage foreclosure. In this scenario, the original property owner will have no collateral for the

---

[22] We assume 100% for purposes of this chapter.

mezzanine lender to pursue since it no longer owns the property. To avoid this result, the mezzanine lender is granted the following two fundamental rights in the intercreditor agreement with the mortgage lender: (1) the right to cure the first mortgage loan default and (2) the right to purchase the first mortgage loan out of the CMBS trust. In each case, the mezzanine lender is subject to payment of certain "make-whole" amounts and subject to certain limitations on time periods.

If the mezzanine lender determines that the value of the property is less than the value of the mortgage loan plus accrued interest, legal fees, and advances (and in some cases, prepayment premiums), then the mezzanine lender will likely not cure or purchase the mortgage loan, and the mortgage lender (acting through the special servicer) will take over the property through a mortgage foreclosure action or deed-in-lieu thereof and proceed with the normal liquidation process. In this case, the value of the mezzanine loan that is in the CRE CDO goes to zero.[23]

However, if the mezzanine lender believes that the property is "undervalued" and that it can "turn the property around" (e.g., retenant the building with better tenants, renovate the property or convert the property to a different use), it can "cure" the mortgage loan (i.e., make the principal and interest payments on the mortgage loan and reimburse any other amounts then due and owing) while finalizing its UCC foreclosure and obtain 100% of the equity ownership interest in the property. If the mezzanine lender elects this course of action, the mortgage lender will be obligated to accept the cure of the mortgage loan.

Given this option and the potential benefit it would have on the CRE CDO and on the CMBS trust, it is important that the mezzanine lender have both the financial capacity to cure the mortgage loan default and the real estate expertise to turn the performance of the property around.

As an alternative to curing the mortgage default, the mezzanine lender also has the right to buy the mortgage loan from the CMBS trust and become the mortgage lender. This option would allow the mezzanine lender to control the entire debt capital stack and foreclose under the mortgage. In this case, the mezzanine lender buys out the mortgage loan at par plus accrued interest, plus any legal fees and servicer advances (and interest on advances).

---

[23] The determination of whether to take either course of action or do nothing is generally viewed by the mezzanine lender as determining the value of the "call option" in owning the property subject to the first mortgage debt. If the mezzanine lender's option is "out of the money," then the mezzanine lender will let the mortgage lender foreclose. If the mezzanine lender's option is "in the money," then it will either cure or buy the mortgage loan out of the pool as described.

If the mezzanine lender chooses this option, then CMBS investors face call risk when the loan is bought out of the deal at par, a loss if the affected CMBS bonds are at a premium or a gain if the underlying bonds are held at a discount. Mezzanine loans, of course, increase the riskiness of the "interest-only" bonds that are stripped off of such CMBS transactions. Although we find many in the CMBS market focusing on extension risk over the next 10 years due to the proliferation of interest-only and low-coupon loans in CMBS originated in the past couple of years, we believe increased callability to be a risk over time. Of course, whereas increased callability could be negative for a CMBS transaction from the perspective of market risk, buying out a credit-impaired loan is positive from a credit perspective. Indeed, if the loan bought out is large enough, it could result in the potential upgrade of some bonds in the CMBS deal if the deal sufficiently delevers.

A collateral manager of a CRE CDO that owns a defaulted mezzanine loan has several options to deal with the situation. First, it could do nothing if it believes its investment is entirely worthless (a possible but less-than-likely situation unless the asset has experienced a significant and permanent reduction in value and/or cash flow). Second, it could sell the defaulted asset out of the CRE CDO. Third, it could decide to keep the first mortgage loan current or buy it out of the CMBS transaction. In either event under this third option, the CRE CDO collateral manager would have to have sufficient resources outside of the CRE CDO to make these payments, as the CRE CDO has no means of its own to make these payments. This underscores the importance of the owner of the mezzanine loan and its ability to directly own and operate real estate as well as access capital to deal with defaulted assets.

In either case, the rating agencies are concerned about how long the mezzanine lender takes to cure the first mortgage loan or buy it out of the trust as these rights delay the CMBS special servicer from taking over the loan and property. Although the mezzanine lender that has decided to cure the loan has done so because it believes the value of the property may go up, the concern here on the rating agencies' part is that the property value could also go down the longer it takes to work out the loan while it is being cured, ultimately resulting in greater losses for the CMBS deal. As a result, the rating agencies typically limit the mezzanine lender to the right to cure the mortgage loan only so long as it is actively and diligently pursuing its UCC foreclosure remedies under the mezzanine loan. Similarly, the rating agencies require the mezzanine lender to exercise its purchase option within a short time frame following a mortgage loan default.

A good, real-life example of a mezzanine lender's cure rights is the workout of a financing secured by an apartment portfolio in Wachovia's CMBS floating-rate deal WBCMT 2002-WHALE 1. In this transaction, a

Wall Street investment bank held a mezzanine loan in excess of 90% of the value of the property, apartments in Houston. Weak market conditions and poor property management by the property owner caused a payment default under the mezzanine loan and the mortgage loan. While curing the mortgage loan, the Wall Street mezzanine lender was able to quickly exercise its remedies under the mezzanine loan and obtain ownership of the properties. As the new owner, the mezzanine lender has since refinanced the mortgage loan, hired independent property management and continues to revitalize the properties. Although there were challenges to this process and attempts to frustrate and delay the transfer of the property to the mezzanine lender by the property owner/borrower in the form of lawsuits and other legal maneuverings, the process moved generally in a reasonably swift and orderly manner, according to Wachovia's servicing group. This example underscores what we have been saying, it is key that the holder of the mezzanine debt (or for that matter the B-note and/or preferred equity) be a seasoned real estate operator with the resources to manage this process through to a successful conclusion.

Predefault: Mezzanine Control Rights

Exhibit 15.9 summarizes the rights of a mezzanine lender before and after a default. The previous paragraphs summarize the fundamental rights of a mezzanine lender after a default under either the mortgage loan or the mezzanine loan. Before a default, the mezzanine lender also has certain rights and protections with respect to the mezzanine borrower. Several key rights of mezzanine lenders versus the borrower typically included in loan documents are the right to approve the annual budget of the property, the right to approve major leases, the right to replace management at the property if financial performance is deteriorating and the right to trap excess cash flow as additional collateral if financial performance deteriorates.[24]

The mezzanine lender also has certain rights with the mortgage lender prior to an event of default. Although these rights are specified in the intercreditor agreement between the mezzanine lender and the mortgage lender, one of the most important rights, prior to any workout of the

---

[24] The mortgage lender is often granted similar rights versus the mortgage borrower based on the mortgage loan documents. Although it is beyond the scope of this chapter to examine the various scenarios wherein a conflict between the mortgage lender, the mezzanine lender, and the borrower could occur, it is generally true that in the case where both the mortgage lender and the mezzanine lender have the same right but disagree (for example the right to replace property management), the mortgage lender's rights prevail.

EXHIBIT 15.9 Principle Mezzanine Lender Rights

Predefault	
Item	**Comments**
Annual budget approval	To ensure proper operation and management of the property.
Approval leases	Typically major ones.
Management kickout	Yes, typically subject to performance criteria such as DSCR test and approved of new manager by mortgage lender. Leasing agent too. Property management.
Cash trap of excess cash flow	Sometimes included in mezzanine loan if DSCR falls below a certain level. However, may be preempted by a similar test in mortgage loan, in which case excess cash flow will be reserved as additional collateral by the mortgage lender.
Rights to approve	Dispersements from escrows and reserves. Mezzanine lender is appropriately focused on operations and management of the property and the cash flow to the owner.

Postdefault	
Scenario 1: Borrower Defaults on Mezzanine Loan Only	**Scenario 2: In addition, Borrower Defaults on First Mortgage Loan**
Exercise remedies under mezzanine loan. Foreclose on equity and become borrower	Unlimited ability to cure first mortgage as long as diligently pursuing rights and remedies under mezzanine loan documents. Buyout first mortgage at: Par + Accrued + Servicer advances

Source: Wachovia Capital Markets, LLC.

mortgage loan, is that the mortgage lender agrees not to make any changes to its loan documents that would be detrimental to the mezzanine lender, e.g., increasing the interest rate of the mortgage loan. In addition, the mezzanine lender is entitled to receive certain copies of notices and financial reporting obtained by the mortgage lender from the borrower.

B-Notes and Participations

B-notes (or *subordinate participations*[25]) are created when the first mortgage loan is split into one or more subordinated positions. The senior loan is referred to as the A-note and the subordinate position as the B-note (see Exhibit 15.7).[26] The most junior B-note holder is the first to absorb any loss on the mortgage loan. In addition, in the case of a material default under the mortgage loan, the B-note is generally not entitled to receive any further payments of principal or interest until the senior A-note(s) has been paid in full (sometimes referred to as the "rainy day" payment waterfall). Of course, when no material default exists under the mortgage loan, the A-note holder and B-note holder will be paid in full each month pursuant to a sequential pay structure, just as CMBS bonds are paid each month in a nondefault scenario (sometimes referred to as the "sunny day" payment waterfall).

One of the drivers behind B-notes is basically a difference in opinion between the rating agencies' and B-note investors' view of a particular loan and property. For example, the rating agency would likely rate and size a loan for an office tower with a 25% vacancy conservatively even if the local office market were improving, thus limiting the amount of proceeds that would qualify as an investment-grade mortgage loan. However, the B-note investor is willing to, in effect, lend more and take the bottom or riskiest part of the mortgage loan because he believes that as the office market continues to improve, the property's cash flow and value will improve as well.

---

[25] The rating agencies prefer that a single note be executed by the borrower and, thereafter, subdivided into senior and junior "participations" in the note rather than the creation of separate and distinct A- and B-notes with the borrower. With one large note, there is only one direct contract between the borrower and the ultimate noteholder. This reduces complications in the case of a bankruptcy filing. Whereas participations are the norm in floating rate CMBS transactions, multiple senior, and subordinate note structures are common (and acceptable to the rating agencies) in fixed rate transactions for reasons beyond the scope of this chapter. Notwithstanding the distinction, the rights and remedies of senior and junior participants are virtually identical to those of senior and junior noteholders. Accordingly, the junior portion of both structures will continue to be referred to as B-notes.

[26] Although B-notes historically have been sold to third-party investors in the form of a separate subordinated note or subordinated participation held completely outside the CMBS pool and trust, increasingly they are being sold in the form of a CMBS certificate collateralized only by a subordinated interest in one mortgage loan (also called a rake bond or directed-pay class). In layman's terms, they are part of the CMBS trust but secured by only one asset, not the entire pool of assets in the CMBS deal. The inclusion of B-notes in a CMBS trust (e.g., a rake bond) provides the B-note with potential added liquidity as they can be resold as a private placement under Rule 144A. Inclusion in the trust also may entitle them to master servicer advancing with respect to current interest payments.

By agreeing to absorb the first loss on the mortgage loan, the B-note holder effectively delevers the A-note, thereby reducing its loan-to-value ratio and improving its credit quality in the rating agencies view.

B-note (and mezzanine) investors are also motivated by the desire to take single-asset, property-specific risk that they can underwrite and monitor carefully. Many investors take a view of their downside as an option to own the entire asset at their debt level (i.e., a cap rate they could not otherwise achieve in the market).

A good way to understand the rights, remedies, and issues regarding B-notes and their differences between those of mezzanine loans is to examine the similarities between B-notes and B-pieces (the most junior class of pooled CMBS bonds relating to a particular CMBS transaction) as they are in a number of respects similar creations. Just as a B-piece is a subordinate class with respect to cash flow derived from a CMBS pool of assets, so too is the B-note a subordinate class, but just with respect to cash flow derived from one loan in a CMBS pool.[27] Just as B-piece holders are typically provided with consultation and approval rights with respect to major servicing actions affecting loans in the CMBS pool and purchase and cure rights with respect to defaulted loans, the B-note holder receives similar (and, in some cases, more extensive) consultation, approval purchase and cure rights, but just with respect to its loan.

B-Note Rights: Differences Between B-Notes and Mezzanine Loans

Not surprisingly, B-note lenders share some of the same rights as mezzanine lenders. Upon an event of default of the mortgage loan, the B-note lender and mezzanine lender are both afforded the two fundamental rights that we discussed earlier in this section—the right to cure the mortgage loan and the right to purchase the mortgage loan.[28]

The calculus of whether to cure or purchase the loan out of the CMBS deal is pretty much the same as for the mezzanine lender. If the B-note holder thinks the market for the particular property associated with the B-note is improving, which would increase the property's value, the B-note holder might "cure" or make all of the mortgage principal and interest payments

---

[27] Whenever a B-note exists, the B-note is subordinate, and junior to the B-piece of a CMBS transaction. In other words, the B-piece is subordinate to all other bondholders with respect to all pooled assets, but senior to any B-note that is secured by a nonpooled asset.

[28] The B-note lender's purchase option is effectively subordinate to the mezzanine lender's purchase option. If the B-note lender purchases the mortgage loan, the mezzanine lender may still elect to purchase the mortgage loan from the B-note lender.

on the A-note. Mortgage loan cure payments by the B-note holder generally prevents the mortgage loan from being transferred to special servicing
(thereby allowing the B-note holder to avoid costly, and potentially unrecov-
erable, special servicing workout fees). These cure payments also generally
allow the mortgage loan to remain in the "sunny day" payment waterfall
thereby preventing the loan from transferring to the "rainy day" cash flow
waterfall, which would prevent the B-note holder from receiving any further
monthly payments until the A-note has been satisfied.

In contrast to the cure period afforded to mezzanine lenders,[29] the period
for a B-note holder to cure is restricted to cures of three to six consecutive
months as it is possible the B-note holder could misjudge the market, and
the property value could deteriorate further creating the possibility of a loss
or greater losses for the A-note holders and the B-note holders.

A key distinction between B-notes and mezzanine loans is the approval
rights and control features afforded a B-note lender as compared with a
mezzanine lender. The B-note lender is granted an additional bundle of
"control rights" that allows it to approve, on behalf of all bondholders having an interest in the mortgage loan, major servicing decisions both prior
and subsequent to a default under the mortgage loan. Common examples of
these pre- and postcontrol rights include the following:[30]

- Right to appoint the special servicer of the mortgage loan.
- Right to approve or reject a proposed lease at the property (in accor-
  dance with the lease approval provisions of the mortgage loan docu-
  mentation).
- Right to approve the annual budget submitted by the borrower.
- Right to approve a new property manager for the property (in accor-
  dance with the provisions of the mortgage documentation).
- Right to approve a transfer of the property by the borrower.
- Post-Default Control Right.
- Right to approve the workout plan for a defaulted loan (often referred
  to as an "asset status report").

Although a mezzanine lender may have a few similar approval rights in
its mezzanine loan documents with the borrower (e.g., approval of borrower's budget, approval of leases or right to replace property manager), the
mezzanine lender does not have the same degree of control as the B-note

---

[29] Mezzanine lenders may generally cure mortgage loan payment defaults for an
unlimited period of time as long as the mezzanine lender is diligently pursuing its
remedies under its mezzanine loan.
[30] A detailed description of the B-note holder's consultation rights and approval
rights is provided in Appendix B to this chapter.

holder, because the mezzanine lender is exercising its approval solely over the borrower. In contrast, the B-note holder exercises its approval authority not only over the mortgage borrower but also over all senior bondholders in the CMBS securitization for which the mortgage loan is included. In other words, the B-note holder is the party that controls most major servicing decisions and approvals required under the mortgage loan without having to obtain approval or be "second guessed" by senior bondholders or the mortgage loan servicer. For example, a mezzanine lender can only approve a lease on behalf of itself vis-à-vis its rights under the mezzanine loan, but a B-note holder can approve a lease on behalf of itself and all other senior interest holders in the mortgage loan.

An additional control right afforded to a B-note holder that has no similar mezzanine loan counterpart is the right to approve (and thereby help formulate) a workout plan once a mortgage loan defaults and is transferred to special servicing. In the case where a loan in a CMBS deal defaults and is transferred to special servicing, the special servicer must submit an asset status report (effectively a plan containing a third-party appraisal of the property and outlining a recommended course of action to deal with the defaulted loan) to the B-note holder for approval. Once approved by the B-note holder, the special servicer must implement the recommended actions contained in the asset status report (perhaps a loan restructuring, foreclosure or other workout solution).

For a summary of the differences between B-notes and mezzanine debt, see Exhibit 15.10.

Limitations on B-Note Control Rights

We have now seen that a B-note holder has much broader rights than a mezzanine lender in that the B-note holder has the ability to grant approvals and make decisions on behalf of all senior bondholders. Constraints clearly need to be in place to make sure that the B-note holder does not abuse its power at the expense of the senior bondholders. After all, the senior bondholders are "senior" in position and have accepted a lower yield in return for the protection afforded to them as a result of their senior position relative to the B-note holder. Two primary protections are standard in the industry to keep in check the power granted to the B-note holder through its "control rights."

The first protection is a standard of care that places limitations on the power granted to the B-note holder. When servicing a mortgage loan in a CMBS transaction, a servicer (or special servicer, as applicable) must always act in accordance with a standard of care commonly referred to as "Accepted Servicing Practices." This standard creates a fiduciary-like relationship between the servicer (or special servicer, as applicable) and the bondholders

EXHIBIT 15.10 Summary of the Principal Differences between B-Notes and Mezzanine Loans

	B-Notes	Mezzanine Loans
Collateral	First mortgage Assignment of rents and leases	Partnership ownership interests in the mortgage borrower
Priority	Subordinate to the A-note, but still part of the first mortgage	Subordinate to the entire first mortgage but senior to preferred equity and equity
Perfection of security interests	Recorded mortgage	UCC filing
Foreclosure	Property foreclosure—Judicial or nonjudicial (6–18 months, state dependent)	UCC foreclosure (60–90 days)
Subordination	Achieved through Participation Agreement	Achieved through intercreditor agreement
Rights on default	Significant consent and consultation rights Input on modifications and workout Purchase option right Cure option	Management kickout Purchase option Cure option
Limits to keep current	Three to four months of consecutive cure	Unlimited provided mezzanine lender is exercising equity foreclosure remedies

Source: Wachovia Capital Markets, LLC.

and requires the servicer to service and administer the loan in a prudent and diligent manner on behalf of such bondholders. The servicer (or special servicer, as applicable) is generally required to enforce this standard of care with respect to any actions taken by the B-note holder. The operative documents governing the relationship between the A-note (i.e., the senior bondholders) and the B-note essentially provides the servicer (or the special servicer, as applicable) the ability to reject (i.e., *trump*) any approval/rejection or other exercise of a B-note holder's control rights if the exercise of such control rights would violate the *Accepted Servicing Practices* standard. The B-note holder can take comfort knowing that even if its exercise of its authority is ultimately rejected by the servicer, the B-note holder can still protect its interest by purchasing the A-note pursuant to its purchase option. A typical definition of the Accepted Servicing Practices standard is provided in Appendix A to this chapter.

The second protection is a confirmation that the B-note holder still holds a meaningful financial interest in the property. If the value of the property has decreased to a level that causes the B-note not to have a significant economic interest in the related property, the related B-note holder may be stripped of its control rights. For example, if the B-note holder's loan is a $50 million loan that represents loan proceeds in the capital stack from $100 million to $150 million but the property is only worth $80 million, it would not be logical for the B-note holder to exercise control rights on behalf of all senior bondholders. Rather, the control rights would shift to the next senior bondholder that has a meaningful financial interest remaining in the property.

This protection is generally known as the *control appraisal period* test and is generally triggered if the value of the property (based on an updated appraisal) has dropped to a level that causes the B-note holder to have less than 25% "equity" in its position based on a comparison of 90% of the then-outstanding value of the property to the then-aggregate outstanding balance of the combined A-note and B-note with accrued interest, advances by the servicer and certain other property expenses. For example, if a mortgage loan balance is $150 million based on an A-note of $100 million and a B-note of $50 million, the value of the property would need to be at least $112.5 million for the B-note holder to retain its control rights. It is important to note, however, that even if the B-note holder is knocked out of the workout process it is still entitled to any residual value once the A-notes, servicer advances, legal, and other fees are paid off.

The need for the B-note holder, master servicer and special servicer to work closely together is readily apparent from Exhibit 15.11. The B-note holder is on the front line of any losses resulting from a defaulted large loan and so has every incentive to minimize his losses. On the other hand, if the B-note holder does not act in the best interest of the CMBS bond holders, does not have

EXHIBIT 15.11 CMBS Fusion Deal

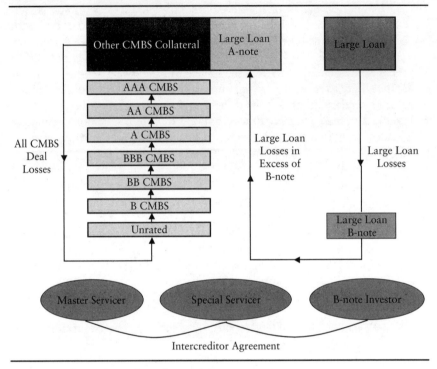

Source: Wachovia Capital Markets, LLC.

deep pockets to buy out or cure the loan or is not a seasoned real estate player then the losses may be excessive and percolate right up through the B-note wiping it out and potentially affecting the A-note and, hence, the CMBS deal, where losses are then directed up through the first loss tranche and so forth like those of any other loan in the CMBS deal. The Accepted Servicing Practices standard and the Control Appraisal Period test are sufficient constraints that must be properly monitored and enforced by the servicer and special servicer to keep the B-note holder from abusing its control rights. As many CMBS deals mature, the inherent tension in the relationship may increase and, accordingly, litigation and loss in the nature of additional expense losses to the affected CDO bonds or CMBS securitization may occur.

The terms of these control rights and privileges enjoyed by the B-note holder (and the limitations placed on the B-note holder) are delineated in a key document, usually the intercreditor agreement or the pooling and servicing agreement. This agreement governs the relationship between the different holders of notes that have an interest in the underlying commercial mortgage loan. Suffice it to say, this agreement is different from deal to deal and is based on the negotiating power between the special servicers, B-note investors and originators. Generally, the market has seen steady increases in the control rights and remedies given to the holders of B-notes. In any case, whatever is worked out, is subject to rating agency approval. Appendix B to this chapter summarizes the rights of B-note holders before and after a default.

Key Differences between B-Notes and Rake Bonds

The key difference between a B-note and a rake bond is that a B-note exists outside the CMBS trust whereas the rake bond is part of the CMBS trust (Exhibits 15.12 and 15.13). This has important implications for the investor or the CRE CDO manager. Because the rake bond is inside the CMBS trust,

EXHIBIT 15.12   CMBS Rake Structure

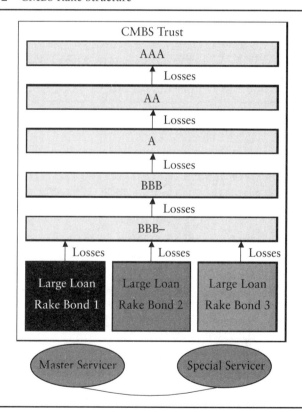

Source: Wachovia Capital Markets, LLC.

EXHIBIT 15.13 CMBS Structure with B-Notes

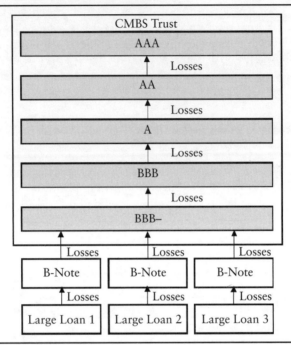

Source: Wachovia Capital Markets, LLC.

it is entitled to servicer advancing with respect to current interest payments and garners all protections associated with any representations and warranties that all of the other bonds in the CMBS deal enjoy, obvious benefits to the managed CRE CDO. B-notes enjoy neither feature unless they are negotiated.

In addition, by being in the CMBS trust, rake bonds qualify as 144A placements and have CUSIPs both of which contribute to potentially superior liquidity. Again, B-notes have neither. In terms of the effect of losses on the CMBS deal, should they occur, there is little difference as the first rated tranche to be hit in either case is the B-note or rake bond, as applicable. Exhibit 15.14 provides a quick summary of the key differences between B-notes and rake bonds.

Preferred Equity Securities

Preferred equity securities are securities that represent equity interests in an entity that owns a commercial property. Operating companies that are

EXHIBIT 15.14 Primary Differences Between Rake Bonds and B-Notes

	Rake Bond	B-Note
Inside CMBS Trust?	Yes	No
CUSIPed?	Yes	No
Part of pooled collateral?	No	No
Benefit of master servicer advancing?	Yes	No
Benefit from collateral depositors reps and warranties?	Yes	No
Offered via	144-A	Privately negotiated
Subordination relationship established via	Pooling and servicing agreement	Participation agreement

Source: Wachovia Capital Markets, LLC.

restricted from arranging mezzanine loans due to covenants signed for first lien mortgages often times may issue preferred equity. In general, preferred equity is senior to common equity with respect to the payments of dividends and other distributions. However, they are generally unsecured and rank below all of the creditors of the issuers, whether secured or unsecured, including the related mortgage loan lenders and mezzanine loan lenders. Although preferred equity is legally equity, from the investor's perspective, it is similar to fixed income securities in that an investor's principal expected source of return is not capital appreciation but rather regular dividend or other payments, not unlike a bond. Liquidity in preferred equity securities is generally limited.

CONCLUSION

Commercial real estate finance has changed more in the past five years than in the previous 50. The evolution and growth of B-notes, *pari passu* securities in CMBS deals, rake bonds, mezzanine loans, preferred equity, static CRE CDOs and managed CRE CDOs have provided investors with a wide variety of investment options. This chapter's purpose is to provide the investor with a greater understanding of these recently developed assets and how they interact with one another. In so doing, we hope it will stimulate new strategies to explore the opportunities offered by these new assets while avoiding inherent risks.

APPENDIX A: DEFINITION OF ACCEPTED SERVICING PRACTICES

Accepted Servicing Practices shall mean the higher of (a) the same care, skill, prudence and diligence with which [A-note holder][31] services and administers similar mortgage loans for other third-party portfolios, giving due consideration to customary and usual standards of practice of prudent institutional commercial lenders servicing their own loans and (b) the same care, skill, prudence and diligence which [A-note holder] utilizes for loans which [A-note holder] owns for its own account, in each case, acting in accordance with applicable law, the terms of this agreement, the loan documents and the loan's insurance policies and with a view to the maximization of timely recovery of principal and interest on a net-present-value basis on the loan as a whole, but without regard to the following:

(i)   any relationship that [A-note holder] or any affiliate of [A-note holder] may have with the borrower or any affiliates of the borrower;

(ii) the ownership of any interest in the loan or any certificate issued in connection with a securitization by [A-note holder] or any affiliate of [A-note holder];

(iii) the ownership of any junior indebtedness with respect to the property by [A-note holder] or any affiliate of [A-note holder];

(iv) [A-note holder]'s obligation to make advances as specified herein;

(v)   [A-note holder]'s right to receive compensation for its services hereunder or with respect to any particular transaction;

(vi) the ownership, or servicing or management for others, by [A-note holder] or any subservicer, of any other mortgage loans or properties; or

(vii) any repurchase or indemnity obligation on the part of [A-note holder] in its capacity as a mortgage loan seller.

---

[31] Intended to cover A-note holder, servicer or special servicer, as applicable.

APPENDIX B: B-NOTES: JUNIOR PARTICIPANTS' RIGHTS

	Predefault
Consultation rights	The servicer will generally be required to consult with the junior participant in connection with a. Any adoption or implementation of a business plan submitted by the borrower with respect to the related mortgaged property. b. The execution or renewal of any lease to the extent lender approval is required in the related mortgage loan documents. c. The release of any escrow held in connection with the mortgage loan not expressly required by the terms of the related mortgage loan documents. d. Material alterations on the related mortgaged property. e. A material change in any ancillary loan documents. f. The waiver of any notice provision related to prepayment. g. Proposals to take any significant action with respect to the mortgage loan or the related mortgaged property. The servicer is also required to consider alternative actions recommended by the junior participant that are related to the foregoing.
Approval rights	The servicer will generally be required to obtain the approval of the junior participant before taking certain significant actions including, but not limited to, a. Any modifications or waivers of any monetary term of the mortgage loan relating to the timing and amount of payments of principal or interest. b. Any substitution or release of collateral for the mortgage loan to the extent not permitted by the related mortgage loan documents. c. Any action to bring the mortgaged property into compliance with environmental laws. d. Certain waivers of "due-on-sale" or "due-on-encumbrance" clauses under the loan documents. e. Any release of the borrower or any related guarantor from liability with respect to the mortgage loan. f. Any material changes to, or any waivers of, any of the insurance requirements. g. Approval/replacement of the property manager.
Termination of special servicer	Generally, the junior participant is permitted to terminate the special servicer at any time, with or without cause, with respect to the related mortgage loan and to appoint a replacement special servicer.

	Predefault
Rights to reports and information	The junior participant is generally entitled to certain reports and information relating to the mortgage loan, including, but not limited to,

    a. Any noncompliance on the part of the related borrower relating to the requirements in the mortgage loan documents regarding the borrower's organization and existence.

    b. A report of account balances in all escrow accounts and a reconciliation statement of all subaccounts.

    c. Copies of all operating statements, financial statements or budgets delivered by the borrower, together with notification of any determination by it that a cash trap period exists under the related mortgage loan documents.

    d. Any adverse changes in any operating statements, financial statements and budgets, or any apparent violation of the provisions of the mortgage loan documents shown by the information set forth on such statements and budgets.

    e. A statement on or before each remittance date reflecting the calculation of the payment due to the junior participant.

    f. Accounting records that reflect the current and correct outstanding principal balance of the mortgage loan and each participation interest, the applicable interest rate during each participation interest, the applicable interest rate during each interest, the applicable interest rate during each participation interest, the applicable interest rate during each interest accrual period relating to the mortgage loan.

    g. Notification of any deficiencies in the required cash management accounts.

Postdefault	
Preevent of default rights	All the rights described above in a pre-event of default scenario continue in a post-event of default scenario.
Cure rights	The servicer is obligated to give notice of any monetary default or nonmonetary default under the related mortgage loan documents to the junior participant (each, a "cure option notice") and must typically permit the junior participant an opportunity to cure such default. If the default is a monetary default, the junior participant will typically have until five business days after the receipt of the cure option notice to cure such monetary default. Cures must include all past due amounts, reimbursement of advances and other trust fund expenses. If the default is a nonmonetary default, the junior participant will typically have until 30 business days after the receipt of the cure option notice to cure such nonmonetary default.
	The junior participant's right to cure a monetary default or a nonmonetary default is often limited to a certain number of cure events over the life of the mortgage loan, and the agreements provide a limit on the number of consecutive months a cure can take place. The number of total cures over the life of a mortgage loan is generally limited to four to six, and the limit on the number of consecutive cures is generally three to four. The rating agencies, although not monolithic on this point, have recently expressed that the number of cures over the life of a mortgage loan be limited to five, with no more than three consecutive cures.
Purchase option rights	Following an event of default, the junior participant will have the right to purchase the senior participation interest at a price equal to the principal balance of the senior participation, together with accrued and unpaid interest thereon up to the purchase date (or through the end of the interest accrual period if the mortgage loan has been securitized), plus some or all of the following:
	a. Any unreimbursed servicing advances with respect to the mortgage loan.
	b. Any reasonable costs and expenses with respect to the senior participation that have not been reimbursed to the senior participant.
	c. Servicing fees payable pursuant to the related pooling and servicing agreement.
	d. Certain additional trust fund expenses in respect of the related mortgage loan.

	Postdefault
Additional approval rights	After an event of default, the servicer will generally be required to obtain the approval of the junior participant before taking any action in foreclosure or any comparable conversion of the ownership of the mortgaged property or any acquisition of the mortgaged property by deed-in-lieu of foreclosure.
Rights to additional reports and information	After the servicing of a mortgage loan is transferred to a special servicer (which generally follows a default), the junior participant is entitled to an "asset status report," which generally sets forth the following:

    a. A summary of the status of the specially serviced mortgage loan and any negotiations with the related borrower.

    b. A discussion of the legal and environmental considerations reasonably known at such time by the special servicer that are relevant to the exercise of remedies with respect to the specially serviced mortgage loan.

    c. The most current rent roll and income or operating statement available for the related mortgaged property.

    d. Recommendations on how the specially serviced mortgage loan might be returned to performing status and returned to the servicer for regular servicing.

    e. The appraised value of the related mortgaged property.

    f. The status of any foreclosure actions or other proceedings undertaken, any proposed workouts and the status of any negotiations with respect to the workouts, and an assessment of the likelihood of additional events of default.

    g. A summary of any proposed actions and an analysis of whether taking such action is reasonably likely to produce a greater recovery on a present value basis than not taking such action.

    h. Other information as the special servicer deems relevant.

The junior participant has the right to approve or disapprove the actions proposed by the asset status report unless such approval or disapproval would be inconsistent with the servicing standard.

Source: Wachovia Capital Markets, LLC.

CHAPTER 16

Synthetic CRE CDOs

Brian P. Lancaster
Senior Analyst
Wachovia Capital Markets, LLC

Anthony G. Butler, CFA
Senior Analyst
Wachovia Capital Markets, LLC

I n the rapidly changing world of *commercial real estate collateralized debt obligation* (CRE CDOs), the application of *synthetic CDO* (SCDO) technology to commercial real estate assets, be they *commercial mortgage-backed securities* (CMBS), *real estate investment trusts* (REITs), on balance-sheet commercial real estate loans or even other cash CRE CDOs, is generating great interest from issuers and investors alike. Starting as a convenient tool for banks to hedge unwanted risk in their corporate loan portfolios or to obtain regulatory capital relief in the late 1990s, SCDOs have become a common fixture in the arbitrage market. Today, the application of this technology to the commercial real estate markets is likely to lead to a similar dominance in the CRE CDO market.[1]

Three key factors have led to the creation of the CRE SCDO market and continue to drive its rapid expansion. First, the creation of a super-senior tranche significantly reduced the cost of liabilities in CRE SCDOs and permits these securities to thrive even when the economics of a cash-based transaction had been less attractive. Second, the development and standard-ization of *credit default swap* (CDS) contracts on CMBS markets and tech-nology has allowed disparate market participants to communicate more effi-ciently, ramp collateral faster, and hedge more efficiently where appropriate.

---

[1] Approximately 13% (8 out of 58) of the deals transacted in the United States and Europe in 2006 were synthetic (or hybrid) CRE CDOs, up from one deal out of 39 in 2005. Through the third quarter of 2007, we have observed that 32% by count (12 out of 38) of the widely marketed deals were hybrid or synthetic.

Finally, the continued growth and evolution of the corporate market has provided a model to follow and tested techniques to draw upon.

Given their advantages, the rapid rise of CRE SCDOs should not be surprising. Compared with cash-based CRE CDOs, CRE SCDOs can be cleaner and more efficient structures. Generally, there is no fixed/floating interest rate mismatch or maturity mismatch between assets and liabilities in a CRE SCDO.[2] There are other advantages as well: quick and easy ramp-up of collateral, greater collateral diversity and generally greater structural flexibility. In fact, transactions can be and have been tailored around the needs of a single investor. See Exhibit 16.1 for a list of the pros and cons relating to synthetic versus cash CDO.

CRE SCDOs have had a large impact on CMBS spreads and credit curve, particularly through the end of 2006 where they were the primary factor in tightening spreads and flattening out the credit curve. Their absence in the market post the various repricing and liquidity waves of 2007 led to a much steeper credit curve in addition to greater volatility.

This chapter reviews the history and segmentation of the CRE SCDO market, explains the basic tools and principles employed in creating a CRE SCDO, compares synthetic and cash-based CRE CDOs, highlights the relative advantages of CRE SCDO investments and discusses investment considerations.

GROWTH AND EVOLUTION OF THE SYNTHETIC CRE CDO MARKET

Noncommercial real estate synthetic CDOs (usually referencing a corporate credit) originated in the late 1990s as a way for banks to transfer the credit risk of their loan portfolios without removing the loans from their balance sheet. In doing so, a bank could lower its regulatory capital requirement on these assets from 100% to 20%[3] and diversify its credit risk while maintaining its relationship with the borrowing client. Transactions motivated by regulatory capital relief or risk management are termed balance-sheet CDOs

---

[2] Should sponsors decide to do synthetic CRE CDOs with loans denominated in different currencies, currency mismatches can be handled seamlessly without the need for explicit currency hedges.

[3] Under Basel I, banks must hold 8% regulatory capital against the par of assets that are 100% risk weighted. Most regulators will lower this regulatory capital requirement to 20% of the 8%, where risk is transferred via a default swap as long as the swap counterparty is an Organisation for Economic Co-operation and Development (OECD) institution. If the risk is transferred in a *credit-linked note* (CLN) format and the collateral for those notes is very high quality, such as Treasuries, the risk weighting could be even lower.

EXHIBIT 16.1   Synthetics versus Cash Deals: Pros and Cons

Pros:

- Using synthetic securities allows a manager the flexibility of gaining exposure to assets that they normally wouldn't see or have the ability to acquire on a cash basis.
- Since the CDS market is a floating market (as the payment is just the spread premium) versus a fixed rate market it removes the need for a swap (in particular a balance guaranteed swap) hence a potential source of basis risk is eliminated from the transaction.
- Given the transparency and availability of the cash market it leads to increased liquidity of the synthetic product from a CDS standpoint.
- Synthetics allow parties to take directional bets on select credits whereas cash positions are long only or no exposure.
- The CMBX index approach creates a universal benchmark for investors to gauge the performance of the markets.
- Synthetics lead to a more global investor based versus CMBS due to their inherent floating rate nature/capability.
- Particularly for hybrid deals, investors are betting on the managers ability to manage a pool of CDS and cash assets and allowed to take further directional bets; that is, shorts or long or credit risk or improved.
- Synthetics offer investors a premium versus CMBS. We will address this in more detail (see Pricing Opportunities).

Cons:

- CDS are not as liquid with respect to transferability of CDS.
- Given the newness and evolution of the market you have some documentation risk (i.e., no deal is the same). Even though the *pay-as-you-go* (PAUG) standard here can be differences.
- CDS spreads have not been correlated with cash spreads to date.
- Short positions in a deal (buying protection) are a drain on the cashflow. It may take some time for the manager's view to play out. In other words if the manager buys an asset that doesn't perform well in the end at least it is generating cashflow in the mean time while a short CDS is only negative cashflow followed by an expected pop in pricing.

(as opposed to arbitrage CDOs discussed later[4]). BISTRO 1997-1, issued in December 1997, was the first bank balance sheet transaction referencing corporate credits[5] that closely resembled the synthetic structures of today.[6]

---

[4] Of course there are *assets under management* (AUM) CDOs and financing CDOs which are more typical of static and managed Cash CRE CDOs.

[5] The deal referenced U.S., European, and Canadian corporates—denominated in USD.

[6] Before BISTRO 1997-1, there were a limited number of SCDOs that were issued without a super-senior tranche and were created purely to decrease regulatory capital charges on the balance sheets of the sponsoring banks. Examples include Triangle Funding Ltd. and SBC Glacier Finance Ltd.

Banks are now beginning to adopt and apply this technology to their on-balance sheet commercial real estate credits for pretty much the same reasons—regulatory capital relief, credit diversification, and maintenance of customer relationships. Additionally the transactions facilitate the further growth of their commercial real estate portfolios and expand distribution capabilities. For example, in June 2006, CRESI Finance Limited Partnership 2006-A, a synthetic CRE CDO referencing some $1.2 billion of commercial real estate loans on the balance sheet of Bank of America was issued enabling the Bank of America to transfer risk on a variety of commercial, multifamily, and land loans.

Synthetic CRE CDOs started first as static-pool, tranched structures, and then progressed into managed tranched structures that incorporate many cash-based CDO features and others such as the ability of the manager to take a short position via CDS or a CMBX index.

The first arbitrage CRE SCDOs were purely synthetic. In other words, transaction assets and liabilities were unfunded and governed solely by a swap confirmation or credit-linked note. From 2005 to 2007, arbitrage-motivated structures have evolved into more broadly syndicated structures issued in both funded and unfunded form. Funded portions are issued in a CLN format.

Although still in its early stages today's CRE SCDO market is increasingly diverse, with a growing list of transaction types. Balance sheet SCRE CDOs now reference structured finance assets as well as commercial real estate loans. Likewise, arbitrage transactions have referenced CMBS, REITs, non-CUSIPed collateral and even other CRE CDOs.

Exhibit 16.2 provides a historical picture of the key events in the development of the SCDO market.

Insurance companies and banks may use synthetic CRE CDOs to lay off risk and maintain customer relationships. Organizational and operational issues at general banks (which are unfamiliar with the securitization process and reporting requirements) are probably the largest impediment to the growth of this sector.

SYNTHETIC CDOs FROM THE GROUND UP

The Building Blocks: Credit Default Swaps

The standardization of credit default swaps on CMBS has enabled the expansion of the SCDO market beyond its use as a balance sheet management tool. In fact, the development of SCDOs has been predicated on the expansion and standardization of the single-name CDS market (and subsequently the CMBX market), which provides the major means for SCDO sponsors to

EXHIBIT 16.2 Key Events That Shaped the Synthetic CDO and Synthetic CRE CDO Markets

First Synthetic Balance-Sheet CDOs	Russian Default Crisis and LTCM Stress CDS Market	Standard ISDA Definitions	First Arbitrage SCDOs	First Structured Finance SCDOs	Conseco Restructuring	First Managed SCDOs	Rise of Single Tranche SCDOs	Revised ISDA Definitions
1997	1998	1999	2000	2001		2002		2003

First CRE CDO Fortress Commercial Mortgage Trust 1999-PC1			First $Billion CRE CDO G-Force 2002-1		First CRE CDO with B-notes Brascan 2004-1	First Synthetic CRE CDO Sorin Real Estate CDO 2005-2	First Hybrid Synthetic CRE CDO Kimberlite CDO I	
1999	2000	2001	2002	2003	2004	2005	2006	2007

Note: CDOs: Collateralized debt obligations; CDS: Credit default swaps; ISDA: International Swaps and Derivatives Association, Inc.; LTCM: Long Term Capital Management; and SCDOs: Synthetic collateralized debt obligations.
Source: Wachovia Capital Markets, LLC.

source (and/or arguably hedge) exposures. Therefore, understanding a CDS instrument is critical to understanding SCDOs.

At the outset, the CDS market was a small interbank market used to transfer corporate credit risk. Lenders looked to distribute the credit risk of large-loan positions to other banks without selling the loans and possibly jeopardizing bank-client relationships. Each CDS contract was highly negotiated and designed to transfer primarily default risk. From this foundation, CDS contracts have become standardized and are now traded by bank portfolio managers, insurance companies and arbitrageurs (e.g., hedge funds and CDOs) to hedge current exposure or accept new exposure to corporate credit risk. According to International Swap and Derivatives Association (ISDA), the notional amount outstanding of CDS grew 32 percent in the second half of 2006, rising from $26.0 trillion at June 30, 2006 to $34.4 trillion at December 31, 2006. This is more than eight times the $4 trillion in corporate debt outstanding per the Securities Industry and Financial Markets Association. The recent dramatic growth of the market may be attributed to a combination of the following:

- Standardized ISDA documentation, which created market conventions and industry wide benchmarks.
- Structured product offerings (i.e., SCDOs) with embedded CDS.

■ A growing educated investor base that has taken advantage of pricing opportunities and technical inefficiencies.

The structured finance market was able to follow in the path developed by the corporate market but needed some alterations to the standards developed by the 2003 revised ISDA definitions. In June 2005, two dealer forms were published by ISDA that governed ABS transactions, namely:

■ CDS on ABS with cash and physical settlement.
■ Pay as you go on ABS or physical settlement (PAUG).

PAUG was developed for the CMBS and RMBS markets with primary differences from the initial corporate form coming from credit events, settlement practices or procedures and notional amount adjustments. The intent of the PAUG form is to mimic or mirror the credit risks that come with owning or shorting an individual (or basket of) reference CMBS or ABS bond(s). The CDS contract runs through the life of the underlying bond and experience any shortfalls or write-downs as well as any reimbursements (interest or principal). In the corporate world, the credit default swap terminates and settles with the occurrence of a credit event or matures after a specific period (e.g., five years). The following discussion will relate to PAUG contracts.

A CDS is a contract between a protection buyer and a protection seller. Under this agreement, the protection buyer pays a premium to the protection seller in return for payment if a credit event (typically principal shortfall, principal write-down and interest shortfalls) occurs with respect to the reference entity—see Exhibit 16.3.

Buying protection is similar to shorting a cash instrument, and selling protection is similar to going long a cash instrument, but credit default swaps and cash bonds are *not* identical investments. Direct investment in fixed rate debt contains interest rate and funding risk, whereas a CDS investment does not. Interest rate risk in a CDS is eliminated because there is no initial cash outlay, and funding risk is mitigated because there is no need to borrow. When an investor borrows money to fund a cash investment, funding risk is created. If the investor's funding cost increases, the spread between the investment and the investor's cost of funds decreases, lowering the economic benefit of the investment while the risk remains unchanged.[7] In short, the unfunded nature of a CDS creates a pure credit risk position.

Emergence of Synthetic CDOs

In its simplest form, a SCDO is the application of a CDS to a reference pool of credits or multiple CDS contracts on individual bonds or credits. The

---

[7] Ignoring any collateral posting requirements relating to counterparty credit risk.

EXHIBIT 16.3 Credit Default Swap Diagram for the PAUG form with Cash Settlement

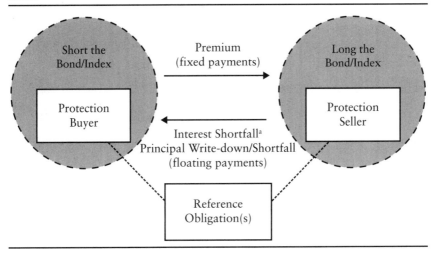

[a] Capped at the fixed premium.
Source: Wachovia Capital Markets, LLC.

pool of reference credits could be tied to loans or to a group of structured finance securities that reside on the sponsor's balance sheet (a balance sheet transaction) or comprise CDS on CMBS bonds or loans. The sponsor of the transaction is a buyer of protection and the investors are the sellers of protection. If certain predefined credit events occur on any of the reference entities, then the sellers of protection must make the buyer whole. For this protection, the sponsor pays a premium based on the notional amount of the pool.[8] If the transaction is entirely unfunded, no cash is exchanged at the outset and, if no credit events occur, the only cash that would be transferred throughout the course of the deal would be the premium paid by the protection buyer. If a credit event occurs, then the seller of protection pays a settlement amount to the buyer of protection. At this point, CDO technology can be layered in to allow investors to participate at different risk levels (Exhibit 16.4).

In unfunded transactions, the sponsor (protection buyer) must rely on the swap counterparty's (investor's or protection seller's) ability to make the required loss payments during the course of the deal. Therefore, counterparties may be required to post collateral based on how the sponsor

---

[8] The *notional amount of a pool* is also known as the face amount and represents the contractual size of the pool on which all calculations of premium and recovery will be based.

EXHIBIT 16.4   Unfunded SCDO: No SPV and No Proceeds Exchanged

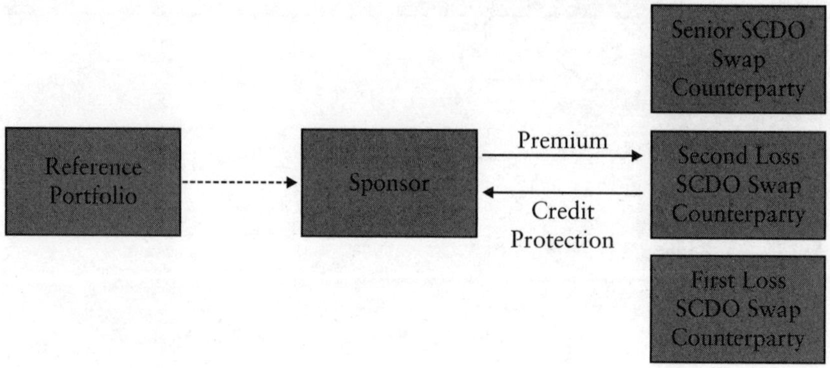

Source: Wachovia Capital Markets, LLC.

views their credit risk. Collateral posting requirements are not generally one-for-one but rather are based on the credit quality of the investor/swap counterparty. In addition, the investor must be able execute a CDS; this requirement (necessitating a negotiated and signed ISDA) often excludes many pension plans, CDOs, and other fund managers. To expand the investor base and to remove counterparty credit risk, sponsors incorporated CLNs, which are funded instruments, into the SCDO framework. Under this format, a *special purpose vehicle* (SPV) is normally created to provide a bankruptcy-remote depository for the high-quality assets (Exhibit 16.5). CLNs were first used in the COBALT 05 CRE CDO, which referenced BB rated CMBS bonds.

Most current SCRE CDO transactions are actually a hybrid of the two structures shown above. A single, highly rated investor (typically a monoline insurance company) will invest in the most senior tranche in unfunded form (CDS), whereas the rest of the liability structure is purchased by various investors in funded (CLN) or unfunded form. The unfunded, senior-most tranche is known as the *super-senior tranche* to reflect its position above the AAA rated tranche.

The super-senior tranche paved the way for the broad scale application of SCDO technology to balance-sheet and later to arbitrage transactions backed by investment-grade assets. Banks have been eager to shed much of their investment-grade bank loan risk because these loans were often extended for relationship reasons and generate low returns. In addition, these assets carry a 100% risk weighting, which means that a bank is charged an 8% regulatory capital charge. Early SCDOs permitted banks to reap the benefits of regulatory capital relief, but they had to bear the cost of the transactions

EXHIBIT 16.5   Funded SCDO: SPV Added and Proceeds Exchanged for CLNs

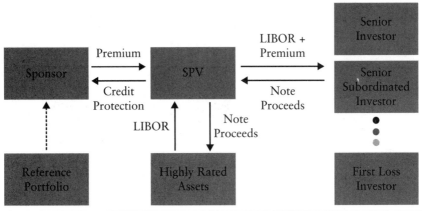

Source: Wachovia Capital Markets, LLC.

which, under traditional tranching (i.e., without a super senior), were not economically attractive. The super-senior tranche dramatically improves the economics and allows more efficient regulatory capital relief.

Senior to the AAA tranche, the super-senior usually accounts for around 90% of the capital structure (assuming an investment-grade pool of assets) and historically carries a low spread that reduces the weighted average cost considerably. A typical balance sheet SCDO in today's market is similar to that shown in Exhibit 16.7.

The credit protection premium is passed from the sponsor to the super-senior investor and through the SCDO and partitioned among the SCDO investors according to the size of their investment and the amount of risk they have taken. When a credit event occurs on a reference entity, high-quality assets are liquidated in an amount equal to the payment obligation on the CDS and the proceeds are then passed to the sponsor. Losses are applied to the investors in reverse order of priority though sometimes the realization of the loss is postponed until the end of the transaction, allowing note holders to earn interest on the entire outstanding amount of their investment.

The structure described in Exhibit 16.6 is typical, but variations are common. In some transactions, the super-senior investor is a counterparty of the SPV and the entire premium is passed from the sponsor to the SPV where it is then partitioned. In other transactions, a portion of the Class A, B, or C notes may be unfunded or partially funded. One of the benefits of an SCDO is the structural versatility afforded to investors and structurers.

The transactions described in Exhibits 16.5 and 16.6 are typical of a balance-sheet-motivated transaction where the sponsor collects interest and

EXHIBIT 16.6   Partially Funded SCDO: Super Senior Added

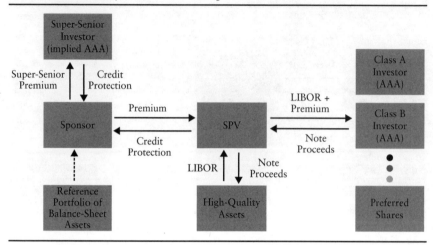

Source: Wachovia Capital Markets, LLC.

EXHIBIT 16.7   Arbitrage SCDO: Reference to a Portfolio of Credit Default Swaps

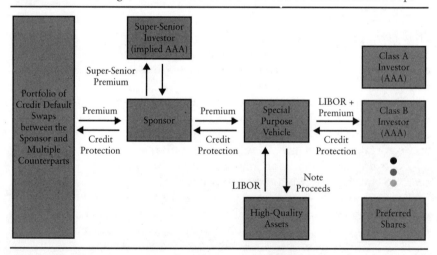

Source: Wachovia Capital Markets, LLC.

fees from cash assets held on its balance sheet. Based on this structure, an arbitrage transaction can be easily constructed if the sponsor selectively enters into CDS contracts with the market (Exhibit 16.7). In this case, preferred shareholders benefit from any premium remaining after payment to the super-senior counterparty and the rated notes.

Life Cycle

The life cycle of an SCDO may look different from a traditional CDO. For instance, SCDOs referenced to IG corporate credits take a short time to ramp up due to a developed and liquid CDS market and will remain outstanding until maturity, which is usually in bullet form. Amortization does not exist because CDS contracts *reference* a particular entity but not a specific security. The termination date of the contract is freely negotiable; therefore structurers are free to arrange for simultaneous maturity of all contracts (Exhibit 16.8).

If the portfolio consists of contracts referenced to structured securities and the transaction is managed, there is little difference between SCDOs and cash-based CDOs because the CDS is tied to specific securities instead of reference credits: The ramp-up period is followed by a revolving period and an amortization period. A typical ramp-up period for a CRE SCDOs is six months to one year. The revolving period is generally three to five years, potentially leaving a 25-year amortization period. As in traditional cash-based CDOs, managed synthetic transactions are subject to early termination of the revolving period and acceleration of payment (through the capture of excess spread) if the collateral pool does not perform well.

EXHIBIT 16.8 Life Cycle of SCDOs Illustrated

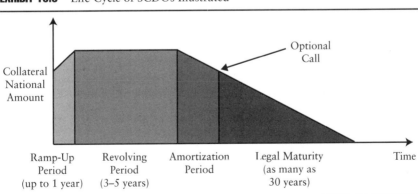

Source: Wachovia Capital Markets, LLC.

Asset Trading

Like cash-based, balance sheet CDOs, balance sheet SCDOs typically are not permitted to trade reference entities in or out of the reference pool on a discretionary basis for regulatory reasons. Limited substitution can take place, however, and both the old and new reference entities are exchanged at a par notional. In contrast, managed arbitrage SCDOs permit trading although the mechanism is different than that used in a cash-based arbitrage CDO.

A position in the reference pool of a managed SCDO can be removed by either terminating the CDS or buying protection to hedge the position (as opposed to an outright sale in a cash-based transaction). If the position is terminated, an early termination payment will be made by the SCDO if there is a loss (the CDS spread has widened) or the SCDO will receive cash if there is a gain (the CDS spread has tightened). If an offsetting position is taken and the credit has deteriorated, causing the CDS spread to widen, the excess spread on the transaction will be negatively affected because the SCDO will pay more in premium on the new CDS than it receives on the original CDS. However, if the credit has improved then the SCDO can lock in a spread premium on the credit and enter into a new contract on another credit.

Rating agencies and note holders typically favor purchasing protection to offset a CDS if the credit has deteriorated (spreads have widened) because cash flow to equity is reduced and the collateral balance is maintained. This prevents cash from "leaking" to equity holders even though significant losses have occurred. To mitigate excessive spread deterioration, investors and rating agencies impose a minimum spread test to ensure that sufficient interest is available to pay rated note holder interest.

Some fully managed SCDOs permit portfolio managers to adopt a net short position in a credit (e.g., Kimberlite). This allows managers to capitalize on a negative view of a particular credit or to take a relative credit view between competitors by going short one and long the other but maintaining a neutral stance on the industry. To the extent the portfolio manager is successful in these strategies, equity holders and note holders will benefit from this added flexibility. As far as we know, there are no cash-based transactions with this feature.

Coverage and Quality Tests

Pure synthetic transactions may not have over *collateralization* (OC) tests but benefit from additional subordination. However, for transactions with OC tests, the senior-most tranche (the super-senior tranche) may be excluded from the OC calculation, which differs from the typical cash OC test. In these synthetic transactions, the OC ratio is calculated as

$$\text{Class X OC ratio} = \frac{\text{Cash collateral account balance}}{\substack{\text{Notional amount of Class X and} \\ \text{notes senior excluding the super senior}}}$$

The OC test is breached if the cash collateral account declines to a level where the OC ratio falls below a certain threshold. Regardless of the method used, credit events and trading losses can result in a breach of the OC test as cash collateral is depleted to cover losses incurred. If the OC test is breached, excess spread is directed away from junior tranches and equity to the most senior bond until the test comes back into compliance. Like cash-based CDOs, quality tests such as the diversity and weighted average rating factor tests are used to maintain portfolio quality during the ramp-up period and revolving (replenishment) periods.

One disadvantage of a SCDO is that there is not as much excess spread flowing through the transactions. Therefore, the OC trigger on a managed or hybrid deal will not react as strongly in covering losses. A cash deal will deleverage faster as it has the LIBOR component flowing through the waterfall (as opposed to just the spread alone).

CREDIT EVENTS: PRINCIPAL WRITEDOWN AND INTEREST SHORTFALL

On June 21, 2005 ISDA introduced a standard confirmation form with terms and definitions for CDS on mortgage-backed securities. The definitions may be modified in any given transaction, but the trade confirm has been successful in creating a common language used by all market participants as well as a standard instrument for trading (a key for market development). Since then, ISDA has issued several *Standard Terms Supplements* to the definitions (five to date with the most recent being August 8, 2007). There is a long and short form available for use today though trades are increasingly cleared through DTCC where no form exchanged. In this case, however, each party fills out a screen with trade details and if they match the trade settles.

As structured finance transactions present a different construct (compared to corporates) there is a different set of credit events. Credit events define the risks that are transferred from the buyer to the seller of protection in a CDS and, theoretically, can be negotiated between the buyer and seller of protection to cover a multitude or only a few risks. With CDS you are not trading bonds but credit events, therefore, great care must be taken to

EXHIBIT 16.9 Settlement Options for Pay as You Go CDS

Credit Event	Settlement Option	Party's Option	Notifying Party
Failure to pay principal	Cash & physical	Buyer	Buyer
Principal write-down	Cash & physical	Buyer	Buyer
Distressed ratings downgrade[a]	Physical only		Buyer
Maturity extension[a]	Physical only		Buyer

[a] Typically does not apply to a CMBS reference obligation.
Source: Wachovia Capital Markets, LLC.

understand these definitions. Initially CDS on CMBS was contemplated to cover two events, failure to pay principal and a principal write-down (this combined with interest shortfalls, though not a credit event covered the economic attributes of a pay as you go CDS trade). Two additional credit events were added to the Standard Confirm—*distressed ratings downgrade* and *maturity extension,* though they are not commonly used or included. See Exhibit 16.9 for a summary of credit events and settlement options.

Given the intent of replicating the underlying cash bond, the CDS contract runs coterminous with the *reference obligation*—(ultimately to its legal final). It doesn't stop after a predetermined amount of time (such as five years with corporate CDS).

There are three options for dealing with interest shortfalls:

1. Provide coverage for 100% of interest shortfalls (uncapped).
2. Provide protection up to the amount of premium (fixed cap, the standard).
3. Have a variable cap (at LIBOR).

As indicated, the most common method for handling interest shortfalls is to cover it with the premium. To the extent interest shortfalls are subsequently made whole on the underlying bond then the protection buyer would need to likewise reimburse any payments received.

ISSUER AND INVESTOR CONSIDERATIONS WITH SYNTHETIC COLLATERAL

There are several benefits to the issuer and investor as well as many considerations when evaluating an SCDO, including:

- Super senior investor
- Ease of execution
- Less spread on the assets (CDS)
- Higher diversity
- Lack of prepayment risk in SCDOs linked to corporate credits
- Shorter average lives
- Bullet maturities
- Low cost of liabilities
- Higher-quality assets
- Precision in credit selection

Super Seniors—Funded and Unfunded

This section is disproportionately larger than the others, however, it corresponds to the importance of placing this class as well as the relative class size in a typical synthetic CRE CDO. As these buyers may have certain negotiated control rights, it is important to understand the triggers, scope, and means by which they can affect the manager and deal.

Types of Super-Senior Buyers

Monoline insurance companies (monolines) are insurance companies that only provide insurance for debt securities. For a premium, they will guarantee or "wrap" a bond or debt issue. They initially provided wraps for municipal bond issues but have since expanded to provide enhancement or guarantees for mortgage backed securities, CDOs, and others. Monolines have been a key player in unfunded super seniors. They, in concert with negative basis lenders, can compete for funded or cash super-senior bonds as well. In order to win the combination of their respective spreads must be inside of the market cash bid as there are additional factors, such as control rights (discussed here), that must be negotiated and dealt with by the issuer and collateral manager. In SCDOs, the super-senior tranche is often unfunded and a monoline will typically write (sell) protection on that tranche in exchange for a premium.

Banks are the institutions that pioneered the SCDO as they were first employed to reduce exposure to corporate loans and bring regulatory capital relief while maintaining the relationship. The same can be done for a bank's commercial real estate portfolio and is referred to as a synthetic balance sheet CDO. The bank will typically retain the super-senior bonds and the equity or nonrated tranche. By so doing they:

1. Accomplish regulatory capital relief.
2. Lay off a portion of their risk.
3. Maintain the relationship with the borrower.

As for nonmonoline insurance companies, it is not clear how many participate but there is at least one major player who participates in the super-senior space.

As monolines are the typical super-senior buyer we will focus the rest of this section on what they bring to the table and how they benefit the other investors including a discussion of key, negotiated, additional control rights, and their potential effects.

Funded or Unfunded Super Seniors: What's the Preference?

Monolines typically prefer to go in an unfunded deal/trade as this removes one party from the mix (the negative basis funder) and can be directly competitive. Simply put, it's less hassle to go unfunded. All in all, they can go either way and the cost of their spread premium will generally be the same. One thing to note, the combination of the two spreads (monoline and negative funder) has to be competitive (better) versus a cash spread level to induce the issuer to undergo the extra work involved in negotiating the control rights required by the monoline. Negative basis funders are typically either European or Asian banks.

Reason Monolines Do Not Buy the Whole Cash Bond and Earn More

The reason that monolines do not buy the whole cash bond is that they are not bank and therefore they do not have that kind of assets or capital. Rather, they are an insurance company with a capital base upon which they write protection (insurance contracts). Their book of business is very highly rated (most likely above single-A), which means that they have very high leverage on their capital.

Note that one of the things the monolines will not do is allow themselves to be a source of liquidity in a transaction. For example, in some CDS of CDOs which have implied write-downs, meaning that the floating-rate payer (protection seller/monoline) could be iteratively paying out and then getting reimbursed if the structure deleverages in time (where your assets eventually exceed your liabilities). This would provide a source of interim liquidity; but that's not what they want to do. Rather, they prefer to pay at the final or pay when losses are final losses (not potentially reimbursable). A monoline will typically have enough liquidity (according to the rating agencies and their own models) to cover losses in a AAA stress case. However, they are meant to be losses and not temporary draws in liquidity.

Challenges Posed by Deals that Have Collateral Consisting of CDS on CRE CDOs

With the ever active search for collateral that provides diversification and correlation benefits, we have lately witnessed a number of CRE CDOs that contain 5% to 12% buckets for either cash or CDS on CRE CDOs (generally anywhere above BB in rating). This creates some issues with respect to credit events defined in the CDS confirm. In the CRE CDO world, you have two types of confirms:

- *Fixed cap with implied write-down (WD)*. If they are giving the floating rate payer the benefit of a fixed cap, meaning that interest shortfall payments are capped or limited to the initial premium, this is good for the monoline as the worst thing that can happen is having the premium go to zero. However, the implied WD feature poses a problem because if you are writing protection at BBB there is a much greater chance of a BBB CRE CDO PIKing than a BBB CMBS having interest shortfalls. If the CDO bond starts PIKing it does not become a credit event (resulting in a floating rate payment), because this is a fixed cap contract. However it's the implied WD that is the problem for the monoline. An implied WD occurs when the value of asset, based on the OC test at that tranche level, is less than the value of the liabilities to that tranche level (OC test below 100). This is an impairment and a floating rate payment is made. This is reimbursable to the extent that later on the OC test is greater than 100. This could happen if the structure hits an OC test and deleverages. But this means that you could have floating rate payments go out and then get reimbursed (back and forth). As mentioned above, monolines do not want to be liquidity providers or be caught in a situation where monies are flowing back and forth too often.
- *Variable cap with no implied write-down*. If there is an interest shortfall you have to pay the interest component (including the LIBOR) so it's possible to have a net floating rate payment. However, under this type of confirm you remove the risk of having OC test breaches. Under this contract your credit event does not occur until there is an actual default.

Note that CRE CDOs are cash flow, not market value, CDOs. Consequently, to generate an OC issue there must be a default or some event that generates a revaluing of the collateral. When you consider the variety of CRE CDOs in the market, among them are CUSIPed deals which have ratings based *haircuts* (HC). For these deals, if the pool starts drifting or experiencing some decent downward collateral ratings migration, the HCs start kicking in and the OC test trips fairly quickly. This is done so the transaction deleverages as things get worse. It is a great feature for investors. However, if a party is writing CDS on one of these deals it means that you are more likely to hit an implied write-down quicker than if you take one of the newer deals, like a whole loan deal, where you do not have ratings HC, you only have the value of nondefaulted collateral plus the calculation amount on defaulted securities which essentially means you have to have whole loans or B-notes in default before you actually HC them. This should be a slower process. Those writing CDS on CDOs would rather not see the HCs but prefer to make payments only on actual defaults. They do not want to see the implied WD, if there is a WD then they want it to be as real as possible.

A monoline in the super senior likes having the HCs because it protects them at the higher ratings by deleveraging the transaction quicker. Whereas in the whole loan deals you are waiting for defaults and recoveries and the transaction is much slower to react.

Increased Complexity of CRE CDO Collateral within a CRE CDO

With 5% to 12% of the assets being synthetic CRE CDOs, all parties have found the need to adjust their modeling and modeling methods to look through the CDOs and model the cashflows for the actual CDO under consideration. CDOs of CDOs are referred to as CDO squared (CDO^2)—you are essential analyzing several CDOs at once. Managed deals are changing all the time. The technical capability of the manager has got to be very high. A key consideration for evaluating mangers that use CDOs as collateral is the quality of their information systems, and the like.

Monoline Influence on Collateral Quality

In general, monolines have varying degrees of influence. An often repeated theme is, "Don't force a manager into a box they don't want to be in as they will have to buy collateral they don't understand, or don't have the risk return relationship they're comfortable with." Anything done would typically be on the margins because it's the firm's origination platform or their investment philosophy or underwriting that you are drawn to and get comfortable with. The issue is making sure that they are comfortable with risk levels and with the platform itself along with a consistent application of the platform. Where a monoline takes issue is if the platform changes philosophy or, more importantly, the actual key people change, then the monolines want to be able to do something about that.

Monoline Control Rights

Two important control language event triggers are:

- *Manager replacement trigger.* The primary concern is being able to jump in and protect their investment should the CDO start heading down (typically defined on an OC test basis). Up front the monoline will seek a manager replacement trigger. This trigger, if breached, gives them the option to terminate the manager, and bring in a replacement. It is not a requirement to replace the manager, but it gives the monoline the ability to evaluate the cause for poor performance. The monoline has the option to act before their super senior position is impaired. This may give investors in the *mezzanine* (mezz) or lower-rated classes some pause for concern. It is important to see where the right kicks in. In the case where it is triggered after significant erosion in the assets such that the equity, all the mezz debt and into the senior level of debt is gone, then all other investors are gone anyway so it should not be a huge concern. If it can trigger with many classes still intact then careful consideration is the order of the day.
- *Event of default OC trigger.* This is typically set to kick in after the management replacement trigger. If the credit situation is not improving/recovering this control right grants the holder the ability to collapse the transaction and liquidate the collateral. Doing so brings the deal to a close and prevents a drawn out experience accompanied by lawyer and trustees fees and so on.

Benefits of Having a Monoline in the Transaction

Monolines will perform their own due diligence on the manager, spending time at their "shop" every time they do a deal. They typically perform a "soup-to-nuts" review of the financial viability of the platform, the personnel, their level of experience, underwriting philosophy, systems, credit process, etc. To the extent that they think the platform relies on a few key people, they will put in a *key man trigger*. In the event that these people actually leave, the monoline will have the option to step in and asses the situation and potentially drive a replacement. They may or may not have a unilateral right to effect the change. Sometimes they share the right with a subordinate not holder or equity or whoever is lowest in the structure and have to act in concert. Given that they will be 70% to 80% of the typical capital structure, they will put a time limit on how long negotiations with "equity" can take place. Ultimately, there will be a point where they require the right to take action. This point is usually found in the documents pertaining to management replacement for cause events (e.g., officers indicted for fraud, criminal activity within the platform, willful breach of covenants, and so on).

For an unwrapped deal, there can be a lengthy process where others have to come together and vote whether the manager should be terminated, followed by a subsequent decision process to determine who the new manager should be. A monoline will seek to hold the time frame to within 10 days to go in and terminate the manager and drive the decision regarding a new manager. The monoline will allow the Equity to vote on the nominee but if there has been fraud there will be a fairly short window for dialogue before they put a new manger in place. After this, they will let the equity vote whether the deal will be static or managed.

One additional benefit is that they are long-term investors committed to the transaction to the end. They can't trade out of their insurance contract.

In summary, a monoline is watching the transaction closely and has some rights to jump in and try to remediate if something is going wrong. There is generally an alignment of interests—they will seek to get the CDO working again. As one person said while explaining such rights, "if we liquidate a deal its not like we get a reward, we stop getting paid."

Efficient Synthetic Execution

Compared with cash-based CDOs, SCDOs are easier and quicker to execute because they generally require shorter ramp-up periods and do not require balance-sheet capacity and may have streamlined documents (for privately negotiated synthetic portfolio trades between two to four counterparties).

Shorter ramp-up periods (can be done in months) are possible in transactions because portfolio managers are usually able to enter into CDS contracts in a more efficient manner than cash bonds. For some time, BBBs off cash CMBS bonds had been highly oversubscribed and available in limited amounts. This was evidenced by the immediate oversubscription or preemptive bids whenever you see a cash deal brought to market. The CDS market is not dependent on specific cash assets. Therefore, SCDO collateral aggregation is not dependent on the forward calendar of issuance, the ability to fill an order on an oversubscribed deal or the availability of outstanding bonds in the way a cash-based transaction is dependent. Theoretically, the sponsor could declare a reference pool overnight and hedge later as it sees fit. Further, the manager can pinpoint the collateral they feel comfortable with and not subject to taking what's available or comes along. They put out the list; they do not have to react to what someone else wants. Additionally they can construct their lists to get collateral in the sizes and proportions they want (which is practically impossible in the cash market).

Synthetic balance sheet transactions tend to have the shortest ramp-up periods because the reference obligations are already on the balance sheet.

For those issuers who do not already have assets on balance sheet or for those with limited balance sheet availability, SCDOs have the added benefit of not requiring any balance sheet to ramp up because CDS are unfunded instruments.

Pure synthetic, privately negotiated transactions may also benefit from simple documentation compared with funded CDOs and SCDOs. Most SCDOs done in the 144A market which are broadly distributed involve a Cayman Island SPE and have documents like an *indenture* and a *collateral manager agreement*. Getting hard numbers is quite difficult but its thought that there are many private synthetic deals that are not done with the aforementioned documents or via a Cayman SPE which are privately negotiated synthetic portfolio trades between two to four counterparties. These types of trades involve just a CDS contract and are simpler from a documentation standpoint. Participants in these transactions generally employ their own legal counsel to ensure that risks are appropriately analyzed.

Maturity/Callability

Many structured finance SCDOs incorporate cleanup calls that unwind a transaction when the economics become unattractive. When the call is exercised, all rated investors will be paid simultaneously. Often, there are yield targets that must be met on bonds in order to call the deal.

Historically Lower Cost of Liabilities

SCDO equity investors benefit considerably from the lower cost of liabilities afforded by synthetic structures. The super-senior tranche typically demands only a fraction of the spread that a traditional AAA CDO investor would require. Because the super-senior tranche represents so much of the capital structure—usually 80% or more—the overall cost of liabilities for the SCDO is reduced dramatically. The "freed" excess cash is passed to the preferred shareholders. Debt holders may also benefit if provisions are made to trap excess cash when credit events occur and losses are realized. Super-senior investors (primarily monoline insurance companies) are willing to accept a low premium because of the considerable structural support provided them (the AAA investors are subordinate to the super senior) and the convenience of making their investment in unfunded form.

Transaction cost is driven down even further by generally lower structuring, administrative and trustee fees. For example, a portfolio manager may earn 50 bps per annum to manage a $300 million pool of collateral

($1.5 million per annum), whereas an equivalent fee for an SCDO manager requires only 15 bps per annum on a $1 billion collateral pool. The same principal can be applied to administrative and trustee fees.

In addition, structuring and placement fees in SCDOs are generally paid over the life of the transaction instead of upfront as is typical for cash-based CDOs. This typically leads to higher leverage, which benefits equity holders, and more collateral at closing, which benefits note holders.

High-Quality Assets

The low cost liability of the unfunded super senior tranche of SCDOs allows these transactions to reference higher-quality collateral (where the arbitrage is thinner) than collateral that is used to collateralize cash CDOs. That said there is little to no supply of CDS on lower-rated credits due to the high premium or carry costs that would be incurred by a protection buyer. Early cash-based CRE CDOs initially referenced BBB CMBS and REIT bonds and were soon followed by deals utilizing collateral rated in the B and BB range. Via SCDOs it is easy to arbitrage the entire capital structure, even highly rated securities. Investors need to be aware that the higher-quality collateral also results in greater leverage and more sensitivity to event risk discussed later.

Single-Tranche Transactions

An expected future variation on the SCDO theme is what is commonly called *single-tranche trades,* which are private in nature. The investor (protection seller) designs a customized SCDO around their credit views and risk tolerance—limited only by the names that are traded in the CDS market. Typically, the investor requests a desired level of exposure to a chosen pool of credits in return for a premium payment. The premium to be received is dependent on the credits selected (spread, quality and default correlation) and the level of risk. For example, an investor may choose 50 credits with an average rating of BBB and total notional value of $500 million and indicate a desire for a $20 million exposure to this pool at an A level of risk. In addition to investment customization, these transactions are characterized by relatively quick closing times.

On the other side of the trade, the protection buyer (typically a CDS dealer) pays the investor a premium for this protection. The CDS dealer will "delta" hedge its position by selling protection to or buying protection from the market in small increments as the probability of default among the underlying reference portfolio increases and decreases (as evidenced by spread widening and tightening). The amount of protection bought or sold will depend on the performance of the CDS reference pool selected by the investor and the risk level (e.g., A level) to be hedged.

Investors will realize several benefits from investing in single-tranche SCDOs, including:

- *Tailored assets.* Single-tranche transactions allow investors to create investments customized for a given risk/return profile. The investor selects the optimal point in the capital structure for investment and actively participates in the portfolio selection.
- *Alignment of investor interests.* Investor involvement in choosing the portfolio of credits eliminates the conflict of interest between senior, mezzanine and equity investors. In a "fully banked" SCDO, where risk is placed to different investors across the full capital structure, the equity investor heavily influences the choice of credits often leading to a riskier, higher-yielding portfolio. In the single-tranche trade, an investor choosing to participate at the mezzanine level would influence the credit choices rather than be subject to the motivations of the equity investors.
- *Ease of execution.* Single-tranche transactions are not dependent on a ramp-up of cash assets or distribution of a full CDO capital structure and therefore can be executed in as little time as it takes to execute the underling CDS trades.

Rating Agencies Accommodate Synthetic "Collateral"

Rating agencies have modified their traditional CDO rating methodologies to accommodate the synthetic nature of the collateral in an SCDO. That said, in general, there are limited differences between synthetic structured finance CDOs, particularly hybrid CRE SCDOs. All of the agencies generally follow their standard quantitative methods with slight adjustments (haircuts to default rates or recovery rates) due to the particular nature of the collateral (CDS), structure or documentation of the transaction.

Some of the agency scrutiny is focused on the documents, and slight changes are made to the standard modeling assumptions accordingly. As one might expect, an area of particular contention involves the definition of credit events. When default swaps reference a CRE CDOs the agencies require changes to the standard form confirm as they are concerned with implied write-downs (where the CDO pays out on this event). The agencies want the buyer of protection to continue to pay the full premium amount (not adjusted down for the implied writedown). This not in the standard form and there will be pricing adjustments by the market (lower premium) to compensate. Issuers/collateral managers may choose not to make this adjustment to the CDS; if so, it will result in larger subordination levels for the deal.

Another important concern, due to the synthetic nature of the transaction, is the collateral posting requirement of each participating party. One of the benefits of a synthetic transaction is the ability for an investor to enter the transaction without an initial exchange of cash. However, the potential for loss is still just as great as an investment in a cash-based transaction. Therefore, it is imperative that each party stand behind its obligation under the CDS contracts and posting requirements are one way to ensure that those obligations are met. For many investors, this occurs naturally when investing in a credit-linked note (full collateral posting in a sense) but for other parties, such as the CDS counterparty (sponsor), the super-senior investor, the *guaranteed investment contract* (GIC) provider (if a GIC is used) or investors choosing to participate in an unfunded manner, collateral posting requirements are established based on the party's perceived risk. Generally, the agencies dictate posting requirements for the CDS counterparty and GIC provider, if any. Posting requirements for the super-senior or other unfunded investors are normally negotiated privately with the CDS counterparty.

SYNTHETIC BALANCE SHEET DEALS

With growing exposure to commercial real estate, increasing scrutiny from the OCC, and desires to boost yields many traditional balance sheet lenders are turning to the commercial real estate synthetic balance sheet CDO (CRE SBSCDO).

There are several reasons for doing a SBSCDO including the following:

- Risk transfer/portfolio management.
- Regulator capital relief (boost return on capital).
- Expand origination markets and facilitate continued growth of the commercial real estate portfolio.

To date there were not many options to address the aforementioned issues. For one thing securitization (CMBS transaction) was not feasible due to limited call protection (if any) and/or short loan terms. Other challenges include adequate systems designed to facilitate risk distribution, data quality and quantity, losing the client relationship, loan standardization, and fixed due diligence costs (for small loans) in addition to the fixed costs for securitization.

The managed CDO addressed many of these issues particularly the call protection and fixed deal costs as short-term loans can be replaced. Rated tranches provide regulatory capital relief (discussed here). Loans can be pinpointed for balance sheet management (geographic, property type, etc.).

The synthetic approach allows the lending institution to maintain the ever important client relationship.

Risk Transfer/Portfolio Management

Whether it is reducing overall exposure or making adjustments to geographic, property type or other risk stratifications, the SBSCDO is an effective means to accomplish these ends. The CRE SBSCDO completes the circle, in a sense, to the beginning of CDOs (corporate) as the balance sheet management or desired risk reduction while maintaining the corporate relation is what gave birth to the synthetic corporate CDO in the first place. Any holder of a large portfolio of commercial mortgage loans can now pare back or sculpt their risk while keeping the loan and the relationship under their control.

Regulatory Capital Relief

A key driver behind doing a synthetic balance sheet deal is regulatory capital relief. This motivation can be shown by looking at how things work under Basel I in Exhibits 16.10 and 16.11. Basel II has been in the works for many years. The latest word, at the time of printing, is that prior to January 1, 2008 European Union (EU) banks and other financial institutions can apply Basel I rules or choose from Basel II or and *internal ratings-based* (IRB) approach. Post January 1, 2008 EU and UK banks must use Basel II. In the US an IRB approach will be used for the largest banks (meaning that no standardized method will apply). U.S. regulators are working hard to get a rule out before the end of 2007. The latest draft would have allowed banks to implement on the schedule they determined as long as they were up and running within three years of the rule being published. Only the top eight or so banks are mandatory. Large investment banks will run under a very similar Securities and Exchange Commission version of the rule. Over time, the next tier of banks is expected to elect to implement that advanced approach. Smaller banks will have a much simpler version of the rule, which is yet to be published.

Basic Setup

The basic CRE SBSCDO set up allows the issuer to sell credit protection for realized losses on a reference portfolio through a credit default swap where the underlying reference portfolio consists of first-lien commercial and multifamily mortgage loans owned by the issuer. Deals are typically set up to have principal payment rules which are similar to a CMBS "sequential pay"

EXHIBIT 16.10   Regulatory Capital Relief Example

Assets Retained	Notional	Risk Weight	Basel I Criteria Capital Ratio	Capital Charge %	Capital Charge Amt
Scenario 1: Loans without Synthetic CDO Protection					
Unsecuritized Loans	[1,000,000,000]	[100.00%]	[8.00%]	[8.00%]	[80,000,000]
					[80,000,000]
Scenario 2: Loans with Synthetic CDO Protection					
Super Senior/[AAA]	[665,000,000]	[20.00%]	[8.00%]	[1.60%]	[10,640,000]
Class A/[AAA]	[166,500,000]	[20.00%]	[8.00%]	[1.60%]	[2,664,000]
Class B/[AA]	[53,000,000]	[20.00%]	[8.00%]	[1.60%]	[848,000]
Class C/[A+]	[19,000,000]	[50.00%]	[8.00%]	[4.00%]	[760,000]
Class D/[A]	[7,000,000]	[50.00%]	[8.00%]	[4.00%]	[280,000]
Class E/[A–]	[6,500,000]	[50.00%]	[8.00%]	[4.00%]	[260,000]
Class F/[BBB+]	[13,000,000]	[100.00%]	[8.00%]	[8.00%]	[1,040,000]
Class G/[BBB]	[8,500,000]	[100.00%]	[8.00%]	[8.00%]	[680,000]
Class H/[BBB–]	[10,500,000]	[100.00%]	[8.00%]	[8.00%]	[840,000]
Class J/[BB+]	[12,000,000]	[200.00%]	[8.00%]	[16.00%]	[1,920,000]
Class K/[BB]	[5,500,000]	[200.00%]	[8.00%]	[16.00%]	[880,000]
Class L/[BB–]	[2,000,000]	[200.00%]	[8.00%]	[16.00%]	[320,000]
Class M/[B–]	[2,000,000]	[1250.00%]	[8.00%]	[100.00%]	[2,000,000]
Equity/[NR]	[29,500,000]	[1250.00%]	[8.00%]	[100.00%]	[29,500,000]
Totals	[1,000,000,000]				[52,632,000]

Assumes CDO liabilities up to and including the respective row are offered to investors and tranche(s) below the respective row are retained as equity.
Capital Charge from keeping unsecuritized whole loans minus Cumulative Capital Charge of retained CDO liabilities.
Source: Wachovia Capital Markets, LLC and Bank for International Settlements.

structure. Thus, absent any credit losses, the structure will delever (credit enhancement increases) as the underlying loans pay off over time. As is the case with synthetics (discussed earlier in the paper) and unlike CMBS, the actual cash flow from the reference portfolio is not paid to the holders of the offered notes. Rather, the transaction is capitalized with the proceeds from the offered securities, which are invested in eligible investments. Interest payable to the holders of the offered notes will be paid from the income earned on the eligible investments and payments from the protected party under the CDS. Principal allocable to the offered notes and excluded classes in any given month will be based on principal payable to or otherwise re-

EXHIBIT 16.11 Regulatory Capital Relief Example

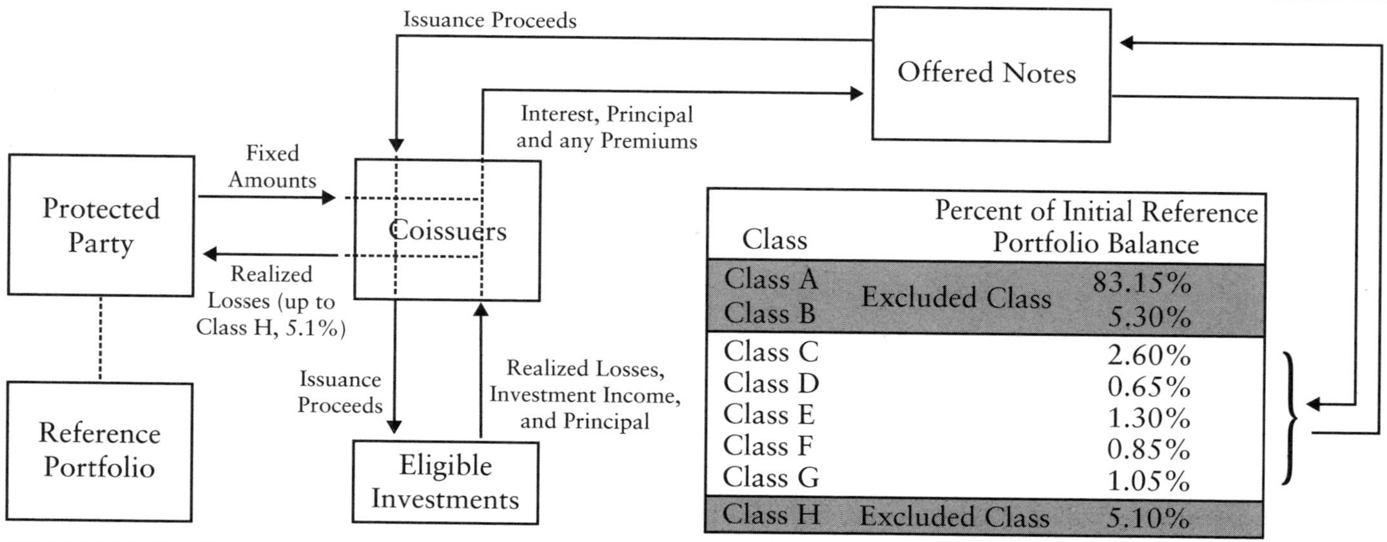

Class	Percent of Initial Reference Portfolio Balance	
Class A	Excluded Class	83.15%
Class B		5.30%
Class C		2.60%
Class D		0.65%
Class E		1.30%
Class F		0.85%
Class G		1.05%
Class H	Excluded Class	5.10%

Offered Notes

Issuance Proceeds

Interest, Principal
and any Premiums

Realized Losses,
Investment Income,
and Principal

Coissuers

Eligible
Investments

Fixed
Amounts

Realized
Losses (up to
Class H, 5.1%)

Issuance
Proceeds

Protected
Party

Reference
Portfolio

ceived by the protected party on the reference portfolio, and the sale or removal of mortgage loans from the reference portfolio.

The CDS will require the issuer to reimburse the party buying protection for realized losses on the reference portfolio in each month prior to the allocation of principal to the offered notes. Realized losses reimbursed under the CDS will be allocated to the offered notes in reverse order of payment priority until their principal balances have either been reduced to zero or are fully impaired.

SBSCDOs can enable or allow the origination arm of the business to run at full capacity without limitations on geography or loan size as excess exposures can be reduced or removed synthetically.

INVESTOR'S GUIDE TO SYNTHETIC CDOs

There are a myriad of investment considerations in connection with CDO investments in general, and SCDOs are no different. However, the emphasis may be different when looking at a synthetic transaction, and we suggest the following considerations be included in an investor's due diligence process in addition to their typical CDO due diligence process:

- Reference portfolio and parameters: quality is key
- Portfolio manager: skills and capabilities
- Event risk: proper modeling
- Additional layer of risk: considering the high-quality assets

Reference Portfolio: Quality Is Key

Investors to pay particular attention to the portfolio of reference credits. Due to the high leverage of investment-grade SCDOs, just a handful of credit events can have significant implications for the performance of the investment. If the transaction is static and motivated by arbitrage reasons, investors should determine how the portfolio was constructed, including the parties involved and their interests, and carefully consider each name in the portfolio.

Many portfolio managers or sponsors retain the equity portion of the liability structure and therefore may be motivated to maximize spread. Equity investors will likely view this favorably, but this could expose note holders to greater risk. To be sure, this is not a unique concern to SCDOs—all managed CDOs are susceptible to similar risk. We simply mention this concern because of the important role collateral manager behavior has played in previous cash-based CDO transactions.

Portfolio Manager: Skills and Capabilities

Portfolio managers should have experience in CDS documentation and established trading relationships with a broad range of CDS brokers, which demonstrates their market access. For more information, this topic is discussed in greater depth in other chapters.

Event Risk: Proper Modeling

Investment-grade SCDOs are susceptible to event risk within the pool of reference assets, just like their cash counterparts. The highly leveraged nature of investment-grade CDOs (the equity tranche can be just a percent of two of the entire liability structure) increases the impact of losses on equity holders and junior note holders. Increasing diversity can mitigate much of the default "lumpiness"; but we recommend that investors also identify and evaluate the weakest credits in the collateral pool. In large part, the performance of their investment will depend on those securities. Therefore, we also recommend that investors measure defaults in terms of the number of defaults and not default rates (e.g., a 0.5% default rate is not possible in a pool of 25 to 50 equally weighted credits), which tends to underestimate the possibility of large losses.

Additional Layer of Risk: Considering the High-Quality Assets

Investors who purchase CLNs depend not only on the creditworthiness of the reference entities, but also on the performance of the high-quality assets that support their position. Typically, the proceeds of the CLNs are invested in a GIC but sometimes highly rated ABS or Treasuries are employed. Regardless, the CLN's performance depends on the performance of those high-quality assets as well as the performance of the reference pool. The insolvency of the GIC provider or a default in any of the high-quality holdings would adversely affect the deal's ability to pay principal and interest when due. Although many market participants may consider default by any of these entities a remote possibility, we suggest investors consider the merits of the high-quality collateral and perform due diligence on the GIC provider, if any.

CONCLUSION

The structured products market and the credit derivatives market have merged to create SCDOs, a product that is attractive to investors and issuers alike. Though the market has been in disarray during the second half of 2007, investors have found SCDOs appealing for a variety of reasons including excess spread, the ability to source credit risk quickly and on a customized set of credits and generally greater structural flexibility. Issuers are also attracted by the potential structural simplicity and how SCDOs can be executed in a shorter time frame.

The learning curve for investors who currently participate in the cash CDO market should be relatively short because SCDO structures bear similarity to the cash market and many cash CDO concepts are transferable. Other concepts such as ISDA documentation and credit default swap mechanics have been presented here to provide investors with the basic tools to understand those areas that are different from the cash CDO market.

CHAPTER 17

European Commercial Real Estate CDOs

Chris van Heerden, CFA
Analyst
Wachovia Capital Markets, LLC

Collateralized debt obligation (CDO) technology was first applied to European property finance in 2006. The active management framework of the CDO structure has increased the accessibility of European commercial real estate (CRE) investments by addressing (1) the high prepayment velocity identified with European CRE; (2) the lack of transparency in investments; and (3) the regulatory morass and country-specific investment nuances.

Although the number of transactions to market has been limited, the variation in managers, collateral, and structures make these deals useful benchmarks for developing an understanding of the market. This chapter reviews European CRE CDO collateral types and structures, and outlines an investor approach to the sector.

CRE CDO COLLATERAL

CRE CDOs in Europe employ a broad spectrum of collateral, generally reflecting the manager's overall portfolio and core competencies. In this section, we examine the major collateral categories, commercial mortgage-backed securities (CMBS), whole loans, A- and B-notes, mezzanine debt, and other sources with mind to the implementation of each in CDOs (summarized in Exhibit 17.1).

Because of a common link to real estate, most assets can be approached first on property fundamentals, including tenant/borrower credit quality, loan terms, and leverage, coverage, or cash flow multiples.

EXHIBIT 17.1   European CRE CDO Collateral at a Glance

Collateral	Description	Leverage
CMBS	Subordinate tranches of commercial mortgage backed securities; publicly rated. Typically issued from AAA to BBB– with occasional lower rated classes. Performance dependent primarily on cash flow from underlying loans. Loans generally have bullet or partially amortizing structures. Deals have varying levels of borrower/tenant concentration. European loans tend to have limited prepayment penalties. Deals more frequently structured as modified pro rata but also sequential. May be synthetic, using credit linked note, credit default swap or total return swap. Cash flow may be diverted from subordinates if deal level income deteriorates due to prepayments or defaults (available funds cap); or cash flow may become sequential on a deterioration in credit support for the senior bonds (sequential trigger events).	65%–70%
A-notes/ whole loans	A single loan, or the senior investment-grade portion of a loan secured by a property or group of properties by a single security package. Performance depends on successful operation of property, market value, and borrowers' ability to refinance at maturity. Usually serviced together with B-note under a single servicing agreement, but with due consideration to seniority of A-note. Commonly directs the enforcement process, subject to the cure and buyout rights of the subordinate lender.	70%–80%
B-notes	Contractually subordinated loan secured by underlying property; with rights detailed in intercreditor agreement. Often ranks *pari passu* with A-note with respect to interest and principal until a "material default or "trigger event," in which case it will likely event of default. The B-note is assumes the first loss in the whole loan. Rights detailed in intercreditor agreement generally include cure rights, enforcement rights, consent rights, and servicing. Some remedies may be subject to control valuation (a test preserving senior lender). These tend to be highly negotiated contracts rather than standardized. May be hypertranched to C- and D-notes	70%–95%
Mezzanine loans	Generally ownership interests in the property owning or related entity. Subordinated to A/B-note, senior to preferred equity. Will have a separate servicer as whole loan. Consent, control, and consultation rights depend on agreement.	
REIT debt	Includes commercial mortgage REITs that invest in commercial mortgages and CMBS, and residential mortgage REITs that invest in single family-residential mortgages and RMBS. Often fund with long-dated (30-year maturity) trust preferred securities to match long-term funding needs. REIT trust preferred securities often do not have dividend.	
Real estate operating companies (REOC)	Debt issued by real estate manager, operator, or developer that is not a REIT or CMBS issuer. REOCs are taxed as ordinary corporations and thus generally have more operating flexibility. Can be secured, unsecured and may be subordinated to other obligations May be in CDS form.	
Other collateral	May include leveraged loans, CDO tranches, whole loan securitizations, opco/propco structures, RMBS, etc.	

Source: Wachovia Capital Markets, LLC.

The evaluation of collateral and an examination of structure are interrelated. Collateral type and quality will be counterbalanced by credit enhancement and higher funding costs. In addition, deal covenants serve to regulate concentration risk and control the potential migration of the pool over time.

Commercial Mortgage-Backed Securities

CMBS has been a natural collateral source, and all European CRE CDOs to date have included allocations to the asset. The acceptance is attributable to the following factors:

- These securities are publicly rated and largely investment-grade debt. Over time, these characteristics should be conducive to the development of a liquid secondary market.
- Diversity is increasing across country and property type. Issuance is expanding by geography (most recently including Greece and Bulgaria), and property types are expanding (loans on car parks, holiday parks, public houses, and bingo halls have appeared in transactions).
- Growth in origination in the past few years raised the availability of collateral.
- CMBS ratings have demonstrated long-term stability (see Exhibit 17.2). Lifetime downgrades totalled 1.6% through year-end 2006, according to S&P, reflecting strong fundamental performance. European CMBS delinquencies have been trending less than 0.1%.[1]

High prepayment speeds and concentration risk are challenges endemic to European CMBS. Loans are often underwritten with weak or nonexisting prepayment penalties, and prepayment speeds have been further exacerbated by low interest rates, competition among lenders, and rising property values. Within the CMBS transaction, this prepayment velocity raises the risk of adverse selection, when good loans prepay and only loans that cannot refinance are left in the portfolio.

Absolute prepayment speeds remain high, although the trend has been slowing. Loans originated in 2003 and 2004 have shown the highest prepayment rates—80% of 2003 issuance has repaid, according to S&P. In the first half of 2007, prepayments slowed to 32% on a rolling 12-month rate, compared with 45% in the first half of 2006.[2] This slowing may be indica-

---

[1] Christina Pries and Esther Robinson Wild, *European CMBS Performance Review H1 2007: Signs of Weakness Despite Robust Performance?* Standard & Poor's, July 19, 2007.
[2] Pries and Wild, *European CMBS Performance Review H1 2007: Signs of Weakness Despite Robust Performance?*

EXHIBIT 17.2 Lifetime Transition Matrix for CMBS

From	Starting ratings (no.)	To									Percentage Upgraded	Percentage Stable	Percentage Downgraded
		AAA	AA	A	BBB	BB	B	CCC	CC	D			
AAA	245	100									0	100	0
AA	238	15.5	83.6	0.8							15.5	83.6	0.8
A	244	7.4	5.7	83.2	3.7						13.1	83.2	3.7
BBB	252	3.2	2.4	5.2	88.9	0.4					10.7	88.9	0.4
BB	92	3.3		2.2	5.4	83.7	3.3	1.1	1.1		10.9	83.7	5.4
B	7						100				0	100	0
Ending ratings (no.)	1,078	311	219	220	238	78	10	1	1	0	106	955	17

Source: Transition Study: 2006 Sees Upgrades Dominate For Third Successive Year In European Structured Finance, 10-Jan-2007, Table 10- Lifetime Transition Matrix For CMBS, This material is reproduced with permission of Standard & Poor's, a division of the McGraw-Hill Companies, Inc.

tive of tightening financing terms and increasing risk premiums (for both debt and equity).

High prepayments elevate the risk of cash flow interruption, especially further down the CMBS capital structure. As loans refinance out of the pool, cash flow diminishes, and the available funds cap may reduce payments to junior classes. Because interest payments on junior classes are not due until there is sufficient yield on assets, liquidity facilities would not cover such a shortfall.

The second challenge for European CMBS, concentration risk, refers to the number of borrowers and properties in a transaction. *Granular* is a frequently used term that describes transactions with a high number of properties and borrowers, which is generally a positive for investors as it reduces idiosyncratic risk. According to S&P, 95% of European CMBS have fewer than 10 loans and more than half of all deals have only one loan. Here, prepayments also come into play, as deals become less and less granular when loans are refinanced out of the pool.

European CMBS have undergone a number of modifications to address the prepayment issue. Transactions have shifted away from the sequential structures to distribute prepayment risk across the capital stack using modified pro rata structures. Some transactions allow for loan substitution and/or replenishment, accompanied by rating agency restrictions on the quality of loans that may be inserted and affirmation of the bond ratings. Deals with substitution features have not been well received by investors. In some cases, the loss of seasoning benefit is addressed by a reduced allowance for leverage.

Within the CDO structure, there are clear advantages to CMBS as a collateral source. The public ratings and information transparency eases the manager's task, especially within a manage-to-model framework. From this perspective, the manager may be able to use modelling software to assess the potential impact of a contemplated CMBS trade on the overall CDO portfolio. Although deal structures are varied, it is relatively straightforward to pinpoint differences and assess the impact of structural variations. On the other hand, managers need to navigate prevailing underwriting conditions (i.e., generous assumptions in the first half of 2007, the propensity to prepay and lumpy borrower/property concentrations in deals.

Whole Loans and A-Notes

Senior-subordinate structures have been used to tranche property loans to most efficiently allocate risk and control rights or workout options. The whole loan describes the undivided loan secured by a property or group of properties. These loans also may be divided into an A/B structure, where the A-loan describes the senior portion of the loan (frequently investment-grade rated). The B-note, then, is secured by the same mortgage and contractually subordinated via the intercreditor agreement. Following the same mechanics, loans may also be further tranched into C-notes, D-notes, and so on. B-notes serve to keep A-note leverage limited, thus facilitating CMBS execution for the A-note. In turn for assuming a subordinated position, B-note lenders are compensated with the granting of certain rights, although these will vary by transaction.

The intercreditor agreement sets forth rights, responsibilities and remedies between the A- and B-note holders. In Europe, intercreditor agreements are marked by less standardization, reflecting regional idiosyncrasies along with the bargaining power and investment strategies specific to individual transactions.

Within the CDO structure, whole loans benefit from a straightforward real estate-driven analysis referencing the property and income in light of debt-service requirements. The valuation of A-notes, on the other hand, also considers the governing intercreditor agreement, but with thought to the benefits of:

- The enhancement to the senior lender's leverage and debt service coverage metrics provided by a subordinated piece.
- The provision for cash flow diversion to the A-loan generally through an escrow agreement or a sequential payment waterfall in an acceleration event.
- Ideally, the alignment of economic interest with a junior party with capacity to remedy default, enhance property value, and enforce security when needed.

There are a number of challenges to whole loans and A-notes as collateral in CDOs. First, information may be restricted for these privately negotiated agreements. Second, for A-notes, the absence of standardization for intercreditor agreements confounds the analysis. Third, workout scenarios for A-notes are untested with regard to stress scenarios where A-note and B-note lenders' interests may diverge.

B-Notes

B-notes have found a constituency among real estate specialist investors, who value property-specific analysis and can benefit from the rights granted to the subordinated lender. Although specifics vary by agreement, junior lenders are generally granted approval rights, enforcement rights, cure rights and buyout rights, along with powers over the loan servicing and administration.

- *Cure rights* refer to a subordinated lender's ability to make an advance to the senior lender to cover a payment shortfall from the borrower. Such a cash injection may stave off default, and thus continue the junior lender's cash flow stream instead of diverting cash exclusively to the senior lender. It may also serve to delay enforcement where enforcement would crystallize losses to the subordinate lender. Cure payments are limited in terms of consecutive cure payments (e.g., two consecutive cures) and cumulative lifetime cures (e.g., four to six cumulative cures). Cure advances are reimbursed after interest and scheduled principal payments are paid to the senior lender.
- *Consent rights* describe the subordinate lender's right to consent to material changes to loan structure, including security arrangements and, possibly, the management of the underlying properties. Some intercreditor agreements will require the consent of both lenders in certain matters. However, the senior lender will typically be able to override consents required from the subordinate lender in a default scenario.
- *Enforcement rights* reference the right of the controlling creditor (likely the subordinate lender) to direct the enforcement process. Enforcement is preceded by a standstill period during which the junior lender would need to obtain consent of the senior lender. The junior lender's control may also be contingent on a control valuation, which tests for the preservation of the junior lender's economic interest in the property.
- *Purchase options* describe the junior lender's rights to buy out the senior lender upon an event of default to become the sole lender and therefore control the workout process. Although the presence of a purchase option is fairly standard, loan agreements differ on what expenses related to the purchase have to be covered by the junior lender, including securitization costs such as liquidity or special servicer costs.
- *Servicing rights* refer to the junior lender's rights to consent to servicing standards and to replace or appoint the special servicer in the event of a workout. The subordinated debt may be serviced together with the senior debt under a single servicing agreement, or separately in some cases.

Intercreditor agreements can be broadly categorized according to (1) the rights of the junior lender regarding loan servicing and administration, especially as it pertains to the initiating and directing of the enforcement process; intercreditor agreements range from granting extensive rights to the junior lender, where all material decisions require B-note consent, to those that minimize the rights and powers of the junior lender in servicing and administration; or (2) the longevity of the junior lender's rights as determined by the provision for writedown through a control valuation event.

A control valuation event describes a test of the preservation of a junior lender's economic interest in the property. Specifically, the control valuation may check that the expected recovery value of a property exceeds the senior debt (often by 110% to 125%). The junior lender's enforcement rights may be contingent on the control valuation, although agreements range between meaningful control valuation events, where the B-note's rights are linked to its economic interests, to agreements where the junior lenders rights cannot be written down.

As CDO collateral, B-note investing relies on intensive property-specific analysis, which should align well with the specialization of CRE CDO managers. The degree of control granted to B-note investors may be valuable within the active portfolio management framework of CRE CDOs. Concerns specific to B-notes include (1) the challenge in diversifying exposure—securitization lenders have tended to make similar loans on like properties with overlapping refinancing risk profiles; and (2) the overall sensitivity of B-notes, given their higher leverage and first-loss position in the whole loan.

Mezzanine Loans

Mezzanine loans are subordinated loans under a separate agreement that is secured by equity interests in the property-owning entity. As such, these loans fill the gap between where whole loan lenders are willing to lend to and the amount of financing borrowers require. In general, prior to a material default, it is not unusual for the mezzanine to receive payments on a pro rata basis with more senior lenders. Following a material default, the mezzanine debt will typically receive consideration below the B-note either through an escrow agreement or sequential waterfall. Also, in the event of a material default, the mezzanine debt would typically have the option to assume the first mortgage.

Other Collateral

Synthetic collateral included in CRE CDOs take the form of euro-denominated credit default swaps, credit-linked notes or total return swaps that reference obligations including whole loans, B- and C-notes, mezzanine loans, CMBS, and real estate entity debt. Synthetics have been useful in overcoming limitations on securitisation in the European market (including secrecy laws and transfer restrictions) and to transfer the risk on portfolios that were not originated with securitization in mind. Aside from the credit quality of the reference credit, synthetic collateral performance also relies on the creditworthiness of the counterparty and may require further legal, tax, and structural consideration.

Real estate investment trust (REIT) and *real estate operating company* (REOC) debt has been used in both secured and unsecured form. The performance of these obligations depends primarily on the issuer or parent's ability to repay debt, and, therefore, real estate entity debt analysis primarily considers the management and overall financial standing of the firm. Even in the case of secured debt, the credit link can not be ignored as the corporate entity is exposed to event risk, changes in management strategy, ownership changes and regulatory changes. Trust-preferred securities have been used as collateral and are generally long-dated deferrable interest instruments. Because of the inherent credit risk, rating agencies may cap the maximum rating achievable by REIT and REOC debt, even when this debt is secured by collateral. For example, S&P caps the maximum rating achievable on secured REIT/REOC debt at two notches above the issuer's corporate credit rating.

In addition to these, CRE CDOs have made allowances to include leveraged loans, whole business securitizations and nonperforming loans. Allowances for the inclusion of these assets increase the flexibility granted to the manager in deploying capital and may increase the overall diversification of the collateral pool, but some assets may be difficult to analyze.

CRE CDO STRUCTURE

Deal structure follows established CDO technology. The collateral manager aggregates a portfolio and then actively trades the assets, within prescribed constraints. The CDO issuer is paid management fees, which include a senior fee and a subordinate management fee. Managers, so far, have retained an equity stake via the subordinated notes. Distributions are made through interest and principal waterfalls, with coverage tests accelerating amortization if collateral deteriorates. Issuance has taken the form of euro-denominated floating-rate notes (with the exception of Glastonbury, a sterling transaction), although multicurrency structures may be a future development.

The CDO lifecycle is divided into the following three stages:

- *Ramp-up period.* Deals have a finite window to fully ramp assets (ranging from 100 days to a year). Funds that have not been deployed by the end of this window would be distributed to noteholders.
- *Reinvestment period.* Typically five years in length, during the reinvestment period the manager monitors and trades the portfolio subject to the constraints laid out in the indenture. Principal proceeds are used to

purchase additional collateral, while reinvestment criteria guard asset quality.

■ *Amortization period*. Prepaying or maturing assets are typically used to retire notes sequentially. Three types of calls serve to limit the life of the deal.

CDOs typically have both investor-driven and event-driven *calls*. These calls are based on time or collateral amortization.

■ The *optional redemption call* is the right of the subordinated noteholders to redeem notes and is be subject to a majority vote. The option is viable only if *net asset value* (NAV) minus transaction costs is greater than the secondary bid for the CDO equity position.

■ The *auction call* acts to limit the final maturity of the transaction. The auction call allows for the assets to be liquidated if the proceeds are sufficient to make all investors whole and achieve the targeted *return on equity* (ROE) for subordinated note investors. In addition to paying all rated notes and subordinated notes, the collateral sale must produce enough to pay all outstanding expenses.

■ The *cleanup call* allows for the sale of all assets when the par value of debt falls below 10% of the original balance. The cleanup call would occur only if the proceeds were sufficient to make investors whole.

Portfolio Profile Tests and Collateral Quality Tests

Collateral tests aim to limit asset and risk migration of the portfolio over time but have to leave enough room for the manager to stay invested in changing markets. For example, a portfolio may strive to maintain 30% minimum whole-loan assets, but high prepayment rates may make a firm covenant to this extent impractical. Collateral tests should line up with a manager's areas of competence as established by track record and dedicated resources.

Portfolio profile tests (PPTs) vet assets in terms of the impact on the overall portfolio by setting minimum and maximum exposures as a percentage of the principal balance. PPTs' criteria can be broadly grouped in terms of asset class, property type, geographic location, structure, obligor concentration, and maturity concentration.

Collateral quality tests (CQTs) screen assets for risk by regulating collateral rating, diversity, spread, coupon, and average life. These tests are generally calculated monthly after ramp-up. Should the deal breach a quality test, the manager may not trade, except to improve the test. For example, the manager may sell lower-rated assets and replace them with higher-rated ones. The cushion between CQT parameters and the actual collateral profile provides a measure of how well the deal is complying with these tests. Exhibit 17.3 outlines commonly occurring CQTs.

Eligibility criteria constrain the universe of assets that can be considered for reinvestment. The list has an overall objective of preserving the purpose and limiting the risk profile of the CDO, with regard to investment risks, but also considering tax implications, regulatory status and other concerns. Generally, only European CRE-linked assets are considered. A limited set of currencies may be eligible; assets must be rated (with some exceptions), must bear periodic interest and must not be defaulted.

Coverage Tests

Coverage tests serve to protect senior classes in the event of a collateral or cash flow deterioration. These tests determine if interest and principal can be paid on the mezzanine notes and below, and whether principal proceeds may be reinvested in substitute assets or be redirected toward amortization.

EXHIBIT 17.3 Commonly Occurring Collateral Quality Tests

Collateral Quality Tests	Description
Ratings and Credit Quality	
Maximum WARF	A rating hurdle for the portfolio, calculated on a weighted average basis.
	Reduces the likelihood of the average probability of default of the pool rising above a given threshold (rating factor increases as credit quality decreases).
Minimum WA Rating	Guides the overall collateral credit quality.
Fitch Default VECTOR Model	Monte Carlo analysis based on probability of default, weighted average loss, and correlation.
Maximum Assets Rated Ba3, B2, etc.	Limits concentration of low-rated assets in the portfolio to reduce the the potential for "barbelled" credit quality. (Average credit quality may mask the inclusion of securities with very low ratings if there are sufficient securities with high ratings.)
Maximum WA Default Probability	Portfolio summary of individual default probabilities, which are based on property quality, debt service coverage, tenant quality, and tenant diversity.
	Expected conditions at the loan refinancing date are also considered.
WA Recovery Test	Portfolio summary of expected collateral recovery rates, which consider property values, loan terms, termination costs, and property jurisdiction.

EXHIBIT 17.3 (Continued)

Collateral Quality Tests	Description
Spread, Coupon, and Average Life	
Minimum WA Spread	Coupon or spread hurdles that mitigate the risk that yield on the collateral will be insufficient to cover the cost of funding for the CDO liabilities and increases the likelihood that the deal will generate excess interest.
Maximum Weighted Average Life	Reduces the likelihood of principal payment on the underlying collateral extending beyond the maturity date(s) of the CDO's liabilities; also limits the average cumulative default probability of the pool.
Diversity	
Diversity Score	Diversity scores rise with perceived diversification. Diversity scores are based on asset default correlations.
Herfindahl Minimum	Reflects diversification as measured by the effective number of assets, which may differ from the actual number of assets, depending on the range of principal balances.
Moody's Maximum Asset Correlation	Quantification of joint asset dependency, using a CDO approach to look underlying collateral to underlying loans.
Largest Origination Year	Limits vintage concentration. Collateral from the same origination year may share similar assets and underwriting characteristics, which may increase correlation.
Other	
Maximum Floating Asset/Fixed	Mitigates the risk that the fixed/floating asset mix will move out of the range for which the interest rate hedge will be effective.
Currency Covenant	Stipulates eligble collateral currencies and currency hedge requirements.

Note: WA: weighted average; WARF: weighted average rating factor.
Source: Wachovia Capital Markets, LLC.

Overcollateralization (OC) tests address the sufficiency of collateral value versus the outstanding debt. *Interest coverage* (IC) tests, in turn, measure cash flow sufficiency.

The *OC test* is similar to an *loan-to-value* (LTV) calculation that measures the ability of the par value of assets to cover the par amount of particular liability tranches (cumulatively). An OC ratio higher than the OC trigger means that a test is in compliance, and no cash flow is diverted. If the trigger is tripped, however, excess interest is diverted from the subordinated notes and is captured to reduce the principal amount of the failing notes. An example of an OC calculation for Class B notes in CDO is

$$OC = \frac{\sum \begin{array}{l} \text{The aggregate collateral principal balance net of any write-downs} \\ + \text{Principal proceeds held as cash and eligible investments} \\ + \text{For defaulted securities, the lesser of market value and} \\ \quad \text{applicable recovery rate} \end{array}}{\sum \begin{array}{l} \text{The outstanding principal amount of the Class A and Class B notes} \\ + \text{Any unreimbursed interest advances} \end{array}}$$

Some transactions have also been structured with haircuts, or discounts, for specified collateral security types (e.g., CCC rated assets and defaulted issues). These reduce the collateral value of lower-rated assets for the purpose of calculating OC tests. In some cases, deals may also have a purchase-price haircut designed to discourage managers from buying discounted collateral to build par. For CRE CDO deals, purchase price haircuts have applied to discounted assets purchased below 85%, for example. When applicable, the discounted par amount is used for test-ratio calculations until the market value exceeds 85% for 45 days. Defaulted assets are generally included at the lower of their purchase price or assumed recovery rate.

IC tests are similar to OC tests but measure the availability of excess spread. The IC ratio divides interest income by interest expense for the given class and any senior classes. Following is an example IC calculation for Class B notes in a CDO:

$$IC = \frac{\sum \begin{array}{l} \text{Scheduled interest payments on the collateral (excluding defaulted} \\ \quad \text{securities) and eligible investments and collection accounts} \\ + \text{Fees received that constitute interest proceeds} \\ + \text{Hedge receipts} \\ - \text{Capped fees and expenses and senior collateral management} \\ \quad \text{fee in interest waterfall} \end{array}}{\sum \begin{array}{l} \text{Scheduled period interest on Class A Notes and Class B Notes} \\ + \text{Any Class A and Class B defaulted interest amount} \end{array}}$$

Where Class X notes are present in the structure, these are not accelerated with other senior classes in the event of a trigger fail.

Deals may be structured with a *turbo* feature to accelerate cash flow when triggered. After the trigger date, a portion of equity cash flow is diverted to pay down outstanding notes sequentially. This may serve to delever the deal after a given date. For example, in the Taberna I transaction, 60% of excess interest is used to pay principal sequentially after year 10.

Cash Flow Distributions

The priority of payments follows standard CDO mechanics—interest proceeds and principal generated by the collateral flow through separate waterfalls. Interest proceeds fund senior fees, expenses and then coupon payments sequentially. If they were not satisfied out of interest proceeds, senior fees and interest on the senior notes are paid out of principal proceeds. Principal allocation is sequential for most transactions. In the event of an IC or OC test breach, available interest would be used to accelerate amortisation of the notes sequentially until the ratios are brought back into compliance. Deferred interest on the junior tranches is paid below current coupons. Exhibit 17.4 illustrates the general priority of payments.

There are some variations in the priority of payments. For example, Duncannon's waterfall structure allows realized trading gains to be treated

EXHIBIT 17.4 Example Priority of Payments

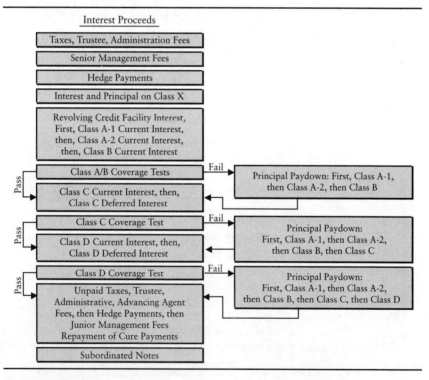

EXHIBIT 17.4 (Continued)

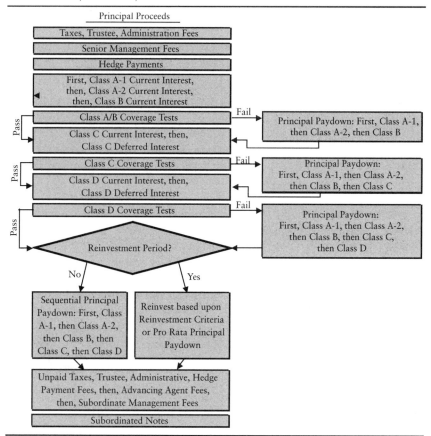

Source: Wachovia Capital Markets, LLC.

as interest (subject to certain conditions), which may send more cash to equity. This contrasts with the typical treatment of trading gains as principal, which would be reinvested or flow through the principal waterfall.

Some transactions may include Class X notes, which are used to finance the issuer's expenses upfront. These notes rank senior to Class A notes in the priority of payments and can be viewed as a senior fee. Generally, Class X notes follow a straight-line amortization schedule. These are not included in credit enhancement calculations, because they are excluded from the OC test and do not benefit from excess spread diversion.

Interest on junior notes is generally deferrable (PIKable) and rated to ultimate rather than timely payment. Deferred interest accrues at the relevant coupon rate and is added to the outstanding principal balance for the calculation of the par value test. For senior notes, nonpayment of interest constitutes an event of default and may result in an acceleration.

Cash Advances and the Revolving Credit Facility

The advancing agent may at times fill the gap where there is an interest shortfall on the senior notes, or to make a cure advance on a B-note. Another form of financing, a revolving credit facility, may be used to aid the acquisition of assets.

An *interest advance* may be made by the advancing agent in the event of an interest shortfall on the senior notes if the advance is deemed recoverable. Such an advance would be reimbursed along with any accrued interest first in the interest waterfall and then with principal proceeds, if interest proves insufficient.

A *cure advance* may be made by a B-note investor to cover a shortfall in property cash flow and forestall a default. In the CRE CDO structure, such an advance may be made by the advancing agent contingent on approval by the majority of subordinate noteholders, if the portfolio manager believes the advance to be recoverable.

The *revolving credit facility* (RCF) may be drawn on to fund the acquisition of assets during the investment period and the reinvestment period. The RCF serves to reduce the negative carry effect of retaining a large cash balance in the deal and gives the manager flexibility with the timing of acquisitions. Draws on the credit facility are reimbursed pro rata with Class A interest.

Currency and Interest Rate Hedges

Funding multicurrency and often fixed rate assets in a CRE CDO requires a mechanism to translate foreign currency and to hedge interest rate movements to correspond to with the single-currency, floating rate CRE CDO liability structure. Most issuers have accomplished this through the use of *perfect asset swaps*. Under a perfect asset swap contract, a swap counterparty would exchange all asset cash flows at a predetermined exchange rate, and accept foreign currency LIBOR indexes in exchange for the funding LIBOR benchmark. The deal would pay a portion of the asset yield to the hedge provider to take the currency risk. If the asset has little call protection, the issuer might also be required to pay an upfront amount to the hedge provider. Because asset default and prepayment are not highly correlated with currency value movements, these instruments are significantly more expensive than vanilla swaps. Rating agencies may prefer perfect asset swaps because they eliminate any market risk related to asset default or prepayment.

One alternative to the perfect asset swap is the use of multicurrency notes to match fund foreign currency assets. These instruments are less expensive and less effective in hedging most of the currency risk. One example of this structure is Glastonbury Finance plc, a sterling deal. To accommodate euro assets, the deal issued dual currency A-1 notes. Up to 35% of assets may be denominated in euros, which would be naturally hedged by a euro-denominated draw on the dual-currency notes. However, investors may be exposed to currency mismatches in the event an asset defaults or prepays. These risks are mitigated by allowing the manager to buy currency options to protect the transaction against prepayment and default risk.

Events of Default

The definition of default (as outlined in the indenture) varies from deal to deal. Some deals have stringent default conditions, such as tripping the OC test of a non-PIKable class. The controlling class or the senior-most class has special rights relative to other classes in the event of default.

When a default event occurs, the controlling class is allowed to vote for the redemption of the deal, usually in whole but not in part. In deals with a super-senior tranche, one party typically may purchase the entire class and thus has a majority control over the vote. Where a deal includes a revolving credit facility (as is the case in Duncannon), the facility provider may also be granted voting rights included with the senior debt to the extent that the facility has been drawn on.

INVESTING IN CRE CDOs

CDO valuation is a sum-of-the-parts process, taking into mind the manager, the collateral composition and weighing those against the deal structure and liability spreads. Clearly, there is no single metric for comparing deals and managers. Exhibit 17.5 summarizes the main components of CRE CDO analysis.

A Few Guidelines

In this section, a framework for CDO valuation that may prove helpful is provided. In general, senior investors should focus on structures, more than managers; mezzanine and equity investors should give equal weight to structures and managers. All investors should consider the following points:

1. *Keep the manager's track record in perspective.* Manager evaluation is a function of (a) the manager's core competencies; (b) the manager's

EXHIBIT 17.5 CRE CDO Analysis

Collateral	Relative Value Analysis
• Diversity • Shadow ratings • Statistical correlation analysis	• Relative credit performance versus similarly rated CMBS • Spread versus similarly rated CMBS • Granularity, diversity considerations • Benefit of collateral manager –Able to act sooner than CMBS special servicers –Frequently reliant on CDOs for term financing on a non-MTM basis –Significant equity retention –Increasing transparency via periodic collateral manager reports to investors
Structure	**Manager Analysis**
• Investing Timeline: –Ramp-up period (how much, types of assets) –Reinvestment period –Optional redemption –Auction call (may help maintain liability maturities) –Clean-up call (10% to 30%) • Structure –Cash flow waterfall –Robustness of IC/OC cushions –Collateral quality tests • Definitions: –Definition and treatment of defaulted assets –Events of default for issued liabilities –Eligible assets • Trading ability/limits – Definitions of defaulted, credit watch, credit impaired, downgraded assets as well as credit improved, discretionary (limit 10%–20%) –Pay attention to the definitions of these terms –Discount purchase limitations	• Balance sheet management, management fees, surveillance – Given the flexibility to reinvest in assets, pay down debt as well as buy/sell assets, the new CRE CDO manager is for all practical purposes engaged in balance-sheet management. – As a result it is critical to have a seasoned manager that has asset experience/access to other capital sources. • Past deal performance –Experience in asset classes –Core competency? CMBS, Whole Loans, B-notes, etc. • Key personnel: dedicated or part-time • Motivation for doing deal (e.g., financing? AUM? Arb?) • Investment process: underwriting, surveillance, loss mitigation trading history, infrastructure and systems adequacy • Equity retention ("skin-in-the-game")

ability to work out assets; and (c) the manager's ability to independently source assets. An unblemished track record may be due to a benign credit environment over the past four years and the longstanding uptrend in the commercial property market. Moreover, personnel changes may diminish the value of past performance records.

2. *Perform due diligence on management teams.* Reward experience, infrastructure investments (such as technology), and controls and administrative procedures, including reporting. Track Fitch CAM rankings.

3. *Focus on the manager's strategy.* Look for managers who say and do things with which you agree. Examine how the manager's WARF, IC, and OC scores evolve through time, after a CDO is issued. Ask managers about their appetite for high-risk investments. Check for consistency between professed and practiced investment strategy.

4. *Check alignment of interests.* Does the manager have an equity stake? Does the manager have a debt stake? How is the manager compensated?

5. *Analyze the structure.* Does the CDO contain par preservation or turbo mechanisms? How much leverage is there? How restrictive are the OC and IC triggers? Perform stress tests and examine the solvency and particular tranches under reasonable default and recovery scenarios. Do not fixate on diversification scores as a proxy for solvency.

6. *Diversify across managers and across CDOs.* With so many moving parts, it is impossible to predetermine the optimal manager or structure. We have found the most experienced CDO investors can list the managers they prefer. These managers employ varying styles and structures.

Based on the newness of the sector, surveillance and information disclosure is still being established. Deals naturally tend to have some lumpy exposures that will require specific disclosure. This disclosure may be made complicated by confidentiality issues. Investors have several information channels:

- Wall Street research, as in other sectors, should provide CDO sector reports and deal surveillance. CRE CDO research focus varies by firm from being a significant focus to a limited coverage area.
- Trustee reports are the primary source for current deal reporting information in terms of compliance with CDO tests, current pool composition, bond pool factors, defaults and prepayments.
- Rating agencies have provided a wealth of information and analysis in the early states of the market. Presale reports have been supplemented by periodic topical reports. Fitch and Moody's also make available their CDO modeling software.

- Third-party tools aid property and bond analysis. Two notable data sources are (1) Intex, a widely used third-party analytics software package; and (2) Trepp, a data source for loan information and deal analytics.

Frequently Asked Questions

1. *Why issue a CRE CDO rather than a CMBS deal?* European CMBS have been structured with provisions for loan substitutions and add-on debt, blurring the clear line between CMBS and CRE CDOs drawn in the U.S. market. Differentiation between the two products focuses on the broader latitude granted to the manager; CRE CDO managers have latitude to manage collateral for prepayments and credit improvements/ deterioration and are apportioned a discretionary trading allowance. For the issuer, this validates the cost of doing a deal, given high loan prepayment velocity; for investors, managed deals are built to stabilize the investment time horizon. We summarize key differences between European CMBS and CRE CDOs in this chapter's Appendix.

2. *Why buy CRE CDOs rather than CMBS?* CRE CDOs are differentiated based on (a) the stable investment horizon achieved by active management to address high prepayment speeds, and multijurisdictional and market nuances endemic to European CRE; (b) broad collateral diversification according by asset class and property type; (c) CDO structural protections, including OC and IC tests; and (d) a yield pickup versus similarly rated CMBS.

3. *Is there enough collateral to support ongoing issuance of well-diversified portfolios?* Prior to July 2007, origination volume was sufficient to support four to five new deals per year. Since then, CMBS and CDO liability spreads have become less certain amid overall capital markets volatility, making it difficult for lenders to originate loans given the unclear exit strategy. We believe clarity around CMBS spreads has to precede renewed CRE CDO origination. In the meantime, some issuers have taken to marketing privately placed static transactions.

4. *Who buys CRE CDOs in Europe? (How established is the investor base?)* CRE CDOs have historically been dependent on CP conduit and SIV buyers for the placement of triple-A notes. Other buyers have included traditional CMBS investors.

APPENDIX: CMBS VERSUS CRE CDOs

	European CMBS	CRE CDO Structure
Issuing vehicle	Corporate SPV incorporated in Europe and listed on European exchange First securitization Static loan pools, fully ramped at issuance No ongoing management fees No call optionality (except cleanup call)	Corporate SPV incorporated in Europe or off shore First, second, or multiple securitization Managed; often no fully ramped as issuance with ongoing management fees Call optionality
Structural protection	Single waterfall	Subordination; OC, IC triggers
Restrictions on collateral	No, typically senior loans secured on investment properties	Wide variety of rated/unrated real estate debt products
Includes junior debt	Rarely	Frequently
Includes unsecured debt	Rarely	Permitted
Tax	Withholding taxes minimized	Some withholding tax risk
Equity commitment of sponsor	Usually limited to excess spread/reputation stake	Manager typically retains material equity exposure with reputation risk
Excess spread	Goes to equity or IO	Goes to equity if performance tests passed
Blind pool of assets	Relatively rare	Partially ramped portfolio at closing; can change over time
Reinvestment	Limited in many transactions—material assets sales require debt/note prepayment	Yes; subject to reinvestment criteria
Rating affirmations	Limited usually to further issuance or restructuring	Necessary for maintaining credit quality over time
Available funds cap issue	Yes, where loan margins are below the tranche coupon	Deal covenants will limit exposure

	European CMBS	CRE CDO Structure
Manager dependency/Assessment	Limited, but greater for single borrower transactions	Critical and with senior fee
Diversion of interest and principal on performance tests	No	Yes, IC and OC tests
Trade out of weakening positions	No	Allowed
Sponsor can make good losses	Considered unlikely	
Interest rate and currency risk	Usually hedged.	Complex
Liquidity facility or advancing	Yes, where loan margins are below the tranche coupon	Servicer advances
Servicing standards/rated servicers/special servicers	In most transactions	Rated servicers not available?
Fixed and floating liabilities	Both, but 10-year maturities or less are usually floating; Assets and bonds can have different basis	Can issue any bond class as fixed or floating
First-loss class	Usually BBB or BB. Class B notes are rare in European CMBS; Fixed coupon Principal writedowns via appraisal reductions and realized losses cash flow terminates on 100% writedown	Equity/Excess cash flow No principal writedowns Cash flow can turn on, off and on
Controlling class	Junior-most class (B-piece buyer)	Senior-most class

Source: Standard and Poor's and Wachovia Capital Markets, LLC.

CHAPTER 18

Government National Mortgage Association Multifamily Deals

Brian P. Lancaster
Senior CMBS Analyst
Wachovia Capital Markets, LLC

Anthony G. Butler, CFA
Senior CMBS Analyst
Wachovia Capital Markets, LLC

Landon C. Frerich
CMBS Analyst
Wachovia Capital Markets, LLC

Stephen P. Mayeux
CMBS Analyst
Wachovia Capital Markets, LLC

This chapter is designed to educate the newcomer about the Government National Mortgage Association (GNMA) multifamily securities market and provide the seasoned investor with an updated view of the sector's credit performance and prepayment speeds. GNMA multifamily securities are backed by U.S. guaranteed pools of multifamily loans.

THE PATH TO A GNMA MULTIFAMILY DEAL

The creation of a GNMA multifamily project loan pool/deal involves essentially three steps: (1) obtaining the Federal Housing Administration guaranty; and (2) obtaining the GNMA guaranty; and (3) GNMA deal creation. (See Exhibit 18.1.)

EXHIBIT 18.1   The Path to a GNMA Multifamily Deal

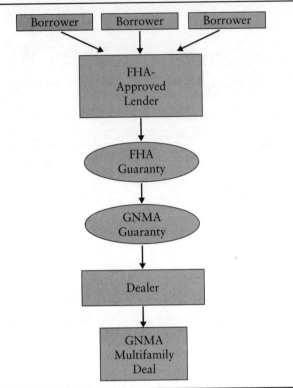

Source: Wachovia Capital Markets, LLC.

Step 1: Federal Housing Administration (FHA) Guaranty

The first step for any GNMA multifamily deal begins with the Federal Housing Administration (FHA).[1] The FHA provides mortgage insurance for multifamily and single-family loans originated by FHA-approved lenders.[2] FHA-approved lenders can be, but are not limited to, commercial banks, insurance companies, mortgage banks, savings and loan institutions, pension funds, and trust companies. This chapter focuses on nonsingle-family mortgages that can be for the construction, rehabilitation, purchase and refinancing of multifamily, and healthcare facilities and make up what is often referred to as the *project loan market*. In total, the FHA has insured

---

[1] The FHA was created in 1934 by the Federal Housing Act with the goal of making it easier for lower- and middle-income families to finance homes.

[2] A list of FHA-approved lenders is provided in Appendix A.

EXHIBIT 18.2 Volume of FHA-Insured Loans and GNMA-Insured Loans ($ billion) 1970–2006: Q3

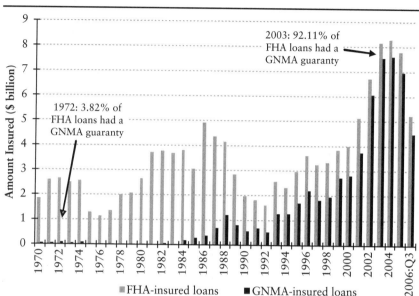

2003: 92.11% of FHA loans had a GNMA guaranty

1972: 3.82% of FHA loans had a GNMA guaranty

▨ FHA-insured loans   ▪ GNMA-insured loans

Source: Wachovia Capital Markets, LLC, GNMA, and HUD.

$144.8 billion (48,916 loans) in multifamily projects, of which $88.1 billion (36,671 loans) has been paid off or terminated and another $56.7 billion (12,245 loans) is still outstanding.

Exhibit 18.2 shows the volume of FHA-insured multifamily mortgages since 1970. Volume has been greater than $5 billion in each year since 2002, and peaked in 2004 at $8.3 billion. A public or private entity can receive financing from an FHA-approved lender as long as the project falls under one of the FHA programs also known as sections in the Fair Housing Act, which are discussed in more detail later in the chapter.

If the loan qualifies for one of the FHA programs, it is given an FHA guaranty. In return, the FHA receives a monthly premium from the lender. Currently those premiums are close to 45 bps for multifamily projects and 57 bps for nursing homes. The FHA guaranty means that the ultimate payment of principal and interest on the loan is backed by the full faith and credit of the U.S. government. The FHA, however, does not guarantee the timeliness of principal and interest payments. In addition, in the event of a default, the FHA charges a 1% assignment fee and only begins accruing interest after the first month of missed payment. This results in a 99% repayment of principal and one month of lost interest.

Step 2: GNMA Guaranty

GNMA[3] provides a second level guaranty for an FHA-insured loan. Essentially, GNMA makes up for the inadequacies of the FHA project loans by guaranteeing both the timeliness of principal and interest payments and by taking care of the 1% assignment fee in the event of a default. Since 1970, GNMA has insured $58.0 billion of FHA project loans. Exhibit 18.2 shows the dramatic growth of GNMA-insured loans, particularly during the past 20 years.

Step 3: A Deal Is Born

The last phase of a GNMA Multifamily REMIC deal involves three parties—an FHA-approved lender, a dealer (investment bank), and the investors. Once an FHA project loan is insured with a GNMA guaranty, a dealer may purchase the loan and place it with an existing pool of GNMA-insured loans. When a dealer has enough loans, typically around 40 to 80, the dealer structures a deal to be sold off to investors. Although the majority of GNMA-insured loans are pooled and placed in REMIC structures, some are left as single pools and sold off directly to investors. The first GNMA multifamily deal to be launched under the GNR shelf name was in 2001 (GNR 2001-12).[4] Since 2001, there have been 94 deals for a total balance of $28 billion, of which $24 billion is currently outstanding. Issuance through Q3 2006 was $4.3 billon versus $4.5 billion for all of 2005 (see Exhibit 18.3).

A CLOSER LOOK AT GNMA MULTIFAMILY DEALS

In this section, we take a more detailed look at GNMA multifamily deals, specifically focusing on the collateral, structure, and the risks involved.

Underlying Collateral (Loan Characteristics)

GNMA loans have fixed rates and accrue interest on a 30/360 day basis. The loans are monthly level pay and generally have 35 to 40 year fully am-

---

[3] The FHA became part of the U.S. Department of Housing and Urban Development (HUD) in 1965. In 1968, Congress created GNMA as a government-owned corporation within HUD with the intent of making a more liquid secondary market for mortgages.

[4] Prior to the GNR 2001-12 deal, GNMA-insured loans were securitized and placed in a number of Fannie Mae REMIC Trust deals, the first of which was Fannie Mae Grantor Trust 1995-T5. Since 2000, however, only a handful of GNMA multifamily loans have been in Fannie Mae deals, the last of which was Fannie Mae Multifamily REMIC Trust 2005-M1.

EXHIBIT 18.3   GNR REMIC Multifamily Deal Issuance ($ million)

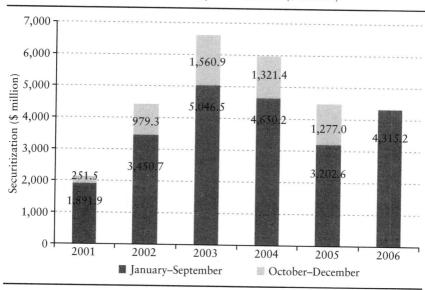

Source: Wachovia Capital Markets, LLC, and Intex Solutions, Inc.

ortizing schedules. The loans always have a minimum spread difference of 25 bps between the interest rate on the mortgage and the interest rate on the security. The 25 bps consists of 13 bps GNMA charges as a guaranty fee and 12 bps kept by the issuer as a servicing fee. Most GNMA loans have some form of call protection, typically a lockout for a certain period followed by penalty points for the remainder of the term of the loan. Until 2005, the predominant structure was five years of lockout followed by five years of penalty points (we use a shorthand notation of 5_5)[5], accounting for 55.4% of all GNMA loans in 2001 (Exhibit 18.4). In 2005 and 2006, however, the more common protection has been two years of lockout and eight years of penalty points (2_8), accounting for 47.4% of the market in 2006 versus only 9.6% for the 5_5.[6]

The shift in call protection has been driven by dealers wanting to achieve better pricing on their deals when they are brought to market. The

---

[5] The penalty points typically decline 1% each year, thus, a 5_5 is five years of lockout followed by penalty points of 5%, 4%, 3%, 2% and 1% for years six through 10, respectively. There are many variations (e.g., a loan in the GNR 2006-30 deal has two years of lockout followed by penalty points of 8% for three years and then 5%, 4%, 3%, 2%, and 1% for the remaining years).

[6] Appendix C provides a more comprehensive look at call protection for years 2001–2006.

EXHIBIT 18.4 Call Protection in GNMA Multifamily Deals: 2001 versus 2006 Deals

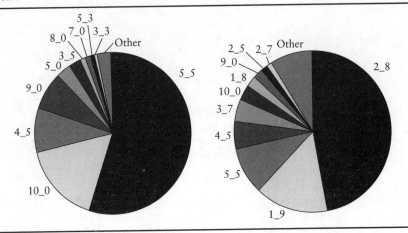

2001 Call Protection			2006 Call Protection		
Type	Balance ($)	% of Total	Type	Balance ($)	% of Total
5_5	1,188,107,742	55.4%	2_8	2,045,442,698	47.4%
10_0	347,173,709	16.2%	1_9	645,809,009	15.0%
4_5	193,283,787	9.0%	5_5	414,592,852	9.6%
9_0	156,293,289	7.3%	4_5	226,801,095	5.3%
5_0	68,898,515	3.2%	3_7	198,521,104	4.6%
3_5	48,949,833	2.3%	10_0	128,866,867	3.0%
8_0	25,245,998	1.2%	1_8	93,034,873	2.2%
7_0	20,552,258	1.0%	9_0	86,101,997	2.0%
5_3	18,685,837	0.9%	2_7	66,775,881	1.5%
3_3	15,726,730	0.7%	2_5	45,669,958	1.1%
Other	60,519,363	2.8%	Other	363,553,629	8.4%
Total	2,143,437,061		Total	4,315,169,963	

Source: Wachovia Capital Markets, LLC, and Intex Solutions, Inc.

newer call protection terms have also allowed borrowers to take advantage of lower rates. We further address this market development and its implications in the prepayment analysis section of this chapter. GNMA loans can be classified into one of following two groups: *project loans certificates* (PLCs) or *construction loan certificates* (CLCs). Many loans begin as construction

EXHIBIT 18.5   Descriptions of Project Loans and Construction Loan Certificates

Project Loan Certificates	
PL	A pool consisting of a single, level payment FHA-insured project loan that has a first scheduled payment date no more than 24 months before the issue date of the securities and has not been modified subsequent to FHA's final endorsement.
PN	A pool consisting of a single, nonlevel payment FHA-insured or Rural Development, RD-guaranteed project loan that has a first scheduled payment date no more than 24 months before the issue date of the securities and has not been modified subsequent to FHA's final endorsement.
LM	A pool consisting of a single project loan with a first scheduled payment date more than 24 months before the issue date of the securities or a loan that has been modified subsequent to final endorsement.
LS	A pool consisting of one or more project loans, each of which is secured by a lien on a small project as determined by FHA or an RD-Section 538 guaranteed loan that has been used for the revitalization of the Section 515 loan portfolio, each of which has a first scheduled payment date no more than 24 months before the issue date of the securities and none of which has been modified subsequent to final endorsement, or issuance of the RD permanent loan guarantee.
RX	A pool consisting of one or more project loans, each of which is secured by a lien on a mark-to-market project as determined by FHA and the Office of Affordable Housing Preservation (OAHP) and each of which has a first scheduled payment date no more than 24 months before the issue date of the securities.

Construction Loan Certificates	
CL	A pool consisting of a single construction loan; the interest rate payable on the securities backed by a CL pool will also be the interest rate payable, upon conversion of the construction loan securities, on the resulting project loan securities.
CS	A pool consisting of a single construction loan; the interest rate payable on the securities backed by a CS pool will differ from the interest rate payable, upon conversion of the construction loan securities, on the resulting project loan securities.

Source: Wachovia Capital Markets, LLC, and GNMA.

loans and, as a project is completed or rehabilitated, a borrower obtains longer-term financing in the form of a PLC. PLCs and CLCs can be further broken up into more detailed categories, the descriptions of these can be found in Exhibit 18.5. GNMA loans are also categorized by the FHA program under which they are insured. We take a closer look at those programs in the following section.

EXHIBIT 18.6   FHA Programs in GNMA Multifamily Deals by Original Balance (2001–2006: Q3 deals)

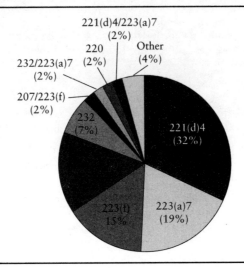

FHA PROGRAM TYPES

GNMA loans are categorized into FHA programs when underwritten. A majority of the loans, 88%, fall into one of five groups. A breakdown of the FHA sections within the GNMA multifamily deals based on original loan balance is shown in Exhibit 18.6. Notice that some loans can fall under more than one FHA program, a considerable amount of loans fall under the 232/223(f) group, for instance. We also provide a brief description of each of the designated FHA programs.

Sections 221(d)4 and 221(d)3 provide insurance for the construction and rehabilitation of multifamily housing for low- and moderate-income families that have lost their homes due to urban renewal, government actions or disaster. Section 221(d)3 applies to nonprofit borrowers where as Section 221(d)4 applies to profit-seeking borrowers. Section 221(d)4 accounts for the largest percentage based on loan balance at around 32%.

Section 223(a)7 allows the FHA to refinance loans that are currently insured under any section, resulting in the prepayment of the existing mortgage. The refinanced loan cannot be greater than the original loan amount and is allowed a term equal to the unexpired duration of the previous loan plus 12 years. Section 223(a)7 accounts for the second largest percentage based on loan balance at around 19%.

Section 223(f) provides insurance for loans originated for the purpose of purchasing or refinancing multifamily complexes, hospitals and nursing homes that are not in need of major rehabilitation. The goal of the program is to allow refinancing to lower the debt service or to purchase existing properties to maintain a sufficient amount of affordable housing. Section 223(f) makes up 15% of the FHA section distribution.

Section 232 provides insurance on construction loans for new or rehabilitated nursing homes, intermediate care facilities, board and care homes, and assisted-living facilities for the elderly. Section 232 represents 7% of the FHA sections based on original balance.

Section 207 provides insurance for FHA-approved lender loans for the construction or rehabilitation of multifamily properties and manufactured home parks.

Section 220 provides insurance for loans collateralized by multifamily properties that are in federally aided urban renewal areas or areas experiencing redevelopment. The purpose of Section 220 is to promote quality housing in areas where revitalization is planned.

Section 213 provides insurance for loans backed by cooperative housing and allows nonprofit cooperative ownership housing corporations to develop the projects.

Section 241 provides insurance to finance property improvements that should enable the property to remain competitive, to extend its useful life and to replace dated equipment without having to refinance.

HOW ARE THE DEALS STRUCTURED?

GNMA multifamily deals are REMIC sequential pay structures with an *interest-only* (IO) bond class. The typical GNMA multifamily deal has six classes—A, B, C, D, Z, and an IO with approximate weighted average lives of 3, 5, 7, 10, and 20 years. The A tranche is a fixed rate class, and tranches B, C, and D are weighted average coupon classes. The 20-year WAL Z tranche is an accrual class in which interest is accrued and added to the principal balance, while the previous classes, A through D, are outstanding. An example of a recent deal—GNR 2006-30, which closed in July 2006—is shown in Exhibit 18.7. In a case where prepayment penalties are collected, all proceeds are distributed to the IO class. Most deals have 40 to 80 loans; although, there have been outliers with as few as 15 loans and as many as 156 loans backing a deal. Deal sizes have typically been in the area of $250 million to $350 million, with the average, since 2001, at $303.8 million (Exhibit 18.8). Because the deals are backed by the FHA and GNMA (the

EXHIBIT 18.7   Example of a Recent GNMA Multifamily Deal (GNR 2006-30)

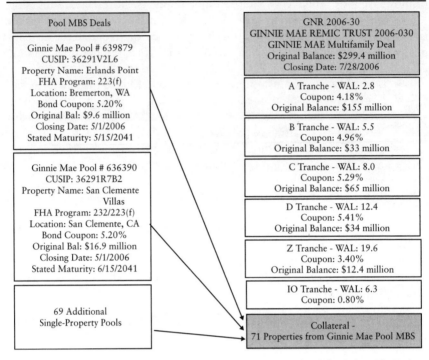

Note: Ginnie Mae Multifamily MBS typically securitize one FHA-insured multifamily loan. The Pool MBS deals are packaged as a REMIC that can be divided into varying payment streams with different expected maturities and coupon rates.

Source: Wachovia Capital Markets, LLC, GNMA, and Intex Solutions, Inc.

full faith and credit of the U.S. government), the classes are not rated but considered AAA.

TRADING GNMA MULTIFAMILY BONDS

When evaluating GNMA multifamily bonds, the most important considerations are the assumptions used when these deals are priced. The standard assumption used by the industry is the pricing speed of 15% CPJ. This assumes that no prepayments occur during lockout, but loans then prepay at a 15% CPR the first year lockout ends through the life of the deal. The second part of the 15% CPJ is the assumption that defaults (involuntary prepay-

EXHIBIT 18.8   GNMA Multifamily Average Deal Sizes ($ million)

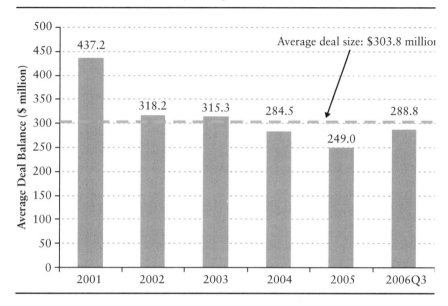

Source: Wachovia Capital Markets, LLC and Intex Solutions, Inc.

ments) follow the timing of the *project loan default* (PLD) curve,[7] which is shown in Exhibit 18.9.

The PLD curve assumes that involuntary prepayments begin immediately, starting at 1.30% in year one and then ramp up to 2.51% in year three before steadily declining to 0.25% for years 15 through 20. The sequential-pay classes (usually A, B, C, and D) are priced to the swaps curve while the accrual class (usually Z) is priced to the U.S. Treasury curve (specifically the 30-year bond). Actual pricing levels are hard to come by as these levels are not typically made public. The most recent deal to publish pricing levels was GNR 2005-89, which priced in December 2005. For current levels, it is best to contact several trading desks that trade the product.

What Are the Risks?

As the principal and interest for these securities are guaranteed, the main concern for an investor is cash flow volatility and the linked reinvestment

---

[7] While not specifically documented anywhere, PLD curve is believed to have been developed by Donaldson, Lufkin & Jenrette in 2000 or 2001 and was based on historical default data. The PLD curve will always be presented in the offering memorandum for the GNMA deals.

EXHIBIT 18.9   Project Loan Default (PLD) Curve

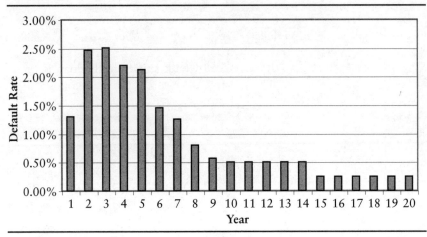

Loan Age (months)	Default Rate
0–12	1.30%
13–24	2.47%
25–36	2.51%
37–48	2.20%
49–60	2.13%
61–72	1.46%
73–84	1.26%
85–96	0.80%
97–108	0.57%
109–168	0.50%
169–240	0.25%
241–maturity	0.00%

Source: Wachovia Capital Markets, LLC, and GNMA.

risk. As the deals are priced at a speed (15% CPJ), there is the risk that the loans will actually payoff at slower or faster speeds. A GNMA loan can prepay in one of the following two ways: as a voluntary prepayment or a default. A voluntary prepayment occurs when a borrower willingly prepays the loan after lockout and incurs penalty points to retire the mortgage. A voluntary prepayment is usually motivated by (1) a rise in property values in which case the borrower may want to sell; or (2) lower interest rates and/or spreads such that the borrower is motivated to refinance the loan. A prepayment, resulting from a default, occurs when a property is struggling financially and can no longer maintain the debt service. Under a default, the lockout period or prepayment penalties no longer apply. When a GNMA loan defaults, one of the following three things occur: a typical default, an override or a modification. In a typical default situation, the loan is given to the FHA, which then liquidates the property. When a loan goes through an override, the FHA works with the borrower to refinance a lower rate of interest. In the case of a modification, the borrower works with the issuer/servicer and the terms of the loan are modified to provide some relief to the borrower. In all three cases, the loans are paid off and the impact to the bondholder is a prepayment.

While often legitimate, there has been concern in recent years of borrowers taking advantage of the system and contriving a default to get out of their current loan without incurring any penalties.[8] Investors should also be aware that while prepayment penalties are passed through to the IO class, GNMA does not guarantee the payment of penalty points by the borrower. The holders of the IO only receive the proceeds if they are received by the trustee. A final consideration for investors is the lack of timely and readily available information regarding the properties backing the deals. In most cases, financial statements and appraisals for the properties are unavailable.

PREPAYMENT ANALYSIS OF GNMA MULTIFAMILY LOANS

As discussed earlier, the main concern for investors is the amount of prepayments both voluntary and involuntary (defaults) within GNMA multifamily deals. In this section, we first show bond performance when prepayment speeds are adjusted to slower and faster levels. Later, we look at what prepayment speeds have actually been using GNMA and HUD loan data.

Speed It Up Slow It Down

The results, in Exhibit 18.10, show changes in *weighted average life* (WAL), spread and yield when adjusting the baseline 15% CPJ rate up and down 10% (to 5% and 25% CPJ). For this analysis, we used generic spread levels

---

[8] A recent example was a case in which Merrill Lynch sued Greystone Servicing and developer Matthews Southwest of Dallas for possibly colluding to engineer a default on a Dallas apartment complex in an effort to avoid prepayment penalties, while acquiring a lower interest rate. The state lawsuit filed by Merrill Lynch was voluntarily withdrawn; however, a substantially similar federal lawsuit was filed and is currently pending.

EXHIBIT 18.10 Changes from 15% CPJ Due to Faster and Slower Prepayment Rates

	15% CPJ	5% CPJ (change)			25% CPJ (change)		
Classes	WAL	WAL	Spread	Yield	WAL	Spread	Yield
A	2.8	+1.7	(54)	(52)	(0.6)	+32	+33
B	5.5	+5.1	(43)	(33)	(1.5)	+29	+26
C	8.0	+7.7	(30)	(21)	(2.4)	+25	+19
D	12.4	+9.9	(20)	(15)	(4.0)	+22	+16
Z	19.6	+10.4	(96)	(93)	(6.2)	+119	+118
IO	6.3	+5.2	(87)	(82)	(1.9)	+272	+271

Source: Wachovia Capital Markets, LLC, and Intex Solutions, Inc.

applied to the GNR 2006-30 deal. When the CPR rate is slowed to 5%, the WAL jumps considerably for all the classes and the spread and yields follow suit. The WALs for classes B and C (the five- and eight-year sequential-pay bonds) nearly double by extending 5.1 and 7.7 years, respectively. When the prepayment speed is increased to a rate of 25% CPR, the WALs shorten and the spread and yields improve as expected for discount-priced bonds.

For a visual presentation of the principal payback window under the three pricing speeds, consider Exhibits 18.11 through 18.15. These graphs clearly show each bond's sensitivity to prepayment speeds.

HISTORICAL PREPAYMENTS

For our historical prepayment analysis, we used loan data provided by GNMA and HUD to determine the speeds at which loans have been prepaying once their lockout period has ended. Our data set begins in 1994 (the year lockout ended), because the amount of loans before then was minimal and prepayment activity was far less representative of today's market.

Exhibit 18.16 shows the prepayment rate for each year following lockout for loans with 5_5 call protection. 5_5 loans have historically accounted for the largest percentage (43.2%) of the GNMA REMIC multifamily market and, thus, give us the most robust and representative data sample. The data shows that the largest percentage (29.8%) of loans payoff during the first year after lockout. The most noticeable drop in prepayments occurs between years six and seven, falling from 12.2% to 2.7%.

Also shown in Exhibit 18.16 are the implied CPR rates for varying time horizons—3, 5, 7, 10, and 13 years. As one would expect, the rate steps down as more years are added. This provides a frame of reference for investors in short-term paper (three-year CPR is 23.9%) and those looking for longer-duration paper (10-year CPR is 13.0%). As discussed earlier, the market benchmark is 15 CPR, which is not far off from both the seven- and 10-year CPRs at 17.1% and 13.0%, respectively. Exhibit 18.17 is the prepayment matrix for 5_5 loans and provides a more dialed-in look at the prepayment activity shown in Exhibit 18.16.

EXHIBIT 18.11 Cash Flow Graph for the Class A: 2.8-Year WAL Bond

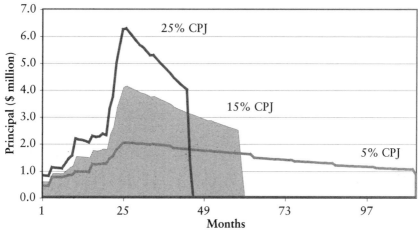

Source: Wachovia Capital Markets, LLC, and Intex Solutions, Inc.

EXHIBIT 18.12 Cash Flow Graph for the Class B: 5.5-Year WAL Bond

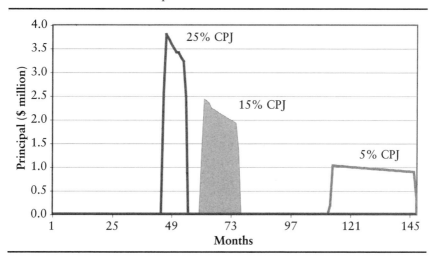

Source: Wachovia Capital Markets, LLC, and Intex Solutions, Inc.

EXHIBIT 18.13   Cash Flow Graph for the Class C: 8.0-Year WAL Bond

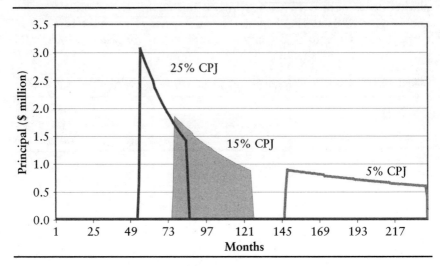

Source: Wachovia Capital Markets, LLC, and Intex Solutions, Inc.

EXHIBIT 18.14   Cash Flow Graph for the Class D: 12.4-Year WAL Bond

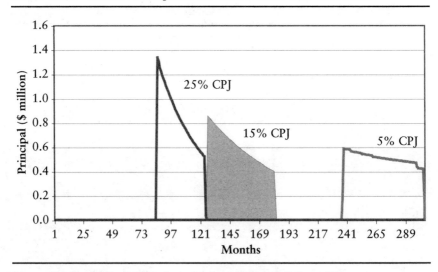

Source: Wachovia Capital Markets, LLC, and Intex Solutions, Inc.

EXHIBIT 18.15 Cash Flow Graph for the Class Z: Accrual 19.6-Year WAL Bond

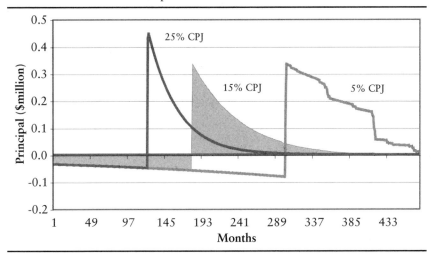

Source: Wachovia Capital Markets, LLC, and Intex Solutions, Inc.

EXHIBIT 18.16 Prepayment Rates for Loans with 5_5 Call Protection (1994–2006: Q3)

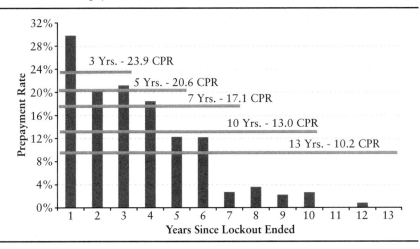

Source: Wachovia Capital Markets, LLC, HUD, and GNMA.

EXHIBIT 18.17 Prepayment Matrix for Loans with 5_5 Call Protection

Year Lockout Ended	Years Since Lockout Ended													Cum. %	Loan Count	Original Balance ($)
	1	2	3	4	5	6	7	8	9	10	11	12	13			
1994	0.0%	0.0%	0.0%	5.6%	15.2%	29.2%	0.0%	14.7%	13.5%	14.5%	0.0%	0.0%	0.0%	92.7%	15	176,548,530
1995	0.0%	0.0%	0.0%	12.8%	3.7%	40.6%	2.9%	2.5%	0.0%	3.4%	0.0%	13.7%		79.7%	14	90,141,674
1996	5.2%	25.3%	14.2%	6.0%	4.5%	2.8%	2.4%	5.6%	6.2%	6.2%	0.0%			78.4%	25	138,768,082
1997	17.8%	45.8%	0.0%	0.0%	3.4%	18.7%	0.0%	8.6%	0.0%	0.0%				94.2%	19	119,931,383
1998	15.6%	3.9%	10.5%	20.3%	20.1%	11.5%	3.8%	0.9%	0.0%					86.6%	111	514,900,446
1999	13.9%	6.9%	22.6%	25.7%	9.7%	4.7%	2.9%	0.7%						87.1%	160	569,070,927
2000	13.0%	19.0%	32.6%	11.3%	6.9%	2.3%	0.1%							85.2%	199	745,493,381
2001	27.6%	22.5%	18.2%	11.0%	0.5%	0.7%								80.4%	202	935,147,582
2002	36.2%	30.5%	10.0%	2.6%	0.6%									79.9%	157	734,235,566
2003	35.5%	15.1%	5.4%	0.6%										56.5%	158	696,482,169
2004	40.5%	10.2%	2.9%											53.6%	171	926,918,146
2005	49.4%	3.7%												53.1%	150	903,289,953
2006	44.4%													44.4%	254	1,436,800,911
% of Orig. Bal.	29.8%	14.3%	11.8%	8.1%	4.4%	3.8%	0.7%	1.0%	0.6%	0.7%	0.0%	0.2%	0.0%	75.5%	1,635	7,987,728,750
CPR	29.8%	20.4%	21.2%	18.4%	12.2%	12.2%	2.7%	3.6%	2.2%	2.6%	0.0%	0.8%	0.0%			

Source: Wachovia Capital Markets, LLC, HUD, and GNMA.

EXHIBIT 18.18 Prepayment Matrix for Loans with 1_9 Call Protection

Year Lockout Ended	Years Since Lockout Ended										Cum. %	Loan Count	Original Balance ($)
	1	2	3	4	5	6	7	8	9	10			
1997	0.0%	0.0%	0.0%	0.0%	0.0%	0.0%	0.0%	0.0%	0.0%	0.0%	0.0%	5	56,000,452
2000	0.0%	0.0%	0.0%	0.0%	0.0%	0.0%	0.0%				0.0%	3	20,954,036
2001	0.0%	0.0%	0.0%	0.0%	0.0%	0.0%					0.0%	1	19,765,194
2002	0.0%	0.0%	0.0%	0.0%	0.0%						0.0%	3	33,457,700
2003	0.0%	0.0%	0.0%	0.0%							0.0%	1	16,713,990
2004	0.0%	0.0%	0.0%								0.0%	3	22,808,900
2005	0.7%	0.0%									0.7%	57	318,356,300
2006	0.0%										0.0%	66	386,508,200
% of Orig. Bal.	0.4%	0.0%	0.0%	0.0%	0.0%	0.0%	0.0%	0.0%	0.0%	0.0%	0.4%	139	874,564,772

Source: Wachovia Capital Markets, LLC, HUD, and GNMA.

EXHIBIT 18.19 Prepayment Matrix for Loans with 2_8 Call Protection

Year Lockout Ended	Years Since Lockout Ended										Cum. %	Loan Count	Original Balance ($)
	1	2	3	4	5	6	7	8	9	10			
1995	0.0%	0.0%	0.0%	0.0%	0.0%	0.0%	0.0%	0.0%	0.0%	0.0%	0.0%	1	8,924,552
1997	0.0%	0.0%	0.0%	0.0%	0.0%	0.0%	0.0%	0.0%	0.0%	0.0%	0.0%	1	6,215,000
1998	0.0%	0.0%	0.0%	0.0%	0.0%	0.0%	0.0%	0.0%	0.0%		0.0%	1	1,323,200
1999	0.0%	0.0%	0.0%	0.0%	0.0%	0.0%	0.0%	0.0%			0.0%	2	18,985,141
2000	0.0%	0.0%	0.0%	0.0%	0.0%	0.0%					0.0%	1	7,098,900
2001	0.0%	0.0%	0.0%	0.0%	0.0%	0.0%					0.0%	6	42,132,100
2002	0.0%	0.0%	0.0%	0.0%	0.0%						0.0%	4	29,594,600
2003	0.0%	0.0%	0.0%	0.0%							0.0%	3	24,661,500
2004	0.0%	0.0%	0.0%								0.0%	8	114,717,523
2005	0.0%	0.0%									0.0%	6	67,182,500
2006	0.0%										0.0%	78	493,214,258
% of Orig. Bal.	0.0%	0.0%	0.0%	0.0%	0.0%	0.0%	0.0%	0.0%	0.0%	0.0%	0.0%	111	814,049,274

Source: Wachovia Capital Markets, LLC, HUD, and GNMA.

EXHIBIT 18.20 Prepayment Matrix for Loans with 3_7 Call Protection

Year Lockout Ended	Years Since Lockout Ended										Cum. %	Loan Count	Original Balance ($)
	1	2	3	4	5	6	7	8	9	10			
1996	0.0%	0.0%	67.6%	0.0%	0.0%	0.0%	0.0%	0.0%	0.0%	0.0%	67.6%	2	14,702,300
2001	0.0%	0.0%	0.0%	0.0%	0.0%	0.0%					0.0%	1	6,465,203
2002	0.0%	0.0%	0.0%	0.0%	0.0%						0.0%	2	24,409,783
2003	0.0%	13.3%	0.0%	0.0%							13.3%	3	19,664,300
2004	0.0%	0.0%	0.0%								0.0%	5	37,267,800
2005	0.0%	0.0%									0.0%	5	42,107,200
2006	0.0%										0.0%	30	226,932,400
% of Orig. Bal.	0.0%	2.5%	13.6%	0.0%	0.0%	0.0%	0.0%	0.0%	0.0%	0.0%	16.1%	48	371,548,986

Source: Wachovia Capital Markets, LLC, HUD, and GNMA.

EXHIBIT 18.21 Implied CPR for 5_5 loans versus All Loans

Time Period (Years)	Implied CPR	
	5_5 Loans	All Loans
3	23.9%	18.6%
5	20.6%	15.5%
7	17.1%	12.8%
10	13.0%	9.9%
13	10.2%	7.8%

Source: Wachovia Capital Markets, LLC, HUD, and GNMA.

An important consideration is the changing nature of call protection among GNMA loans from longer to shorter lockout periods with higher penalty points. The historical 5_5 curve is not going to be as representative of the deals that have been done in the past few years. We have a hard time believing that many loans with 8%, 9%, and 10% penalty points will prepay immediately in the first or second year after lockout. Currently, there is not a great deal of data for the forms of call protection that have been most prevalent over the past couple of years (i.e., 1_9, 2_8, and 3_7), but they do appear to be prepaying much slower than historic levels (Exhibits 18.18–18.20).[9] Only one 1_9 loan has prepaid thus far during the penalty point phase (within one year of lockout), and no 2_8 loans have prepaid during the penalty point period. Data are sparse for the 3_7 loans; although, it does show at least some prepayments.

In Exhibit 18.21, we show the implied CPR rates when using loans with all forms of call protection versus using only 5_5 loans. The CPR for all loans is roughly 5% lower than the 5_5 CPR when looking at the three-, five- and seven-year time horizons and roughly 2% to 3% below for the 10- and 13-year time horizons. This is due to loans with the newer forms of call protection (shorter lockout periods and higher penalty points), which are not prepaying as quickly.

DEFAULT ANALYSIS OF GNMA MULTIFAMILY LOANS

For our default (involuntary prepayment) analysis, we again used historical loan data from the GNMA and HUD databases. We used loan data starting in 1984 to have enough years to accurately compare with the market standard PLD curve, which spans 20 years. Exhibit 18.22 shows the historical

---

[9] This is in combination with favorable market conditions such as strong price appreciation and historically low interest rates and spreads.

EXHIBIT 18.22 Historical Default Rates (based on 1984–2006: Q3 data)

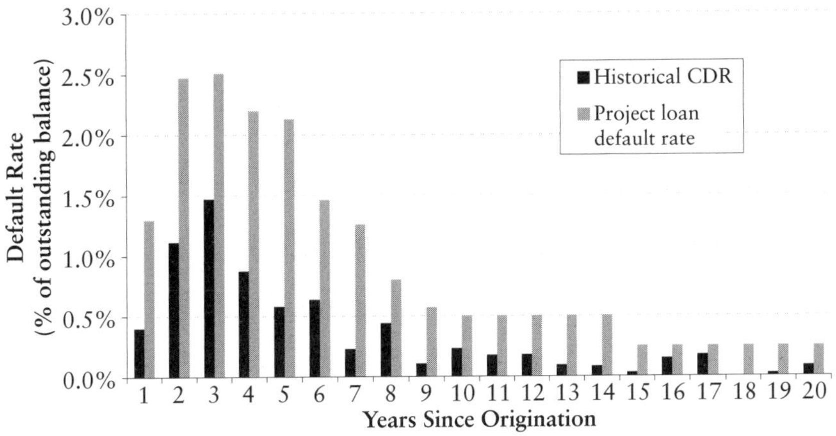

Source: Wachovia Capital Markets, LLC, HUD, and GNMA.

default rates for each year since origination for GNMA loans compared to the PLD curve. Our historical default rates are lower than the PLD rates in every year following origination. Both curves peak in year three, with the PLD rate at 2.51% versus 1.47% for the historical data. On a cumulative basis, we found that over a 20-year period defaults have been 6.89% of the original balance (Appendix D). The cumulative PLD rate (when converted from percentage of outstanding balance to percentage of original balance) is 17.18%, or close to 2.5 times higher than our historically derived number.

Appendix D provides the data backing Exhibit 18.22.

CONCLUSION

While relatively small, the GNMA multifamily market presents unique investment opportunities to the project loan investor. The intent of this primer is to give a thorough overview of the GNMA market to equip investors with a base of knowledge that may open the door to a more in-depth and actionable look at these securities. Beyond the background, structuring and trading of GNMA multifamily deals, the key takeaways for investors are (1) the awareness of the effects and possible implications of the evolution in the call protection toward shorter lockout periods; (2) that historical prepayments over a 10-year time horizon for 5_5 loans have been at a 13 CPR, which is just below the 15 CPR market standard; and (3) in aggregate, default rates for vintages since 1984 have been lower than the rates assumed by the PLD curve.

APPENDIX A: FHA-APPROVED LENDERS IN 2006

Active Mortgage Corporation
American Mortgage Solutions, LLC
American Property Financing, Inc.
Arbor Commercial Mortgage, LLC
Armstrong Mortgage Company
Bankers Mortgage & Investment Group, Inc.
Beacon Hill Mortgage Corporation
Bedford Lending Corporation
Berkshire Mortgage Finance
Cambridge Realty Capital Ltd. of Illinois
Capital Funding Group, Inc.
CapitalSource Mortgage Finance, LLC
Capmark Bank
Capmark Finance Inc.
Capstone Realty Advisors, LLC
Centennial Mortgage, Inc.
Century Health Capital, Inc.
Charles River Mortgage
CharterMac Mortgage Capital Corporation
CMC Mortgage Services, Inc.
Collateral Mortgage Capital, LLC
Columbia National Real Estate Finance, LLC
Column Guaranteed, LLC
CWCapital, LLC
Davis-Penn Mortgage Company of Texas
Deutsche Bank Berkshire Mortgage, Inc.
Evanston Financial Corporation
First Housing Development Corp. of Florida
Forest City-Capital Corporation
Gershman Investment Corporation
Great Lakes Financial Group Limited Partnership
Greystone Servicing Corporation, Inc.
Harry Mortgage Company
Heartland Bank
KeyCorp Real Estate Capital Markets, Inc.
Lancaster Pollard Mortgage Company
Links Mortgage Corporation
Love Funding Corporation
M&T Realty Capital Corp.
MMA Mortgage Investment Corp.
New Trier Mortgage Company
P/R Mortgage & Investment Corporation
Phares Company

PNC Multifamily, Inc.
Prudential Huntoon Paige Associates, Ltd.
Quaker Capital, L.P.
Red Mortgage Capital, Inc.
Reilly Mortgage Group
Renaissance Mortgage Financial Services
Rockhall Funding Corporation
Rockport Mortgage
St. James Capital, LLC
Suburban Mortgage Assoc., Inc.
Wachovia Multifamily Capital, Inc.
Wells Fargo Multifamily Capital

Source: Wachovia Capital Markets, LLC, and HUD.

APPENDIX B: GNMA REMIC MULTIFAMILY DEAL LIST, 2001–2006: Q3

Ticker	Original Balance ($)	Current Balance ($)	Settlement Date	Dealer
GNR 2001-12	291,790,179	122,618,229	29-Mar-01	Nomura Securities/Merrill Lynch/Utendahl Capital Partners
GNR 2001-16	884,145,441	302,051,473	30-Apr-01	Credit Suisse First Boston
GNR 2001-34	266,332,857	158,392,490	30-Jul-01	Merrill Lynch/Newman & Associates/Utendahl Capital Partners
GNR 2001-44	487,683,196	238,852,079	27-Sep-01	Credit Suisse First Boston
GNR 2001-58	256,062,088	194,594,847	30-Nov-01	Merrill Lynch/Utendahl Capital Partners
GNR 2002-9	761,392,461	407,790,181	28-Feb-02	Credit Suisse First Boston
GNR 2002-25	426,879,656	294,986,952	30-Apr-02	Credit Suisse First Boston
GNR 2002-26	321,946,488	214,989,877	30-May-02	Merrill Lynch
GNR 2002-28	204,844,762	156,075,429	30-May-02	Nomura
GNR 2002-35	293,530,264	182,010,090	30-May-02	JPMorgan/GMAC Commercial Capital Markets/Utendahl Capital Partners
GNR 2002-37	291,803,072	216,685,579	30-May-02	Credit Suisse First Boston
GNR 2002-53	292,159,318	200,500,543	30-Jul-02	Credit Suisse First Boston
GNR 2002-56	237,050,618	219,448,269	29-Aug-02	JPMorgan
GNR 2002-61	354,332,282	223,670,172	26-Sep-02	Credit Suisse First Boston
GNR 2002-62	280,636,363	173,889,382	30-Sep-02	Nomura, Utendahl Capital Partners, LP
GNR 2002-81	220,767,128	176,735,702	29-Nov-02	Greenwich Capital
GNR 2002-83	280,086,256	244,675,996	27-Nov-02	JPMorgan/GMAC/Blaylock & Partners LP
GNR 2002-85	133,929,008	65,961,071	27-Nov-02	Citigroup
GNR 2002-91	355,026,384	244,411,694	30-Dec-02	Merrill Lynch

Ticker	Original Balance ($)	Current Balance ($)	Settlement Date	Dealer
GNR 2002-94	364,336,619	185,978,074	30-Jan-03	Credit Suisse First Boston/Myerberg & Company, LP
GNR 2003-5	313,119,601	238,822,027	30-Jan-03	Nomura/Utendahl Capital Partners, LP
GNR 2003-16	243,739,873	222,573,331	28-Feb-03	JPMorgan/GMAC/Blaylock & Partners
GNR 2003-17	218,770,416	205,038,735	28-Mar-03	RBS Greenwich Capital/Utendahl Capital Partners
GNR 2003-22	302,511,362	270,389,145	28-Mar-03	Credit Suisse First Boston
GNR 2003-36	337,293,176	302,857,715	30-Apr-03	Credit Suisse First Boston
GNR 2003-38	409,502,595	260,061,925	30-May-03	Merrill Lynch/Myerberg & Company
GNR 2003-43	258,881,113	203,576,960	30-May-03	Nomura, Utendahl Capital Partners
GNR 2003-47	312,769,053	225,723,783	30-May-03	Credit Suisse First Boston
GNR 2003-48	259,820,985	225,919,347	29-May-03	JPMorgan/GMAC Commercial Holding Capital Markets/Blaylock & Partners LP
GNR 2003-49	246,045,012	234,301,130	30-Jun-03	RBS Greenwich Capital
GNR 2003-59	429,244,805	382,028,813	30-Jul-03	Credit Suisse First Boston
GNR 2003-64	490,479,090	353,340,748	29-Aug-03	Credit Suisse First Boston
GNR 2003-72	282,021,643	236,486,129	29-Aug-03	JPMorgan/GMAC Commercial Holding Capital Markets/Blaylock & Partners LP
GNR 2003-73	244,583,130	235,243,737	30-Sep-03	RBS Greenwich Capital
GNR 2003-78	338,320,206	316,430,447	30-Sep-03	Nomura/Utendahl Capital Partners, LP
GNR 2003-87	288,072,418	252,190,976	30-Oct-03	Credit Suisse First Boston
GNR 2003-88	269,816,271	246,888,748	30-Oct-03	JPMorgan/GMAC commercial Holding Capital Markets/Blaylock & Partners LP
GNR 2003-96	328,882,516	295,488,398	28-Nov-03	Merrill Lynch
GNR 2003-108	307,319,619	268,520,877	28-Nov-03	Credit Suisse First Boston
GNR 2003-109	376,174,193	355,024,787	30-Dec-03	RBS Greenwich Capital

Ticker	Original Balance ($)	Current Balance ($)	Settlement Date	Dealer
GNR 2004-6	345,434,760	335,343,188	30-Jan-04	Credit Suisse First Boston/Myerberg & Company, LP
GNR 2004-9	276,509,789	243,592,922	27-Feb-04	Nomura
GNR 2004-10	310,839,946	293,034,238	27-Feb-04	RBS Greenwich Capital
GNR 2004-12	300,007,070	268,017,245	26-Feb-04	JPMorgan/GMAC/Blaylock & Partners, LP
GNR 2004-20	284,137,414	250,744,369	30-Mar-04	Credit Suisse First Boston
GNR 2004-23	241,978,574	233,003,649	30-Apr-04	Greenwich Capital
GNR 2004-25	246,737,423	236,913,329	30-Apr-04	JPMorgan/GMAC Commercial Holding Capital Markets/Blaylock & Partners, LP
GNR 2004-43	299,078,863	284,699,535	30-Jun-04	RBS Greenwich Capital
GNR 2004-45	317,333,060	308,230,818	30-Jun-04	Nomura
GNR 2004-50	391,732,720	360,929,723	30-Jun-04	Credit Suisse First Boston/Myerberg & Company, LP
GNR 2004-51	252,525,771	232,751,788	30-Jul-04	JPMorgan/GMAC Commercial Holding Capital Markets/Blaylock & Partners, LP
GNR 2004-57	227,918,179	213,793,011	30-Jul-04	RBS Greenwich Capital
GNR 2004-60	205,895,662	193,716,151	30-Aug-04	Nomura
GNR 2004-67	371,230,900	317,506,232	30-Aug-04	Credit Suisse First Boston
GNR 2004-77	323,118,173	300,334,304	30-Sep-04	RBS Greenwich Capital/Utendahl Capital Partners
GNR 2004-78	257,965,001	250,806,065	30-Sep-04	JPMorgan/GMAC Commercial Holding Capital Markets/Blaylock & Partners, LP
GNR 2004-84	334,839,017	326,448,081	29-Oct-04	Nomura/Deutsche Bank Securities/Myerberg & Company, LP
GNR 2004-97	208,535,992	201,826,741	30-Nov-04	RBS Greenwich Capital/Utendahl Capital Partners
GNR 2004-100	230,765,000	225,385,528	30-Nov-04	JPMorgan/GMAC Commercial Holding Capital Markets/Blaylock & Partners, LP
GNR 2004-103	295,383,790	267,781,793	30-Dec-04	Nomura/Deutsche Bank Securities/Myerberg & Company, LP
GNR 2004-108	251,917,433	245,016,819	30-Dec-04	RBS Greenwich Capital/Utendahl Capital Partners

Ticker	Original Balance ($)	Current Balance ($)	Settlement Date	Dealer
GNR 2005-2	283,641,946	278,668,654	31-Jan-05	Deutsche Bank Securities/Nomura/Utendahl Capital Partners
GNR 2005-9	287,557,651	282,037,787	01-Feb-05	RBS Greewich Capital
GNR 2005-10	242,112,424	238,518,506	28-Feb-05	Nomura
GNR 2005-12	257,602,908	243,466,246	28-Feb-05	Credit Suisse First Boston
GNR 2005-14	268,360,000	259,043,654	28-Feb-05	JPMorgan/Blaylock & Partners, LP
GNR 2005-29	262,806,267	253,169,990	29-Apr-05	RBS Greenwich Capital
GNR 2005-32	232,340,001	228,431,240	29-Apr-05	JPMorgan/Blaylock & Partners, LP
GNR 2005-34	194,781,033	178,823,081	27-May-05	Nomura
GNR 2005-42	202,007,124	198,860,675	30-Jun-05	Deutsche Bank Securities/Nomura/Utendahl Capital Partners, LP
GNR 2005-50	261,389,492	257,451,321	29-Jul-05	RBS Greenwich Capital
GNR 2005-52	225,037,001	220,100,834	29-Jul-05	JPMorgan/Blaylock & Company, Inc.
GNR 2005-59	237,993,901	222,735,188	30-Aug-05	Nomura
GNR 2005-67	249,434,289	246,322,272	29-Sep-05	Deutsche Bank Securities/Nomura/Utendahl Capital Partners, LP
GNR 2005-76	307,085,958	303,553,169	28-Oct-05	RBS Greenwich Capital
GNR 2005-79	209,667,002	207,412,833	28-Oct-05	JPMorgan/Blaylock & Company, Inc.
GNR 2005-87	297,327,185	289,750,142	30-Nov-05	Nomura, Wachovia Capital Markets, LLC, Myerberg & Company, LP
GNR 2005-89	201,957,692	200,236,064	30-Dec-05	Deutsche Bank
GNR 2005-90	260,949,927	258,461,487	30-Dec-05	RBS Greenwich Capital
GNR 2006-3	400,814,985	397,772,318	30-Jan-06	Banc of America Securities, LLC/Deutsche Bank Securities/Myerberg and Company, LP
GNR 2006-5	457,455,307	453,724,784	28-Feb-06	RBS Greenwich Capital
GNR 2006-6	236,055,606	232,961,721	28-Feb-06	JPMorgan/Blaylock & Company, Inc.

Ticker	Original Balance ($)	Current Balance ($)	Settlement Date	Dealer
GNR 2006-8	344,469,091	342,634,711	30-Mar-06	Banc of America Securities, LLC/Deutsche Bank Securities/Myerberg and Company, LP
GNR 2006-9	259,766,827	254,947,725	30-Mar-06	Nomura
GNR 2006-15	328,851,198	327,058,455	28-Apr-06	RBS Greenwich Capital
GNR 2006-18	211,412,460	210,279,169	28-Apr-06	Deutsche Bank Securities/Banc of America Securities LLC/Utendahl Capital Partners, LP
GNR 2006-19	225,052,331	221,315,823	28-Apr-06	JPMorgan/Blaylock & Company, Inc.
GNR 2006-30	299,422,868	298,533,972	28-Jul-06	RBS Greenwich Capital
GNR 2006-31	259,413,673	258,786,046	28-Jul-06	Credit Suisse/Myerberg & Company, LP
GNR 2006-32	353,701,785	353,037,528	28-Jul-06	Banc of America Securities, LLC/Deutsche Bank Securities, Inc.
GNR 2006-39	262,325,596	261,886,755	30-Aug-06	Nomura
GNR 2006-42	225,053,000	224,742,900	30-Aug-06	JPMorgan/Blaylock & Company, Inc.
GNR 2006-46	180,074,998	179,780,087	30-Aug-06	Deutsche Bank Securities/Banc of America Securities LLC/Utendahl Capital Partners, LP
GNR 2006-51	271,300,234	271,300,234	29-Sep-06	Banc of America Securities, LLC

Source: Wachovia Capital Markets, LLC. and Intex Solutions, Inc.

APPENDIX C: CALL PROTECTION BREAKDOWN IN GNMA MULTIFAMILY DEALS BY YEAR

2001			2002		
Call Protection	Balance ($ million)	% of Total	Call Protection	Balance ($ million)	% of Total
5_5	1,188.11	55.43%	5_5	2,508.67	56.63%
10_0	347.17	16.20%	10_0	685.80	15.48%
4_5	193.28	9.02%	4_5	502.32	11.34%
9_0	156.29	7.29%	9_0	271.93	6.14%
5_0	68.90	3.21%	5_0	103.49	2.34%
3_5	48.95	2.28%	3_5	71.01	1.60%
8_0	25.25	1.18%	0_5	36.81	0.83%
7_0	20.55	0.96%	7_0	30.29	0.68%
5_3	18.69	0.87%	8_0	29.41	0.66%
3_3	15.73	0.73%	7_3	27.32	0.62%
Other	60.52	2.82%	Other	162.88	3.68%
Total	2,143.44		Total	4,429.93	

2003			2004		
Call Protection	Balance ($ million)	% of Total	Call Protection	Balance ($ million)	% of Total
5_5	4,363.92	66.05%	5_5	2,953.48	49.46%
4_5	420.10	6.36%	3_7	948.41	15.88%
10_0	321.94	4.87%	4_5	374.12	6.26%
9_0	305.65	4.63%	1_9	277.37	4.64%
6_5	198.75	3.01%	2_8	217.35	3.64%
3_7	119.39	1.81%	3_5	146.52	2.45%
3_5	99.96	1.51%	10_0	133.88	2.24%
5_0	92.00	1.39%	3_3	129.73	2.17%
3_3	88.45	1.34%	9_0	124.05	2.08%
0_3	75.19	1.14%	5_0	96.02	1.61%
Other	522.07	7.90%	Other	570.76	9.56%
Total	6,607.42		Total	5,971.69	

2005			2006Q3		
Call Protection	Balance ($ million)	% of Total	Call Protection	Balance ($ million)	% of Total
2_8	1,637.91	36.56%	2_8	2,045.44	47.40%
5_5	919.68	20.53%	1_9	645.81	14.97%
3_7	783.90	17.50%	5_5	414.59	9.61%
1_9	327.04	7.30%	4_5	226.80	5.26%
4_5	220.25	4.92%	3_7	198.52	4.60%
3_5	61.04	1.36%	10_0	128.87	2.99%
0_10	50.20	1.12%	1_8	93.03	2.16%
9_0	44.33	0.99%	9_0	86.10	2.00%
10_0	42.48	0.95%	2_7	66.78	1.55%
4_6	34.82	0.78%	2_5	45.67	1.06%
Other	357.91	7.99%	Other	363.55	8.42%
Total	4,479.56		Total	4,315.16	

Source: Wachovia Capital Markets, LLC, and Intex Solutions, Inc.

APPENDIX D: HISTORICAL GNMA DEFAULTS, 1994–2006: Q3

Origination Year	Years Since Origination																				Cum. %
	1	2	3	4	5	6	7	8	9	10	11	12	13	14	15	16	17	18	19	20	
1984	0.00%	0.00%	0.00%	0.00%	0.00%	1.67%	0.00%	0.00%	0.64%	0.00%	0.00%	0.00%	0.00%	0.00%	0.00%	0.00%	0.00%	0.00%	0.00%	7.47%	9.78%
1985	0.00%	0.00%	0.00%	0.00%	0.00%	0.00%	0.00%	0.00%	0.00%	0.00%	0.00%	5.21%	0.47%	0.00%	0.00%	0.00%	6.19%	0.00%	0.00%	0.00%	11.87%
1986	0.00%	0.00%	0.00%	0.00%	0.00%	0.00%	0.00%	0.00%	0.00%	0.00%	0.00%	0.00%	0.00%	0.00%	1.96%	1.05%	0.00%	0.00%	0.00%	0.00%	3.02%
1987	0.00%	0.00%	0.00%	0.00%	0.00%	0.00%	0.00%	2.08%	0.00%	0.00%	0.00%	0.00%	0.70%	0.29%	0.00%	0.00%	1.01%	0.00%	0.00%	0.00%	4.08%
1988	0.77%	0.00%	0.00%	0.00%	0.00%	0.00%	0.00%	0.00%	0.00%	0.00%	0.38%	0.00%	0.68%	0.00%	0.00%	0.93%	0.16%	0.00%	0.00%		2.91%
1989	0.00%	0.00%	0.00%	0.00%	0.00%	0.00%	0.00%	0.00%	0.00%	0.31%	0.00%	0.00%	0.00%	0.00%	0.00%	0.86%	0.00%	0.00%			1.18%
1990	0.00%	0.00%	0.00%	0.00%	0.00%	0.00%	0.00%	0.00%	0.00%	3.23%	0.00%	1.35%	1.89%	0.97%	0.00%	0.00%	0.00%				7.45%
1991	0.00%	0.00%	0.00%	0.00%	0.00%	0.00%	0.56%	0.00%	0.00%	0.00%	1.28%	1.61%	0.91%	0.00%	0.00%	1.20%					5.56%
1992	0.00%	0.00%	0.00%	0.00%	0.47%	0.00%	0.00%	0.00%	0.00%	0.35%	0.00%	0.00%	0.00%	0.00%	0.00%						0.82%
1993	0.00%	0.00%	0.00%	0.00%	0.18%	0.00%	0.00%	0.40%	0.00%	0.00%	1.41%	0.00%	0.00%	0.00%							2.00%
1994	0.00%	0.00%	0.00%	0.00%	0.18%	0.14%	0.00%	0.00%	0.00%	0.00%	0.53%	0.00%	0.00%								0.90%
1995	0.00%	0.16%	0.97%	0.85%	0.03%	0.16%	0.23%	0.84%	0.53%	0.88%	0.00%	0.04%									4.11%
1996	0.15%	0.00%	1.54%	0.30%	0.00%	1.01%	0.48%	0.73%	0.33%	0.22%	0.00%										4.77%
1997	0.00%	0.00%	0.14%	0.38%	1.37%	0.00%	0.14%	0.62%	0.21%	0.17%											3.04%
1998	0.19%	0.30%	1.40%	1.75%	0.00%	0.83%	0.77%	1.17%	0.00%												6.41%
1999	0.21%	1.08%	0.96%	0.75%	2.17%	0.87%	0.35%	0.00%													6.39%
2000	0.65%	2.25%	1.86%	0.85%	1.16%	1.83%	0.00%														8.60%
2001	0.88%	2.10%	2.08%	2.14%	0.29%	0.50%															7.99%
2002	0.75%	1.83%	3.69%	1.20%	0.43%																7.89%
2003	0.53%	1.29%	1.22%	0.31%																	3.34%
2004	0.42%	1.76%	0.63%																		2.81%
2005	0.45%	0.18%																			0.62%
2006	0.00%																				0.00%

Origin-ation Year	Years Since Origination																				Cum. %
	1	2	3	4	5	6	7	8	9	10	11	12	13	14	15	16	17	18	19	20	
% of Orig. Bal.	0.40%	1.11%	1.45%	0.85%	0.56%	0.61%	0.22%	0.42%	0.10%	0.22%	0.17%	0.17%	0.09%	0.08%	0.03%	0.14%	0.17%	0.00%	0.02%	0.08%	6.89%
CDR	0.40%	1.12%	1.47%	0.88%	0.58%	0.64%	0.23%	0.44%	0.11%	0.23%	0.18%	0.18%	0.09%	0.08%	0.03%	0.15%	0.18%	0.00%	0.02%	0.09%	
PLD	1.30%	2.47%	2.51%	2.20%	2.13%	1.46%	1.26%	0.80%	0.57%	0.50%	0.50%	0.50%	0.50%	0.50%	0.25%	0.25%	0.25%	0.25%	0.25%	0.25%	

Source: Wachovia Capital Markets, LLC, HUD, and GNMA.

Commercial ABS

CHAPTER 19

Aircraft-Backed Debt Securities

Chris van Heerden, CFA
Vice President
Wachovia Capital Markets, LLC.

P ooled lease aircraft-backed securitizations have been used since the early
1990s to finance the aircraft portfolios of leasing companies. This chapter reviews the development of the aircraft *asset-backed securities* (ABS)
market and its overall place in aircraft financing. This is followed by an
overview of deal modeling.

The aircraft ABS market can be divided into deals issued before and
after 9/11. Over time, many of the original structuring assumptions for pre-
9/11 transactions have proved optimistic and most securities in this group
trade at distressed prices. Bonds in these deals tend to trade at significantly
discounted prices and the majority of the subordinated bonds have stopped
performing. Post-9/11 transactions have employed monoline insurance, and
have been structured with newer aircraft financed at lower leverage.

All transactions in the sector are characterized by complex amortization
formulas and limited protection against deterioration in performance and
therefore require careful analysis based on independently derived assumptions.

HISTORICAL BACKGROUND TO THE
AIRCRAFT-BACKED DEBT MARKET

Before deregulation of the airline industry, which started in the United States
in 1978, the industry was financed primarily by the banking sector with a
combination of loans and mortgages on aircraft. A few large carriers maintained monopoly pricing in protected markets. Service levels were high with

This chapter was originally coauthored with Mark Heberle.

hot meals and drinks provided. Air travel remained the domain of business travelers and only wealthy individuals and their families used airlines to travel on vacations. Systemwide load factors were near 50% in the early 1970s; fully half of the seats were unoccupied.

Deregulation allowed airlines to compete directly by letting market forces determine routes and fares while allowing for an influx of new entrants. Prices dropped and airlines were forced to focus on cost containment. During the 1980s, airlines were able to remain relatively profitable by developing a system of yield management to maximize revenue on a particular flight. In effect, passengers were charged different amounts for similar service. Price-insensitive business travelers were charged significantly higher prices for the convenience of last-minute bookings, which subsidized the lower cost being charged to vacation travelers with the flexibility of booking travel farther in advance, and load factors increased.

By the 1990s, the largest U.S. airlines had developed hub–and-spoke networks to more efficiently provide service to their extensive route structures when the first Persian Gulf War sent the sector into a three-year downturn. As airline credit deteriorated, traditional sources of financing that relied heavily on corporate credit dried up and new structures evolved that migrated to a higher reliance on asset value and structure for the repayment of debt.

Exhibit 19.1 depicts the various alternatives available to finance aircraft, as they range along a continuum from reliance on corporate credit risk at one end to reliance on assets and structure at the other. Early forms of finance in the sector, such as bank loans, leveraged leases, and mortgages, relied primarily on the airline credit for repayment. *Equipment trust certificates* (ETCs), and *pass-through certificates* (PTCs) were rudimentary forms of structured finance where airlines would finance individual aircraft in standalone structures.

EXHIBIT 19.1 The Movement from Credit Risk to Asset Risk

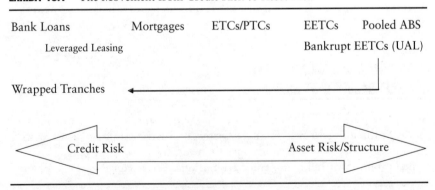

Source: Wachovia Capital Markets, LLC.

These structures gave way to *enhanced equipment trust certificates* (EETCs, pronounced double-E TCs). The enhancement to these securities came from adding larger pools of aircraft, with more than one aircraft type, then issuing several tranches of debt. A final enhancement over ETCs was the addition of a liquidity facility that would continue to service interest payments for 18 months in the event of default by the airline.

As banks withdrew from direct lending to airlines, the void was partially filled by specialized leasing companies with the expertise to maximize the value of commercial aircraft through active management of their aircraft portfolios. These operating lease companies were able to diversify the credit risk across a large number of operators in diverse geographic locations, and they had the asset-specific expertise to be able to move aircraft out of low-growth markets and redeploy them in high-demand areas of the world.

Aircraft ownership has been tied to the efficient allocation of the tax benefit associated with a depreciating asset: as airlines have been largely unprofitable, ownership has shifted to operating lessors that are typically owned by profitable parent companies. The privatization of airlines elevated the importance of balance sheet management and shareholder value, while more competition in a liberalized market has raised the need for flexible fleet management, driving airlines to look to the operating lease market. Low inflation rates have also decreased the attractiveness of owning aircraft while airlines have been able to reduce exposure to residual value risk and shift the burden of potentially "owning the wrong aircraft" to lessors. Airline ownership of aircraft (western-built aircraft in airline use) declined to 45% in 2007 from 59% in 1990. Planes transitioned to operating lessors (that grew ownership to 14% in 2007 from 11% in 1990) but also to the capital markets. In Exhibit 19.2, EETC and ABS ownership shows up under the "Broker, Bank and Manufacturer" category, which grew ownership share to 38% in 2007 from 28% in 1990.

THE MARKET FOR AIRCRAFT-BACKED SECURITIES

The first pooled ABS transaction was done in 1992, whereas the earliest EETC transactions were done in 1994 (see Exhibit 19.3). Issuance peaked in 2000 with a total of $16.0 billion from 28 transactions. In 2001, issuance in the sector appeared headed toward record levels until the terrorist attacks of 9/11 halted issuance of pooled aircraft lease ABS.

The EETC market remained open after 9/11 as Delta Air Lines, Inc., came to market just days after the attacks with a $1.4 billion EETC transaction. In the fourth quarter of 2001, the EETC market remained open to American Airlines, Inc., and Southwest Airlines Co. as they brought to

EXHIBIT 19.2 Changing Ownership of Commercial Aircraft

	Aircraft Market by Manager Category					Aircraft Market by Ownership Category				
	Airlines	Broker, Bank or Manufacturer	Operating Lease Company	Other	Total	Airlines	Broker, Bank or Manufacturer	Operating Lease Company	Other	Total
1990	76%	8%	15%	1%	100%	59%	28%	11%	2%	100%
1991	72%	8%	18%	2%	100%	54%	31%	13%	2%	100%
1992	71%	9%	19%	1%	100%	53%	32%	14%	2%	100%
1993	70%	8%	20%	1%	100%	51%	33%	14%	2%	100%
1994	70%	7%	21%	1%	100%	51%	33%	14%	2%	100%
1995	71%	6%	22%	1%	100%	50%	35%	13%	2%	100%
1996	71%	6%	22%	1%	100%	51%	35%	13%	2%	100%
1997	72%	5%	22%	1%	100%	51%	34%	13%	2%	100%
1998	71%	4%	23%	2%	100%	50%	35%	13%	2%	100%
1999	72%	4%	23%	2%	100%	49%	36%	12%	3%	100%
2000	71%	3%	24%	1%	100%	49%	37%	12%	2%	100%
2001	70%	3%	25%	1%	100%	49%	37%	11%	2%	100%
2002	68%	3%	27%	1%	100%	48%	38%	12%	3%	100%
2003	66%	4%	29%	2%	100%	46%	39%	13%	3%	100%
2004	64%	4%	30%	2%	100%	45%	39%	13%	3%	100%
2005	64%	4%	30%	2%	100%	44%	39%	13%	4%	100%
2006	63%	5%	31%	2%	100%	44%	38%	13%	4%	100%
2007	63%	4%	31%	2%	100%	45%	38%	14%	4%	100%

Source: Ascend Online Fleets.

EXHIBIT 19.3   Aircraft-Backed Debt Issuance

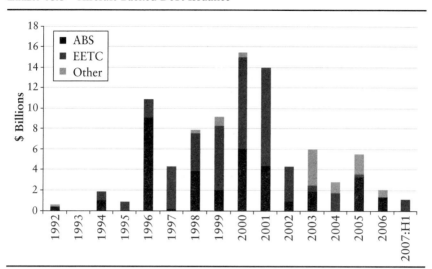

Source: Wachovia Capital Markets, LLC.

market deals of $1.7 billion and $614 million, respectively. As deliveries slowed and unencumbered assets decreased, issuance across the aircraft-backed market dropped dramatically in 2002 with eight deals pricing for a total of just $4.3 billion. Post-9/11 EETCs have been less leveraged and have typically issued wrapped floating rate liabilities.

In 2003, pooled aircraft ABS returned to the market with the Wachovia Securities-led Aviation Capital Group 2003 transaction. The deal featured a supplemental rental facility, which helped provide cash flow to the transaction in the event that lease rentals dropped below a threshold amount. The year also marked the emergence of the repacked transaction of existing securities and the use of monoline wraps to increase liquidity. In Exhibit 19.4, we highlight the repackaged and wrapped transactions that have been brought to market since 2003.

The Bear Stearns-led Aircraft Certificate Owner Trust 2003 is the largest repackaged transaction at $1.3 billion. The deal was a repackaging of the guaranteed portions of US Airways EETCs. This was also the only repackaging of EETC collateral at the time. The most popular securities for wrapped transactions have been the senior securities of the LIFT transaction that was initially brought to market in 2001. These securities appealed to the monoline wrap providers, because they had been rated by S&P and were investment grade at the time the transactions were wrapped.

EXHIBIT 19.4 Repackaged and/or Wrapped Secondary Aircraft Securities

Date	Deal	Amount ($ million)	Credit Enhancement	Underlying Security	Lead
4/22/03	ACBN 2003-1	1,365	MBIA	A Classes of US Air EETCs	Bear Sterns
9/23/03	CSTLE 2003-1W	75	MBIA	CSTLE 2003-1 A1s	Lehman
11/13/03	LIFT 1W A3s	47	Ambac	LIFT A3s	Wachovia
12/4/03	CRABS 2003-1	200	Subordination	AIRPT A9s/Zero CPN	Morgan Stanley
1/14/04	CSTLE 2003-2W	125	MBIA	CSTLE 2003-2 A1s	Lehman
3/31/04	ARTS 2004-1	312	Subordination/ MBIA	$156 million LIFT A1s/A2s	Morgan Stanley
4/15/04	ARTS 2004-2	60	Subordination/ MBIA	$30 million LIFT A1/A2s	Morgan Stanley
5/17/05	UCAT 2005-1	203	Ambac	$145 million LIFT A1s/A2s	United Capital
11/3/05	P-JETS 2005-1	100	Subordination	UAL 2001-1 A-3, B Classes	Piper Jaffray
9/13/06	P-JETS	142		UAL 2000-2 notes	Piper Jaffray
11/1/06	P-JETS	151		UAL 2001-1 A-3, B and C Classes	Piper Jaffray
12/14/06	P-JETS	250		DAL 2000-1 and 2006-3	Piper Jaffray
1/5/06	Acapulco Funding	50	Ambac	ACAP 2000 A1	Wachovia
2/26/07	P-JETS 2007-1A	158	Subordination	PALS 99 A1, A2, and B1	Piper Jaffray
		3,238			

Source: Data from Bloomberg L.P., Rating Agencies, and Wachovia Capital Markets, LLC.

There were no pooled aircraft ABS deals brought to market in 2004 with a sectorwide issuance of a mere $2.8 billion. The pricing of the AERLS transaction that financed Cerberus Capital's acquisition of debis AirFinance marked the reopening of the aircraft ABS market in 2005 and was followed by the Aviation Capital 2005 for total securitization issuance of $4.87 billion for the year. In 2006, two low-leverage transactions followed; the Aircastle serviced ACS Pass Through Trust and the Genesis Lease Ltd. serviced Genesis Funding Ltd. The first deal in 2007 was the refinancing of AERLS 2005-1A with a single-tranche wrapped deal, and three more transactions made it to market through the third quarter.

In terms of market size, issuance of aircraft-backed securities since 1992 total approximately $77.4 billion, of which about $48.2 billion is outstanding (see Exhibit 19.5). The EETC market represents 52% of issuance and 51% of the outstanding. The next largest segment is pooled lease ABS, which represents 38% of total issuance and 33% of the current market.

The greater contraction of the ABS market is partially explained by the fact that, in 2001, Morgan Stanley called its entire MSAF program, which had been a major issuer in this market. The EETC market benefits from greater liquidity with a current market size of $24.5 billion versus approximately $15.9 billion in the ABS sector (Exhibit 19.6). The "other" category of aircraft-backed securities includes the WESTF engine deal, the funded portions of synthetic transactions and deals backed by loans on corporate jets.

Continental Airlines, Inc., represents 25% of the EETC market with approximately $10.6 billion in issuance from 22 transactions (Exhibit 19.7), followed by, United and Delta, each with 12% market share. The top five issuers represent 70% of the market. Investors interested in evaluating cross-sector opportunities between pooled aircraft ABS and the EETC market need to understand that moving from EETCs into ABS requires giving up liquidity for structure.

EETCs AND POOLED LEASE ABS COMPARED

Aircraft-backed debt securities follow along a continuum based on a reliance on corporate credit from the unsecured debt and ETCs at one end of the spectrum to a reliance on structure and collateral in the EETC and ABS markets on the other. EETCs are corporate debt securities with certain characteristics of securitized assets. In the aftermath of 9/11, the corporate credit component weakened and the securities traded more on the reliance on their structural support and the quality of their aircraft.

EXHIBIT 19.5   Total Issuance of Aircraft Backed Debt (total issuance: $77.4 billion)

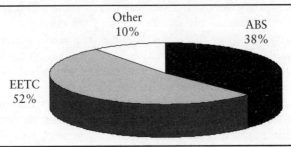

Source: Data from Bloomberg L.P. and Wachovia Capital Markets, LLC's estimates (April 2007).

EXHIBIT 19.6   Estimated Current Outstanding Aircraft-Backed Debt (total outstanding: $48.2 billion)

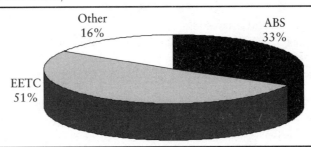

Source: Data from Bloomberg L.P. and Wachovia Capital Markets, LLC's estimates (April 2007).

EXHIBIT 19.7   EETC Issuance by Airlines

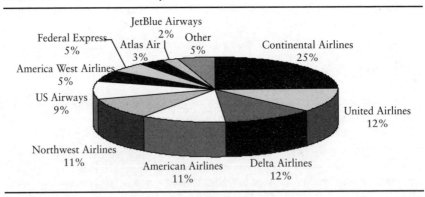

Source: Data from Bloomberg L.P. and Wachovia Capital Markets, LLC's estimates (April 2007).

Weakening airline credit quality and eroding LTV levels due to the assumed reduction in aircraft values post-9/11-affected EETCs and pooled aircraft ABS. To address the ramifications of these stresses, we compare EETCs with aircraft lease ABS based on diversification, re-leasing risk, and risk due to the erosion of aircraft values.

- *Diversification.* Aircraft pools diversify the risks to lessees, aircraft, and geographic regions. As aircraft become available from either normal lease maturities or default by an individual airline, the aircraft can be marketed in other regions. EETCs, by comparison, have concentrated exposure to an individual lessee and a narrow range of aircraft types. On the other hand, EETCs are typically backed by newer aircraft and the credit quality of the individual lessee is usually higher in a EETC than the overall credit quality in a pooled transaction. However, U.S. airlines have been the most drastically affected by the terrorist attacks, and most EETCs are issued by U.S. airlines, highlighting the strength of regional diversification.
- *Re-leasing risk.* Pooled aircraft ABS have come under stress due to lessee credit weakness and, to varying degrees, the number of aircraft types coming on the market due to U.S. and foreign fleet reductions. EETCs, on the other hand, are generally fully amortizing corporate obligations over the life of the security. In other words, the aircraft lease securitizations have re-leasing risk, whereas the EETCs have individual credit risk and the risk that, in the event of default, the aircraft will have to be marketed in a distressed market.
- *Risk of aircraft valuations.* Protection is provided to pooled aircraft ABS deals and EETCs in the form of overcollateralization. As discussed earlier, the typical LTVs of the EETCs are lower than those of a pooled aircraft lease securitization for a given rating level. Although both asset classes are exposed to the risk of declining aircraft values, the structure of the pooled aircraft lease securitizations is more resilient to short-term shocks and recessions. However, in the event of long-term cash flow impairment, ABS structures offer little recourse to bondholders, whereas EETCs have been restructured in bankruptcy to preserve value for senior investors. To understand differences in leverage, we need to take a closer look at aircraft valuation methods.

Within the context of airline finance, valuations are described as being either *base value* or *market value*. The *base value* of an aircraft is an appraiser's opinion of the underlying economic value of an aircraft in an open, unrestricted, stable market environment with a reasonable balance of supply and demand. These values assume that aircraft can be marketed under stable market conditions. *Market value,* on the other hand, is the appraiser's opinion of the most likely trading price for the aircraft in the then-current economic environment. Differences between base values and market values become important in times of severe stress. Base values will be more stable than market values.

Aircraft lease securitizations will generally have annual reviews to update their base values. To the extent that base values drop more than 5% below the expected base values in the deal, the scheduled amortization of senior classes is generally accelerated at the expense of the junior classes to bring LTVs in the deal back into balance. EETC securities, on the other hand, do not have annual appraisals, and investors need to take this into account when looking at cross-sector opportunities.

EETCs are more exposed to market value risk, whereas pooled aircraft lease securitizations are more exposed to base value risk. Although EETCs are structured with liquidity reserves that can cover interest payments for 18 months while an aircraft is being marketed for sale, the risk in a downturn is that the stress on aircraft values will keep market values below base values for an extended period. For EETCs, this effect is partially offset by newer collateral and lower LTVs. Many investors have mistakenly assumed that these lower LTVs are a sign of a more conservative structuring of EETCs. This is not so; the lower LTVs associated with EETCs are warranted due to the reliance of these structures on realizable asset value.

Changing View of Pooled Aircraft ABS versus EETCs

Exhibit 19.8 summarizes the changing view of pooled aircraft ABS versus EETCs. When these deals were first being done, one positive feature of EETCs was that they were backed by newer aircraft that were core to the issuing airline's fleet. EETCs were almost all issued by the major U.S. carriers, which was viewed as a good thing until the downturn in the U.S. market that was exacerbated by the events of 9/11. The downside of the EETC was that there was no diversification in credit exposure and there was little diversification among aircraft types.

Another drawback of these structures was the lack of a dedicated servicer. This was not generally viewed as a major negative, however, because there was no expectation of having to remarket the aircraft during the life of the deal. Unfortunately, as a number of these transactions faced issuer bankruptcy, the lack of professional servicers became an issue as creditors with limited industry knowledge had to enforce their rights.

The pooled lease transactions, on the other hand, were issued with a broad diversification across lessees, aircraft and regions worldwide. The negatives for the pooled lease deals were that their aircraft were older on

EXHIBIT 19.8   Pooled Aircraft ABS versus EETCs

	EETCs	Pooled Aircraft ABS
At time of issuance		
Pros	Newer aircraft	Diversified by aircraft, geography and
	Generally core to airline fleets	lessee
	Low investment-grade lessee	Actively managed pool
Cons	No lessee diversification	Generally unrated lessee base
	No geographic diversification	Aircraft generally older than in EETCs
	No servicer	
In the Current Market		
Pros	Newer aircraft	Most managers have been able to keep
		aircraft flying, albeit at lower lease rates
Cons	Major U.S. airlines in trouble	Some deals have older aircraft types
	Structures not working as	All deals are suffering from lower lease
	contemplated in bankruptcy	rates and higher expenses

Note: ABS: asset-backed securities; EETCs: enhanced equipment trust certificates.
Source: Wachovia Capital Markets, LLC.

average than the EETCs and their lessee base generally consisted of unrated entities around the world.

In the current environment, many of those unrated companies have fared better than the major U.S. airlines that issued EETCs. However, due to the severity of the decline in commercial aviation, some older aircraft types are being retired early and the shorter expected useful lives of these aircraft have a greater effect on the pooled lease deals than the EETC deals. In addition, the global nature of the downturn temporarily reduced the value of regional diversification in 2003–2004.

The active management aspect of pooled lease deals has gained value over time. Transactions were structured with the full knowledge that aircraft would have to be placed with more than one lessee over the life of the transaction. The ability of servicers to repossess and re-lease aircraft has been tested over the past several years, and most succeeded at keeping aircraft flying. As with the EETC market, relative value will hinge on a thorough analysis of the aircraft backing the transactions and the structural support given a particular security.

AIRCRAFT ABS DEAL STRUCTURES

Pre-9/11 pooled aircraft ABS transactions were intended to pay down the liabilities of the structure in advance of the projected depreciation of the aircraft in the portfolio. Generally, commercial aircraft are expected to fly in revenue service for 25 to 30 years with many examples flying for much longer.

Each transaction has its own set of assumptions related to useful life and depreciation based on the particular makeup of the portfolio of aircraft with some deals using 25-year useful lives and assumptions of residual value, while others assumed 30-year useful lives and no residual value.

A typical pre-9/11 pooled aircraft ABS transaction was structured similar to the example shown in Exhibit 19.9. The A classes in these deals typically represented 70% to 75% of the liabilities in the transaction and were generally issued on a floating rate basis. Subordinated tranches were amortizing securities with fixed and floating coupons. The payment of principal was based on a minimum principal paydown curve as well as a scheduled principal paydown curve.

In Exhibit 19.9 there are two second-pay securities, originally structured as soft bullets, that were projected to be refinanced 2 to 3 years from the time of issuance. Failure to refinance these securities was to result in the payment of a step-up coupon of 50 bps. Since the downturn in the aviation sector that followed the events of 9/11, none of the pre-9/11 transactions have refinanced their soft-bullet securities. These deals have all experienced reductions in lease rate cash flow and have, therefore, not had sufficient funds available to pay the subordinated step-up coupons.

Given the low cost of funds represented by these original transactions, we do not anticipate any of these transactions refinancing any of these existing structures. Although severely distressed, these securities are very resilient

EXHIBIT 19.9   Typical Pre-9/11 Deal Structure

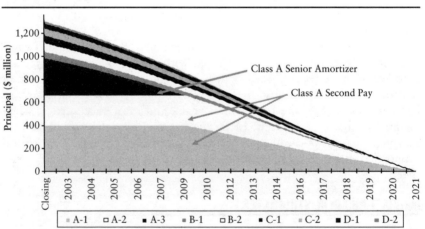

Source: Wachovia Capital Markets, LLC.

to indenture events of default. The most likely event of default in the current market is the failure to pay senior class interest. Due to the resiliency of their structure and their prevalence in the capital structure, many senior second-pay securities have extended out to their minimum principal curves and, in many cases, are trading at distressed levels. Senior second-pay securities represent the largest portion of the tradable supply of securities in this sector.

Despite the stresses in deal performance in the past six years, a number of issues inherent in deal mechanics have generally been left unchanged in post-9/11 transactions. The treatment of expenses—the most significant driver of underperformance—has not changed from deals issued in the 1990s. Money paid by lessees as reserves for future maintenance expenses are treated as revenue and distributed to note holders rather than being reserved against upcoming expenses. Other areas, such as weak reporting for an asset class with no reasonable proxy for performance, the absence of bondholder remedies before collateral becomes impaired and complex amortization formulas, have not made the progress that may have been expected.

MODELING AIRCRAFT CASH FLOW

Dramatic declines in deal cash flow from 2001 to 2003 highlighted the need to forecast deal revenue based on prevailing market conditions rather than the assumptions that were made at issuance. Early models that used haircuts to the *offering memorandum* (OM) base case did not have the ability to specify values for variables such as time on ground or early asset sales. These models also failed to apply a homogenous set of inputs across deals that were structured with varying OM base case assumptions. Over time, the market began evaluating deals with models built up from the individual aircraft level.

Wachovia, for example, publishes the *Aircraft Analytics Sourcebook* quarterly to review changes to our cash flow models and summarize the resulting analytics. The purpose of the sourcebook is to evaluate deals based on consistency in approach rather than presenting these cash flows as our best guess of the income stream likely to be experienced. The static nature of these scenarios makes them inadequate for a full evaluation of subordinate tranches in this sector. Pricing on subordinate tranches reflects significant option value and represents leveraged bets on further recovery.

To estimate future lease cash flow for aircraft, we use a lease rate factor curve model. The lease rate factor curve describes monthly leases rate as a percentage of aircraft value (Exhibit 19.10). This approach has the advantage of giving weight to aircraft depreciation in calculating forward lease rates. We also assume that aircraft depreciation follows an accelerated

EXHIBIT 19.10 Lease Rate Factor Curve

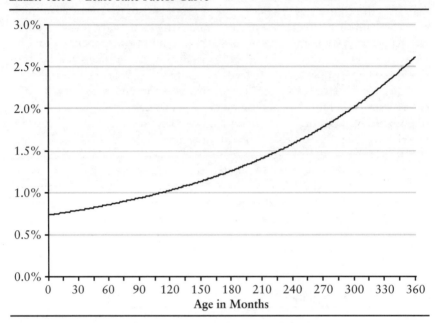

Source: Wachovia Capital Markets, LLC.

depreciation curve (Exhibit 19.11). Multiplying aircraft value by the lease rate factor generates a lease rate forward curve.

Lease factors are based on the historically observed relationship between aircraft values and lease rates. For example, a new narrow body may command 0.89% of its market value in monthly lease rentals in its first year and 1.7% when it is 20 years old. As the example shows, lease rate factors for older aircraft exceed those of new aircraft as owners need to recover their invested capital over a shorter remaining economic life and assume the greater volatility associated with older aircraft residual values. In reality, the factor-derived lease rate is an approximation, and the realized rate will vary based on the length of the lease term, the perceived residual value of the aircraft and the credit quality, among other factors.

Our aircraft value assumption is based on the Ascend market value rather than appraisal base value. The base value represents the stable, long-term economic value of an aircraft assuming a balance of supply and demand. (Base values can be found in yearly appraisals for each deal.) The market neutrality of base value would appear to make this a better driver for the lease rate calculation as opposed to market value, which will fluctuate based on supply and demand. In practice, however, we find that appraisal

EXHIBIT 19.11 Aircraft Value as a Percentage of Original Market Value

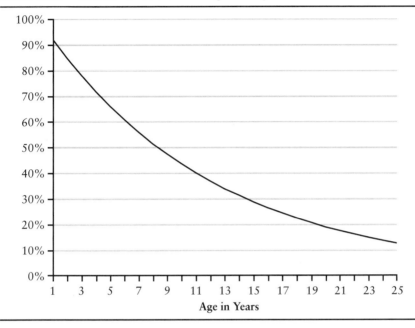

Source: Wachovia Capital Markets, LLC.

values easily vary as much as 120% for the same aircraft between different transactions. Also, given the rebound in aircraft demand after 2003, it became difficult to give credence to base values that were still significantly above market values, in some cases, even at a late point in the cycle.

Deals in sector were structured with a straight line depreciation assumption, compounded by an inflation factor. The result was a convex shaped depreciation curve, where depreciation expenses increased later in the life of the asset. In reality, aircraft maintenance expense increases with age. Using straight line depreciation translates to substantially higher ownership cost later in the aircraft life (Exhibit 19.12), whereas an accelerated depreciation schedule shows rising maintenance cost offset by declining depreciation expense (Exhibit 19.13).

Beyond aircraft values and lease rates, our methodology in evaluating pooled aircraft ABS transactions involves further estimates, including the following:

- Estimating or using actual lease rollover dates. We assume future lease terms of five years. We also assume downtime between leases of 30 to 360 days depending on the aircraft type.

EXHIBIT 19.12 Ownership Cost with Straight Line Depreciation

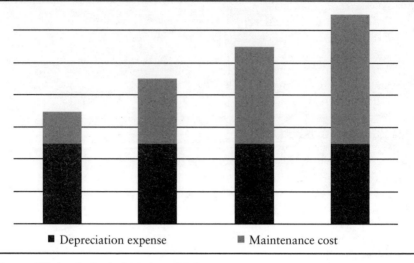

■ Depreciation expense   ■ Maintenance cost

Source: Wachovia Capital Markets, LLC.

EXHIBIT 19.13 Ownership Cost with Accelerated Depreciation

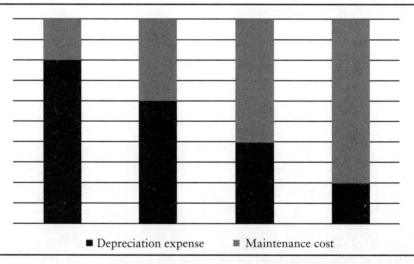

■ Depreciation expense   ■ Maintenance cost

Source: Wachovia Capital Markets, LLC.

■ Estimating useful life. Here we adopt the industry standard assumption for passenger aircraft useful life of 25 years and model a 15-year useful life for freighters from the time of conversion.

- Making a reasonable assumption for collection of maintenance reserves as a percentage of lease revenue.
- Estimating the residual value of aircraft at the end of their useful lives. To this end, we use a centralized database to ensure consistency across various transactions.
- Running the resulting cash flow through the liability waterfall of the transaction using forward LIBOR.

DATA QUALITY AND MODEL RISKS

Modeling risk can be associated with the data quality as well as simple bugs in the calculation engine. The sector came of age at a time when the reporting requirements were minimal. Some servicers have voluntarily increased the volume of reported data. Best practices for disclosure in the sector include web-posted reports, detailed lease rollover information and investor updates detailing extraordinary items—especially related to expenses. Other securitized assets tend to have reasonable proxies for collateral performance, such as loans of a similar credit profile and vintage. There is no market indicator for the risk and performance of an aircraft lease contract, which means the servicer has a monopoly on the pieces of information necessary to forecast deal performance.

Investors in the aircraft ABS sector must be diligent about doing the work to become comfortable with the risks inherent in this asset class. Modeling aircraft lease cash flow and then evaluating the corresponding liability waterfall is fraught with potential modeling risks. Even though the focus of this discussion is on asset-side modeling, the resulting analytics will also depend on the assumptions made in the liability model. From this perspective, the modeling of interest rate hedges represents a risk. The swap notional amount varies as a percentage of the Class A balance outstanding on each deal with varied standards of disclosure to help or hinder modeling.

Investors should avoid the pitfall of attributing too much predictive power to even the most elegant models. The key from the investor viewpoint is to evaluate opportunities in the sector in such a way as to gain comfort that model error is skewed to the upside.

WORLDWIDE MARKET FOR COMMERCIAL AIRCRAFT

Commercial aircraft leasing companies market aircraft to airlines around the world. The vast majority of the aircraft managed by these operating lease companies are Western-built jets. At this point, it is worth a few mo-

EXHIBIT 19.14   Worldwide Fleet of Aircraft in Airline Usage

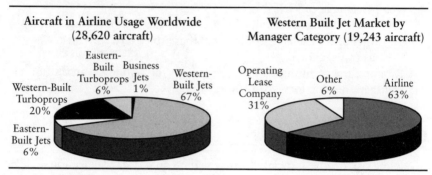

Source: Ascend Online Fleets (April 2007).

ments to look at how this market relates to the broader world market for commercial aircraft. In the left pie chart of Exhibit 19.14, we summarize the total worldwide fleet of 28,620 aircraft being flown in standard airline usage, either passenger or cargo aircraft flown by airlines, as of April 2007.

Roughly 67% of the world airline fleet is made up of Western-built jets, the vast majority of which are built by Boeing, Airbus, Embraer and Bombardier. Boeing and Airbus are the primary Western manufacturers of *large commercial aircraft* (LCA), and Bombardier and Embraer are the main Western manufacturers of *regional jets* (RJs).

The pie chart on the right breaks down the world fleet of Western-built jets by manager category. Of the 19,243 world fleet of Western-built jets, 31% are managed by leasing companies, whereas 63% are managed by the airlines. This equates to 5,974 Western-built jets managed by the leasing companies.

Commercial Aircraft Leasing Companies

Leasing companies control a large and growing percentage of the world fleet of commercial jet aircraft. Lessors are ranked by fleet size in Exhibit 19.15. Over the past two years, a number of leasing companies have changed ownership. Some portfolios have transitioned to large sponsors that are efficient owners of assets with resources to fund long-term growth. Examples include the acquisition of Singapore Aircraft Leasing by Bank of China, the purchase of the GATX aircraft leasing business by Macquarie Aircraft Leasing Ltd. and the consolidation of Boullioun Aviation into Aviation Capital Group.

After several years of inactivity, leasing companies, in 2005, again resumed placing orders for new aircraft with the manufacturers. According to Ascend Online, lessors had 781 aircraft on order in April 2007. A large portion of these were from ILFC and GECAS with orders for 205 and 151 aircraft, respectively.

EXHIBIT 19.15 Top Lessors by Total Aircraft Managed and on Order, as of May 2007

		Managed	Owned	On Order	Average Age
1	GECAS	1,716	571	151	9
2	ILFC	932	851	205	6
3	Boeing Capital Corp	267	217	0	10
4	AerCap	242	126	96	13
5	Aviation Capital Group	213	131	15	12
6	CIT Aerospace	208	198	77	8
7	Babcock & Brown Aircraft Management LLC	204	57	0	7
8	RBS Aviation Capital	197	190	41	3
9	Pegasus Aviation Inc.	181	24	8	6
10	AWAS	142	45	0	13
12	Macquarie Aviation Leasing Ltd.	137	88	3	8
14	ORIX Aviation Systems Ltd.	94	29	0	8
15	BCI Aircraft Leasing Inc.	87	21	0	18
16	Singapore Aircraft Leasing Enterprise Pte. Ltd.	70	45	66	3
17	Aircastle Advisor LLC	66	59	0	11
18	Pembroke Group	66	15	0	6
19	Nordic Aviation Contractor A/S	58	50	0	19
20	Aircraft Leasing & Management	54	0	0	1
21	Aergo Capital Ltd.	52	14	0	24
22	World Star Aviation	50	0	0	1
23	Q Aviation LP	49	23	0	9
24	Sumisho Aircraft Asset Management BV	44	17	0	7
25	Allco Finance Group	43	21	0	4

Source: Ascend Online Fleets and Wachovia Capital Markets, LLC.

Much of the investment activity since 2005 came as private equity funds aimed to capitalize on the recovery in the industry. Lease rates for commercial aircraft hit bottom in mid-2003 in the wake of the SARS epidemic and the active portion of the Iraq War. At that time, the monthly lease rate for a mid-1990s 757 had dropped from a pre-9/11 level of $300,000 a month to around $100,000. By late 2006, individual aircraft were being placed for more than $200,000. In the next section, we look at the changes in lease rates across a wider cross-section of aircraft that are relevant to pooled aircraft ABS investors.

Aircraft Lease Rates

In reviewing long-term lease-rate trends, the production status is significant in determining the resilience of monthly rates to recover. Lease rates weakened in 2000, tracking the broader economy. But it was not until 2003 that rates reached their post-9/11 trough, as renegotiated lease contracts, bankruptcies and fleet reorganizations took time to work through the system.

In-production narrow-body aircraft have recovered to pre-9/11 rates for Boeing aircraft but not for Airbus narrow bodies (Exhibit 19.16). Airbus values were affected by sustained high production rates through the downturn: 233 A320 family aircraft were delivered in 2003 versus 236 in 2002. In comparison, 737 deliveries were reduced to 173 in 2003 from 223 in 2002. During this period, a number of A320 operators collapsed, including Swiss, Sabena and Aero Lloyd, also increasing the number of available aircraft. For fairness in comparison, it is important to keep in mind that the A320 has been in production since 1988 compared with 1998 for the 737NG.

EXHIBIT 19.16 In-Production Narrow-body Lease Rates

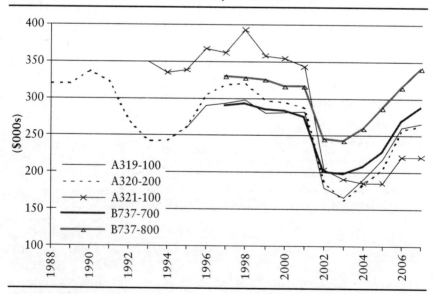

Source: Data from Ascend Online Fleets and Wachovia Capital Markets, Ltd.

Wide-body aircraft have historically proven to be more susceptible to downturns, as these are operated by fewer airlines with less diverse business models. Indeed, in the most recent downturn, the in-production passenger widebody aircraft group faced lease rate declines of 35% to 50% (Exhibit 19.17). Here lease rates have been slower to return to pre-9/11 levels.

Despite the strong market recovery for current technology types, the experience for out-of-production aircraft has been mixed (Exhibit 19.18). The shortage of newer narrow-body aircraft benefited 737 classics, which recovered 51% from the lows. Another narrow body, the 757–200, also benefited from the overall market recovery, but other types such as the MD-80, Fokker 100 and A310 were unable to gain solid footing again. To understand variations in the performance of different aircraft models, it may be helpful to look at characteristics of desirable leasing assets.

What Makes a Good Leasing Asset?

The marketability of an aircraft is affected by a variety of factors. From a lessor's perspective, a good leasing asset is one in that can be marketed to a large number of airlines and face limited competition from other available aircraft. In general, the following are drivers of marketability of a commercial aircraft type:

EXHIBIT 19.17 In-Production Wide-body Lease Rates

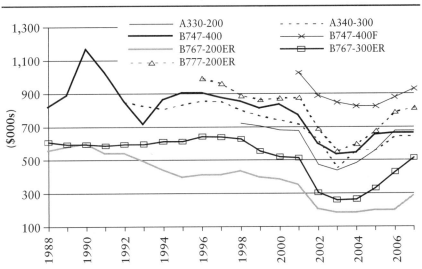

Source: Data from Ascend Online Fleets and Wachovia Capital Markets, Ltd.

EXHIBIT 19.18 Out-of-Production Aircraft Lease Rates

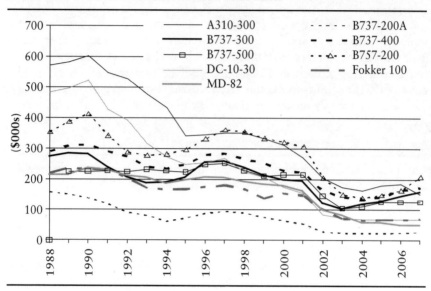

Source: Data from Ascend Online Fleets and Wachovia Capital Markets, Ltd.

- *Number of current operators.* A high number of current operators is always preferable as lessors benefit when multiple carriers compete for a limited number of available aircraft. Higher numbers of operators are associated with regional diversification and a greater variety of operator business models, which provide stability for values.
- *Number of aircraft in production run.* A long production ensures a solid installed base of users and a broad market for used aircraft as well as spare parts.
- *In-production status/backlog.* Large order backlogs ensure that aircraft remain in production for years to come and that carriers will need to look to the leasing market to service unanticipated demand. Conversely, when an aircraft goes out of production, late-production cycle aircraft can be expected to depreciate at a significantly faster rate than their midproduction examples.
- *Existence of a cargo conversion program.* The potential for cargo conversion will act as a support to aircraft values and can extend revenue service of an aircraft for as much as 15 years after conversion.
- *Number of young aircraft on ground.* High numbers of available aircraft hurt the lessor's ability to capture attractive lease rates for their aircraft. However, a distinction must be made between newer vintages, which will have a material negative impact on lease rates, and older

vintages approaching the end of their useful life that will have less of an effect.

The combination of the first two drivers is referred to as the market mass for the aircraft. Exhibits 19.19 and 19.20 show the market mass for various aircraft types. For the top 35 aircraft types, we have provided additional details of marketability in Exhibit 19.21. Attractiveness as a leasing asset will also be influenced by the age, engine type and maintenance condition.

The Impact of Fuel on Aircraft Operating Expenses

Although airline bankruptcies and restructuring served to reduce labor costs, they were not helpful in addressing fuel costs, which have become the largest operating expense for U.S. airlines. Due to dramatic increases in the price of refining, jet fuel prices have outpaced the already steep price trajectory of crude oil.

Airlines have had limited success in passing higher fuel prices on to consumers. For the aircraft market, the bottom line is that total cost per available seat mile will be an important driver in decisions about which aircraft to use for a particular mission. However, we have learned over the past several years that other factors can have as much or more weight in

EXHIBIT 19.19   Narrow-body Aircraft Market

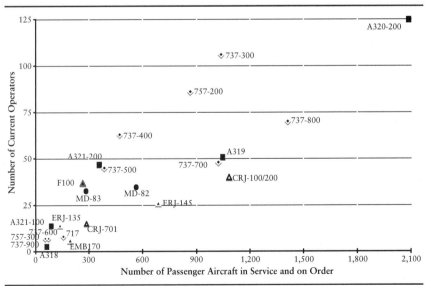

Source: Aviation Specialist Group, Inc.

EXHIBIT 19.20   Wide-body Aircraft Market

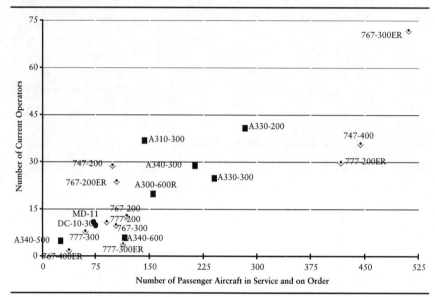

Source: Aviation Specialist Group, Inc.

the decision-making process. These other factors include the availability of alternatives and the ability of a carrier to finance those alternatives. After all, more than five years after 9/11 a great many older fuel-inefficient aircraft are flying because the financial condition of many airlines precludes replacing these aircraft with newer models.

Exhibit 8.23 lists web sites that can be used to find additional data on the sector. Included in this listing are a number of manufacturers and industry groups that provide their own forecasts of aircraft demand. Over the next 20 years, the number of aircraft in service is widely expected to double and require financing of more than $2 trillion in investment by airlines.

SUMMARY

As the leased portion of the worldwide commercial aircraft fleet continues to grow, pooled lease aircraft ABS has remained a viable financing vehicle. Despite improvements in leverage levels and collateral quality in post-9/11 transactions, investment in the sector continues to require an asset-level-up valuation approach that relies on independently derived assumptions regarding forward aircraft cash flow.

EXHIBIT 19.21 The Top 10 Aircraft Types by Fleet Size

	Aircraft Type	Body Type	In Service	Stored	Curren Total	On Order	Grand Total	Option
1	Boeing 737 (NG)	Narrow body	2,107	7	2,114	1,486	3,600	953
2	Boeing 737 (Classic)	Narrow body	1,814	98	1,912	0	1,912	0
3	Airbus A320	Narrow body	1,629	20	1,649	1,088	2,737	454
4	Boeing (McDonnell-Douglas) MD-80	Narrow body	937	153	1,090	0	1,090	0
5	Boeing 747	Wide body	894	122	1,016	118	1,134	56
6	Boeing 757	Narrow body	983	30	1,013	0	1,013	0
7	Bombardier (Canadair) CRJ Regional Jet	Regional Jet	916	91	1,007	0	1,007	51
8	Airbus A319	Narrow body	924	9	933	559	1,492	239
9	Boeing 767	Wide body	838	54	892	59	951	30
10	Boeing 727	Narrow body	414	324	738	0	738	0

Note: Excludes special use aircraft. May include freighters.
Source: Ascend Online Fleets as of April 2007.

EXHIBIT 19.22 Airline Cost Index: Breakdown of Operating Expenses

	ACI (2000 = 100)	Percent of Operating Expenses	Percent Change Yr/Yr
Fuel per gallon	282.0	27%	23%
Labor per FTE	111.5	24%	0%
Transport-related per ASM	404.3	14%	6%
Professional services per ASM	104.1	8%	−4%
Other operating per RTM	90.8	7%	−11%
Aircraft ownership per operating seat	75.4	7%	−10%
Nonaircraft ownership per enplanement	92.1	4%	2%
Landing fees per capacity ton landed	136.6	2%	0%
Food and beverage per RPM	59.8	2%	−3%
Maintenance material per revenue air- craft hour	53.2	1%	−4%
Passenger commissions as percent of pas- senger revenue	31.0	1%	−4%
Communication per enplanement	72.1	1%	−7%
Advertising and promotion per RPM	63.4	1%	−8%
Utilities and office supplies per FTE	82.5	1%	7%
Nonaircraft insurance per RPM	234.1	1%	−20%
Aircraft insurance as percent of hull net book value	141.4	0%	12%
Interest as percent of outstanding debt	136.5	nmf	−19%
COMPOSITE	176.7	100.0%	19.3%

Note: Interest cost not included in composite.
Source: ATA Airline Cost Index as of January 2007.

EXHIBIT 19.23 Useful Web Sites for Additional Data

Websites	Link
Deal Pages	
Aerco	www.aerco-group.com
AFT	www.aftreports.com
Airplanes Group	www.airplanes-group.com
ALS	www.alsreports.com
EAST	www.eastreports.com
LIFT	www.liftreports.com
Pegasus	www.pegasusaviation.com/login.php
Servicers	
AerCap	www.aercap.com
Aircastle Ltd.	www.aircastle.com
Aviation Capital Group	www.aviationcapital.com
AWAS	www.awas.com
Babcock & Brown Ltd.	www.babcockbrown.com
GE Commercial Aviation Services (GECAS)	www.gecas.com
Genesis Lease Limited	www.genesislease.com
International Lease Finance Corp.	www.ilfc.com
Pegasus Aviation Finance Co.	www.pegasusaviation.com
World Star Aviation, Ltd.	www.worldstaraviation.com
Manufacturers	
Aibus SAS[a]	www.airbus.com
The Boeing Co.[a]	www.boeing.com/commercial/
Bombardier Inc.	www.bombardier.com
Embraer (Empresa Brasileira de Aeronautica S.A.)	www.embraer.com
News and Industry Data Sources	
Air Transport Association of America (ATA)	www.airlines.org
Bureau of Transportation Statistics	www.bts.gov
Federal Aviation Administration[a]	www.faa.gov
International Air Transport Association (IATA)[a]	www.iata.org
SpeedNews	www.speednews.com
The *Monitor*	www.monitordaily.com

[a] Proprietary market forecast made available.
Source: Wachovia Capital Markets, LLC.

CHAPTER 20

Intermodal Equipment Securitization

Chris van Heerden, CFA
Analyst
Wachovia Capital Markets, LLC

Securitization has been used by lessors to raise secured financing against pools of marine shipping containers (i.e., intermodal equipment). In short, the asset class is marked by (1) sound long-term fundamentals of increasing global trade; (2) deals structured with a dependency on the servicer reflected in leverage restrictions; and (3) callable, wrapped securities that have performed consistently over the history of the asset class. This chapter provides an overview of the container shipping business and a brief review of the securitization of the asset class.

MARKET BACKGROUND

Container use has grown rapidly because it is internationally standardized, deployable in intermodal transport, and relatively inexpensive. As a result, the container has played a major role in the international division of labor that has allowed manufacturing to be located wherever it is most economical. Before the use of containers, the process of handling, gathering, and distributing cargo had changed little since the time of the Phoenicians.

Oceangoing cargo ships started using containers in the 1950s. In the late 1960s, an international agreement was reached that standardized the sizes of containers to be used for sea and land transportation. *Container-ization* was a major improvement to the *break-bulk shipments* that were prevalent before the advent of containers. Break-bulk shipments involved manually packing and unpacking ships with pallets full of cargo. A shipment would be packed, unpacked, and repacked several times along its journey as cargo changed from ship to rail to truck along the delivery route. With containers, cargo is loaded into the container at the point of departure and then the container is loaded onto the ship. Goods remain in the container while the container is transported from the ship, double-stacked on a railcar, and then placed on a chassis for delivery by truck to its final destination.

Information on the sector is scarce. Container trade data are derived from ports and customs data by a handful of consultants in the sector (e.g., Global Insight, Drewry's Shipping Consultants Ltd., and Ocean Shipping Consultants Ltd.) Primary data sources are extremely limited. As a result, industry reports involve broad estimates and are published yearly.

High growth in container and chassis fleets is due in part to the expansion of shipping lines and the cost savings of transporting goods using containers, resulting from increased efficiency and security in packing only once at the source when transporting goods. Industry growth may also be attributed to changes in manufacturing practices, such as the growing reliance on *just-in-time* (JIT) delivery methods, and increased exports of component parts by technologically advanced countries for assembly in other countries and the subsequent reimportation of finished products.

Containerization has revolutionized transportation and increased productivity in shipping, rail, and trucking. Exhibit 20.1 shows productivity gains in rail and trucking have far outstripped the productivity gains in business as a whole over the past 30 years. This increased efficiency was driven by containerization and has helped to spur globalization as the growth in international trade in goods and services has grown from 10.7% of U.S. GDP to 26.9% over the past 30 years.

EXHIBIT 20.1 Productivity Trends in the U.S. Transportation Industries (1955 = 100)

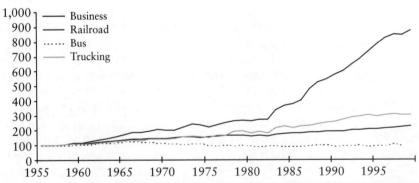

Source: U.S. Bureau of Transportation Statistics.

DEAL STRUCTURE

The typical intermodal deal is structured using a *master indenture* structure, meaning that a single pool of collateral backs multiple series of notes. Issuance is typically in the form of wrapped senior notes. Exhibit 20.2 provides an illustrative transaction diagram. Over time, additional containers can be added to the collateral pool and additional notes issued as term funding. The addition of assets is subject to the overall leverage limits of the master indenture and requires rating agency approval.

Container transactions benefit from a significant amount of overcollateralizaiton. Assets exceed the amount of debt issued by 15% or more, depending on the deal. The addition of assets to the transaction is limited by this leverage limit.

Cash inflow consists of lease rental income and proceeds from residual sales. Revenues net of expenses are used to make payments on the notes. Principal payments are divided into two layers: paid first, the minimum pay-

EXHIBIT 20.2   Illustrative Transaction Diagram

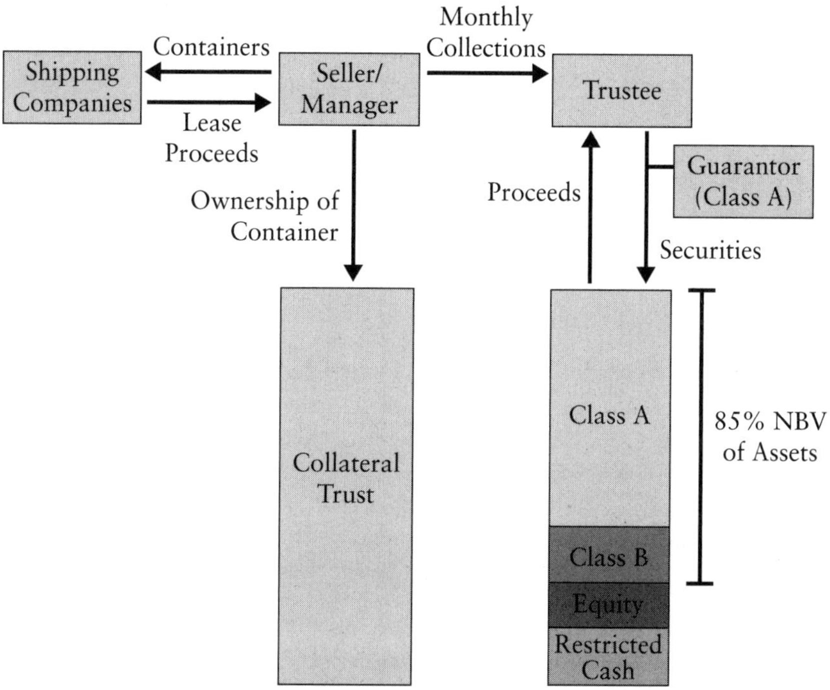

Source: Wachovia Capital Markets, LLC.

ments are set to a 15-year amortization schedule, and scheduled payments are set to a 10-year amortization schedule. Deals in the sector have consistently paid in accordance with the 10-year amortization schedule. Notes are generally callable three to four years after issuance.

A number of trigger events provide for early amortization of the notes in response adverse developments. These triggers may include a failure to pay monthly interest or principal at maturity, a servicer default, and deterioration in asset value.

ISSUER OVERVIEW

Securitizing has been used by some lessors to finance a portion of their fleets. Historically, ocean carriers split the majority of the container market with leasing companies, with each laying claim to a 46% to 47% share, the remainder resting in the hands of rail and trucking companies.

Lessors can time asset purchases by based on leasing economics. In periods of high box prices, lessors can scale back orders while ocean carriers time orders to coincide with new vessel deliveries. This was the case in 2005 and 2006 when lessors took delivery of only 32% and 35%, respectively, of new containers. In terms of fleet growth, this means the leased container fleet added less than 3% in 2005, after average gains of 8.5% in the preceding three years.

Lessors have slowed purchases to avoid owning overpriced assets. The previous run-up in newbuild container prices in the 1990s meant that a container purchased in 1995 at the then prevailing price of $2,400 had a depreciated cost that exceeded newbuild prices until 2003. Ocean carriers, on the other hand, are concerned with having containers available to service new ships, and are therefore less price-sensitive buyers.

Consolidation has been a theme in the container leasing industry in the past decade as operators aimed to enhance returns through economies of scale. It is also the largest lessors that have been the most frequent users of securitizations, with Triton Group, Textainer Marine Containers, and GE SeaCo issuing most frequently.

Return Analysis

Lessors' return on investment has been in a long-term decline as the leasing market matures. During the 1980s, returns exceeded 30%, but have since declined to 13.8% in 2006. Returns have been eroded as per diem lease rates have declined faster than new box prices. In turn, lessors have responded by increasing scale and increasing the share of containers placed

EXHIBIT 20.3 Rate-of-Return Calculation

Cost	$1,850
Useful Life	15 years
Five-Year Term Lease per Diem Rate (5 years)	$0.70
Master Lease Rate per Diem Rate (10 years)	$1.15
Master Lease Utilization Rate	80%
Residual Value	15.0%
Rate of Return	13.8%

Source: Wachovia Capital Markets, LLC.

on long-term lease. Fortunes of leasing companies have also been aided by a high utilization level and the associated reduction in storage costs, lower repositioning costs, and strong secondary values.

Lessors are increasingly rolling containers to a second long-term lease following the initial lease. Typically in the past, a new container was placed on an initial five-year lease and then served out the remainder of its life under a master lease agreement, where rentals were paid on a daily use basis. Lessors are showing a preference for fixing containers on a second long-term lease. In mid-2005, almost 62% of the lessors' TEU were on long-term lease, up from 37% in 1995. Exhibit 20.3 outlines an approximate rate-of-return on a new container, as at year-end 2006.

OUTLOOK FOR ISSUANCE

Long-term demand for containerized trade has been supported by a trend toward globalization and lower trade barriers, the shift of consumer goods manufacturing to developing countries and the efficiency gains realized from using intermodal transport. Benefiting from these fundamentals, the container fleet has sustained an average annual growth rate of 8% a year since the mid 1990s. Trade expansion, ship slot additions and the replacement cycle of the wave of mid-1990s production boxes should support future fleet growth.

CONCLUSION

The container securitization market is a niche corner of structured products with a limited number of potential issuers. Deal performance, so far, has been pristine. This consistency has been reflected in new issue pricing, which has narrowed the gap versus other wrapped paper. Future issuance will likely be tied to lessor fleet growth, which is supported by the sound long-term fundamentals underpinning container shipping. This suggests a continuation of the two- to three-deal pace that the sector averaged per year.

CHAPTER 21

Life Insurance Reserve Securitization

Chris van Heerden, CFA
Analyst
Wachovia Capital Markets, LLC

Regulation Triple X, implemented in 2000, stipulates reserve requirements for term life insurance policies. Intended to standardize reserve requirements in the industry, the statutory reserve requirements set out under this regulation has been viewed as conservative. Insurers have used the securitization market to fund the reserve requirement, thereby obtaining match term funding, advantageous rating agency treatment and potential tax benefits. This chapter reviews the motives for securitization, its implementation and the outlook for future issuance.

For investors, Triple X securitizations offer exposure to a nonsystematic asset class. The underlying drivers of performance, lapse rates and mortality, perform independently of business cycles and financial instruments. Deals benefit from large asset pools, where the large number of policies smoothes performance around the expected mortality rate. Furthermore, triple X transactions are supported by direct capital contributions from the insurer and the retention of future embedded profits from policy premium payments. Financial guaranty insurance policies have been employed by all transactions to date.

THE LIFE INSURANCE SECURITIZATION MARKET

Triple X is one subgroup in the broader life insurance securitization market. Total life insurance securitization reached roughly $18 billion in outstanding volume in mid-2007, with issuance of approximately $5 billion in 2006 and $2 billion year to date through June 2007.[1]

The life insurance securitization market divides into the following:

- *Triple X* securitization, which funds the regulatory capital requirement for level premium term life insurance policies. Deal terms may be as long as 30 years,
- *Embedded value* securitizations (also referred to as value-in-force monetization) release the profits "embedded" in future cash flows from a defined block of business,
- *Catastrophic mortality bonds* pay the issuer in the event of spikes in general population mortality by referencing a mortality index. These bonds can provide insurers with a level of protection that may not be available in the reinsurance market, and
- *New business strain* funding has been used to finance the upfront costs of writing new business by raising debt against future premiums.

Aside from the difference in motivation, embedded value and Triple X securitization differ in terms of collateral. Triple X transactions retain cash from the debt raised as collateral in the deal, whereas embedded value transactions are collateralized by future profits from a defined block of business. Whereas Triple X securitization is specific to U.S. law, embedded value transactions have also been executed in the United Kingdom.

RESERVE FUNDING SECURITIZATION

Regulation Triple X sets reserve levels, known as statutory reserves, specifically for guaranteed premium life insurance policies. The margin of conservatism and lack of risk differentiation built into the regulation mandate reserves that may be multiples of what insurers deem economically required. Insurers calculate economic reserves based on their best estimate actuarial assumptions. The difference between the statutory reserve and the economic reserve is known as redundant reserves, or excess reserves. Redundant reserves arise because statutory reserves may not reflect improvements in mortality, have a built-in margin of conservatism, have limited risk differentiation and assume that policies do not lapse. It is the redundant reserves that are financed in through securitization.

Life insurers historically met the redundant reserve requirement directly or indirectly (e.g., via offshore life reinsurers) through renewable bank-issued *letters of credit* (LOCs). This has been an imperfect funding source because

---

[1] Rodney A Clark, *The Booming U.S. Life Insurance Securitization Market Shows Signs of Diversifying*, Standard & Poor's, June 8, 2007.

the short-term nature of these LOCs (most often only one year) does not match the 20- to 30-year life insurance reserve liabilities. Also, because LOC capacity from banks is limited, the cost can potentially increase significantly over time. As an alternative, insurers have turned to the securitization market to address the shortcomings of the LOC market.

In essence, a Triple X securitization involves the sponsoring insurer or reinsurer passing a defined block of business to a *special purpose reinsurance vehicle* (SPRV) and contributing the risk-based capital requirement for the transaction. Capital markets notes are issued in the amount of the redundant reserves. Funds raised in the capital markets are placed in a reserve credit trust, invested in qualified assets and held for the benefit of the issuer to provide statutory reserve credit.

The economic reserves are raised from policy premiums retained in the transaction. When the reserve need declines later in the transaction, funds are released to amortize the notes. For the ceding insurer, the transaction addresses the statutory reserve for the given block of business on a match-term basis. Capital markets notes may take the form of long average-life notes and short-term refinancing auction-rate money market notes.

Regulation XXX

Regulation XXX became effective in 2000 with the purpose of standardizing reserve requirements for U.S. life insurers. "Regulation XXX" was the name assigned to the new rule during the drafting stage and has remained in use after final adoption of the code as the Valuation of Life Insurance Model Regulation.[2]

When it went into effect in 2000, Regulation XXX referenced a 1980 Commissioners Standard Ordinary Mortality table (CSO table) as the basis for calculating statutory reserves. Because the 1980 CSO table assumed no policy lapses and was based on data collected in the 1970s, neglecting 30 years of mortality improvements, insurers saw a dramatic increase in the required capital that had to be set aside for term life insurance policies.

Since the original implementation of Regulation XXX, reserve requirements have been reduced by the introduction in 2003 of updated mortality assumptions, the 2001 CSO table, and then in 2006, with the introduction of the 2001 CSO Preferred Class Structure Mortality Table. Although these revisions have eased the reserve strain on insurers, the CSO data are inherently conservative.

---

[2] Insurance companies are regulated at the state level, and the National Association of Insurance Commissioners (NAIC) coordinates insurance regulation and supervision between various state insurance commissioners, promoting uniform laws and regulations.

EXHIBIT 21.1   Excess Reserve Illustration

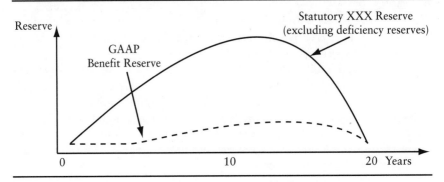

Note: Based on a 20-year term policy issued to a male preferred nonsmoker, aged 45. GAAP benefit reserve based on pricing assumptions with no PADs (provision for adverse deviation).
Source: Towers Perrin, Tillinghast insurance consulting practice.

Redundant Reserves

Statutory reserves are calculated based on the CSO tables, whereas the theoretical economic reserve is the present value of future liabilities net of the value of future premium income. The gap between statutory reserves and economic reserves is the excess reserves (see Exhibit 21.1).

Life insurers historically funded excess reserves directly or indirectly (e.g., via off-shore life reinsurers) through short-term, renewable bank-issued LOCs. These have been an imperfect funding source because the short-term nature of the LOCs (typically one to three-year terms) does not match the long-term reserve requirement. Also, because LOC capacity from banks is limited, the cost can potentially increase significantly over time. Triple X securitizations have allowed insurers to finance excess reserves while addressing the shortcomings of the LOC market.

THE LEVEL PREMIUM GUARANTEED POLICY

A level premium term policy provides insurance for a specified number of years (usually 10 to 20) at a fixed premium. Payments stop when (1) the policy expires, (2) the policy lapses, or (3) the policyholder dies and the insurance company has to pay a death benefit (Exhibit 21.2). Mortality is the only event that produces a negative cash outflow. In a lapse scenario, the insurer loses future premium income but is also released from having to pay a future death benefit.

EXHIBIT 21.2 Cash Flow of a Level Premium Term Policy

Year	1	2	3	4	5	6	7	8	9	10	Total CF
No Events	$300	300	300	300	300	300	300	300	300	300	3,000
Lapse	300	300	300	300	300	0	0	0	0	0	1,500
Death	300	300	300	300	300	300	300	300	300	-1,000,000	-997,300

Note: Assuming a $300 annual premium and a $1.0 million death benefit.
Source: Wachovia Securities, LLC.

In the context of the securitization, mortality and lapsation are the primary risk factors. A death benefit payment leads to a cash outflow and reduces future premium income. As a risk factor, mortality is unrelated to business cycles, or credit and equity markets. It is also a well-analyzed risk factor with extensive data history. Within a Triple X transaction, a large sample size reduces variability in mortality around the expected value as the number of policies in a pool can reach up to 1 million.

TRANSACTION STRUCTURES

In a reserve funding securitization, the insurer cedes a defined block of business to a captive SPRV, thereby delinking the book business (policy block) from the credit risk of sponsor. Two types of structures have been used to achieve this objective: the *downstream* structure used by First Colony Structure (Exhibit 21.3) and the and the *upstream* structure used by Scottish Re and RGA (Exhibit 21.4).

Despite the differences between the two structures, the securitization process encompasses similar basic transaction steps:

1. The sponsoring insurer/reinsurer cedes its Triple X reserves for a defined block of business to a SPRV (captive reinsurer) by entering into a reinsurance agreement.
2. The captive reinsurer funds the capital requirement via either the capital markets trust (downstream structure) or LLC (upstream structure), which, in turn, is funded by selling securities to investors.

EXHIBIT 21.3   Downstream Transaction Structure

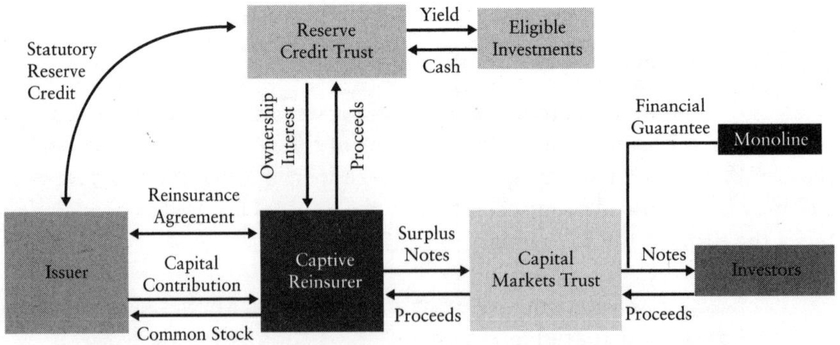

Source: Wachovia Capital Markets, LLC.

EXHIBIT 21.4   Upstream Transaction Structure

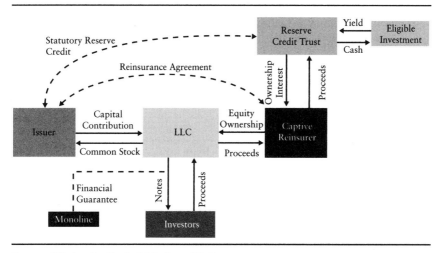

Source: Wachovia Capital Markets, LLC.

3. The captive reinsurer deposits the required capital to the reserve credit trust as statutory reserve credit for the issuer. Proceeds raised from the issuance of capital markets notes are invested in highly rated investments.

The downstream structure is differentiated by its ability to raise additional tranches of debt over time by using an auction rate program. As the statutory reserves increase over time, the structure can issue additional tranches of debt. On the other hand, the upstream structure prefunds the full required reserves upfront.

Credit Enhancement

A significant amount of credit enhancement is structured into Triple X transactions and serves to reduce the sensitivity of the senior debt in the light of the complexity of these transactions and compensates for the risk that policies may be mispriced or misclassified by the issuer. This credit enhancement takes the form of the following:

- *Economic reserves* contributed by the issuer that are based on the issuer's base-case actuarial assumptions,
- *Equity* invested by the issuer that serve as a first loss position, and
- *Future embedded profits* that can be retained in the structure if performance deteriorates.

At any point in the transaction, the size of these assets relative to the amount of notes outstanding is a useful metric for the creditworthiness of the transaction.

Ongoing Performance

Ongoing cash flow to the transaction comes from reinsurance payments made by issuer. The reinsurance premiums are affected by mortality, lapses and refunds/dividends paid to the issuers.

- *Mortality.* Covered death claims lead to an immediate cash outflow (reducing overcollateralization) and also diminish future premium income.
- *Lapses.* Lapses reduce future premium income but also reduce the reserve requirement.
- *Experience refunds.* Reinsurance contracts are commonly structured to allow the ceding company to recapture profits on the book of business subject to specified financial thresholds. Because experience refunds effectively reduce credit, refunds are restricted in the event of adverse performance on the policy block.
- *Shareholder dividends.* Equity contributions may be allowed to be returned to the issuer in the form of shareholder dividends after the reserve requirement has peaked subject to certain conditions.

The Bonds

Securities issued by Triple X securitizations have included wrapped floating rate term notes and *pari passu* auction rate money market securities. Term notes have long average lives of around 20 years, as amortization begins after the reserve requirements have reached their peak. Auction rate money market securities may be monthly refinancing obligations and may pay a step-up rate in the event of a failed refinancing. Bonds are typically callable in full at any payment date to allow the sponsor to recapture the risk, although a call premium may apply early in the life of the deal.

Issuers

Securitization reduces required reserves and gives the issuer the ability to recover transaction costs and emerging profits (via experience refunds and shareholder dividends). On the issuer's balance sheet, this may have the effect of reducing liabilities and increasing equity. To access the securitization market, issuers are required to present a track record of mortality and lapse experience that is credible and be able to potential increases in earnings

EXHIBIT 21.5 Triple X Securitizations

Issue Year	Deal	Ceding Insurer	Amount Issued ($ million)	Monoline
2003	River Lake Insurance Co. I	First Colony	1,100	MBIA
2004	Potomac Trust Capital I	Banner Life	550	AMBAC
2005	Orkney Re I, plc	Scottish Re	850	MBIA
2005	River Lake Insurance Co. II	First Colony	600	MBIA
2005	Orkney Re II, plc	Scottish Re	457	Assured
2006	River Lake Insurance Co. III	First Colony	750	FGIC
2006	Ballantyne Re PLC	Scottish Re	2,102	Ambac, Assured
2006	Potomac Trust Capital II	Banner Life	450	Unknown
2006	Timberlake Financial	RGA	850	Ambac
2007	River Lake Insurance Co. IV	First Colony	540	MBIA
			8,249	

Note: Amount issued column includes subsequent offerings.
Source: Wachovia Capital Markets, LLC.

volatility from retained mortality risk. Total Triple X issuance passed the $8 billion mark in 2007 with issuance dominated by Scottish Re and First Colony.

CONCLUSION

The magnitude of the Triple X reserve requirement is large and growing. Moody's estimates that demand for Triple X reserve credit will reach $45 billion in 2007 compared with $9 billion at year-end 2002. The share of reserves funded through securitization has been limited by the complexity of executing transaction, which requires coordination between the issuer, underwriter, monoline guarantor, actuarial consultants, lawyers, accountants and tax advisors, rating agencies and regulators. Transaction costs have been high relative to other structured products, and $300 million is commonly viewed as a minimum size. Given the early stage of the market, we expect these costs to decrease over time as standardization increases with more issuance.

The steep growth trajectory of the industry wide Triple X reserve requirement is a positive for future issuance. However, insurance reserve securitization is fundamentally a response to insurance regulation, and changes to reserve requirements or adverse developments in accounting or tax treatment of SPRVs would undermine the growing use of securitization.

Index